The U.S. Military in the Print News Media

The U.S. Military in the Print News Media

Service and Sacrifice in Contemporary Discourse

Luke Peterson

ANTHEM PRESS

Anthem Press
An imprint of Wimbledon Publishing Company
www.anthempress.com

This edition first published in UK and USA 2024
by ANTHEM PRESS
75–76 Blackfriars Road, London SE1 8HA, UK
or PO Box 9779, London SW19 7ZG, UK
and
244 Madison Ave #116, New York, NY 10016, USA

British Library Cataloguing-in-Publication Data
A catalogue record for this book is available from the British Library.

Library of Congress Cataloging-in-Publication Data: 2023949127
A catalog record for this book has been requested.

ISBN-13: 978-1-83998-871-4 (Hbk)
ISBN-10: 1-83998-871-1 (Hbk)

Cover Credit: Air Force Senior Airman Jonathan Valdes Montijo

This title is also available as an e-book.

To Callan. To Teagan. And to a world without war.

CONTENTS

ACKNOWLEDGMENTS

Books don't appear out of a vacuum. This may be even truer for academic treatises like this one that came out of years of thought, conversation, research, preparation, and aspiration in the time since the completion of my PhD at the University of Cambridge and the subsequent publication of my first manuscript considering print news media discourse in 2014. It would be impossible, therefore, to credit all those who contributed in some measure to this project over a decade-long period that took place in far-flung localities like Austin, Texas, West Sussex, England, and Pittsburgh, Pennsylvania. As such, these acknowledgments are necessarily abridged. For that, I can only apologize. And to all who guided me, coached me, or listened to me, to all who helped in any capacity over these last ten years, I am eternally grateful.

But to those who had a direct hand in this book being in the world and traveling the long road from germinating idea, to all-consuming research project, to published manuscript, I thank you most especially. I am incredibly grateful to Scott Smith for long and expertly informed conversations about U.S. politics and social dynamics, which were foundational elements in the histories I recount in the case study chapters here. To Mary Snyder and Bob Concilus, for your mentorship, guidance, and investment in this project, I thank you both so much. Your contributions were invaluable to my research and writing process. To Harry Gunkel, my uncle, my comrade, and my dear friend, your championing of this project motivated and inspired me more than you can know. To have you in my corner in this work, and in all things, is a blessing beyond measure. And to Derek Long, for your friendship, your enduring confidence, and for your contributions to this project, I am eternally grateful. I have always been lucky with my friends, and I count you at the top of that exclusive list. Thank you.

And to my wife, Katy, my best friend and my keenest editor, thank you. Nothing I do in the world happens but for you, and with you, always.

Luke Peterson
Pittsburgh, Pennsylvania
October 2023

Chapter One

EMPIRE, LANGUAGE, AND DISCOURSE: THE U.S. MILITARY IN THE PUBLIC IMAGINATION

There is no stronger or more persistent strain in the American character than the belief that the United States is a nation uniquely endowed with virtue.[1]

—*Stephen Kinzer, 2006*

The Great American Lie

America[2] is a nation at war. Between 1776 and the most recently completed year at the time of this writing, the United States has been involved in either open or clandestine warfare for 225 out of the 243 years of its existence.[3] Said another way, America can then be considered a nation *of* war, not just a nation *at* war, wherein a foundational part of the fabric of American society, American policy, and even American identity itself is inextricably bound up in warfare. Further, and as the full scope of this study intends to show, America might be more accurately described as a nation *of* war given the numerous, avoidable, and unnecessary wars of choice that this country has undertaken during its 243 years of existence. In spite of the fact that the United States consistently presents itself as a reluctant combatant both at home and on the global stage, this record of bellicosity indicates that war, and the myriad forms of death and destruction that come with it, is a deeply seeded aspect of America's political identity.

Indeed, it is plain to see that American foreign policy and its attendant military-industrial complex have been dependent upon and bound up within campaigns of warfare for the majority of the country's history. And over the course of the last 125 years, the majority of that warfare has been exported to distant points on the globe, ensuring that the American landscape and both its urban and rural infrastructure have stayed all but completely intact while foisting devastation upon the citizenry of other nations from Southwest Asia, East Asia, Latin America, and many points in between. Through this period of history, the United States has seen war as a preferable policy choice even when other, far less destructive avenues of conduct on the international stage have been readily available. In the words of a former participant in some of the most brutal aspects of this macabre historical period: "If the American military-industrial complex believes anything, it's that for any problem there exists a military remedy."[4] Truly, and as this study intends to show in detail, it has become impossible to suggest that the United States, its political elites, its economic power brokers, or its military leadership, with a particular eye on the last century of international activity, dislike warfare. War is our policy of choice.

The idea, then, that the United States is a peaceful nation, or that it is, in any way, a force for stability and passivity on the global stage is a lie. This lie encapsulates the notion that political and military elites working within agencies embedded within the American military-espionage-industrial complex of the government of the United States have as their primary raison d'être the best interests of the people of the United States. This lie presupposes that elected officials, representatives, government agents, bureaucrats, and other official functionaries *serve* in their respective roles to carry forward the best interests of the people of the United States and, in so doing, uphold the highest, most moral, and most altruistic ideals, often touted as the most laudable rationale for governance upon which a country has ever been founded. The lie here referenced further asserts that these ideals still hold any water whatever in the political structure or policy decisions of the United States, or that these laudable precepts still permeate the very fabric that continues to hold the country's social and political institutions together. This lie further indicates that the main current of thought, deed, and practice in government is in pursuit of truth and justice, that government, military, and intelligence officials embody the best qualities and attributes of the country, and that, in the main, the structures and institutions of the country are righteous and just because the individuals operating within them are composed in a likewise manner.

This oft-repeated and subtly woven deception compels the American citizenry, and large portions of the global citizenry as well, to the inevitable conclusion that, on the basis of this altruism and purity of motivation, on the basis of the benevolence of the organizing principles of the country, and on the basis of the desire to extend those laudable principles to every corner of the globe, that the United States was and is a force for good in the world. That is to say, the idea that the American experiment is unique in the community of nations and is a bastion of peace and tranquility on the global stage is so pervasive and presumptive within contemporary American society that quibbles of policy preference and noisy domestic arguments aside, the United States is presumed by huge swaths of the American public in the current political moment to be a harbinger of good to the global populace. As such, where goes America, good goes with us, trafficked by a highly respected and uncritically lauded, dressed up and decked out, and well-funded warrior caste: the U.S. military.

The following work intends to show that subtly worked and oft-repeated lie for precisely what it is: a deception foisted upon the media-consuming public of the United States consistently and repeatedly over the course of the last century. To put a finer point on it, the analysis that follows on these pages intends to unpack, uncover, and critically examine how the history of the last century plus of the American experiment has been, in large part, formulated by reliance upon certain unquestioned and unexamined precepts that are embedded deep within the American sense of self. Among those precepts are included the ideas that the United States is a protector of peace in the world, that the United States has only ever committed soldiers to war reluctantly and with good reason, and that, above all, those soldiers, sailors, and marines sent to do the actual fighting in the name of American values are altruistic, honorable, strictly moral, and altogether laudable. Indeed, it is this latter trope of the American sense of self whence derives the primary thrust of this work and to where I will direct the majority of my pointed criticism throughout the chapters that follow.

In identifying the presence of this pervasive and oft-reified lie within contemporary American society, I do not intend to suggest that one side or the other of the vehemently demarcated political divide in twenty-first-century America has exclusive responsibility for the dissemination of this deception. Nor do I intend that my characterization of the American self-conception presents a singularly viable or otherwise monolithic view. By any standard of assessment, the United States in the twenty-first century does not concur across ideological lines as to who we are or where we are going. That is to say, within contemporary American political discourse, there are clearly allowed differences of belief, ideology, practice, and/or opinion. Honest individuals can disagree even when the assembled facts are not in dispute. And when they are in dispute, as has increasingly become the case for social and political discussions in the twenty-first century, those disputes between national political and economic elites can become vehement, vitriolic, personal, and quite public. Nevertheless, even at the point of this type of irreconcilable dispute, neither the structure of the state nor the overall design of the American political system, nor particularly the altruistic motives guiding the U.S. military, none of these foundational societal elements are impugned from within the operation of these systems themselves. A colloquial way to phrase this assertion is as the so-called "bad apple" argument, a defense of the righteousness of the status quo put forward innumerable times by ranking guardians of the political, economic, and military institutions of the United States (this specific form of discursive justification is examined in some detail in the news media analysis portion of Chapter 7 in this book, "Iraq Part II: Invasion, Occupation, and Imperial Overreach"). This thinly crafted justification instructs that individuals are impeachable while institutions are not. What this book sets out to accomplish is to demonstrate that those institutional gatekeepers come from either side of the ideological divide present within the United States and that they all traffic in, defend, and dispense the American lie that our institutions are just and equitable, that our military acts in ways that are exclusively lawful and righteous, and that our country, in its dynamic self-conception, is always well-intentioned and is always beyond moral reproach.

This narrative of the government operating for the people, of the military serving the best and only ever the defensive interests of the people, and the intelligence agencies being secretive though ultimately trustworthy operatives of the state has been foisted upon the American people via authoritative sites of media discourse for more than a century. That the people en masse are served by the U.S. government, that American society writ large is benefited by American military commitments around the world, and that the U.S. intelligence agencies operate on behalf of Americans everywhere is part and parcel of the grandiose lie. Rather, this book will demonstrate that the government and its membership, the military and its leadership, and the intelligence community and its operatives exist for their own benefit. They exist to perpetuate themselves, to extend their influence, and ultimately and most importantly, to enrich their leadership and their allies from corporate America (more often than not, former or future policymakers themselves) while at the same time expanding the power base from which they operate in the country and in the world. This book will further demonstrate that, through authoritative news media discourse, particularly of the print variety, that the U.S. military is an accepted, protected, and substantially defended institution whose scope, breadth, and motivations are not to be questioned wholesale. Individuals may be impugned, and policy decisions may be questioned, but the necessity, indeed, the right-eousness of the institution of the U.S. military itself is constructed as an unimpeachable fact within contemporary news discourse in the country today.

That these assertions are controversial or otherwise unpopular as analyses of the contemporary status quo in American politics, industry, and society is, in and of itself, an indication of the extent to which media and cultural products within the United States have been successful in inculcating this deliberate doctrine of American altruism and best interest operations of the offices of the state on behalf of its people. Further, an additional argument might be asserted that indicates that the timeline suggested within this book for an examination of the ramifications of this pervasive American self-decep-tion is too narrow in scope in order to be able to fully encompass the lengths of time during which the global juggernaut of American politics and military industry has been predicated upon deception in its practices, both domestic and foreign. Nevertheless, it is the purview of this book to demonstrate the presence of this protective discourse and the successful distribution of this ideology in the American public mind from the period of the Spanish-American War through to the earliest phases of the second American intervention in Iraq in the first decade of the twenty-first century, leaving the remaining elements of the American military legacy beyond this arguably narrow historical scope for another author on another day.[5]

In each of the case study chapters to follow, then, the actor at the center of this highly critical examination, that group already argued to be protected by a righteous discourse and wholesale positive valuation within mainstream news media discourse and cultural products, is the institution of the U.S. military. Inferring from media in the contempo-rary social sphere in the United States, the individuals who constitute members of this gilded institution as a collective believe in the righteousness of America and demon-strate this belief by subjecting themselves to rigorous training, ritualized traditions, and, on occasion, abhorrent violence ostensibly in service of higher objectives. Theirs is a commitment that demands loyalty over logic while impelling a boundless faith in flawed and corrupt institutions through often bizarre, communal rituals, including "antiquated haircuts, peculiar dialects and communal running [that] perform the same function as church liturgies, national pledges of allegiance, fraternity hazing rituals and the secret handshake. They create a culture that separates adherents from non-adherents."[6] More to the point, theirs is a community that, through news media and cultural products, is draped in honor of action and legitimacy of purpose, bestowed with ribbons and med-als, and praised on high days on holidays for their *service* to the American experiment. Rarely if ever criticized for its abject legitimacy or discursively assaulted as a whole body, the U.S. military, hung with banners, billboards, bunting, and flags, occupies a profoundly influential position within contemporary American society, substantially informing Americans about who we are, where we have been, and where we are going.

This book takes that construction head-on, challenging pervasive notions, both implicit and overt, that the U.S. military exists for the benefit of the citizenry, that war as policy is always applied sparingly, precisely, and carefully, and/or that membership in that fraternity is universally undertaken for selfless, altruistic purposes. Rather, in subsequent chapters, this study will show how the public and news media discourse surrounding U.S. military action has time and again glossed over or covered up grotesqueries conducted by American soldiers, sometimes on a grand scale. Or, as is consistently the case, this study will identify when and where crimes committed by Americans in the name of American citizens are treated as flukes of individual incompetence by authoritative news outlets rather than evidence of institutional rot, from the March across Samar to the My Lai Massacre and from the Caco Wars to Abu Ghraib. In each of these cases and in the many others to be documented in this study, the problems inherent to the political system of the United States, the problems inherent to the foreign policy decisions made within the United States, and in particular, the problems inherent to the operations of the U.S. military are represented as problems of individual incompetence, incidental mistakes, or unintended abuse. This work will demonstrate how that system of representation functions and point to the consequences of those representations for the news-consuming Americans and for the rest of the world as well.

In sum, this book deals with U.S. military aggression against global populations throughout the course of the last 125 years, demonstrating that, at an institutional level, the U.S. military is deliberately violent and negligent, that its masters are callous and self-interested, and that the sum of the institution that is the U.S. military exists not to serve the American people but to serve its corporate and political paymasters. Finally, and critically, this book will demonstrate how an attendant American public has been deceived in all of these things for more than a century, deliberately misguided by an authoritative, mainstream news media and cultural discourse into uncritical praise of the very individuals and institutions about whom we should be the most circumspect, and the most cautious. It is to the definition of that critical idea, discourse, already mentioned in this introduction as well as in the subtitle to this book, and to a consideration of the manner in which this dynamic, theoretical concept will be applied throughout the course of this book that this introduction now turns.

Discourse, Language, and Knowledge

This book will argue that the deliberate praise and protection of the U.S. military, its membership, and the policymakers that have directed it over the course of the last century constitute a discourse in the contemporary United States. A discourse represents a diffuse, diverse, malleable frame of knowledge surrounding a topic or set of related topics held as true by an attendant public.[7] Indeed, the term *discourse* makes an appearance in this book's title, suggesting a critical focus not simply on an alternative history of the events surrounding a century of American military engagements but rather on the absorption of information and the creation of legitimated knowledge surrounding those events. A discourse exists as a frame of knowledge, an intellectual trope, or a presumed set of assumptions or foundational knowledge that can influence the structure, function, and purpose of subsequent, connected discourses within a given intellectual environment. In order to become more conversant with this idea as it will be used and referenced in this specific study, and given that the concept of discourse has been applied very differently by a highly diverse group of social science researchers since the development of the concept, a more robust definition of the idea of discourse is provided next.

Following the work of French philosopher and social critic Michel Foucault, the intellectual most closely associated with the concept of discourse,

> Whenever one can describe, between a number of statements, such a system of dispersion, whenever, between objects, types of statement, concepts, or thematic choices, one can define a regularity [...] we will say for the sake of convenience, that we are dealing with a *discursive formation*.[8] (emphasis in original)

The existence of discursive formations as intimated here by Foucault implies the presence of both a creator and a receiver, a distributor and an audience, through which a power-based dialectic of information exchange takes place. Such is the malleability of discourse construction, though, that the idea of bilateral exchange oversimplifies the intellectual environment in which discursive constructions exist. Rather, discourse is energized by the participant as well as the distributor, generating intellectual power and cultural influence through its diffusion in a public space, its interaction in a communal body, and/or its reassertion in subsequent intellectual environments. Returning to Foucault, then, it is understood that "discourse and system produce each other,"[9] and it is this interaction of discourse production and systemic reification that is of interest here, and in the pages that follow.

Discourses flourish among attendant publics who collectively relate to a statement or set of statements about a given topic or set of related topics. They can be understood as constructed, contingent aspects of knowledge whereby details of a historical event, a contemporary moment, or a novel concept are crafted, polished, and then, as is often the case, replicated by individual actors within the aforementioned attendant public. As has been discussed, discourses are non-linear and non-binary. Rather, they are expansive, flexible, and adjustable creations in the intellectual space that can influence individuals or groups toward a certain understanding, however subtle or overt, of a concept or set of ideas. Discourses can reinforce power-based institutions, or challenge them. They can confront injustices or exacerbate them. To be engaged in discourse construction, circulation, or criticism, then, is to be engaged in a relational process, one in which the individual, the public, and the institution are each connected in a specific role defining, fostering, or contradicting a particular social, cultural, or intellectual environment. Put succinctly, "Discourses are [...] constructions or significations of some domain of social practice."[10] They are not reality per se, but they can inform the reality of the attendant public to a substantial degree, enacting power dynamics within institutions and interpersonal dynamics within social relationships to affect the public view and potentially to alter the collective public course.

Key to understanding the structure and function of a discourse, then, and especially key to understanding its application and meaning within the pages to follow, is the idea that a discourse has powerful potential to affect public cognition and social understanding of a given topic under consideration. Discourses can be local and relational, yes, but the analysis of a discourse typically, and specifically in this study, presumes the assessment of a power-based relationship wherein a department, a corporation, or an institution impacts individual or public interpretation of an idea via asymmetrical size and/or influence within the distributive environment. Even states have an interest, typically through power-based influence, in crafting a particular discourse, or subverting antithetical or otherwise critical discourses invoked to challenge the power, authority, or legitimacy of the state's position. Considerations of certain forms of discourse, then, require the ability to analyze a statement, a concept, or a set of related ideas within a power-laden environment, one that very often purports simply to put forward facts rather than rendering information within a leveraged or contested environment. This type of discourse production has been identified and analyzed before and recalls an academic tradition in the study of discourse and language, namely Critical Discourse Analysis (or CDA), within which this study is firmly located.[11] Among other elements of critical academic inquiry, CDA contends: "that a 'system' for knowledge production dominates our political and cultural discourse, and this production is an expression of (and a reinforcement of) power and the powerful."[12]

As such, and according to the theoretical foundations provided by CDA, not all producers of, or contributors to, discourse are weighted equally within sites of discourse creation and/or replication. CDA then implies a revision to the idea of totally lateral or egalitarian methods of discourse creation and absorption, wherein power within states, societies, governments, or institutions impinges upon or otherwise significantly influences the energy and viability of a given line of discursive knowledge. This theoretical structure connects elements of language and meaning at the heart of the broader concept of discourse with the state, society, or even the time and temporality of a distributed discursive construction: "CDA aims to demonstrate that semiotic and linguistic features of interaction are systemically connected with what is going on socially, which in turn is also happening semiotically or linguistically."[13] In the current work then, the "system of knowledge" under investigation is the one responsible for constructing and disseminating information regarding the U.S. military and its wartime operations. The vast majority of this work will concentrate on one such institution, the print news media, but will also seek to investigate cultural products such as television and sporting contests for their role in enforcing and/or solidifying those discursive conditions created and distributed by the authoritative print news media. In order to better frame the criticism on the following pages, though, a foundational text establishing the regimens and the conditions within which CDA takes place bears specific examination here.

Language as Power: Orientalism and the Discourse of the Elite

In the late 1970s, the publication of a seminal work of intellectual criticism from a Palestinian-American scholar placed the tradition of elite, institutional representation under intensive scrutiny. It was through that magnum opus—Edward Said's *Orientalism*[14]—that the academic reliance upon tradition, hierarchy, and power in the study of the Middle East, North Africa, and the Indian subcontinent was laid bare. In speech, in act, but particularly via text, according to Said, conventional, expert knowledge was disseminated by means of direct, practically hereditary transmission: an unbroken line of inheritance funneling subjective, orientalist tropes from source material to new generations of enthusiastic scholars searching for firm footing in unsteady academic environs. In many cases, the texts in question and the problematic assumptions that rested at the core of their analyses retained an unnaturally long life because of a lack of willingness or ability on the part of the recipient parties to redress the established canon. Through this process, text itself—ostensibly ideologically neutral historical, sociological, and cultural study—was remade into an agent of power, transmitting value-laden information about the Orient and the dialectical Other, but made all the more insidious, according to Said, precisely because of the attribution of the aforementioned ideological neutrality to these scholarly works and to their oft-lauded creators.

Following Foucault and Said, then, the linkages between text and knowledge, and between print and understanding could not be more profound nor more influential upon the intellectual environment in a given community. Indeed, in Said's own view, texts and their authors retain such import within approaches to criticism precisely because of their ability to mold reality, to create knowledge, and to structure the boundaries of the rational and the real:

> A text purporting to contain knowledge about something actual [...] is not easily dismissed. Expertise is attributed to it. The authority of academics, institutions, and governments can accrue to it, surrounding it with still greater prestige than its practical successes warrant. Most important, such texts can *create* not only knowledge but also the very reality they appear to describe. In time such knowledge and reality produce a tradition, or what Michel Foucault calls a discourse, whose material presence or weight, not the originality of a given author, is really responsible for the texts produced out of it.[15] (emphasis in original)

It is evident, then, as given in Said's institutional criticism, that textual representations have a particularly influential role in structuring a discourse. Put another way, information contained within a text that is presumed to be authoritative contains a certain amount of intellectual power, creating the possibility of delineating the true nature of a particular topic or concept. If so, texts retain within them an intrinsic power within discourse construction, a power to impart knowledge, to shape the intellectual environment, and, to an extent, to influence the perception of reality itself when it comes to the adoption of frames of knowledge about a particular subject. Indeed, disconcerting though it may be at times, the import attributed by Said to text and to text language can be extrapolated to contribute to a subjective form of reality where individuals are guided in their approach to an understanding of the world based upon the text and the language in their immediate intellectual environment. Truly, if the culture wars of the contemporary political moment in the United States have instructed anything, it is the veracity of this idea, even to the point of prideful declarations based upon "alternative facts" that have no relationship whatsoever to quantifiable, observable phenomena.[16] Perhaps, then, we should no longer proclaim, "You are what you eat." Instead, we are all, demonstrably, what we read, what we study, and what we come, through discourse, to know.

In a later work speaking specifically to news media representations about the East, and particularly concerning Islam, Said emphasizes this very point, acknowledging the precarious nature of discourse and knowledge dependent to a substantial degree upon the intellectual resources serving to contribute to that discourse, and, consequently, to that knowledge:

> In other words, what we are dealing with here are in the very widest sense communities of interpretation, many of them at odds with one another, prepared in many cases to go to war with one another, all of them creating and revealing themselves and their interpretations as very central features of their existence. No one lives in direct contact either with truth or with reality. Each of us lives in a world actually made by human beings, in which such things as "the nation" or "Christianity" or "Islam" are the result of agreed-upon convention, of historical processes, and, above all, of willed human labor expended to give those things an identity we can recognize.[17]

A number of critical elements emerge here that are both foundational to a working understanding of discourse as a concept (applied in the academy general and here in this particular work), but beyond that, to consider how a staid public and institutionally supported discourse in a given community, like that of the mainstream discourse on the U.S. military in the contemporary United States, can impact an entire, attendant community, shaping their knowledge, their version of reality, and even their sense of self.

Said begins by acknowledging the high stakes involved in discourse creation, suggesting that differences in interpretation of the wider world can impel opposing groups "in many cases to go to war with one another." And as is plainly evident in ongoing rhetorical combat within the United States today, whether on the efficacy of vaccination, the results of a free and fair election, or anthropogenic climate change, there are clearly vastly different intellectual resources being applied in order to structure discourse and knowledge in the United States at the present moment. Said would go further, though, to intimate that none of the cacophony of voices engaged in the contemporary culture wars have exclusive access to the truth, despite the fervency of their beliefs. Rather, following this criticism, Said would have us all living in an intellectual world of ideas, of connected and repackaged concepts—in short, in a world of discourse. Crucially, that world is "made by human beings," a contingent and dependent discursive universe in "which we depend for our sense of reality not just on the interpretations and meanings we form individually for ourselves, but also on those we *receive*"[18] (emphasis in original). And when in lockstep or reflective of not an inconsiderate amount of unison within elite institutions of distribution, these frames of knowledge begin to ossify approaching something like an irrevocable aspect of the lived and shared reality of a given attendant public: "As officials repeat a discourse, it becomes [...] potentially a dominant discourse. Once it attains dominance, criticism often becomes confined to operating within the discourse, rather than a critique of the discourse itself, since the legitimacy of the discourse has become internalized."[19] It will be these strictures within the contemporary print news discourse on the U.S. military that serve as focal points of the power-laden, discursive analysis to come in the case study chapters to follow.

This final element of Said's philosophy, connecting text to language to discourse to knowledge, should remain well within the frame of reference for any discourse analyst. Indeed, while subsequent pages will cite verifiable source material in a broad-based effort to criticize an authoritative, mainstream discourse, the parameters of discourse as a concept, in addition to the transitory nature of the intellectual environment in the twenty-first century, make this process a subjective one no matter the care taken in research and in writing. Following Foucault and Said, as well as the tradition of CDA that they helped to found, the intellectual inputs applied in this work will produce certain discursive outcomes in their own right, establishing new realities and new contingencies that might be subject to their own critique or contestation. The act of criticizing a discourse retains within it this unavoidable dilemma: the reliance upon selective materials and contingent tropes within discursive processes that retain as their end the mitigation of rigid, traditional, and institutional frames of knowledge. As such, the potential for creating a productive, dynamic, and even egalitarian analysis of a discourse represents a kind of production of knowledge itself within a given intellectual environment and will be subject to the parameters of those environments even while working tenaciously to tear them down.

But while the analysis of such a thing as discourse and the presumption of the existence of such a thing as knowledge can result in unwieldy, even unsatisfactory forms of scholarly production, the assessment of the vehicle through which these concepts are transmitted, namely language, might succeed in landing audiences onto a more stable footing from within the confines of this critical approach. More tangible still is the assessment of those highly visible and highly influential *institutions* responsible for authoritative language production and distribution within communities, publics, nations, and societies: the authoritative print news media.[20] As has been emphasized, the work to follow will substantially focus on an analysis of U.S. military action and reputation through a series of historical military engagements for the purposes of determining the parameters as well as the consequences of authoritative discourse on that subject. This work stands firmly, then, as an institutional, not an individual critique, given that "the real political task in a society such as ours is to criticize the workings of institutions, which appear to be both neutral and independent; to criticize and attack them in such a manner that the political violence which has always exercised itself obscurely through them will be unmasked."[21] It is to these institutions, and the intellectual power they are able to wield within language and discourse distribution, that this study now turns.

Language and the News Media

Discourses are distributed via language. They are those pervasive intellectual frames where language is applied as a vehicle, a set of meaningful symbols and/or sounds through which semantic structures and discursive iterations are distributed from one individual, one group, or one institution of discourse creation to another.[22] The application of language within the print news media must inevitably involve the assertion of intellectual frames (what will be called throughout this study, "frames of representation"), given that "framing essentially involves selection and salience. To frame is to select some aspect of a perceived reality and make them more salient in a communicating text, in such a way as to promote a particular problem definition, causal interpretation, moral evaluation and/or treatment recommendation for the item described."[23] As such, language embeds within discourse what can be called ideology, given that the distribution of language on related topics or systems of information necessarily comes with in-built assumptions, presuppositions, and/or intellectual positions. Put another way, "a discourse [is] a type of language associated with a particular representation, from a specific point of view, or some social practice."[24] As mentioned, it is the position of critical linguists and philosophers alike that these representations carry a significant cognitive weight throughout the publics in which they circulate. They can confirm or reject, create community, and/or isolate individuals and groups from one another within a common intellectual environment. They hold sway over large and small groups and posit powerful frameworks within those communities in the construction of collective and individual identities. Discourses are powerful elements within attendant societies, and the language through which they are trafficked is likewise powerful. As such, a great deal of this work and the case studies to follow will focus on language and its particular form of selective representation. In fact, it would not be untoward to say that this study is obsessed with language and the myriad potential views it can create. This is quite simply because, as discourse analyst and prominent media scholar Norman Fairclough once put it: "The ideological work of [...] language includes particular ways of representing the world."[25] The remainder of this study will closely follow this guiding principle in the analysis of news texts purporting to narrate elements of American wars for news-consuming audiences within the United States.

It would be a mistake in this assessment, though, to consider that all language from all sites of discourse creation is created equally. The position of certain sites of language production, their reach, their audience size, their economic leverage, and their sheer productive capabilities mean that within discourse creation, certain sites of language production retain a much greater influence in the shaping of the intellectual environment than others. Of course, we recognize these sites of discourse production and distribution as news media institutions with the capabilities to create and distribute language via text, video, audio, and/or combinations of media production. And as previously mentioned within this introductory chapter, the theoretical frames guiding analytical approaches to text and language study under the auspices of CDA attempt to account for this differentiation of influence and balance. The analysis of these kinds of productive sites, then, constitutes a particular process, one in which the weight of the institution and its impact upon the intellectual environment are considered concomitant with the content of their media products and the impact of their reach upon the attendant community. Put another way, the analysis of news media discourse cannot be considered in the same fashion as the analysis of individual or small group discourse. What discourse analysts looking at the news media must consider is the power of these language creators to formulate "(1) social realities, (2) social relations and (3) systems of knowledge and belief."[26] It is not an exaggeration to view these sites of discourse creation as masters of linguistic manipulation, discursive construction, and/or reality formation. As such, "What we are getting at becomes plain; Mastery of language affords remarkable power."[27]

Situated within this form of discourse criticism, though, questions still remain: Who or what constitutes the news media as an institution? What makes them an authority within discourse, and which forms of their productions retain the most influence within a given discursive environment? Some of the answers to these questions will become illuminated throughout the case study chapters dealing with U.S. military engagements around the world over the course of the last century. After all, the news media as an institution has changed considerably during that span of time, as has the recipient public in the United States attending to those media products. In general terms, though, it is possible to sketch out some characteristics of the news media institution that will be under examination in subsequent case study chapters. While undoubtedly dynamic in the current intellectual, political, and technological moment, it is the broadly termed authoritative news media as a singular contributor to a national discourse on the U.S. military that will receive a standalone treatment in the discourse analysis to come within the following pages. For a general description of who or what comprises the authoritative news media and what the impact of their contributions in language and discourse is, I return to an earlier analysis of this organization and its coverage of ongoing political conflict in the Middle East:

> institutionally vetted, authoritative news text remains a crucial avenue of investigation into considerations of discourse, thought, and language [...] Often repetitive or recurrent themes—such as the frames of representation identified in the case studies in this book— deepen this cognitive impact. Ultimately, conceptual relations, positive and negative associations, and functional memory is significantly informed in each of these processes. It is this value of [media language] in the construction of knowledge, and the value of text and its influence upon individual and social memory that renders the printed news so influential in the construction and distribution of contemporary discourse. Consequently, items in [the print news media] receive significant investigative attention [...] in the discussion to follow.[28]

Effectively, then, what this study attempts is a positioning of sorts, a locational placement of the language and contributive ideology of the authoritative news media in the discursive environment of the United States. That environment is itself subject to analysis, though, given the span of time under examination in this study and the dynamic social elements at work within the societies under investigation. For the purposes of this study, however, all of those elements are possible sources of analysis and are made all the more relevant as actors within the intellectual environment owing to the fact that "the media are shaped by the wider society, but they also play a vital role in the diffusion of such social and cultural changes."[29] It is the society contributing news media creators, the language produced by them in those authoritative roles, and then the subsequent impact of that language within that same society that constitute the sites of analysis here. As evident, it is a dynamic and cyclical framework, and one that will receive further commentary in the case study chapters to follow.

A final, as yet underrepresented actor within the intellectual and discursive framework under discussion is the state, including its role in news media production and subsequent discourse creation. Clearly, the topic under consideration in the current study—the discourse on the U.S. military throughout the last century—is one that would be of interest to the state, writ large, and in particular, to the organs of the state concerned with military action, so-called defense budgeting and spending, and intelligence gathering. In sum, these state organs represent some of the most visible and legitimated branches of the state that is able to manipulate violence for state-sanctioned ends.[30] They are among the most organized, well-funded, and well-regarded branches of the state, particularly the United States, and as has already been asserted, their membership constitutes a virtually unimpeachable warrior class through which we view exclusively laudable, reputable, and respectable characteristics of ourselves and of our nation as a whole. Leveraged to its fullest extent, then, and in particular as it regards authoritative discourse openly critical of state action, "The state does have an interest in controlling media output."[31] And amid an increasingly dynamic and decentralized media environment, this impulse of the state continues to seek influence over large, powerful, and authoritatively placed institutions. The news media thereby becomes implicated in discourse construction. Even now, in the presence of an undeniably diffuse media environment, discourse as constructed by the authoritative news media has substantial significance, and when that discourse is endorsed or even crafted by the organs of the state itself, that influence grows even more. The specific role of the news media in crafting, refining, and disseminating discourse is thereby tied to state auspices, and as will become clearer in the specific case studies to follow, elements within the state are, at varying times, aware of the national news media discourse and are intent upon curbing open criticism of state actions or of state functionaries.

If, then, it is in the interest of the state to disseminate information to the public about the laudable nature of its armed forces and/or the general beneficence of military action as conducted by that state, it stands to reason that a robust news media would serve expertly well as the vehicle for delivery of that message even in states with substantially large and diverse intellectual communities. As such, the historical case studies in the chapters that follow will examine the impact of the news media as it has inhabited that role over the course of the last century and more, analyzing the extent to which the news media of the United States has acted to authoritatively challenge the positionality of the state vis-à-vis its military actions throughout the globe or whether, in fact, it has been a complicit institution in those activities. Part and parcel of the analysis to follow will examine, through critical assessment of news media discourse, the role of the news media in America's wars and the extent to which that institution, via commission or omission, framing, selection, salience, lexical choice, and/or via other methods of discourse creation, endorsed America's brutal military activity throughout the twentieth and twenty-first centuries and championed the warrior class who trafficked in that brutality.

The object in this assessment is not simply to lambaste the media as an institution; this much has been done and is being done on a regular basis, whether online or via vehement public remonstration. Rather, the object in this case will be to delineate the role played by the news media in providing the discursive space for the state to engage in war. This, again, will be a process of analysis considering language, lexical choice, naming, story selection, story positioning, audio and video accompaniment, and other forms of linguistic and textual analysis to discover the discursive positioning of a given author, news item, or overall publication. The consequences of that advocacy, of that support, of that role as a vocal champion of state objectives, or, when it occurs, of the role of a particular news item as critical of state action, will likewise be illuminated in each of the case study chapters to follow.

It is with this consideration of discourse, language, and thought, and with a firm conception of the role of the news media and its connection to state objections firmly in mind, that this study now pivots to an examination of the history of U.S. military involvement around the world in the twentieth and twenty-first centuries and to the frames of representation and subsequent impact upon individual and collective knowledge created around those engagements for and by an attendant American public. It is to that bloody and contingent history, and to its expression in news media language and in popular discourse, that this study now turns.

Notes

1 Stephen Kinzer, *Overthrow: America's Century of Regime Change from Hawaii to Iraq* (New York: Times Books, 2006), 315.

2 It is a lexical gloss to conflate the term "America" with the nation-state, the United States of America. Considering the expanse of the continents of North and South America with their many and varied indigenous and immigrant populations, the term "America" should be considered nebulous at best and could be used in reference to a wide variety of peoples, cultures, political bodies, and/or national groups. For the purposes of shorthand, though, and to be able to vary what will be a consistent and regular reference to the United States of America, this work will sometimes employ "America," as it is used in common parlance, to mean the United States specifically, not the other, more numerous, and more ancient peoples of the Americas more broadly. Using this term in this fashion is in no way intended to undermine, ignore, or disrespect the peoples of the American continents who arrived there thousands of years before European colonial settlers, and who continue to provide vibrant and vital contributions to the culture, character, and history of those continents as a whole.

3 Sabir Shah, "The US Has Been at War 225 Out of 243 Years since 1776," *The News International,* January 9, 2020. https://www.thenews.com.pk/print/595752-the-us-has-been -at-war-225-out-of-243-years-since-1776.

4 Andrew Bacevich, *America's War for the Greater Middle East: A Military History* (New York: Random House, 2016), 337.

5 To be specific, the case study chapters in this work will explore U.S. military intervention in the following conflicts: the Spanish-American/Philippine-American War, World War I, World War II, Vietnam, the Persian (or First) Gulf War, and the Iraq War beginning in 2003. As this study intends a sweeping critique of language and discourse surrounding American wars overall, some might suggest these military engagements constitute too narrow a scope to be able to proffer the conclusions that are drawn by the end of this investigation. According to these criticisms, a more complete vision of the American military compulsion might start with an examination of the so-called "Indian" Wars of the nineteenth century or the American Civil War before those. To be clear, while this criticism may have some merit,

this work does not purport to be the final word on the subject of the U.S. military in the national discourse. Rather, the intent here is to explore that national discourse as it has been engaged under the banner of the American Empire, a cultural and political imperium that was engaged in earnest with the actions and outcomes of the Spanish-American War in 1898. This military imperium extends to the present political moment, with U.S. military interventions, overt and clandestine, exercised in locations around the world. And while some major American military actions during this period are omitted in this study, the Korean War and the U.S. occupation of Afghanistan to name just two, the record assembled here stands on its own merit as evidence of a concerted pattern of language and representation over the course of more than a century of American warfare. Further research and additional manuscripts are no doubt required in order to examine additional American military ventures within the framework of the methodology provided within this work.

6 Steele Brand, "What Ancient Rome and Greece Can Teach Us About the Modern American Military," *Time.Com*, September 20, 2019. https://time.com/5681715/citizen-soldiers -history/.

7 The conception of such a grouping as the "public" has been a source of much theoretical speculation and debate within the social sciences from the latter part of the twentieth century and through to the present day. Suffice it to say here that for the purposes of this study, while this author acknowledges that a great many reputable theorists have taken up this debate with varying levels of impact upon the discourse surrounding this term, in applying this term here, this study will revert back to one of the earlier articulations of the concept in recent academic history, that of German philosopher Jurgen Habermas. Habermas articulated the conception of the public as a community, or in his term, a "sphere," wherein members of a community may choose to attend to, or reject, discussions of a given idea. For Habermas, the public sphere, then, refers to, "a specific domain—the public domain versus the private. Sometimes the public appears simply as that sector of public opinion that happens to be opposed to the authorities. Depending on the circumstances, either the organs of the state or the media, like the press, which provide communication among members of the public, may be counted as 'public organs'." Singular though this definition is, for the purposes of the current study, it will be the definition recalled in order to assert public action or public engagement with the discourse on the U.S. military throughout subsequent discussions (Jurgen Habermas, *The Structural Transformation of the Public Sphere* (Oxford, England: Polity Press, 1989), 2).

8 Michel Foucault, *The Archaeology of Knowledge and the Discourse on Language* (New York: Harper and Row, 1972), 38.

9 Ibid., 76.

10 Norman Fairclough, *Media Discourse* (New York: Bloomsbury Academic, 1995), 94.

11 This type of discourse analysis, beyond the broad frames established and concretized by the work of Michel Foucault, is known as Critical Discourse Analysis (CDA) and is closely associated with the work of linguists, sociologists, and social critics like Edward Said, Teun Van Dijk, Norman Fairclough, and Ruth Wodak. Also in the tradition of CDA, see this author's *Contending Discourses: Palestine—Israel and the Print News Media* (London: Routledge, 2014).

12 John Tirman, *The Deaths of Others: The Fate of Civilians in America's Wars* (New York: Oxford University Press, 2011), 15.

13 Mia Fischer, "Commemorating 9/11 NFL-Style: Insights into America's Culture of Militarism," *Journal of Sport and Social Issues* 38, no. 3 (2014): 206.

14 Edward Said, *Orientalism* (New York: Vintage Books, 1978).

15 Ibid., 94.

16 The phrase "alternative facts" is most closely associated with Kelly Anne Conway, press adviser and counselor to Donald Trump, shortly after he was inaugurated as the 45th president of the United States. Intending to soft-peddle Trump's deceitful claims that his inauguration event was the largest in American history, Conway suggested that actual facts referenced by the press corps at the White House can be countered by Trump's "alternative facts" in the White House analysis of the situation (W. Cummings, "'Alternative Facts' to 'Witch Hunt': A Glossary of Trump Terms," *USA Today*, January 17, 2018. https://www.usa-today.com/story/news/politics/onpolitics/2018/01/16/alternative-facts-witch-hunt-glossary -trump-terms/1029963001/).

17　Edward Said, *Covering Islam* (New York: Vintage, 1981), 45–6.

18　Ibid., 46.

19　Jeffrey H. Michaels, *The Discourse Trap and the U.S. Military: From the War on Terror to the Surge* (New York: Palgrave Macmillan, 2013), 4.

20　For a complete treatment of the institution referred to here as "the authoritative print news media," see, by this author, "Chapter 3: Nations, Publics, and the Print News Media," in *Contending Discourses: Palestine—Israel and the Print News Media* (London: Routledge, 2014).

21　Michel Foucault in Noam Chomsky and Michel Foucault, *The Chomsky-Foucault Debate on Human Nature* (New York: The New Press, 2006), 41.

22　There are many scholarly works that have contributed to a robust debate on the impact of language upon cognition and its function as an internal guide toward social and political realities. Key to this study is the internal function of language, which works at least subtly, but perhaps altogether unconsciously, in the structuring of forms of knowledge in recipient individuals, given that "there is no symbolization without symbols, there is no internal representation without an internal language" (J. Fodor, *The Language of Thought* (Sussex, England: The Harvester Press, 1975), 55). See also Pierre Bordieu, *Language and Symbolic Power* (Cambridge: Polity, 1991); J. B. Caroll, *Language and Thought* (Englewood Cliffs: Prentice Hall, 1964); and Talbot, et al. *Language and Power in the Modern World* (Edinburgh: Edinburgh University Press, 2003).

23　R. M. Entman, "Framing: Toward Clarification of a Fractured Paradigm," *Journal of Communication*, 43, no. 4 (1993): 52.

24　Fairclough, *Media Discourse*, 41.

25　Ibid., 12.

26　Ibid., 55.

27　Frantz Fanon, *Black Skin, White Masks* (New York: Grove Press, 1967), 18.

28　Peterson, *Contending Discourses*, 7–8.

29　Fairclough, *Media Discourse*, 51.

30　In a 1918 lecture entitled "Politics as a Vocation," German sociologist Max Weber famously equated the state with that "human community that (successfully) claims the monopoly of the legitimate use of physical force within a given territory." This author finds this definition substantially characteristic of states and state action in the twentieth and twenty-first centuries and will be relying upon this description throughout this study (Max Weber, *Politics as a Vocation* (Philadelphia: Fortress Press, 1965)).

31　Fairclough, *Media Discourse*, 45.

Chapter Two

FIN DE SIÈCLE: THE BEGINNINGS OF AMERICAN EMPIRE

Imperialism is a depraved choice of national life, imposed by self-seeking interests which appeal to the lusts of quantitative acquisitiveness and of forceful domination surviving in a nation from early centuries of animal struggle for existence.[1]

—*J.A. Hobson, 1902*

Spanish Conquest of Cuba

The Spanish acquisition of Cuba as a colonial possession is generally dated to that seminal year in the Age of Exploration, 1492, when Christopher Columbus[2] himself is credited with landing on the island in fulfillment of his commitments to the centralized Spanish monarchy under King Ferdinand II of Aragon and Queen Isabella I of Castille. Having brutally ended nearly 800 years of Muslim governance in Spain in the consolidation of their own political power on the Iberian Peninsula, Ferdinand and Isabella famously dispatched Columbus as the commander of three vessels intending to gain land, gold, and converts to the Spanish kingdom. No less bloodthirsty than his employers, Columbus and his men (mariners, seamen, and soldiers reputedly much more able and seaworthy than Columbus himself)[3] landed in the fabled New World and quickly began torturing and murdering its indigenous inhabitants in pursuit of wealth, fame, and Christian glory for their own sake, and on behalf of the Spanish royals.

Cuba managed to escape permanent Spanish settlement until the year 1511 when Diego Velazquez de Cuellar landed on the island not as an explorer but as a conqueror with an army and new orders from Ferdinand and Isabella to take the island for Spain. The Taino, Ciboney, and Guanajatabey people resisted de Cuellar's army and engaged in a three-year guerilla campaign against the conquering Spaniards that exacted a hefty toll upon the militant conquistadors, very nearly undoing Spanish designs there before they had begun. Over time, though, new diseases and new technologies[4] began to overwhelm indigenous resistance, and with the capture, torture, and murder of Taino leadership in 1514, de Cuellar took complete control of the island, laid the foundations for the port city of Havana, and instituted the nearly four-century Spanish rule over Cuba and its indigenous populations that lasted into the twentieth century.

The Spanish possession of Cuba, along with their numerous other holdings throughout the Caribbean and the rest of Central and South America, was obsessed with two primary objectives: specie and souls. Convinced that Cuba was littered with easily obtainable gold deposits, de Cuellar and subsequent Spanish governors pressed the remaining indigenous inhabitants of Cuba (a population in steep decline from their peak of 500,000 upon first contact with the Spanish)[5] into forced labor and forcible conversion to Christianity. Formalized by the extension of the encomienda system, which originated in Spain, Spanish conquerors were assigned indigenous Cubans as slaves, after which they were compelled to learn Spanish, abandon their traditional religion, and, above all, work tirelessly for the benefit of the Spanish governor. The subject populations also owed taxes to their ruling conquistadors in the form of meat, crops, and manufactured goods. The Spaniards, for their part, promised to maintain order and infrastructure while enriching themselves on the backs of native labor and ingratiating themselves to the crown with a steady supply of exotic goods from the New World. Havana became a wealthy commercial port city specializing in the export of resources and manufactured products ripped from indigenous possession, and over time, the import of slaves stolen from Africa and pressed into brutal labor in order to expand the production of sugar on the island.

It was this new, globally cherished super crop that propelled the Spanish Empire in the Caribbean and resulted in the slavery of more than a million and a half Africans kidnapped, trafficked, and forced into grueling labor in the New World (those who survived the trans-Atlantic passage, at least).[6] The sheer productivity of the sugar plantations in Cuba even after the official end of brutal chattel slavery there gave Cuba critical leverage on the international, political stage during and after widespread industrialization across the planet. Indeed, throughout the nineteenth century, and still bound by the political and social structures imposed upon the island by a European colonial power, Cuba continued to punch well above its international weight in sugar production, outdoing much larger agricultural systems in the development of this highly sought after commodity:

> Cuba has been called the sugar bowl of the world. Although the island is no larger than the state of Mississippi, it produces every year a million more tons than India, the second largest producing country. Cuba [in the late nineteenth century] produce[d] 28 per cent of the world's sugar cane and over 85 per cent of Cuba's yearly sugar crop is sold to the United States.[7]

By the late nineteenth century, sugar had become the defining crop of the island's economy and would lead to interest, investment, and competition from other imperial powers across the globe, including one located much closer to the island of Cuba itself than Spain's traditional European rivals. Before that imperial competition was to become fully realized, though, a critical capacity in the politics of the island itself was to unfold.

The Ten Years' War: The First Cuban Revolution

By the latter third of the nineteenth century, Europe's grip upon its colonies had begun to weaken. Across the Americas, nationalist movements began to form to fight against paternalistic, imperial control. In 1866, Spain assembled the *Junta de Información,* a maneuver that acknowledged the desires of Cuban nationalists to be guaranteed equal rights under Spanish rule. Cuban nationalists petitioned the *Junta* to be granted

a substantially reduced tax burden, to liberate slaves held in bondage on the plantations, or, failing these allowances, to be granted complete autonomy and independence.
Perhaps unsurprisingly, the Spanish government acceded to none of these demands and
instead used the *Junta* to ban nationalist meetings on the island of Cuba and to raise
taxes on the island's inhabitants. Peaceable voices for change in Cuba were overwhelmed
by those calling for armed rebellion, and on October 10, 1868, nationalist organizer
Carlos Manuel de Céspedes proclaimed Cuba's independence from Spain at his sugar
plantation at La Demajagua. In April of 1869, Céspedes was officially elected president
of an independent Cuba, and a state assembly published a new constitution abolish-
ing slavery and viewing with favor the annexation of Cuba by the United States, both
controversial policies within the ranks of the revolutionary movement. Nevertheless, by
the end of the first month of the revolution, Céspedes counted among his cohort 12,000
men and women at arms, a substantially mixed demographic and economic group that
included freed slaves, plantation owners like Céspedes himself, and an assortment of
merchants and laborers willing to fight to overthrow the callous Spanish overseers.

A combination of Spanish incompetence, guerilla warfare, nationalist fervor, and
indigenous disease extended this first Cuban revolution for a decade, during which time
landed rebels like Céspedes fought alongside revolutionary leaders of African descent
like Antonio Maceo. As a result of this representative coalition of revolutionary fighters, the United States ignored the winds of change in Cuba, and Civil War hero cum
President Ulysses S. Grant never gave public support to the revolutionaries, despite a
number of civic groups within the United States pressuring him to do so. Instead, the
Grant administration vacillated, preferring to mitigate Spanish imperial control over
Cuba rather than seeking its end. Not even the continuation of slavery under Spanish
rule, the said same slavery Grant's Union Army fought to extinguish in the United
States during the Civil War, prompted Grant to consider intervention in Cuba. Instead,
the United States preferred to keep Spain and Old Europe within diplomatic circles
while at the same time coveting the colonial control Spain had over Cuba despite their
abusive, racist, and autocratic methods:

> [T]he Grant administration largely resisted the pressure to support the insurgency, and its
> criticism of Spanish rule was consistently muted as important figures in Washington sought
> to modify rather than end Spanish colonial practices [...] the Grant administration [...]
> even supported the continuation of Spanish sovereignty over the Cuban population as a
> part of a drive to enhance its own material interests in Cuba.[8]

The possibility of a true multiracial and economically egalitarian nationalist movement
was too much to bear in the halls of power in Washington, and the rebellion proceeded
apace in Cuba without American support. Grant, like subsequent U.S. administrations,
would only see the developing situation in Cuba through the eyes of American interests
and would only move to favor the end of Spanish control of the island when it became
expedient to do so.

Differing visions for Cuba's future combined with the death by ambush of Céspedes
in 1874 and the eventual redeployment of Spanish forces in Cuba took the wind from

the sails of the 1868 revolution (better known now as "the Ten Years' War"). As of the signing of the Pact of Zanjon on February 10, 1878, the war was over and the newly independent government of Cuba was dissolved. But the period that followed the Ten Years' War would not be a stable one. Other independence movements rose to challenge Spanish authority and to push for economic and social reforms centered on the island's continued use of slave labor to produce its chief global export. Between 1879 and 1890, the Little War (in Spanish, *La Guerra Chiquita)* picked up where the Ten Years' War left off, and a new round of fighting between Cubans and Spanish imperial forces was engaged. More than a decade of continual armed conflict took its toll on Cuba, though, leaving more than 200,000 dead and contributing to an island-wide economic depression.[9] U.S. tariffs on Cuban imports further punished the island's farmers and merchants and portended further disturbances in the relationship between the island and the economic giant to the north.

The Origins of the American Imperium: 1890–1898

Though officially unmoved during the Ten Years' War, which saw Cuban nationalists resist European imperialism in the western hemisphere, by the end of *La Guerra Chiquita* in 1890, big business in the United States took a very serious interest in the world's sugar bowl. Propelling this interest were the election results of 1896, in which Republican William McKinley defeated Democrat William Jennings Bryan by 271 Electoral College votes to 149. McKinley's victory was based primarily on support from big business and the propertied classes of the Northeast and was fueled by an injection of campaign financing totaling more than $3.5 million (over $118 million in 2022 dollars)[10] solidifying the marriage between big business, social conservatism, and political expansionism. From McKinley's Washington, Cuba loomed as an intriguing imperial prize for the president and for Gilded Age capitalists of the latter nineteenth century.[11] It was nearby, and it was resource-rich. It was known to be abundant in agricultural produce, especially sugar. It had deep water ports, a critical attribute for policymakers eyeing imperial expansion based upon naval power, and finally, and arguably most critically, the island provided quick and easy access to Panama and therefore potentially through the envisioned Panama Canal: "The importance of the Caribbean region to the United States lies in its proximity, its commercial advantage as a source of raw materials and a market for manufactured goods, and as a strategic military addition to the Panama Canal."[12] This final attribute was discussed openly in the halls of Washington and elsewhere as a nearly irresistible attribute coloring U.S. dealings with Spanish officials and within Cuban nationals in the 1890s. Imperial possession of Cuba was seen as a first step toward remaking the Caribbean as a whole into an "American lake."[13]

These factors drove massive private investment in Cuba in the latter half of the twentieth century from business elites who were intricately connected with policymakers in Washington. Interests in agricultural production, transportation, public utilities, and tobacco topped the list of aggressive economic imperialists based in the United States: "American investments in Cuba by 1893 amounted to over $50,000,000; the trade of the United States with the island had reached a value of $100,000,000; while American claims amounted to over $16,000,000."[14] In the months after his election, though, McKinley remained publicly cool toward the idea of military intervention in Cuba, careful not to commit his administration to a policy that would offend Europe and/or chastise foreign investors. Likewise, by early 1898, even for the most ardent imperialist voices in the United States, a *casus belli* had not revealed itself in Washington. With unprecedented cash flow going into Cuba-based businesses, though, and coming out of that island in the form of profit, the writing was most decidedly on the walls as "more and more business spokesmen urged acquisition of the (Caribbean) islands as a stepping stone to the supposedly lucrative Oriental trade."[15] With public opinion somewhat lagging when compared to that of the business elites in the country, though, a groundswell was needed to convince the average American that invading Cuba was the right thing to do.

By 1897, Spanish suppression of Cuban nationalism took the form of organized reconcentration camps in and around many Cuban cities. As thousands were dying from hunger and disease, the conditions of the camps were graphically portrayed for the U.S. public by sensationalist newspapers of the day. If these papers weren't focusing on the hardships endured by Cubans under Spanish rule, they were emphasizing the bravery of Cuban patriots desperate to overthrow the yoke of foreign imperialism. This quality had been aptly demonstrated in the decades-long Cuban uprising against the Spanish monarchy and revealed the Cuban people to have common cause with the American people, a citizenry who envisioned themselves as anti-imperialist freedom fighters: "It was no stretch for public and press alike to link the *Grito de Baire* [announcing Cuba's revolt against Spain] to the 'shot heard round the world' at Lexington 120 years before."[16] Further, graphic depictions of Spanish oppression gave rise to a new kind of journalism, a method of reportage in which rival newspapers competed for readership using increasingly shocking descriptions of unrest in Cuba to whip up public sentiment for a new American war. Under these unique conditions, yellow journalism was born:

> With increasing competition for readership by the major newspapers (such as William Randolph Hearst's *New York Journal*) and the rise of yellow journalism in the United States, reports of Spanish cruelty and atrocities became commonplace as the American public began to demand that [the] President [...] do something about Cuba.[17]

Along with Hearst's *New York Journal*, Joseph Pulitzer's *New York World* played its part admirably, sensationalizing the oppression of the Cubans while expanding the influence of a media industry now firmly entrenched in the business interests of the era. For each of these media tycoons, war in Cuba made good business sense, and they were happy to oblige their fellow robber barons by pushing the reading public in the United States to an increasingly belligerent attitude throughout 1897 and into 1898.

In December of 1897, widespread civil unrest broke out in the port city of Havana. Swayed by the aforementioned yellow journalism, "American popular reaction to the Cuban insurrection instinctively backed the rebels and cast Spain in the role of brutal oppressor."[18] With a groundswell of popular support, Washington decided that the time had come for direct action. The McKinley administration dispatched the U.S.S. *Maine* to Havana under the auspices of safeguarding U.S. citizens and property in Cuba. Tensions between Washington and Madrid were at a fever pitch when, in February of 1898, the *New York Journal* printed a private letter from the Spanish minister in Washington, Enrique Dupuy de Lôme, that described President McKinley as "weak" and a "popularity-hunter." Upon publication of the letter, De Lôme immediately resigned, and the Spanish government issued an apology, but the incident increased the strain between Spain and the United States. American interest in Cuba was at an all-time high, and with a dedicated military presence on the island, war was imminent.

"Remember the *Maine*! To Hell with Spain!"

On February 15, 1898, a huge explosion sounded in Havana Harbor, ripping through the *Maine* and instantly killing hundreds. Other U.S. naval vessels along with Spanish boats docked nearby made a beeline to the crippled vessel in a desperate attempt to rescue what men they could, but such was the violence of the explosion in Havana Harbor early that morning that their efforts were largely futile. One account of the explosion and its aftermath explains that: "Of the 355 officers, sailors, and marines on board at the time of the destruction, 252 were killed outright; 8 others would die of wounds in Havana hospitals. Many of the dead were never recovered, nor were their body parts identified."[19] The days to follow the explosion, an accident resulting from poor storage of

Photo 1 Theodore Roosevelt and the so-called "Rough Riders," one of three units of the 1st United States Volunteer Cavalry during this period and the only one of the three to see active combat during the Spanish-American War (circa 1898).

flammable ammunition in the bowels of the ship,[20] were a diplomatic disaster for Spain. Desperate to establish their innocence and keenly aware that they were not prepared for a war with the United States, Spain offered to investigate the tragedy and to accept American assistance in doing so. The McKinley administration was unmoved by this offer as newspapers around the country leaned into their basest inclinations in reporting the incident as a Spanish plot to the attendant public:

> Shameless pains were taken to gather or manufacture the smallest speck of "news." For a week, the *New York Journal* devoted an average of eight and a half pages of news, editorials, and pictures to the *Maine*. [...] William Randolph Hearst offered a fifty-thousand-dollar reward "for the conviction of the criminals who sent 258 American sailors to their death."[21]

The culmination of this explosion of jingoism from the yellow press was undoubtedly the *New York Journal* headline on February 18th that screamed in huge letters: "REMEMBER THE *MAINE!* TO HELL WITH SPAIN!"[22]

As the crisis mounted, Spain sought support from other European governments, which gave verbal support to the idea of arbitration. In April, representatives from Germany, Austria, France, Great Britain, Italy, Russia, and even Pope Leo XIII begged McKinley not to turn the unexpected naval disaster into an excuse for war and intervene in Cuba, "in the name of humanity." Spain followed this international plea with still more concessions toward the American position, promising to end the re-concentration policy and to embolden the Cuban representative body, the *cortes,* in order to quell domestic strife on the island. Spain did not vow to grant Cuba full independence, though, thereby providing room to maneuver for McKinley and other unabashed expansionists within his administration. Despite Spanish efforts to achieve a compromise, when he gave a report to a joint session of Congress as to the unfolding diplomatic situation between Washington and Madrid on April 11th, President McKinley made no mention of Spanish concessions. The decision for war had already been made.

A week later, Congress passed a resolution declaring that "the people of the Island of Cuba are, and of right ought to be, free and independent, and that the Government of the United States hereby recognizes the Republic of Cuba as the true and lawful government of that island."[23] Unable to achieve a diplomatic resolution to the issue, the Spanish government severed diplomatic relations with the United States and declared war. The United States reciprocated, having already begun to prepare the army and navy to make war against Spanish holdings in the Caribbean and in the Pacific. And despite the fact that "no one in the Administration, of course, bothered to ask the Cubans who were fighting in the island whether they wanted American military intervention," the United States was off to war, settling their dispute with Spain "by war for its own purposes" without any consideration of "the wishes of the Cuban people."[24] It was in this war that the characteristics and behaviors of the American imperium that are all too visible to pundits and commentators two decades into the twenty-first century were unveiled: "the Spanish-American War led to a new role for the American state as an imperial power."[25] America had arrived.

But at only "28,747 officers and enlisted men, against a U.S. population of 73 million people," the standing army at the time of the U.S. declaration of war was "the smallest proportionally under arms at the beginning of any war, except the Revolution of 1776."[26] As such, Congress hastily rushed through a massive $50 million spending bill to bolster troop numbers and upgrade the weaponry and materiel required for the upcoming military action. And despite being relatively unprepared and undermanned in a war against an imperial, European power, the United States still held a critical military advantage in the coming fight. In fact, the accidental explosion of the USS *Maine* was politicized and the advantages of a possible U.S. presence in Cuba were exploited, at least in part, because U.S. military leadership knew that "Spain had no chance of winning the war [...] The Madrid government, debt burdened, with scarcely any ready cash and with dried-up credit, was placed at a severe handicap when compared to the United States."[27] This was especially true of the Spanish position in Cuba, where U.S. Army regulars began to experience quick and consistent success in combat with Spanish troops. After the institution of the naval blockade by the newly minted North Atlantic Squadron at Santiago, U.S. soldiers, including Roosevelt's Rough Riders and units of Buffalo Soldiers, redeployed from the ethnic cleansing of the American Southwest[28] fought into the interior of the island. On July 1st, at the Battles at El Caney and San Juan Hill, U.S. troops penetrated the outer defenses of Santiago itself. Complementing this thrust was heavy artillery fire from the U.S. fleet that, by July 3rd, had beached or sunk all of the Spanish ships in the port of Santiago.

Photo 2 A hastily constructed army encampment in Pennsylvania assembled in order to train newly inducted recruits ahead of the Spanish-American War.

By August, Spain was suing for peace despite their weakened military position, leaving them vulnerable to a highly unfavorable settlement. In the final accounting, Spain surrendered all authority over Cuba and ceded Puerto Rico and Guam to the United States as well (a separate consideration for the Philippines, the other Spanish possession highly coveted by U.S. policymakers, will be discussed next). Fewer than 400 U.S. soldiers were killed in these engagements, facing, as they were, ill-fed and poorly equipped Spanish soldiers already exhausted from years of guerilla warfare against Cuban nationalists. One enemy did exact a substantial toll on American soldiers, though: the heat. More than 2,000 would lose their lives to heat exhaustion and tropical disease in fighting on the island of Cuba, fully sixfold more than died by Spanish bombs or bullets. The same would not be true of the U.S. military's experience in the Philippine Islands over the course of the next five years.

The Philippine-American War: 1898–1904

While U.S. Army units engaged beleaguered Spanish soldiers in the Caribbean, the McKinley administration made a concomitant decision to take possession of the roughly 7,000 islands and 7,000,000 inhabitants of the Philippines. Like Cuba, the Philippines constituted an imperial Spanish holding within which nationalist resistance to European rule had taken root. But while American officials had at least sporadically acknowledged the legitimacy of the indigenous Cuban claim to independence, the Philippines were viewed, both within the popular press and within the halls of Washington, with a more naked imperial ambition. These islands were considered valuable territorial possessions given their proximity to trade routes with China and because of the potential they represented for American diplomatic ambitions in the East. The casual racism asserted by print news coverage of the time likewise presumed that indigenous Filipinos were incapable of self-governance, possibly unlike the nationalist Cubans. Securing this expansive island chain, then, would entail the military defeat of both Spanish imperial forces as well as indigenous, nationalist troops. As such, while many Americans were convinced of the benevolent nature of the U.S. mission in Cuba during the Spanish-American War, the goal of U.S. policy in the Philippines was plainly one of conquest, a conquest for which the new American imperium was ready.

To secure American control of the Philippines, "Commodore George Dewey, in command of the Asiatic squadron at Hongkong [*sic*], was ordered to proceed to Manila Bay in the Philippine Islands [...] and to capture or destroy the Spain fleet there."[29] On May 1, 1898, at the Battle of Manila Bay, Dewey led his squadron into the bay before dawn and destroyed the Spanish ships anchored there. Between May and July of that year, more than 11,000 U.S. troops arrived in the Philippines and by August 13th, all of the capital of Manila was under U.S. control. Contrary to U.S. designs for the island nation, though, in June of 1898, indigenous forces under the command of the charismatic nationalist Emilio Aguinaldo declared their independence and established a provisional government over virtually the entire archipelago outside of Manila. Aguinaldo initially hailed the United States as liberators throwing off the yoke of Spanish oppression, proclaiming that "the great and powerful North American nation have [*sic*] come to offer disinterested protection for an effort to secure the liberation of this country."[30] Hopeful of a cooperative military venture against the Spanish, Aguinaldo's forces attempted to assist the U.S. military in the capture of Manila in the summer of 1898. But the true nature of the U.S. mission in the Philippines would soon be revealed to Aguinaldo.

The U.S. commander in the Philippines, General Wesley Merritt, had, in fact, arrived on the scene with specific orders not to recognize any Filipino Republic. Instead, he was tasked with establishing complete, though nominally provisional, American governance on the islands. Aguinaldo and his government were ordered to withdraw from the city under threat of force by the U.S. commander, and by the winter of 1898, the only military and political authority in Manila was that of the Americans. For a time, a détente existed between the American forces and those of Aguinaldo, but with U.S. troop numbers swelling up to 120,000 throughout the Philippines,[31] a war between U.S. soldiers and indigenous nationalists became inevitable. In February of 1899, fighting broke out between U.S. troops and Aguinaldo's forces on the outskirts of Manila. McKinley blamed the fighting on Aguinaldo and his men, but "After the war, [a U.S.] army officer speaking in Boston's Faneuil Hall said his colonel had given him orders to provoke a conflict with the insurgents."[32] The McKinley administration was committed to the takeover of the Philippine Islands, and the U.S. military was the broadsword sent to carry forward that imperialist policy.

Brutal warfare ensued between U.S. forces and Filipino nationalists. For his part, Aguinaldo was a talented leader who, even with "no previous fighting experience, succeeded in leading a guerilla resistance, which sprang up across the islands."[33] But the American war in the Philippines was intimate and cruel. Civilians were frequently targeted by U.S. forces' intent upon the eradication of the highly effective Filipino insurgency and the total seizure of the Philippine Islands. The U.S. military establishment informed their soldiers that this manner of conquest and dispossession was right and good, and the racist language used by American soldiers served to create the intellectual distancing necessary in order to brutalize the innocent. The civilian inhabitants of the towns and villages set upon by the American military were referred to as "goo-goos," "gooks," or "niggers," a term as familiar as it was offensive to African American soldiers who participated in the war.[34] And like subsequent U.S. wars throughout the twentieth century, this dehumanizing language had substantial military utility. As such, so-called rules of war were systematically trampled by American commanders and their junior officers during the course of this fighting. Even the recently concluded Hague Convention of 1899 governing lawful war and laying out terms for the consideration of war crimes was thoroughly ignored:

> From the first days of fighting, Americans violated even the new rules—such as the require-ment to accept surrender—that would have applied had they recognized the Hague treaty as relevant. Worse, from the early phase in and around Manila, Americans assumed that most of the people they met were hostile, and shot many without a second thought.[35]

More horrors ensued. In a chilling parallel with the behavior of U.S. forces in Southeast Asia decades later, Filipino women and children were targeted as civilian collaborators with Aguinaldo's militia. A U.S. Marine, Littletown Waller, described how these considerations were put into grotesque practice in the field during postwar trial testimony, in which he informed that his commander, one General Smith, "instructed him to kill and burn, and said that the more he killed and burned the better pleased he would be." When Waller asked to clarify who among the indigenous population should be targeted for this killing and burning, General Smith informed him that included anyone "over ten" years of age.[36]

The predictable result of the Americans voluntarily abrogating established rules of warfare was mass civilian death, resulting in dubious political and military outcomes. Nearly five years of fighting left between 20,000 and 34,000 Filipino fighters killed, with civilian casualties of at least 200,000 dead. Other sources put the figure of Filipino civilians dead as a direct result of U.S. military action much higher, "between 300,000 and 500,000 in a population of 7 million."[37] Whatever the precise number of wartime dead among the civilian populace of the Philippines, though, these figures clearly establish a targeted American campaign against noncombatants during the war. Around 4,300 American soldiers died during this campaign too, either wounded by enemy fire or brought down by tropical disease.[38] What's more, the Philippine-American War cost the United States Treasury over $600 million to prosecute and would see an American military presence on those islands well into the twentieth century. The U.S. role on those islands would not come to an official close until the presidential administration of Woodrow Wilson, who acquiesced to persistent Filipino demands for sovereignty over their own territory and an end to American conservatorship over their country. These costs, the lives lost, the infrastructure destroyed, and the gluttonous sums of money spent, all of them were justified by the American imperial oeuvre and the popular discourse that countenanced it as it burst onto the geopolitical scene at the end of the nineteenth century.

Frames of Representation: Constructing Discourse in the Print News Media

What we were telling ourselves about these pursuits, however, through the print news media, the accepted, authoritative narrators of the American story at the time of these events, led the American public to very different conclusions about our political goals, our global purpose, and, critically, about the role of the U.S. military within those domains. That is to say that through the print news media of the late nineteenth and early twentieth centuries, the attendant American public seeking information about the war and the role of the U.S. military in it would likely not have been provided with the criticisms of policy and performance asserted here. Rather, with a substantial amount of crossover and uniformity across publications, readers of the major newspapers in the United States during this period of time would have been presented with a paean to both American political figures and the U.S. military. These intellectual directives resulted from coverage of events connected to the Spanish-American War, which created a discernible discourse among the American public. Within this discourse, a form of curated or contingent knowledge about the events of this global crisis was disseminated. The American press as an institution contributed mightily to the dissemination of this discourse to U.S. readership of the era, a number of interested and literate citizens in the tens of millions. This discourse did not emphasize moneyed interests in the United States pushing for economic control over Cuba, nor did it emphasize the American imperial gambit that saw the domination of huge sections of the globe by military, political, and economic means as the righteous position of the American state in the twentieth century. What it did emphasize about American politics and, critically, about the U.S. military is examined next.

Given the provision of the theoretical context surrounding language, knowledge, and discourse in the opening chapter of this book, it will be evident that a textual examination of *all* connected, related, and/or relatable statements connected to a social and political conflagration as dynamic and wide-ranging as the Spanish-American War would be an impossibility. Instead, and in reliance upon a technique applied by this author in the 2014 work *Palestine-Israel in the Print News Media: Contending Discourses*, the following examination will identify certain prominent or otherwise widely distributed tropes contained within the print news media coverage of the Spanish-American War in order to elucidate a number of oft relied upon elements within the print media's coverage of the war. These elements will be referred to throughout the remainder of this chapter and the remainder of this work as tropes, frames, or more fully frames of representation, wherein a specific theme, characteristic, trait, or leitmotif is either overtly asserted or subtly relied upon by the author or editorial board of a given news publication. Put another way, the analysis of frames of representation within the print news media surrounding coverage of the Spanish-American War will highlight a few of the critical elements that were asserted and repeated by the period press within their retelling of wartime events. Taken together, these frames begin to paint a picture detailing the way in which the print news media discussed U.S. policy and the U.S. military during the prosecution of the Spanish-American War. The examination to follow substantially defines the shape, angles, and vibrant colors of that picture as it landed in the minds of newsreaders all over America at the turn of the twentieth century.

The frames to be examined further were those determined by this author to be among the most prominent, most often repeated, and/or the most discursively impactful upon review of the thousands of news articles examined during the course of the research for this study (see Appendix A of this book for more detail on specific publications and news items that were reviewed for this chapter). Upon extensive review of the products of the news industry during the period under examination, these were the discernible frames of representation that revealed the most about the presumptions and preconditions maintained by the journalistic classes while at the same time being those that would have made the most significant impact within the formation of knowledge about the war among the reading public. These tropes and conditional narratives were repeated time and time again across multiple large media markets as geographically disparate as Los Angeles, Seattle, and New York, often landing with the same vehemence and the same emphasis across those distant locales, and potentially even across years of coverage of events connected to the war.

In identifying these frames of representation within media coverage, then, I am dissecting the story (or more accurately, the stories) within the story of the Spanish-American War, the manner in which knowledge about the war was conditioned, shaped, and reshaped for the duration of the war in American living rooms and American boardrooms. The examination to follow is, therefore, a critique of American knowledge and culture, an imaging of that section of the national mind crafted and mediated by the print news media of the day. This idea of a mediated or mediatized culture is intimately connected to conceptions of media discourse, given the widespread and lasting impact considerations within the media have within a given national polity: "A media culture has emerged in which images, sounds, and spectacles help produce the fabric of everyday life, dominating leisure time, sharing political views and social behavior, and providing the materials out of which people forge their very identities."[39] That is to say, an examination of media discourse and media culture is a delineation of not only knowledge but also of the identity of a given community, in this case, the public readership attending to the Spanish-American War. And while discourse is dynamic and while cultures change over time, the intent of this study is to encapsulate media discourse and its connected formations of knowledge and culture within a specified period of time. It is hoped that extending this method of language, discourse, and news media examination over the events and actions of many American wars throughout the nineteenth, twentieth, and twenty-first centuries will, thereby, lead to more thorough descriptions of a national knowledge, a national culture, and a national mood surrounding our conceptions of the U.S. military, its place within our society, and its place within the world. What follows immediately below, then, is the articulation of the first pillar in that intellectual structure: an examination of prominent frames of representation articulated by the print news media in the United States in descriptions of the Spanish-American War.

Reluctant Warriors: America the Beneficent

Among the most prominent tropes discernible in period media coverage of the Spanish-American War was the idea that the United States had no desire for war, either as a national, political body or as a military institution. Quite separate from the years-long machinations seeking influence and/or control over Cuba and the Caribbean Ocean that were known to have occurred, this frame of representation posits the soldiers and sailors of the U.S. military as reluctant warriors, soldiers of a country that will go to war if a just cause necessitates it but will not run headlong into a conflict if one can be avoided. This frame constructs the United States as a peaceable, non-violent nation, one that never invites war or seeks conflict in order to extend global power but rather only goes to war reluctantly and then only with good reason to do so. The following discussion will detail the manner in which print media coverage asserted this frame of representation in the popular discourse during the Spanish-American War, but this specific trope of media coverage representing the actions of American politicians and the American military will also be revisited in subsequent chapters as well, given its ubiquity of media coverage in American wars throughout the twentieth and twenty-first centuries.

As tensions built within official channels between Washington and Madrid, the print media within the United States insisted upon informing its readership of America's reputation for beneficence, in so doing assuring them that there would be no war between the United States and Spain. In May of 1898, for example, the *New York Times* declared that "We have not, happily, the reputation of being fighters"[40] reassuring their readers of the non-aggressive posture of the United States and its military. On the contrary, the *New York Times* insisted throughout the late winter and early spring of 1898 that cooler heads would prevail in the ongoing dispute with Spain and that their readership should have faith in the elected leaders then presiding over these diplomatic issues. Readers were further encouraged to chastise those who attributed belligerent motives to the McKinley administration or members of the military, explaining in an article entitled "Alarmists Rebuked Again" that "the situation is declared to be grave enough to induce thoughtful and calm consideration of facts, without recourse to displays of brazen fiction calculated groundlessly to inflame or alarm the people."[41] Calm was the order of the day in the Caribbean, a political and diplomatic calm guided by rational and sober men within the Washington establishment who clearly wanted to avoid war with Spain, no matter the largesse that such a war might bring the country. This prevalent narrative trope in print coverage of the Spanish-American War both presumes and insists upon American non-violence and, more particularly, reluctance to join a fight where other political or diplomatic options present themselves. As will be made evident throughout the course of this study, this narrative trope, while common across the multitude of American wars investigated for this work, has little basis in fact when it comes to the ubiquity of the American military around the world and the very common use of war as policy emanating from Washington across multiple generations of the country's history.

Indeed, the readership of the print media was regularly informed of these beneficent intentions within the entire political and military establishment, from the office of the president to the average soldier, as headlines broadcast America's self-conception as an anti-imperial, anti-war force for good in the western hemisphere. Widely distributed news articles informed that "it is the firm intention of the administration not to provoke war with Spain. It is hoped by the president and his advisers that war can and will be avoided"[42] as well as notifying the readership of the "almost superhuman" efforts the Administration has made and is making to preserve the peace."[43] Headlines in other news items blared the country's "Hopes to Avoid War"[44] while also informing the public that there were "No Extraordinary War Preparations Afoot."[45] Hence, it was all but guaranteed through media declarations and via commentary or intimation from official sources that the United States would not be going to war before the end of the nineteenth century. A certain pride was attached to this reluctance to belligerence as a number of news articles across multiple and diverse authoritative publications applied the same repetitive narrative structure. America was not, in fact, a nation of war, nor were we in any way hopeful for war or military conquest. Reluctance to fight as a pillar of national character took pride of place within coverage of diplomatic tensions between the two would-be belligerents.

Truly, throughout the first half of 1898, the press as an institution proudly boasted of America's desire to avoid war at all costs, lauding pacifism as a national trait and abjuring hawkish institutional voices. In fact, these representations would continue beyond the United States' commitment of military personnel to the Caribbean in order to intervene in the burgeoning crisis between Spain and Cuban nationalists. Even after the U.S.S. *Maine* was dispatched to the port city of Havana, for example, the media were at pains to emphasize the friendly intentions of the ship and its crew and to declare unequivocally that a warship was somehow not dispatched on a mission of war: "In official circles the tendency is to accept the argument that the United States is friendly, and that it is needless to attach importance to the visit of an American vessel to Havana."[46] In other instances, news reports actually used the *Maine's* mission as evidence of America's friendly intentions, suggesting it would be folly to view the presence of a foreign warship in Caribbean harbors as a hostile act: "all classes of people will greet the Maine as a representative of a friendly Nation."[47] Credit was given to military personnel but also, overtly, to the McKinley administration, which was repeatedly lionized for their even-handedness and balanced decision-making: "Administration officials miss no opportunity of declaring their confidence in the promise of the maintenance of peace."[48] A military buildup in the Caribbean coupled with an increasingly bellicose administration, then, should have informed the news-reading public of the opposite intent. Neither McKinley nor military leadership wanted war, the press assured its readers, given the peaceable, amicable, and rational nature of the United States and its leadership.

In sum, and in particular, during the run-up to the war in the early months of 1898, the print media within the United States consistently embraced the idea of peace as they featured voices and perspectives that denied the eventuality of war. Through these representations, America was continually categorized as a friendly, peaceable, and peace-loving nation that was reluctant to go to war, even determined to find any other solution but armed conflict with Spain. This frame carried substantial discursive import during the period of coverage reviewed here in that it conditioned the reading public to view military action as alien within American policy designs. In fact, it may be argued that this frame of representation was so regular and so impactful within this period of coverage that readership and the attendant public following news stories about the growing international flap could have reasonably concluded that war itself was singularly un-American. This discursive trope will continue to inform the readership of the print news media within the United States about the supposed intentions of American policy-makers and military leaders as the United States dives headlong into various wars into the twentieth and twenty-first centuries.

Bravery, Discipline, and Endurance: The Story of the American Soldier

War narratives in the contemporary United States are the stuff of legend. They tell of a singular form of bravery and commitment to a cause, of duty and discipline in unimaginably adverse conditions, and of loyalty, camaraderie, and a kind of brotherhood between men under fire that can be found nowhere else in human society. These narrative frames are ubiquitous in contemporary popular culture, particularly in films, television shows, and widely consumed video games such as the now-infamous series of graphically violent first-person shooter simulations known as *Call of Duty*.[49] But depictions of war as thrilling and of the soldiers in them as brave, selfless, and disciplined did not appear in American culture from out of nowhere. The discourse on war and the U.S. military has centered upon these tropes for generations, a fact that serves to justify the imperialist notions of the policymakers designing the wars themselves as effectively as it excuses the grotesque expenditure of American wars in terms of money, materiel, and human lives. These frames of representation predate the U.S. military commitment in the Spanish-American War and would certainly be discernible in period publications during the American Civil War, for example, in news articles from both the Union North and the Confederate South. Nevertheless, it is our purpose here to identify and examine this collective frame of representation, encapsulating soldiery within cherished ideals of bravery, discipline, and/or endurance, in descriptions of American fighting in the Caribbean and the Pacific at the turn of the twentieth century.

That soldiery requires supreme bravery is a foregone conclusion within contemporary American culture. That American soldiers are the bravest of soldiers is likewise presented as a given in all U.S. military conflicts, past and present. Examples of this singular bravery and uncommon valor abound in period news pieces during the Spanish-American War and cut across both theaters of war and all branches of U.S. military service. In an article more akin to a pulp novel than a fact-based news piece, the *New York Times* reported that "the Americans retired, carrying their wounded under fire [...] being closely pursued, the fog enabling the enemy to creep up to them. Two men who were carrying a comrade were shot in the arms, but they continued with their burden."[50] The tone is of a gallant quest, a daring escapade under gunfire while being pursued by the enemy, and it would be as readable as text in an adventure novel as it is here, as news of the war. Furthermore, these epic descriptions were ever-present in the pages of the *Times* throughout the war, adding weight to this discursive construction via sheer volume of repetition as the war dragged on. Another plaudit of American soldiers from the same publication read: "Approaching under cover of the bushes, to about 60 yards from the trenches [...] the Americans appeared, they gave a great yell and the Filipinos became panic-stricken, about a hundred seeking safety in flight, while a white flag was raised by those who were in the trenches who also shouted 'Amigos!' (friends)."[51] Here, American soldiers are dynamic and stealthy and are adept at using foreign terrain to their advantage. Further, they are intimidating to the enemy so as to force their surrender by their mere appearance from undercover. When pressed to fight, American forces are cunning and daring but also stalwart and robust. Where enemy soldiers might sneak, Americans only "approach under cover." Where enemy soldiers become "panic-stricken," Americans show no cowardice whatsoever. From these and many other news narratives like them, attendant audiences back home in the United States were assured of the ultimate prowess and bravery of American men in uniform overseas.

In a complimentary frame of representation to ubiquitous conceptions of American bravery, American soldiers were presented as rigidly disciplined and highly orderly, especially when compared to the slovenly and disorganized enemy. While encamped or on patrol, the American soldier was sober and focused, maintaining his health and hydration in order to be able to accomplish his mission: "On the march he has learned to avoid excessive drinking of water and to have his canteen filled with water which has been boiled, or, better yet, with weak tea, slightly sweetened before starting."[52] When engaged in battle, American discipline truly shone through, becoming a leading factor in American successes in the war: "It was noted that the movement was being executed like clockwork. It was necessarily one of great rapidity, yet the officials noted with delight the perfection of the arrangements as revealed in the press dispatches."[53] Discipline, order, and even perfection of action classified American troops and their maneuvers according to the authoritative press during this period. The American military comes across to the readership in these descriptions as well-organized, well-oiled, and well-intentioned. American soldiers were so disciplined, in fact, that they were able to avoid any kind of wartime atrocities during their deployment.

Or were they? One embedded journalist with the U.S. Army during combat operations attempted a version of the accepted narrative trope pronouncing American discipline, noting that "The Americans refrained from burning the town and are resting there to-night."[54] The disturbing implication in this declaration of American restraint is the idea that on other occasions, American soldiers *had* burned Filipino hamlets and villages in order to punish the local populace, hence the overt praise for resisting that destructive inclination here. In once again praising the discipline of action and attitude present among the American soldiers, this narrative ploy may have thereby inadvertently revealed a disturbing counter-narrative. Indeed, postwar accounts from both American documentarians and Filipino sources inform us that civilian communities were deliberately destroyed or denuded as part of the U.S. campaign to dominate the Philippines. These and other American tactics targeting civilian populations in the Philippines and Cuba made it to the pages of the authoritative news media of the day only in the rarest of cases, typically, as in the example provided, via accidental disclosure rather than as an intentional mea culpa.

A final attribute to be added to the repeated declarations of American valor and discipline within news articles covering the Spanish-American War in this frame of representation is the idea of endurance. American soldiers were able to fight longer and harder than their counterparts on the whole. Through this narrative, news readers were regularly reminded that Americans could endure greater depredations than their enemies. Headlines bellowed out the toughness of the American soldier, and their attached reports confirmed as much, going to great lengths to assure the reading public of the staying power of the average American soldier: "Every officer and man is tired [...] and attacking during the day through the mire of rice paddies and deeply plowed sugar fields, wading and fording streams without a moment's pause to learn of depth or bottom."[55] American soldiers are eager to endure difficulty if it aids the war effort. One article simply titled "The Brave Work of Marines" informed that "they have rushed into the hardships and the dangers of a guerilla campaign with the steady nerves and patient endurance of veterans of a dozen wars."[56] Truly stalwart, the American advantage in manpower is made clear through this frame of representation, adding endurance to that unique combination of American military traits while reassuring readers of an inevitable and honorable victory. Through these attributions, period discourse espoused through the print media assured readers of American superiority in all martial endeavors, educating readers about "The Difference In Men," itself the head-line of a *New-York Tribune* article. Our boys were simply better, the article informed, as it praised "the superior intelligence and skill of the American [soldier]."[57] Often coupled with complimentary frames of representation cataloging American discipline and bravery, the added measure of American endurance completes a narrative loop in this discursive construction describing American soldiers as peerless and heroic with nearly superhuman capacities in wartime and beyond. With such a plain and qualita-tive advantage in manpower, the impending American victory was a mere formality to be lauded and lionized when it arrived in the same manner as we glorify our own, superior soldiers.

The Cowardly, Lazy, and Destitute Enemy

Following on from their characterization of American soldiers as brave, earnest, and disciplined even in the midst of wartime chaos, the authoritative news media of the Spanish-American War era was at great pains to inform its readership of the lowly and destitute nature of America's enemies, representing both Cuban fighters and Filipino nationalists as cowardly, dim, and lazy. Within this frame of representation, character-izations of American enemies as inept and incapable were juxtaposed with high praise of American bravery and skill, a narrative strategy within the broader discourse that served to deepen the dichotomy between the warring sides for attendant American audiences while simultaneously identifying the morality and righteousness of the American cause. These representations were especially discernible in descriptions of battles wherein U.S. soldiers were elevated within a given news narrative over and above hapless and ill-disciplined foreign troops. But in truth, the denigration of for-eigners within the period press was not reserved for fighters alone; sweeping condem-nation of entire national groups or racial categories was also common, revealing the true character of the news industry within the United States to be as unapologetically racist as it was jingoistic and inflammatory in descriptions of those regions conquered by American soldiers. Overall, these descriptions of America's enemies definitively judged and condemned communities throughout the Caribbean and Asia, an intel-lectual rendering which in turn enhances the words and deeds of the American soldier within news media discourse in the mind of the reading public within the United States.

   In one clear example of this highly partial representation, an article that ran under the title "Worthless Cuban Rebels" classifies the entire island of Cuba as bankrupt and backward, declaring clearly in favor of American seizure of the island upon defeat by the Spanish and its recreation as an American protectorate:

> According to one careful observer, progress will be to the average Cuban a deep disap-pointment. It will mean labor, the care of family, the payment of taxes to support schools, living in a place something better than is found for cattle, instead of idly roaming the land to rob when possible, fight Spaniards, when they are in inferior numbers and position, and of never working, even if starvation is to be the penalty of refusal to labor.[58]

This brief assessment in a news piece about the war plainly condemns en masse the entire population of Cuba, relegating them to a backward existence in opposition to hard work, honesty, or social progress of any kind. Here, Cubans are idle, violent, and shiftless beings without hint of either societal organization or intellectual redemption. The assertion within this piece is of a people incapable of organization or modernity, an island of misfits ripe for conquest and crying out for organization by a more capable, guiding hand, namely the United States. This categorical condemnation is extended even further by the racist diatribe of one General Young, a commanding officer in the conquering U.S. Army whose own scorn and vitriol is quoted at length in a news article praising American successes in the war: "The Cubans are no more capable of self-government than the savages of Africa. The average Cuban is a very low order of mankind. He is a mixture of Spanish, Indian, Italian, and negro, and he inherits the bad qualities of all."[59]

Given the respect afforded to an American general during wartime, the inclusion of General Young's racist treatise within a news piece ostensibly covering wartime events is as telling as it is common during authoritative news coverage of American wars. Having obtained the highest military rank possible, Young's opinions carried considerable weight within the period discourse; his diatribe here could well be seen as a standard U.S. Army perspective on Cuban society. And who would know better than an army officer who had participated in the fight to pacify the island? Young's testimony, therefore, constitutes a powerful nail in the coffin of Cuban dignity and autonomy within print news discourse in the United States. As similar testimonies from military and political leadership as well as editorial condemnations mounted during news media coverage of the U.S. military presence in the Caribbean, a specific narrative espousing the hapless and pitiful nature of each of these societies became increasingly prevalent. From within the authoritative press, their undoing was complete.

Not that nationalists, fighters, rebels, or even average citizens on the Philippine Islands were spared this castigation by the American press. In like manner to Cuba, Filipino soldiers and civilians alike were represented within the U.S. press as being ignorant and destitute. Their fighters were ragtag and poorly organized, and their citizens were uneducated and backward. The press discourse of the U.S. war in the Philippines left no doubt as to who the superior fighters were, and beyond that, no doubt as to who the superior society was on the whole. One report of American fighting in the Philippines described a deplorable enemy amid a destitute society: "The insurgents are an armed mob [...] incapable of government, and are angry with Admiral Dewey for seizing vessels flying Filipino flags."[60] In other representations, and in keeping with exhaustive narrative frames portraying American military bravery, they are full of cowardice and are therefore no match for the disciplined, focused, and superior Americans under arms opposite them: "The cowardly retreat of the enemy under the Marblehead's guns had led the American officers to believe that there was little possibility of an attack."[61] The Filipino fighters are, like the Cubans, shiftless and dishonest. They fly false flags of truce, and they seize advantage by sneak attack, not through honorable means of warfare: "A Filipino Colonel came out this morning from Caloocan under a flag of truce. Several American officers promptly went to meet him; but when the parties met the Filipinos opened fire."[62] Honest warfare is, in fact, a foreign concept to these people who complain bitterly about the disciplined and relentless American soldiers: "The Filipinos say 'Los Americanos don't fight fair. Instead of going back after a battle to have dinner and smoke cigarettes, they keep on going ahead and want to fight again'."[63] Laziness, dishonesty, and cowardice are, according to this authoritative news framing, endemic to the Filipino people. By contrast, the American bearing, behavior, and overall way of inhabiting the world are far superior.

Nor was it only enemy soldiers or nationalist fighters described in pejorative terms within the authoritative press. Many Filipino civilians were attached to U.S. Army encampments as aids or employees, taking advantage of the presence of tens of thousands of American soldiers to seek employment in one of the various logistical services that accompany the billeting of U.S. soldiers on foreign soil. This group of Filipino nationals was likewise the target of prejudicial ire from the print news media in the United States even as they were working to facilitate the U.S. presence in their country, for example, as nurses in hospital wards tending to sick and injured U.S. soldiers: "There are Filipino servants in these wards. They are, as a rule, lazy and [...] very dumb. They cannot stand cold at all, and during these chilly nights in December, they beg the nurses very earnestly for blankets."[64] Further insults and racist assumptions are added in another article referring to this same group of service workers and ostensible allies of the U.S. position in the Philippines, which declares, "You would be surprised at the number of them who can read and write."[65] Racist condemnation and prejudicial abuse were not reserved for American enemies, then, but rather were applied generously and frequently by authoritative news articles ostensibly describing Filipino society to attendant American readership at home in the United States.

Conclusions: Media Morality in the Spanish-American War

These and other prolific descriptions dotted the pages of major newspapers in the United States throughout the Spanish-American War, providing a virtually inexhaustible number of references to categorically destitute populations. These communities' entire raison d'être was to subsist through dishonesty and trickery, to avoid work, to steal, rob, or kill, and to in essence remain in a state of backward social and political development into perpetuity. To contrast these representations distributed widely for the attendant American public, consider descriptions of the American soldier and his perspective on the war and the world in general. He is moral and righteous. He is upright and hardworking. He is disciplined, stalwart, and competent in all things. He is educated, knowledgeable, determined, and sober. The disparities between these two descriptive categories could not be more evident. The American soldier and, therefore, America in the world, is a beacon of order and certitude in a wilderness of chaos and corruption. Cubans, Filipinos, enemies, and allies alike are to be forced into the world of order and discipline and remade in the image of the American social system. The Spanish-American War is thereby recast not only as an exercise in extending the righteous American imperium but also as a martial effort to uplift the wayward peoples of the world as we thrust them forcibly into the twentieth century. The U.S. military is further endowed with rectitude and righteousness, therefore, given the expansive extent of their purpose in the world. They don't simply destroy; they uplift and rebuild as well.

Demeaning the enemies of the U.S. military also serves to sustain the morality of war and the righteousness of the American cause within popular discourse. If the enemies of American military action are lazy, ignorant, immoral, and incapable of organizing themselves into a recognizable form of civil society, then the idea of their conquest by American hands becomes excusable, even laudable within American culture. Further, if authoritative voices are given space to denigrate the capacities of the enemies of the United States then the idea of their subjugation, even their death at the hands of American soldiers, is softened substantially, leading observers of war and the American military conquest in little doubt as to which side of the combat line is virtuous and just. It is not surprising, therefore, to see representations of the low state of both Filipino and Cuban society abound in print media coverage of the Spanish-American War from publications across the country. Quite aside from details of the acts and deeds of American policymakers or the average American soldier, these constructions serve to implant a comforting level of certainty and unequivocal moral rectitude within the American discourse about the war itself. Upon repeated exposures to this oft-asserted frame of representation, there can be no doubt within the record of the war that the American enemy was wretched, that the American cause was just, and/or that the American soldier fighting in this war was above moral or ethical reproach during the course of this fighting.

Notes

1 J. A. Hobson, *Imperialism: A Study* (London: George Allen & Unwin, Ltd., 1902), 368.

2 On those few occasions in this work where he is mentioned, Columbus will be referred to using the anglicized version of his name, given its ubiquity in common parlance.

3 Accounts of Columbus' incompetence and cruelty abound in historical revisions of the previously unchallenged narratives that declared him an explorer, a hero, and one of the most important figures in the founding of the United States of America. Specifically, new evidence points to the preeminence of Basque sailors and traders as being key to the trans-Atlantic voyages of both Columbus, whose first mate, Diego Arana, was Basque, and Magellan, whose Basque navigator, Juan Sebastian de Elcano, took command of Magellan's ship after his death and led the remainder of his crew in the first documented circumnavigation of the globe (Michael Upchurch, "The Little Culture that Could," *The Washington Post*, January 30, 2000). See also Mark Kurlansky, *The Basque History of the World* (New York: Walker Books, 1999)).

4 For more details on the methods by which this tectonic historical shift took place, which brought avaricious European conquerors to the established peoples and nations of the Americas and not, say, the other way around, see Jared Diamond's seminal work on the subject, *Guns, Germs, and Steel: The Fates of Human Societies* (New York: W.W. Norton & Company, 1999).

5 In fact, while there are those who point to the vestiges of indigenous culture still prominent in Cuba today, others have argued that the entirety of the Taino people was wiped out by the onslaught brought by the Spanish: "Within 100 years of Columbus' landfall, virtually the entire indigenous population—heavily concentrated in the fertile lowlands of eastern Cuba—had perished" (Christopher P. Baker, "Cuba's Taíno People: A Flourishing Culture, Believed Extinct," *BBC News: Culture and Identity*, February 6, 2019. https://www.bbc.com/travel/article/20190205-cubas-tano-people-a-flourishing-culture-believed-extinct).

6 For more on the role of sugar in the Age of Empires, see April Merleaux's detailed study, *Sugar and Civilization: American Empire and the Cultural Politics of Sweetness* (Chapel Hill: The University of North Carolina Press, 2015).

7 Scott Nearing and Joseph Freeman, *Dollar Diplomacy: A Study in American Imperialism* (New York: Monthly Review Press, 1970 [1925]), 173.

8 Andrew Priest, *Designs on Empire: America's Rise to Power in the Age of European Imperialism* (New York: Cambridge University Press, 2021), 87.

9 H. W. Morgan, *America's Road to Empire: The War with Spain and Overseas Expansion* (New York: John Wiley and Sons, 1965), 6.

10 As a share of the country's GDP, this would render the election of 1896 as the most expensive election in American history (Matthew O'Brien, "The Most Expensive Election Ever: [...] 1896?" *The Atlantic*, November 6, 2012. https://www.theatlantic.com/business/archive/2012 /11/the-most-expensive-election-ever-1896/264649/).

11 In fact, U.S. imperial ambition directed at Cuba goes back much further than the nineteenth century. As indicated by one historian, "Almost from the founding moment of the American republic, its statesmen considered the island part and parcel of the national polity. Cuba's European ties were considered an accident of history." So Thomas Jefferson wrote, "I have ever looked on Cuba as the most interesting addition which could ever be made to our system of States." In 1823, the year the Monroe Doctrine was formulated, Secretary of State John Quincy Adams, having acquired Florida from Spain and recognizing the independence of the revolting Spanish colonies in the hemisphere, found it "scarcely possible to resist the conviction that the annexation of Cuba [...] will be indispensable to the continuance and integrity of the Union itself." (Ivan Musicant, *Empire by Default: The Spanish American War and the Dawn of the American Century* (New York: Henry Holt Publishers, 1998), 78).

12 Nearing and Freeman, *Dollar Diplomacy*, 122.

13 Ibid.

14 Ibid., 249.

15 Morgan, *America's Road to Empire*, 87.

16 Musicant, *Empire by Default*, 78.

17 Clifford L. Staten, *The History of Cuba* (Santa Barbara: Greenwood Press, 2015), 42.

18 Musicant, *Empire by Default*, 78.

19 Ibid., 140.

20 In the immediate aftermath of the explosion, despite the lack of U.S. cooperation, a Spanish investigation was conducted into the causes of the blast aboard the U.S.S. *Maine*. Their initial conclusions supported the theory that the explosion was an unfortunate accident: "what the Spanish divers found was significant [...] the hull plates were bent outward; 'the entire vessel forward appears open,' noted their report, 'having undoubtedly burst toward the outside.' Thus, it had been an *internal* explosion." In 1976, a team of American investigators also determined the explosion to have been accidental resulting from high internal temperatures in the ship's storerooms that contained volatile black powder: "It contained between eight and nine tons of black powder, and in hot weather, the temperature of the compartment had been measured at 110 degrees" (Musicant, *Empire by Default*, 142–43 (emphasis in original); Ibid., 138).

21 Ibid., 143–44.

22 Ibid., 144.

23 Nearing and Freeman, *Dollar Diplomacy*, 251–52.

24 Philip S. Foner, *The Spanish-Cuban-American War and the Birth of American Imperialism 1895–1902. Volume I: 1895–1898* (London: Monthly Review Press, 1972), 253.

25 Ibid., 29.

26 Musicant, *Empire by Default*, 235.

27 Ibid., 275.

28 As to these related martial purposes for which Buffalo Soldiers were used by the U.S. government, author Benjamin Wetzel informs that the authority of the federal government was built upon the destruction of Native America: "the American government assiduously went about extending its authority over the American West [...] conflicts with the Sioux and Cheyenne at Little Big Horn in 1876, the Apache in 1886, and the Lakota at Wounded Knee in 1890 serve as only the most well-known of the violent encounters between American forces and

Native American groups." Without the establishment of this military and political authority on its own continent, Wetzel argues, the imperial war against Spain years later would not have occurred (Benjamin Wetzel, *American Crusade: Christianity, Warfare, and National Identity, 1860–1920* (Ithaca: Cornell University Press, 2022), 74).

29 Nearing and Freeman, *Dollar Diplomacy*, 252.

30 Ibid., 197.

31 Robert P. Saldin, *War, the American State, and Politics since 1898* (Cambridge, England: Cambridge University Press, 2011), 46.

32 Howard Zinn, *A People's History of the United States* (New York: HarperCollins, 2003 [1980]), 314.

33 Samuel Moyn, *Humane: How the United States Abandoned Peace and Reinvented War* (New York: Farrar, Straus and Giroux, 2021), 110.

34 Author Willard Gatewood describes an "unusually large number" of desertions among black troops in the U.S. Army in the Philippines in protest of their racist treatment at the hands of their commanders as well as in sympathy with population of the Philippines themselves. In describing this account, activist-author Howard Zinn goes on to describe the Filipino rebels who "addressed themselves to 'The Colored American Soldier' in posters" pleading with them to find common cause between the Filipino villagers and their own struggle for dignity and equality back home (Zinn, *A People's History of the United States*, 319).

35 Moyn, *Humane*, 111.

36 Waller's testimony here is also quoted at length in Zinn's *A People's History of the United States*, 316.

37 John Tirman, *The Deaths of Others: The Fate of Civilians in America's Wars* (New York: Oxford University Press, 2011), 45.

38 According to researcher and author John Tirman, who is an expert in war and wartime casualties, most of the more than 4,000 American deaths in the Philippine campaign were due to disease, not enemy fire: "The war in the Philippines took 4,000 U.S. soldiers' lives, most by disease" (Ibid).

39 Douglass Kellner, *Media Culture: Cultural Studies, Identity and Politics between the Modern and Postmodern* (London: Routledge, 1995), 1.

40 "Not Evil, But Good," *New York Times*, May 6, 1898, 6.

41 "Alarmists Rebuked Again: No Extraordinary War Preparations on Foot. Both Secretary Long and Secretary Alger Authorize an Emphatic Denial of Sensational Rumors—'Public Judgement should be Suspended' Still The Administration's Watchword. Military and Naval Activity Explained. Things Looking Better, Mr. Long Says. Confidence in the Court of Inquiry," *New-York Tribune*, February 27, 1898, 1.

42 "Hopes to Avoid War: Administration will not Rush into a Conflict. Waiting Naval Court's Report. Policy of the President as Outlined to Friends at the White House—Spanish Government not Believed to Have Been Involved in Any Plot to Blow Up the Warship—Any Demand for Indemnity, It Is Said, Is Likely to be Met Promptly. Expects Spain to Pay. Would Congress Agree to It? No Important Developments. Public is Fully Informed. Secretary Long's Statements. Information from Sigsbee. Sigsbee's Recommendations Approved," *The Washington Post*, February 25, 1898, 1.

43 "A Crisis Imminent: Cuban Complications Threaten Immediate War With Spain. President McKinley's Patience Almost Exhausted—Inexplicable Delay of the Foreign Relations Committee—Additions to the Spanish Navy," *Los Angeles Times*, February 6, 1898, 6.

44 "Hopes To Avoid War," *The Washington Post*, February 1, 1898, 1.

45 "Alarmists Rebuked Again," *New-York Tribune*, February. 27, 1898, 1.

46 "Maine Now at Havana: Exchange of Courtesies with Spanish Officials. Sigsbee Confers With Gen. Lee. Arrival of Warship Occasioned Surprise and Aroused Curiosity, but City Remains Tranquil—Maine Likely to Remain in Port Some Time—Commander Sigsbee to Call on Acting Captain General Parrado—Much Gratified by His Reception," *The Washington Post*, January 26, 1898, 1.

47 "The Maine Sent To Cuba: Battleship Leaves Key West for Havana, Supported by the Whole of Admiral Sicard's Fleet. Secretary Long Explains It, Says It Is a Friendly Call Merely—Spain Notified of the Course to be Taken—A Concession to the Demand for Action," *New York Times*, January 25, 1898, 1.

48 Ibid.
49 For more on the ubiquity of positive war imagery in American video game culture, see Chapter 8 in this book entitled "Selling the Drama: Culture, Media, the Military, and the American Self."
50 "Fierce Battle With The Filipinos: Six Killed and Forty-three Wounded on American Side. Rebels Were Finally Routed. Col. Stotsenburg and Lieut. Sisson of Nebraska Regiment Dead. Fourth Cavalry Loses Two Men—Enemy Fought Behind Breastworks Near Quingua—Thirteen of Their Force Killed," *New York Times*, April 24, 1899, 1.
51 "Fighting Their Way To Malolos: Americans Defeat Aguinaldo, Leading His Army. The Enemy Forced Back. Left 100 Dead on the Field, Losing Many Prisoners. MacArthur Advances, Result of Seventy-Two Hours of Battle Complete Rout and Flight of the Filipinos," *New York Times*, March 28, 1899, 1.
52 "Army Life Around Manila: Regulations for the Bivouac After the Fighting of the Day—Outposts Detailed—Health Precautions," *New York Times*, October 20, 1899, 5.
53 "Otis Describes the Battle: Administration Officials Note the Brilliancy of the Movement to Crush the Filipinos' Army," *New York Times*, March 26, 1899, 1.
54 "Fighting Their Way to Malolos," *New York Times*, March 28, 1899, 1.
55 "Army Life around Manila," *New York Times*, October 20, 1899, 5.
56 "Brave Work of Marines: Full Story of the Fighting at Guantanamo Camp. In Fancied Security the Midnight Surprise Second Night's Fighting Cubans on Skirmish Duty. Final Rout of the Spanish," *New-York Tribune*, June 27, 1898, 3.
57 "The Difference in Men," *New-York Tribune*, June 20, 1898, 6.
58 "Worthless Cuban Rebels: Described by Returning Army Officers as Fit for Nothing but Loafing and Pillage. Means Trouble For America. Insurgents' Continuance of the Fighting Considered a Bad Sign—Plans to Feed the Needy Poor," *New York Times*, August 24, 1898, 2.
59 "Cannot Trust The Cubans: Gen. Young Says It Would Be Folly to Give Them the Island. His Estimate of Their Character Based Upon His Experience at Santiago—Praises the Conduct of Maj. Gen. Joe Wheeler," *The Washington Post*, August 6, 1898, 4.
60 "Filipinos Fleeing Before Americans: Aguinaldo's Forces Driven Back from Manila. Their Loss in Battle 5,500. Rebel Leaders Declare Americans Forced the Engagement," *New York Times*, February 7, 1899, 1.
61 "Brave Work of Marines," *New-York Tribune*, June 27, 1898, 3.
62 "Americans Hold Manila Securely: Lines Extended Nine Miles to the North and South. No Fear of Water Famine. The Works Captured and Missing Machinery Recovered. Natives Put To Rout. One-third of the Hostile Body of Filipinos Incapacitated and the Survivors in Full Retreat," *New York Times*, February 8, 1899, 1.
63 "Army Life around Manila," *New York Times*, October 20, 1899, 5.
64 "In the Hospital at Manila: Comfortable Home Provided for Sick American Soldiers in the Philippine Islands," *New York Times*, January 26, 1900, 3.
65 "Filipinos Becoming Friendly: A Volunteer Soldier's Estimate of the People of Manila—They Are Learning to Like the Americans," *New York Times*, November 20, 1898, 14.

Chapter Three

WORLD WAR I: AMERICAN SERVICE

We are about to do the bidding of wealth's terrible mandate. By our act we will make millions of our coun-
trymen suffer, and the consequences of it may well be that millions of our brethren must shed their lifeblood,
millions of brokenhearted women must weep, millions of children must suffer with cold, and millions of
babes must die from hunger, and all because we want to preserve the commercial right of American citizens
to deliver munitions of war to belligerent nations.[1]

—*Senator George Norris, April 4, 1917*

A House Divided: America in World War I

World War I, or the Great War as it was then known, was a slaughter of epic proportions. Devastating new military technologies merged with age-old continental rivalries
and imperialist ambition in an exhaustive war of attrition, one that bled armies on both
sides of the gore-soaked trenches of energy, equipment, and, most tragically, the soldiers
themselves. And though this conflagration would rend the world for four long years,
from the summer of 1914 through to November of 1918,[2] the United States of America,
led by effete, southern-born Democratic president Woodrow Wilson, was a latecomer
to these horrific events. Sustained by the majority of public opinion in the United States
at the time, isolationism was the buzzword that encapsulated U.S. foreign policy of
the era: leave European problems to Europe while America tackles its own. When the
American Expeditionary Force finally did enter the war in April of 1917, compelled
most forcefully by the business elites who stood to profit from the bloodshed, the entire,
brutal episode was just 18 months from its conclusion. After armistice, state and society
in the United States embraced a new model of foreign policy, one that would guide
them substantially throughout the twentieth century. In this new ethos, isolationism was
abandoned as folly as the United States donned the garb of increasing militancy and
nearly endless warfare for the remainder of the era. The characteristics of the society
that launched us into perpetual conflict, militarizing our sidewalks, streets, and schools
along the way, therefore bear closer examination here.

At the outset of hostilities in the summer of 1914, the United States of America was
a decidedly racist, unjust, and, in many ways, authoritarian country. From sanctioned
segregation in the former Confederate South to strike-breaking and union-busting in
the industrial north, America on the precipice of World War I was deeply unequal. At
the time, as it is now by most valuations, the country contained a variety of intractable
social, economic, and political problems within its own borders, and it was this collection of problems that drove the public imagination of the nation far before any consideration of international political rivalries might even have been entertained. In the

words of one historian, America in 1914 was in turmoil, at war with itself, and deeply at odds with the motions and movements of twentieth-century modernity:

> [G]iven the underlying fissures within a formerly colonial society, originating in the triangular Atlantic slave trade, expanded by means of the violent appropriation of the West, peopled by a mass migration from Europe, often under traumatic circumstances, and then kept in perpetual motion by the surging force of capitalist development, America's problems with modernity were profound.[3]

In short, the problems faced by American society at the outbreak of World War I were enormous. As such, it is likely that the assassination of the heir to the Austro-Hungarian throne by Bosnian-Serb nationalist Gavrilo Princip on June 28, 1914, had little bearing on the day-to-day activities of most Americans. Soon, though, it would become apparent that this singular act would be used as a catalyst for global war on an unprecedented scale, involving U.S. allies as well as newly created enemy states. The United States of America would become a direct player in these events, sending a largely conscripted and mostly untrained army to join in the fight, adding the deaths of thousands and the maiming of thousands more to the already staggering weight of social and political strife borne by America in that troubled decade.

Illegal Dissent: The Espionage and Sedition Acts

In the buildup to World War I in the United States, hundreds of thousands of Americans across diverse ethnic, economic, and ideological communities would come to be at the receiving end of exclusionary policies and targeted discrimination orchestrated by the primary organs of the state itself under the government of Woodrow Wilson. Within the wartime government in Wilson's Washington, state-sponsored policies led to unconscionable levels of sanction and discrimination directed at citizens deemed to be critics of the war or of U.S. participation in it. Through legal action, explained by their proponents as necessary public safety measures during the crisis of wartime, socialists, labor leaders, immigrants, and hundreds of others would become targets for censure and imprisonment along with random episodes of communal violence for the duration of the war. And as with the institutional racism within the United States directed at the country's African Americans and other minority groups within the country discussed in some detail later, in many ways, the suspension of previously guaranteed civil liberties and the violent eruptions that it impelled would have lasting consequences for the social values of the country for decades to come.

In the spring of 1917, some measure of debate rippled through the halls of political power in the United States regarding the impending U.S. entry into World War I. For many analysts today, though, despite vocal calls from many within the country for the United States to maintain its neutrality,[4] American participation in the war with the Allies was a matter of when, not if.[5] Business elites and firms connected to the manufacture of war materiel were deeply entrenched with the Allied powers and, at the same time, were highly eager to join in the European bloodshed given that "by 1917, when America entered the war, its trade with Britain and France had increased by 184 percent"[6] over previous decades. As such, on the evening of April 2, 1917, President Woodrow Wilson addressed a joint session of Congress and passionately called for a declaration of war against Germany. Two days later, the resolution easily passed the Senate by a vote of 82 to 6, with a notable no vote from Nebraska Senator George Norris, who cautioned his colleagues presciently: "We are about to do the bidding of wealth's terrible mandate."[7]

With the die cast, the economics and logistics of warfare became the primary preoccupation of Wilson and his cabinet; with equal fervor, though, they threw themselves into the creation of a nationwide propaganda campaign designed to silence criticism of the war and censor the press. With the Orwellian title of the Committee on Public Information (CPI), this official propaganda department was headed by former journalist George Creel, who was directly appointed by Wilson to head the campaign to control information as it related to the U.S. prosecution of the war. Creel was afforded a staff of thousands who worked in the production of pro-war materials, including pamphlets and posters, while they simultaneously reviewed news publications, scouring millions of column inches for any whisper of a critique of ongoing U.S. policy from the fields of France to the firms of Wall Street.[8] Key to this naked propaganda campaign were the Four Minute Men, roughly 75,000 civilian volunteers who traveled to civic centers and schools in order to sing the praises of war and glory while condemning any criticism of the United States as un-American. Millions of Americans were witness to these ostensibly patriotic spiels, and at least thousands felt the wrath of their neighbors for not being fully and blindly committed to American involvement in World War I.[9]

The effect of the CPI was almost immediate. Just weeks after the congressional vote to commit the United States to war, Creel and his staff had generated enough paranoia within Washington and in the popular discourse to compel the passage of a federal censorship bill designed to prosecute any and all critics of the war effort:

> The Espionage Act, as it was known when finally enacted into law on June 5, 1917, furnished the government with ample instrumentalities for the suppression of those who opposed the war. It provided for $10,000 fines and imprisonment up to twenty years for persons obstruction military operations in wartime, and $5,000 fines and up to five years' imprisonment for use of the mails in violation of the statute.[10]

The Espionage Act equated dissent with terrorism remaking any and all who opposed the war or America's role in it as an enemy of the state. Protections previously guaranteed to all citizens were reduced to unaffordable luxuries as the America of the Great War generation was compelled to fall into lockstep with the militaristic program of the day at risk of fine, imprisonment, or worse. Under the Espionage Act, the Postmaster General was permitted to read suspicious mail and to impede its transport if he deemed its contents nefarious. In the era of the handwritten letter, this effectively severed communication for hundreds of thousands of Americans from scores of targeted groups, including immigrants from new enemy states and so-called political dissidents who had rallied or organized on behalf of damnable ideologies like socialism or communism. In the chilling assessment of one author: "The Espionage Act was the legal beginning of America's surveillance state."[11]

But Wilson, the CPI, and the military leadership of the country were not done there. Not even a year after the passage of the Espionage Act:

> [t]he administration instigated [...] the Sedition Act of May 1918 [which] provided for the arrest of those deemed guilty of utterances or actions that might impede the war effort, including the providing of advice to men subject to the draft [...] The Sedition Act went farther than any previous federal legislation in its negation of the essential elements of the Bill of Rights, barring any "disloyal, profane, scurrilous or abusive language about the form of government of the U.S. or the Constitution of the U.S., or the military or naval forces of the U.S. or the flag of the U.S. or the uniform of the army or navy."[12]

In tandem, the Espionage Act and the Sedition Act became powerful tools in the hands of Wilson administration officials in the silencing of dissent and the suspension of civil liberties in the United States. With this legislation in hand, the administration had the backing of federal, state, and local police as well as all affiliated courts to seek out critics of U.S. policy and to punish them as they saw fit within the letter of these new, repressive laws. All forms of demonstration or dissent via speech were free and fair targets for prosecution, too, given that the Sedition Act included statutes against any form of expression that even sought to encourage others to draw contemptuous or scornful conclusions about the U.S. government or its policy.

The effects of these repressive government measures seeking to outlaw free speech and compel the citizenry to support the war were as immediate as they were wide-ranging. Leftists and labor organizers, suffragists and supporters of women's rights, communists, student groups, and immigrant communities were all targeted by these draconian measures and were all made to suffer because of them: "About nine hundred people went to prison under the Espionage Act. This substantial opposition was put out of sight, while the visible national mood was represented by military bands, flag waving, the mass buying of war bonds, the majority's acquiescence to the draft and the war."[13] Jail terms of six months were not uncommon. In West Virginia, the secretary of the Socialist Party received that sentence for suggesting that America had become "militarized." In Philadelphia, jail terms were handed down for even the possession of a pamphlet entitled "Long Live the Constitution of the United States."[14] Hard times and little comfort awaited these prisoners, jailed for the assertion of previously guaranteed rights now suspended by a government obsessed by war. And like so many freedoms mythologized as divine, the right to free speech died in the dark in World War I era America and arguably still remains a tenuous liberty more than a century later.

Racism in America: From the Compromise of 1877 to the Red Summer of 1919

Among the most durable of the social issues plaguing the United States in 1914 was its intractable racism. This was because America in the 1910s was the social and economic product of policy decisions made two generations earlier during the Presidential Election of 1876. Prior to that election, federal troops had been billeted across the former Confederate South in order to forcibly impose the Reconstruction Amendments, the 13th through the 15th, passed a half century before World War I, in order to ostensibly grant equal status under the law to all people within the borders of the United States. The death knell of the concerted effort toward political, economic, and critically, cultural reunification of the post–Civil War United States came with the decision of the newly minted Rutherford B. Hayes administration in 1877 to shift federal troops billeted in the former Confederate states to rail yards and mines across the industrial north, where laborers and workers of all stripes were striking en masse.[15] The now-famous Compromise of 1877 assured Republican Hayes the White House despite his defeat in the 1876 election to Democratic rival Samuel J. Tilden by more than 247,000 popular votes.[16] The might of the Army of Reconstruction, some 43,000 soldiers still clad in their Civil War era blue coats, facilitated the breaking of worker strikes by industrialists, managers, and business elites from West Virginia to Cleveland and many spots in between.[17] The only cost in advancing this so-called compromise was the protection of the newly acquired rights of freedmen, former slaves, and their descendants in the violently racist American South. It was a price that those united, elite interests were all too happy to pay.

As such, several complimentary priorities within the American value system were firmly established with the Compromise of 1877. Arguably the most lasting pillar of American society stemming from this policy decision was the abandonment of America's newest citizens, the people of color, who had won the greatest gains during the conflagration of the 1860s. Left to the whims of the local authorities across the southern slave states, African Americans lost what they had gained in the intervening years between 1863 and 1877, rendering the Reconstruction Amendments worth little more than the paper they were written on. 1877, therefore, marks the year in which federal protection for, and enforcement of, the rights of African Americans was deemed of secondary importance to concentrated business interests in the North. Many would suggest that the clear articulation of the priorities as embodied in the Compromise of 1877 established a value system within the United States that remains highly recognizable today, decades into the twenty-first century.

The constitution of American society during the Great War was naturally the product of these decisions. In all measurable ways, America was a racist nation, but it was singularly so when it came to the makeup of the American military preparing to fight in the great European conflagration. African Americans were drafted at a higher rate than whites, and they were offered less opportunity to claim an exemption from forcible military service given the racially motivated standards of the more than 4,000 national draft boards created by the Wilson administration to bolster troop numbers once the U.S. commitment to war had been made. According to historian David Kennedy:

The Selective Service System also treated blacks unfairly, especially with respect to exemptions. Thirty-six percent of black registrants were pronounced eligible for service compared with only 25 percent of whites. In part that differential derived from the effective ban on black volunteering, which left the black pool of able-bodied men, in contrast to the white, undepleted by voluntary enlistments. But to a great extent, the inability of blacks to secure exemptions at the same rate as whites owed to their inferior position in American society.[18]

As a result of the decision-making made by American draft boards in 1916 and 1917, more than 13 percent of the involuntary army that comprised the American Expeditionary Force was African American, even though at the time, only 10 percent of the American population was black.[19] Even the eventual head of the American Expeditionary Force, the U.S. Army's name for their World War I contingent, carried a racist moniker as his nickname, known as he was as "Black Jack" Pershing for his previous command of African American units in the Spanish-American War.[20] (For more on the specious and anti-democratic nature of the World War I-era draft boards and the Selective Service Act of 1917, see the subtitled section in this chapter, "'Selective' Service: Conscription and Discourse in World War I").

Perhaps unsurprisingly, then, the American Expeditionary Force (AEF) was segregated upon its constitution. In fact, in military encampments during basic military training, black troops billeted in southern cities were saddled with so many restrictions as to remake their time in the AEF into a form of compensated incarceration: "black soldiers were in effect prisoners restricted from off-base recreational facilities and subjected to the segregationist practices of the host communities."[21] Upon completion of their training and their decampment to European battlefields, these segregated units were unofficially barred from serious combat roles, instead being designated for menial labor as dictated by their white commanding officers. Racial epithets, taunts, jeers, and physical abuse hampered these men in all of their activities within the AEF, given that "neither the army nor the government nor the American people in general included the 400,000 African Americans who served with the U.S. Army during the Great War in their definitions of common citizenship."[22] It seems clear, then, that the U.S. military during World War I took its moral compass from American society writ large, heaping abuse and degradation upon its African American membership before, during, and after combat operations in the war had long ceased.

The predictable culmination of this institutional racism exemplified by, but certainly not limited to, the era's military was undoubtedly the summer of 1919, when race riots tore through more than 25 American towns and cities. In what came to be aptly known as the Red Summer, white mobs, largely motivated by jealousy at black soldiers returning to their communities with positive military records and a small amount of pay earned during their time in the army, attacked black youth and black veterans, in some cases with the cooperation and/or coordination of local police. Poor federal planning for the reintegration of soldiers into the postwar economy inflamed racial tensions throughout the country, leading to a catalyst in the summer of racist rage:

Late in July, a huge riot exploded in Chicago when whites stoned a black teenager who accidentally drifted across a marker segregating a Lake Michigan beach. A rock struck the boy in the head and he drowned. The resulting riot engulfed Chicago's business district, killing 38 people and seriously injuring 500. More than 1,000 people were left homeless when arson was added to the rioters' weaponry.[23]

The Red Summer of 1919 cost hundreds of lives, with the largest single mass casualty attack killing as many as 200 African Americans in Elaine, Arkansas, in September of that year.[24] Federal leadership in the resolution of this violence was nonexistent, leading one historian to assert that then President Woodrow Wilson,[25] considered for a time a progressive reformer, simply "never contemplated using the moral and political authority of the presidential office to condemn racial bigotry or direct public attention to the chronic perpetrators of racial violence."[26] In the absence of any federal policy addressing such ghastly racial violence, towns and cities in post–World War I America were left to their own devices, with many falling deeper into segregationist and exclusionary policies. It wouldn't be until the Civil Rights legislation of the 1960s that federal leadership would take a role in attempting to ameliorate America's most intractable social disease.

The Business of War: American Interest in Europe

If the constitution of American society and its value system during the era of the Great War was the direct product of the Reconstruction Era, then it is critical to further explore the relationship between business, the military, and the American society during that period. With the rights of African Americans duly forfeited via the abrogation of federal protections in the Reconstruction South and with free speech in full retreat thanks to the Espionage and Sedition Acts, the U.S. in the early 1900s was able to revive another policy priority for the oncoming century: the guaranteed political protections of concentrated business interests no matter the human cost. As it happened, the exclusively profit-minded priorities of Morgan, Rockefeller, Carnegie, and Mellon et al. eventually came to support American entry into the war, where their European markets for all goods, civilian and military, could be expanded under the auspices of vague notions of American national interest. And since the industrial classes could no longer count people as property,[27] market expansion needed to run parallel with the suppression of labor costs in order for these magnates to maintain their gluttonous fortunes. As a result of these hand-in-glove considerations between policy construction and business expansion, a clear priority emerged in early twentieth-century America: the protection of business interests and the propertied classes. And if the story of America in World War I is the story of a society struggling to contend with the fateful consequences of the decisions of generations past, then we too must come to terms with the priorities and the pronouncements of this generation of financial and martial arbiters of the Great War.

Industrial firms and large business holdings began to sway American policy before the war, while the ramifications of American entry were still being debated by U.S. citizens and their representatives. Far from neutral observers, the United States contributed heavily to the Allies selling bombs and bullets to France, Great Britain, and Russia while also loaning huge sums of money to Allied governments to facilitate their prosecution of the war: "American bankers and corporations were reaping enormous benefits by selling weapons and munitions to the British, the French, and the Russians. Now these profiteers wanted to take this covert alliance a step further, into actual war."[28]

Using Washington-based policy tools, J.P. Morgan and Co. benefited substantially from this wartime profiteering before U.S. entry into the contest, drawing the United States ever closer to a military commitment to the Allies. But forcing Washington's hand in that policy shift was precisely the point: "J.P. Morgan and Company acted as agents for the Allies, and when, in 1915, Wilson lifted the ban on private bank loans to the Allies, Morgan could now begin lending money in such great amounts as to both make great profit and tie American finance closely to the interest of a British victory in the war against Germany."[29]

But these methods still didn't satisfy the need for profit. In the logistical scramble that resulted from the U.S. declaration of war against Germany in April of 1917, Morgan and others leaned heavily on the Wilson administration to influence the appointment of one of their own, Bernard Baruch, to the head of the War Industries Board.[30] With that appointment confirmed, industrial firms across the country could use their direct connections to that board to press for manufacturing and logistical contracts that were deemed necessary for wartime production. In these efforts, the industrialists of the era were creating a macabre blueprint for developing a permanent relationship between industry, the military, and the perceived national interest within the United States. Whether by intentionality or opportunism, war created business expansion, and easy access to policymakers in Washington made the wealthy even wealthier during the Great War. The price of this colossal wealth was, of course,

Photo 3 A soldier of the U.S. Army's 32nd Division in the trenches during World War I.

the millions of dead across the battlefields of Europe, or closer to home, the 116,000 American dead (times two catastrophically wounded) as a result of the war.[31] Naturally, the rich became richer while thousands of poor and working-class soldiers were made to pay the bill. Put another way, "American capitalism needed international rivalry—and periodic war—to create an artificial community of interest between rich and poor, supplanting the genuine community of interest among the poor that showed itself in sporadic movements."[32]

World War I marked the first declared war in the United States in the twentieth century. It also represented full-scale economic production alongside a concomitant federal commitment to the manufacture of public consent for a controversial military engagement. The parameters of these relationships, those connecting policymaking to industry and profiteering to the average, everyday soldier, remain instructive when it comes to recognizing the size and scope of these institutions within the United States today. As such, World War I permanently established "the tightening bonds between capital and the military" in this country and, in so doing, "changed the nature of warfare in the twentieth century."[33] The costs of these developments were staggering; civil liberties were compromised, and whole segments of the American populace were sacrificed in aid of expanding profits on the basis of artificial consent. As ever, the poorest among us, those of us with the least choice in a top-heavy capitalist system, paid the dearest price, with more than 116,000 families deprived of a loved one as a result of the marriage between profit and patriotism. In the end, the American legacy in World War I can be recognized as "the product of a globalizing militarism that promotes economic profit over people's lives."[34]

"Selective" Service: Conscription and Discourse in World War I

Another American liberty that came to be sacrificed at the altar of the Great War was the right not to join the military. This new loss of individual freedom stemmed from the fact that the Wilson administration and its financial backers had badly overextended themselves with their April 1917 declaration of war against Germany. As it existed at the time, the sum total of U.S. forces available for action was a mere 98,000 men, half of whom were billeted in U.S. colonies and territorial possessions abroad, a force size far too small to make a substantial difference in the bloody fighting on the continent.[35] And even if such a force had been called up, trained, outfitted, and prepared for deployment, logistical matters, not least of which was the problem of transport across the Atlantic, loomed large in the aftermath of the April 1917 declaration. What would be needed should the United States truly seek to influence the outcome of the macabre events transpiring in Europe in 1917 would be a doubling in the size and reach of the U.S. military and a concomitant increase in the number of ancillary personnel able to outfit those soldiers with the materiel they would need once they arrived at the blood-soaked trenches of France.[36] The will of the political and economic elite to make war may well have been present, but the means to do so remained out of reach.

The surest way to an expansion of the kind that would be necessary for the United States to enter World War I was conscription. Yet the idea rankled Wilson and his

Secretary of War, Newton Diehl Baker. Both officials expressed their beliefs in volunteerism and ultimately "refused to endorse proposals for universal training,"[37] the so-called UMT, or Universal Military Training, endorsed by the more rightist elements of Wilson's government. In the war of ideas that would follow, Wilson and Baker would assert that the idea of conscription violated a key principle of American values, intimating that, in some intangible way, Americans had a natural integrity and would rise to the challenge posed by authoritarian Europe on the basis of moral rectitude alone. This persistent American self-conception bears further discussion in the closing chapter of this work, "Selling the Drama: Culture, Media, the Military, and the American Self," but for our purposes, suffice it to say here that in 1917, Wilson and Baker were wrong. The belief that these men at the top of the administration had that Americans would rally to war on behalf of the political and economic elites on the basis of the principle and principle alone would not be borne out. With time of the essence and recruitment numbers lagging far behind their targets, Wilson and Baker acquiesced to a reversal of policy, and on May 8, 1917, the euphemistically named Selective Service Act was hastily passed through the 65th United States Congress.

This act was a crucial piece of legislation for the wartime era, but would also come to signal a critical shift in the discourse on the U.S. military within the country. For practicable purposes, the Selective Service Act allowed the federal government to use conscription to expand military rosters around the country in preparation for its mission to European shores. Eventually, though, after the official expiration of the act in 1947, it would be reasserted and indeed, extended, to require all men of fighting age (at the time defined as ages 21 to 45, now as young as 18) to register for military service. This registration system would be used to devastating effects in order to press-gang vulnerable young men around the United States into military service during the reinstitution of the draft in World War II, the Korean Conflict, and perhaps in its most infamous application, during a decade of American brutality in Vietnam. In fact, the Selective Service Act is still in place today should the federal government ever choose to reinstate forcible military service.[38]

Discursively, though, and within the American conception of military action over the course of the next century, the passage of the Selective Service Act of 1917 was a watershed moment in American intellectual history. This act was the first piece of federal legislation to attach the idea of "service" to the role of soldiery in the United States. The attendant conceptions of this naming convention brought into sharp focus what had been more vaguely appended to citizen soldiers in the country's history prior to 1917. Included among these conceptions are the by now ubiquitous plaudits of sacrifice, bravery, honor, and integrity, among other exclusively positive attributions. Beginning with this naming convention, ideas of self-sacrifice and service have remained irrevocably attached to participation in the U.S. military, whether during peacetime or during open war, and whether performing clerical or administrative duties or positioned in a combat unit and engaged in live fighting. Indeed, it is difficult to overstate the staying power of the linkages between service and military employment created as a result of the passage of the Selective Service Act in 1917 within the American imagination. Previously disparate and intellectually distant notions were thereby remade and permanently connected. As a nation, we have been subject to the intellectual fallout of these processes ever since.

Writing about the power of the discourse connecting conceptions of service and sacrifice with employment in the U.S. military during World War I, historian David Kennedy elucidates the notion of all military activity being part and parcel of some grand, altruistic cause as a known aspect of the self-ascribed American character in the early part of the twentieth century:

> A word so reverently repeated had obviously been heavily freighted with meaning. Some of that meaning derived from the quite natural wish of Americans, like all peoples, to think well of themselves—especially to think of themselves as an exceptionally altruistic nation. But to a still greater extend, the wide currently of the term "service" reflected the particular dilemmas of the historical phase through which American society was then passing.[39]

As it happened, though, this "freighted" notion of service was not just linked to a particular historical phase of the American story. Rather, it was a characterization that was appended to a specific moment, that being conscription and mobilization in preparation for war in Europe in 1917, that became a vital tool for policymakers and defense contractors alike with which to append every American military venture from 1917 forward to the present day. Contrary to Kennedy's assertion, the United States has not passed through the "particular dilemmas" that granted this intellectual juxtaposition its utility. Rather, we have compelled ourselves, using the most uncritical of methods, to remain in that historical and intellectual moment, to content ourselves with the unquestioned linkages between the military and service, between the grotesqueries of war and saccharine notions of sacrifice. What first appeared in a flurry of practical legislation during the era of Wilson, then, became a staple of American popular discourse and an immovable pillar of the self-conception embodied by participation in the military through to the present day.

The Discourse on World War I in the United States: Frames of Representation

In his harrowing analysis of war memoirs, aptly titled *The Soldiers' Tale: Bearing Witness to Modern War*, author Samuel Hynes provides a brief description of the defining narrative of World War I, as the majority of us have absorbed it in history classes or within popular culture. He informs us starkly that:

> For most of us, the soldiers' tale of the First World War is the story of four years of fighting along a narrow band of earth that stretched across norther France from the Channel to the Swiss border. Along that band two lines of trenches face each other across a dead space that was called no-man's-land. From time to time through those long years men rose out of one trench or other to attack across that dead space and were cut down by artillery and machine gun fire, in the battles whose names for us are weighted with pointless death: Ypres, Loos, Arras, Verdun, the Somme, Passchendaele. Eventually, the tale goes, the Germans were forced by hunger and attrition to retreat, and the war ended.[40]

And so it was for the American soldiers compelled either by forced conscription or reverential notions of service to participate in the so-called Great War. And although the American commitment to the European savagery, wherein men were "cut down by artillery and machine gun fire" by scores of thousands, was much abridged compared to the rest of the Allied states, it was no less horrifying a crucible that they were forced to endure. While Hynes and others like him provide a profoundly valuable service to our historical memory by cataloging and analyzing the horrors of warfare through the words of the soldiers who lived it, this work now turns to an illumination of what might be called a more cynical element discernable within wartime texts. Specifically, the remainder of this chapter concerns itself with the discourse on the U.S. military as observed within widely distributed print news articles that were published and distributed to an engaged American readership during the war. In examining this element of the public discourse, this narrative will unearth assumptions, predilections, and biases present within journalistic descriptions of war while also investigating potential purposes that might be served in the assertion and widespread distribution of these discursive structures within American society.

To be clear, this exercise in no way seeks to discount or discredit the suffering endured by American soldiers in European trenches during the World War I, nor does it seek to diminish the profound loss felt by 116,000 American families whose loved ones perished by the bomb, the bullet, or the bayonet while fighting on the battlefields of Europe (to say nothing of the rampant disease that accelerated virtually unchecked through army camps during this time). Rather, the investigation to follow, much like the intellectual act performed by Hynes in his examination of war memoirs, is an evaluation of collective memory. By circumscribing the attribution of political utility to yet another American war piled up with yet more "pointless death," the remainder of this chapter seeks to illuminate a connected set of values, norms, and assumptions that were being attributed to the U.S. military during the height of World War I. In this evaluation, the war dead are neither dismissed nor diminished; rather they are centralized as subjects in an elaborate discursive structure, the consequences of which continue to unfold today.

In the following examination of language and discourse surrounding the U.S. military in World War I, it is noteworthy that conceptions of service and sacrifice are conveyed largely as assumptions to the American public that was reading news stories during the war. That is to say that in nearly all of the news articles examined for discursive structures within this chapter, the element of American service to a greater cause and/or American sacrifice for a global good was readily observable. These frames of representation guiding public knowledge around the U.S. military then continued as staple messages within news coverage of the United States military for the remainder of the twentieth century, no matter how dubious the *casus belli* or how politically or morally questionable the prosecution of the war. What follows below, then, is not a description of the subtle ways in which period journalists and major news publications inserted elements of sacrifice or service into their coverage of World War I. Indeed, this frame of representation of American action during the war was nothing short of ubiquitous and could have been singled out in every news piece of the period here examined. Rather, in the following analysis, the coverage is examined for tropes adjacent to or in concert with conceptions of American sacrifice based upon the actions or attitudes of U.S. soldiers in Europe during World War I.

As before, each of these distinct tropes is examined using texts from news coverage of the war published in nationally circulated and widely regarded news publications such as the *New York Times* and the *Los Angeles Times*. These frames of knowledge provide a broader view of an American self-conception seen through the popularly absorbed news media of the era focused, as it was, upon three distinct tropes, each unique and compelling in the ongoing construction of the American story in intellectually informative ways. Those tropes in question are an image of the thrilling nature of war itself, the decidedly humble nature of the average American soldier despite his heroism and bravery, and the overwhelming superiority of American society and American soldiery itself. An exploration of these frames of representation within the period discourse will serve to further elucidate ideas about the war, about the military, and about U.S. soldiers from within the stories we told ourselves at the time. Concluding remarks in this chapter connect conceptions of the American military at the beginning of the 1920s and its new role in international politics with the country's ongoing domestic demons of racism, classism, and exclusionism that could not, or would not, be exorcised.

The Thrill of War

Among the more consistent frames of representation present upon examination of hundreds of period new articles covering the American military during World War I (see Appendix B) was the indication that the war was thrilling, that American soldiers were dashing heroes, and that the entire experience of American deployment was joyful and/or exhilarating. The assertion of this frame of knowledge came with descriptions of youthful exuberance on the part of American soldiers, even when in life-and-death scenarios. Journalists during this time saw fit to include narratives of Americans fighting as if contesting a college football game or laughing or whooping in the face of grave danger. There was a Hollywood quality to many of these descriptions; news writers in these pieces slid into the role of war advertisers as much as behaving as war reporters as they endeavored to sell the war to home audiences as exciting and adrenaline-inducing rather than harrowing, terrifying, or disturbing. This narrative frame substantially diminishes the brutal, even consciousness-altering contest that this war became for participating soldiers, repackaging it instead as a jaunt, a bit of excitement to be experienced by Americans overseas at this time.

One *New York Times* journalist captured this sentiment in his descriptions of the interactions between American soldiers and their counterparts in other Allied armies. The Americans are presented as raucous and coarse but ultimately, as effective soldiers:

> The Americans charged to the shouts of "Lusitania!" After this battle, a story was circulated throughout the British Army and in England that the Australians remarked to some American soldiers: "You'll do me, Yank, but you chaps are a bit rough!" When the four American companies were returned to their commands the day after the engagement they were met by an Australian Colonel who started to address them in a very formal fashion but ended by blurting out, "Yanks, you're fighting fools; But I'm for you!"[41]

Whatever the provenance of this tale of allied camaraderie, its inclusion in a regular news article about the progress of the American war is telling. The atmosphere described is one of ribaldry and joviality, where shouts, jeers, and jests were all too commonplace. The Americans, herein "Yanks," were chastened for being undisciplined or "rough," but were ultimately singled out by an Australian officer and commended for their martial prowess, earning the nod as "fighting fools." The narrative is hardly one of high stakes or life-and-death challenges typically associated with period trench warfare. Rather, readers are invited into a world with jokes, jibes, and, at the end of the day, with low stakes. The discursive construction is of a stimulating environment with attractive levels of camaraderie and joyfulness. War is thrilling. War is fun.

Extending this atmosphere, an embedded reporter from the *New York Times*, whose regular cables back to the home front painted a vibrant picture of the American role in the war for the *Times'* readership, provided a description of battle as exciting and collegial. The narrative he relayed depicts American soldiers passing by German prisoners and jeering at them, taunting them with jibes equivalent to participation in a local sporting event spectated back home:

> I saw infantry this afternoon passing German prisoners coming back from the front, and our lads yelled at them in the same spirit that fans for a victorious football team yell at their vanquished opponent. Frankly, the Americans are proud of themselves tonight. They sort of feel that they are coming into their own after being out of the spotlight for some time, and they have the spirit to bring fresh victories.[42]

Two discursive elements within this description stand out. In the first place, the jocular nature of the interaction between American soldiers and German prisoners informs once again that war is an elaborate game replete with taunts and jeers and other associated, low-stakes consequences. The description provided does not relay military tactics, nor does it depict Americans risking their lives or dying (which we know they did in large numbers). It is a relaxed and sporting atmosphere where soldiers taunt each other like "fans for a victorious football team" might.

Second, this journalist is at pains to cover the American soldiers with glory, announcing that they feel "proud of themselves tonight" for whatever battlefield heroics that have gone unmentioned and that they "have the spirit to bring fresh victories" in the future. The defining action in this episode is of secondary importance to the lessons to be taken from it; war is jovial and sporting, and Americans are good at it. The narrative choices made here by a regular contributor to America's newspaper of record during the war present telling evidence of the wartime environment being constructed and relayed to American audiences. These choices inform that the stakes for American soldiers are low and that the atmosphere in which they operate is relaxed. American soldiers are thrilled by the war and are enjoying it immensely.

Other descriptions of Americans in battle refer to their indomitable spirit or their youthful vigor. Even when pressed to acknowledge the challenging or trying nature of the contest in which American forces were engaged, these descriptions emphasize the American ability to overcome on the basis of youthful energy and martial zest: "The spirit of the youthful American soldiers remains excellent under trying conditions."[43] Wonder and awe accompany these descriptions, informing the readership of the beauty of battle and ultimately the righteousness of war. Americans thrill at the victories they achieve and marvel at the wonders of war; descriptions provided by journalists using this trope within their commentary on American soldiers during the war enhance the thrilling nature of the warfare being described, creating images of U.S. soldiers as warrior-heroes taking part in a glorious contest: "I was with them on that morning they started, and I came back today to the scene of the greatest battle in which troops of America ever engaged."[44] Pressed to their limits given the challenges of trench warfare, Americans persevere, and when they do, "It [is] impossible to view the progress of the battle without exhilaration."[45] The narrative is one of exuberance and triumph in the face of danger or death, leaving the readership on the home front to marvel at the defining action of war.

Occasionally, the headline of a war story would itself have been enough to relay thrilling episodes of war or to construct a Hollywood quality around the real-life actions of American soldiers in the European trenches. Battles were described as wondrous or exciting; military action was dressed up in superlative language replete with thrilling conclusions. The outcomes of these engagements were secondary to these headline stories commanding the attention of readership and relaying information about military adventure and wartime thrills. One such headline proclaimed: "Most Wonderful Fortnight in War: Events of Last Two Weeks Make Them Without Parallel"[46] declaring for readers that war can be "Wonderful" and that American soldiers have seen it firsthand. Another headline adds to this dramatic and dashing atmosphere, reading as if scripted for a television or film production: "Beat Enemy's Best on Hindenburg Line: Americans Smash Prussian Guard's Resistance in Formidable Trenches. New Troops Fight Well, Young Soldiers Show Excellent Discipline As Well As Dashing Courage."[47] The news story attached to this headline informs of American glory and unparalleled courage in the face of a stalwart enemy, the elite Prussian Guard (even though the action in question was against a retreating German army). Here, the journalist and his editors are at pains to describe for American audiences how exciting and riveting war can truly be and to sell the idea of a glorious, thrilling, and exhilarating war to the largest number of readers possibly picking up morning newspapers back home in the United States. War involves dashing "Young Soldiers" experiencing the intensity of battle only to come out heroic and unscathed upon the cessation of the battlefield guns.

American Bravery, American Humility

Along with pervasive ideas concerning the thrilling, dashing, and/or dynamic nature of the fighting in World War I, American audiences reading war coverage during the U.S. commitment to the European theater of war were also informed, both subtly and overtly, as to the unique bravery and unparalleled courage of the American fighting forces. American soldiers faced great odds, and they persevered; their accomplishments on the battlefield were second to none in the Allied armies despite their comparative lack of fighting experience. Within this frame of representation conditioning stories about the American war, there were no American deserters, no American timidity, and no such thing as American cowardice. Soldiers fought bravely down to the last man, and the war was won because of this singular heroism, this unparalleled valor. Through these descriptions, it was as if "medieval notions of battle as an arena for individual heroism [arrived] intact into the early twentieth century."[48] As with elements of service and sacrifice endemic to news media representations of war for American audiences, the discursive element of heroism is likewise nearly ubiquitous throughout the discursive framing of U.S. wars fought over the course of the last century and could therefore have been included in any or all of the media analysis provided in this work's case study chapters.

And yet, with some regularity in the news articles reviewed for this study, juxtaposed with assertions of American gallantry and fighting prowess were oft-asserted notions of American humility, graciousness, and even reluctance to fight in various military engagements. Far from impugning cowardice, this news coverage began to establish a critical trope that will become a staple of the American self-conception surrounding U.S. military engagements and our own attitudes toward war. Unlike frames of knowledge cataloging the thrilling nature of war, this frame of representation asserts that American soldiers do not relish in the fighting of the killing that comes along with the duties borne by soldiers. Rather, connected with new media characterizations of bravery and courage are undercurrents of humility and self-effacement. Taken together, the connection of these representations paints a distinct picture for attendant audiences back in the United States of the U.S. Army, comprised of reluctant heroes, steadfast men bent on doing their duty if and when it is required but without bloodlust or particular zeal for battle for the sake of it. The connection of these two frames of representation within authoritative news coverage of World War I will establish lasting, indelible patterns of American self-consideration that will carry through the remainder of the twentieth century and will follow U.S. military action into twenty-first century warfare as well.

As for the first component within this multifaceted frame of representation, the idea of domestic news media coverage uncritically portraying American soldiers as courageous or heroic in the midst of military action abroad may demonstrate bias within the news media, but it can hardly be said to be uniquely American. In a 1918 speech, expressing his staunchly isolationist stance, Republican Senator Hiram Johnson famously quipped "The first casualty when war comes is truth."[49] Though it is unlikely Johnson was speaking specifically about the way in which soldiery is lionized by a country when its citizens go to war, media coverage of soldiers as unfailingly brave may certainly fall within his categorical assertion of truth, or at least objectivity, as a wartime casualty. As such, it is not surprising that news stories during this period informed that: "The fighting was in the open and the American infantrymen showed great courage";[50] or that: "Among the combat divisions of the American Expeditionary Forces, there is none whose gallant exploits have been so widely disseminated [...] as those of the 2d division";[51] or that: "the glory of Belleau Wood belongs almost exclusively to the Marines."[52] Other descriptions emphasized the difficulties of the fighting conditions or the skill of the American enemies so as to enhance the achievements and considerations of the Americans taking part in the war.

Typical coverage informs readers that: "It is no reflection on other units of the Second Division to say that the job of driving the Germans out of the wood was the toughest of all. It was finished only after twenty-three days of desperate fighting."[53] as well as "It is a feather in the cap of the American Army to have brought up against it a crack unit like a division of the [Prussian] Guard, which expects only to be used in major operations."[54]

Clearly, news outlets in the United States had a penchant for emphasizing American bravery and bravado, but such coverage may well be expected during times of war. More telling, perhaps, in examining war reportage in the United States during this period were the multiple examples emphasizing American humility, American modesty, and the self-effacing nature of American soldiers at war. These descriptions did not describe the actions of soldiers in battle or their achievements in the face of a daunting enemy. Rather, the purpose of these frames of representation was to emphasize the attitude of the average American soldier, to inform the reading public on the home front that American soldiers may be engaged in grotesque fighting and killing, but they were still good, wholesome boys, near sheepish in the reluctant performance of their duty. One such description let readers know that the U.S. Army was made up of "men of few words, intent on doing the day's work well, and built no castles in the air."[55] Another article assures readers that "the absence of boastfulness and the shamefacedness before even deserved praise have been traits of our returned veterans that have caused wide comment by the public. They fought and do not talk."[56] And finally, and perhaps most descriptively, a journalist embedded with American soldiers in France fawns: "As to the army, its spirit, even more distinctly as one approaches the firing line, is one of cheerful fortitude, supported by confidence confirmed on many a stricken field, that its quality is worthy of its cause. There is no touch of boastfulness or flamboyance about it."[57]

These flattering descriptions of the humility and modesty of American soldiers during World War I help to construct a distinctive discourse among the reading public within the United States. In concert with commonly distributed descriptions of American bravery and heroism in the face of dastardly enemies, the overall construction of the American soldier begins to take shape. He is a dedicated and dutiful fighter, a soldier, and a son doing his duty for God and country, but he takes no pleasure in the act of killing. He is never boastful, never braggadocios. The average U.S. soldier does not gloat or crow about his deeds, and he never glories in the killing of others. The American soldier within this frame of representation is a soldier for the sake of duty, because soldiering has to be done, but he is not a killer in the literal sense. He is moral. He is loyal. He is workmanlike, competent, able, and brave. The American soldier gets the job done without frills, without fanfare. Readership at home would come to possess a clear picture of this brave yet reluctant hero from the frequent reports of his courage and humility that dotted the pages of major news publications throughout the various phases of the war.

American Superiority

The structure of this frame of representation includes the core idea that America is a superior nation, one whose morals, values, intentions, and actions are simply divined as more righteous and more perfect in the existing community of nations within the world. Within this frame, the concept of nation becomes broad, encapsulating all of the men at arms under the banner of the United States as superior beings whether in their strength, their endurance, their courage, or their moral rectitude. Located within this discursive frame, the American soldier can fight longer and harder than the enemy, endure greater burdens and more grievous injury than the enemy, and achieve greater accomplishment than the enemy simply by attribution of his superiority to the enemy in every measurable quality. Concomitant to this presumption of superior status, Germans and Austrian enemies of the American soldier, when permitted to render their opinions on the war and its potential outcomes, reinforce these notions. As such, when German prisoners are given voice in the period news articles analyzed within this study, they express their desire to leave Germany behind, to move to America, and/or to adopt the American way of life given its obvious advantages over desiccated European society.

The element of superiority most clearly manifests in news coverage of World War I in descriptions of the American fighting prowess, which were often presented with an almost natural understanding that Americans were simply superior to the Germans in measurable physical attributes. The correlation to that physical superiority, then, was superior soldiery, and newsreaders in the United States at the time would have been able to absorb a number of these descriptions in authoritative news media sources of the period. One description of American physicality described a sense of national pride at the "appearance of our sturdy Westerners with their clear skins and fine physiques."[58] Along with this physical prowess came precision and overall excellence in soldiery, as many period journalists were quick to attest: "The excellence of the American artillery fire was largely responsible for the capture by American Marines of approximately 400 prisoners in the fighting."[59] Plaudits continued to describe for readers an artillery barrage "so perfect that the Germans were cut off from escape."[60] As evidenced, the physical superiority of the Americans led them to superiority in all aspects of soldiery, ultimately, but not surprisingly, winning the war on behalf of the Allies.

Descriptions of expert soldiery transitioned seamlessly to descriptions of exceptional American endurance, a consistent element throughout news coverage of the war and frequently linked to American successes in the face of a weaker, less determined foe: "Almost constant rains, with cold, have forced great suffering and tested the limit of physical stamina of the men in the front lines."[61] And with this combination of physical fitness and unyielding endurance came American victories on the battlefield typically against elite units of the German or Austro-Hungarian forces opposing them: "It evidently was not possible for the guards to stop the Americans."[62] where the "guards" referenced in this blurb referred to the Prussian Guard, an elite unit among the German Army conquered by the stronger, more determined Americans within this narrative. From this series of successes came heaps of praise from journalists cataloging battlefield results for stateside readership. U.S. troops were naturally called courageous and brave as writers pointed out the inevitability of American victory: "From the minute the Americans swarmed, the inferiority of the enemy resistance was marked."[63] And yet even after victory, such was the makeup of the American forces as to desire to push on despite danger in keeping with their indubitable fortitude and determination: "The American soldiers are anxious to keep going at the enemy, despite considerable losses."[64]

Finally, the frame of representation intimating American superiority and strength was perhaps most clearly and convincingly communicated by the enemies of American forces themselves, German or Austrian forces captured as a result of American action, and then interviewed by embedded U.S. journalists reporting the war for audiences back home. Naturally, the decision to include testimony from the enemy remained within the purview of the journalists and editors crafting wartime stories for American audiences. And in addition, the provenance of several of these testimonies may rightly be called into question within this frame of representation, as a structured discourse on the superiority of American forces is bolstered substantially by confirmation of these ideas from the mouths of foreign soldiers. In all, though, whether by honest journalism or by massaging the truth in encounters with captured enemy soldiers, the decision to include paeans to American food, American culture, and the American way of life would have had a profound effect upon readership absorbing news about American action in World War I within the United States. This commentary served to underscore the righteousness of the American cause, the virtue of American society, and the overall value of the United States, newly thrust by war into the global community of nations.

As such, those journalists who encountered captured German soldiers were quick to inform audiences about German admiration for their American counterparts: "All the prisoners expressed admiration for the fighting qualities of the Americans."[65] It is interesting to note the ubiquity of this approbation and respect given within this article as coming from the mouths of "all" of the captured prisoners, meaning that evidently none of the German soldiers expressed disdain for the enemy that they had been fighting and killing for months on end at the time of this report. And far beyond a lack of resentment or disdain, captured German soldiers apparently expressed not only their fondness of Americans but were also quick to confess their desire *to be* American to passing U.S. journalists embedded at the front: "The prisoners said they were glad to be captured, and several expressed a desire to go to the United States after the war to live."[66] Other reports simply praised American cultural products, noting their desirability among the captured enemy: "One interesting subject discussed in our leaflets is the good food supplied to the German prisoners, not forgetting the excellent quality of our tobacco."[67]

The sum total of this testimony, in combination with consistent reporting of American fighting prowess and physical dominance when compared to the European armies, is to create a vivid picture of American superiority. In the main, this superiority was expressed in the arena of war; American soldiers fought longer, harder, and were better at the art of war than were their German or Austrian counterparts. As evidence of this fact, the Allies won the war, and the American war efforts were singled out in U.S. news reports as being the single most impactful element in that ultimate victory. Beyond fighting abilities and physical strength, though, the readership of authoritative news media reports during World War I would have also learned of American cultural superiority through both covert suggestions of this truism on the pages of the nation's newspapers and also through testimony given by captured enemy soldiers who were full of praise for American soldiers and American society alike. Overall, there could be no escaping the discursive construction of American dominance during World War I, as it was represented by the authoritative news media. And like conceptions of American bravery and humility, this form of self-aggrandizement would become a standard feature of American storytelling about our wars and about our military for many years to come.

Conclusions: American Soldiers, American Service

If the Spanish-American War was the inauguration of the twentieth-century American imperium, World War I was the crucible by which the United States forged a critical and unwavering pillar in its own self-conception. Beset, though the United States was, by racism and drippings of authoritarianism combined with an elitist clique of business interests set against workers, we told ourselves a different story. As evidenced by the analysis of major print newspapers rendered earlier, from a period of time beginning with the earliest drippings of war in Europe through until many months after its end, the American story of itself remained glimmering and undeterred by nagging social or political realities. Rather than a divided nation guided by uber-wealthy, unapologetic businessmen, we told ourselves in print news story after print news story that we were a nation of self-sacrificers in service to a just cause. Rather than a nation dogged by Jim Crow codes and legal institutions enshrining white supremacy, we told ourselves we were a diverse group of young heroes, fighting for liberty and justice in far-flung places like the Meuse-Argonne and the Belleau Wood. And rather than violent reactionaries who used force to dictate the rules of society from Lake Michigan to Appalachia and many places in between, we assured ourselves that we were peaceable, principled creatures dragged into the fray only when all avenues of avoidance proved immoral and therefore impossible.

Discourse, specifically a discourse on the U.S. military throughout its engagements in World War I, informed us of these things. Through these narrative frames, we tell ourselves a story about the role of the U.S. military in this war and about the role of the United States in the world writ large. By applying selective language, presumptive constructions, by including or excluding narrative tropes, and through sheer self-selected bias among journalists and their editorial overseers, distinct but complimentary notions describing who the U.S. military become clear. Taken as a whole, these frames of knowledge substantially contribute to the formation of the American identity, a complimentary set of interconnected and inter-influenced self-conceptions that situate America and Americanness in any given political or social moment. This discourse further establishes expectations for frames of representation and narrative constructions in successive social and political moments as well given the tendency for new narrative constructions to rely upon existing tropes and established narratives even in descriptions of novel political developments. As such, the frames of representation described here as connected to a foundational, national knowledge surrounding the U.S. military and its actions during wartime retain within them substantial longevity, lending themselves to the construction of new frames of knowledge in subsequent descriptions of the U.S. military into the future.

The frames of representation in question include those discussed at length within this chapter. They indicate that war is a thrilling venture performed by dashing and daring men. Within this frame, the concept of war is remade as a wholly joyful and attractive spectacle, an adventure that young men should aspire to participate in, as their older brothers and fathers were participating in the fighting in World War I. This particular narrative trope ensured that public knowledge around World War I remained positive and exciting while reconstructing the men who participated in the war as heroes of the kind portrayed in comic books or action movies. These men were further associated with beneficent attributes to include bravery and humility, making it clear to attendant American audiences following the war that American soldiers were not simply exciting and able; they were brave, too. All of these qualities contributed to a firm understanding, as carried forward by news media discourse, that Americans were a superior stock of people far stronger and far more accomplished in their endeavors than their European cousins. America as a whole is remade in this narrative trope as a New Jerusalem, a shining city upon a hill and the envy of the rest of the world's citizens, even captured and disgraced wartime enemies.

Above all, though, news coverage during the period is at pains to demonstrate that the American soldiers who fought in World War I were humble and dutiful. Multiple period news pieces make it plain to readers that the U.S. Army is populated by self-effacing and reticent young men, brave and capable when it comes time to fighting, but only because they must and only when they have to. The vision of the American soldier carried forward in this discourse is of a man in the service of a grand ideal, a man who sacrifices for comrade and country, a devoted warrior-citizen of a kind that we should all aspire to be. The through line of all of these descriptions of American soldiers, then, is the concept of service, a critical narrative underpinning U.S. soldiers, the military as an institution, and conceptions about the country itself as it drifted toward more brutal warfare, the vast majority of which being avoidable and unnecessary. Returning to historian David Kennedy, this linking notion of service in connection with military action from World War I onward was anything but accidental:

> "[S]ervice" [was] a fittingly ambivalent term, at once connoting the autonomy of the individual will and the obligation of the individual to serve a sphere wider than his own. For men deeply committed to individual freedom, but increasingly forced to recognize the necessity of cooperative endeavor, "service" was a marvelously reconciling concept, seeming to stand midway between two equally insistent and apparently incompatible value systems. Small wonder, then, that the word crept into the discourse of the day whenever those systems threatened to conflict.[68]

The uncritical nature of the conceptual connections that still exist, identifying soldiery as inseparable from service within a contemporary American context, testifies to the accuracy of Kennedy's analysis here. For while related characterizations of soldiery are identifiable within a given discourse on the U.S. military outside of conceptions of service—bravery, capability, humility, superiority—the centralizing frame, the notion that connects and grounds those descriptions for American audiences across the multiple decades of U.S. military hegemony, is the ambiguous notion of service to the country, no matter how questionable the country's motives happen to be. Each subsequent analysis of a discourse surrounding an invasion or a foreign war engaged by the U.S. military will return to this ubiquitous descriptor, then, and will catalog the ways in which authoritative institutions such as the news media reify America's conceptions of its own warriors as brave, dutiful, and critically, as reluctant servants of some grandiose national notion. It is to these other American wars and violent military engagements now etched into our collective history that this study now turns.

Notes

1 Senator George Norris, "Against Entry into War" speech before the Senate, April 4, 1917. 65th Congress, 1st Session.

2 The catalyst of World War I was the assassination of the Austro-Hungarian Archduke Franz Ferdinand by Bosnian-Serb nationalist teenager Gavrilo Princip. The war ended with the silencing of all guns along the front and official armistice on November 11, 1918 at 11:00 a.m., the eleventh hour of the eleventh day of the eleventh month of the fifth year of war.

3 Adam Tooze, *Deluge: The Great War, America and the Remaking of the Global Order, 1916–1931* (New York: Viking Press, 2014), 27.

4 Many immigrant communities in the United States during this period had well-established loyalties to the countries of the Central Powers as they were the countries of their origins. Equally, many other Americans preserved powerful resentments toward the Allies: "Millions of German-Americans preferred neutrality, as did many Irish Americans. Jewish Americans were hard pressed not to celebrate the advances of the Imperial German Army into Russian Poland in 1915, where they brought welcome relief from Tsarist anti-Semitism" (Tooze, *Deluge*, 43).

5 Historian Thomas Fleming has gone so far as to call American neutrality in the run-up to World War I a "sham," pointing out that the overwhelming business interests in the country at the time were indelibly tied to the Allied powers. In this thinking, no amount of hue and cry from Americans protesting participation in the war, whatever their reasoning, was going to keep the country out of the conflict (Thomas Fleming, *The Illusion of Victory: America in World War I* (New York: Perseus Books), 23).

6 James Tyner, *Military Legacies: A World Made by War* (Abingdon, Oxfordshire: Routledge Press), 14.

7 Norris, "Against Entry into War."

8 Robert H. Zieger, *America's Great War: World War I and the American Experience* (New York: Rowman & Littlefield Publishers, Inc.), 78.

9 Carol Oukrop, "The Four Minute Men Became National Network during World War I," *Journalism Quarterly* 52, no. (December 4, 1975): 632–37. https://doi.org/10.1177/107769907505200404.

10 David Kennedy, *Over Here: The First World War and American Society, 1916–1931* (New York: Oxford University Press, 1980), 26.

11 Garret Peck, *The Great War in America: World War I and Its Aftermath* (New York: Pegasus Books, 2018), 121.

12 Zieger, *America's Great War*, 197.

13 Howard Zinn, *A People's History of the United States* (New York: HarperCollins, 2003 [1980]), 368.

14 Fleming, *The Illusion of Victory*, 107.

15 Zinn, *A People's History of the United States*, 362.

16 Among the most authoritative accounts of the controversy surrounding the elections of 1876 is C. Vann Woodward, *Reunion and Reaction: The Compromise of 1877 and the End of Reconstruction* (New York: Oxford University Press, 1991 [1966]).

17 Mark L. Bradley, *The Army and Reconstruction, 1865–1877* (Washington, DC: Center of Military History, 2015).
18 Kennedy, *Over Here*, 162.
19 Ibid.
20 Zieger, *America's Great War*, 103.
21 Ibid., 104.
22 Ibid., 103.
23 Fleming, *The Illusion of Victory*, 399.
24 "Red Summer: The Race Riots of 1919," *The National WWI Museum and Memorial*. https://www.theworldwar.org/learn/about-wwi/red-summer.
25 Perhaps this inaction should not be surprising, though, coming from the president who famously called D.W. Griffith's film *The Birth of a Nation*, a shameful black faced, minstrel vision of postwar America, "writing history with lightening," further lamenting, "My only regret is that it is all so terribly true" Mark E. Benbow, "Birth of a Quotation: Woodrow Wilson and 'Like Writing History with Lightning'," *The Journal of the Gilded Age and Progressive Era* 9, no. 4 (2010): 509–33. http://www.jstor.org/stable/20799409.
26 Zieger, *America's Great War*, 197.
27 The text of the 13th Amendment, which officially became law in the United States in December of 1865, still allows for slavery for any individual who has committed a crime. It reads, in part, "Neither slavery nor involuntary servitude, except as a punishment for crime whereof the party shall have been duly convicted." The fact that convicted criminals, even those convicted of minor offenses, can still be legally forced into labor against their will in the United States has led to the rise of practices such as convict leasing for profit maximization during the early decades of the twentieth century, as well as the exploitation of captive laborers in prison being preyed upon by companies in order to increase profits to the maximum quarter after quarter.
28 Fleming, *The Illusion of Victory*, 32.
29 Zinn, *A People's History of the United States*, 362–63.
30 Ibid.
31 Peck, *The Great War in America*, xii.
32 Zinn, *A People's History of the United States*, 363.
33 Tyner, *Military Legacies*, 15.
34 Ibid., 157.
35 Tooze, *Deluge*, 201.
36 Eventually, some two million men and women would participate in a military capacity during World War I (Kennedy, *Over Here*, 205).
37 Ibid., 147.
38 According to the Selective Service System registration website, nine eras of the U.S. military have categorized the country's level of belligerent readiness throughout our history and have been used to describe the degree to which forcible participation in the country's military would be required during that period. The current period in U.S. military history and the one in which I was compelled to register for Selective Service encapsulates the period of time between 1980 and the present and is named "Out of Deep Standby."
39 Kennedy, *Over Here*, 152.
40 Samuel Hynes, *A Soldiers' Tale: Bearing Witness to Modern War* (New York: The Penguin Press, 1997), 74.
41 "Hard-Hitting 33rd Division: Not One Enlisted Man as Tried by General Court-Martial after the Training Period in Attack at Hamel. The Big Offensive. Astride the Meuse. Fought to the Last Minute. Division's Unique Record. Advances of the Division," *New York Times*, May 18, 1919, 63.
42 Edwin L. James, "Drive Goes On. Joined with the French. Advance on the Meuse. Three Miles from Stenay. Magnitude of Our Victory. Mud and Mines in Roads. Four Defense Lines Broken. Disorganization of Enemy," Special Cable to the *New York Times*, *The New York Times*, November 4, 1918, 1.
43 Edwin L. James, "Fierce Fight in Argonne: Americans Push Ahead in the Face of Desperate Resistance," Special Cable to the *New York Times*, *The New York Times*, October 1, 1918, 1.

44 Edwin L. James, "Desolation Reigns North of Verdun: Silence Where American Cannon Roared Year Ago. Shunned by Its Owners, Debris of Battle and Bones of the Dead Tell Tragic Story of Historic Ground," *New York Times,* September 21, 1919, 1.
45 "Beat Enemy's Best on Hindenburg Line: Americans Smash Prussian Guard's Resistance in Formidable Trenches. New Troops Fight Well, Young Soldiers Show Excellent Discipline As Well As Dashing Courage," *New York Times,* September 28, 1918, 1.
46 *New York Times,* October 6, 1918.
47 *New York Times,* September 28, 1918, 1.
48 Kennedy, *Over Here,* 178.
49 It is possible that in this speech, Johnson was recalling Aeschylus who is attributed as having said, "In war, truth is the first casualty" around 2,500 years before World War I.
50 "Sweep All From Path: Franco-Americans Drive Ahead; Our Whole Line Crashes for War as German Flanks Are Pressed In; No Stand of Enemy Was Ex-Pected [sic] Before Vesles Forest Reached," *Los Angeles Times,* August 3, 1918, 1.
51 Major A. W. Greely, "Gallant Record of 2d Division," *New York Times,* June 15, 1919, 36.
52 "The Marines at Belleau Wood," *The New York Times,* July 24, 1923, 20.
53 Ibid.
54 G. H. Perris, "Loss of Belleau Crippled Germans: Wood Taken by Americans Was an Important Base for Further Advance," Special Cable to the *New York Times, The New York Times,* June 17, 1918, 1.
55 "Pershing," *New York Times,* September 7, 1919.
56 Greely, "Gallant Record of 2d Division," 36.
57 Perris, "Loss of Belleau Crippled Germans," *The New York Times,* June 17, 1918, 3.
58 "City Boys as Soldiers," *New York Times,* May 4, 1919, 1.
59 "American Barrage Traps 400 Germans: Headed Off by Hail of Shells as They Fled Before Marines in Belleau Wood," *The New York Times,* June 14, 1918, 4.
60 Ibid.
61 Edwin L. James, "Americans Win Battle For Hill: 1,000 German Dead Left on the Field After Fierce Struggled in the Argonne. Fight in Blinding Storm Gains Toward Lancon and West of Fleville Weaken Foe's Hold in Forest," Special Cable to the *New York Times, The New York Times,* October 9, 1918, 8.
62 Edwin L. James, "Joint Sweep 50 Miles Wide: Gourand's French Army Co-Operates and Gains Four Miles. Americans Go On At Night: Pennsylvania, Kansas, and Missouri Troops Defeat The Prussian Guards," Special Cable to the *New York Times, The New York Times,* September 27, 1918, 1.
63 Ibid.
64 Edwin L. James, "Marines Drive Germans Back; Foe Sends Up Crack Divisions," Special Cable to the *New York Times, The New York Times,* June 11, 1918, 1.
65 "American Barrage Traps 400 Germans," *New York Times,* June 14, 1918, 4.
66 Ibid.
67 "Germans Impressed By Our Propaganda: Leaflets Showered on Enemy Come from Paris Printing House Directed by Americans," *New York Times,* November 9, 1918, 5.
68 Kennedy, *Over Here,* 154.

Chapter Four

WORLD WAR II: THE GOOD WAR

War is not an occasional interruption of a normality called peace; it is a climate in which we live.[1]
—*Samuel Hynes, 1997*

War Making in America

The enormity of World War II is difficult to overstate. Beginning with the Japanese invasion of Manchuria in 1937 and lasting roughly until the destruction of two Japanese cities by American nuclear bombs in August of 1945,[2] the conflict embroiled dozens of nations and tens of millions of people and spread previously unimaginable horror throughout the globe. As many as 70 or 80 million people died in this war, the vast majority of them civilians who were starved, shot, stabbed, or burned to death in fires that consumed entire cities or in the barbaric ovens of Nazi death camps. Perhaps up to 20 or 25 million were soldiers who died in the fighting itself, making what many consider to be the ultimate sacrifice on behalf of intangible, even ephemeral political ideals such as fascism, communism, or democracy. Countless others were wounded physically or psychologically or were otherwise permanently affected as a result of the war by the loss of a loved one or the loss of livelihood. The war was widespread and all-encompassing; it was the defining political, cultural, economic, and martial event of the first half of the twentieth century. The consequences of World War II, however, would extend much farther into the future.

The United States entered the war on the side of the Allies via declarations of war against both Japan and Germany in December of 1941, just after the Japanese destruction of the American Naval Station at Pearl Harbor in Hawaii.[3] By the end of the war, more than 16 million Americans had been active in the military during the conflict, meaning that more than 10 percent of the overall population of the country had direct involvement in the war. The American war effort incorporated unprecedented industrial production, innovating new avenues for transportation and distribution among civilian and military personnel alike. Beyond logistics and production, capacities creating the nuts and bolts of warfare though, the culture of the United States was indelibly altered by the war. The massive gravity of the American military effort provided jobs and a measure of financial security to new segments of society (especially women), but the engine of martial success exposed as much tension in the American social fabric as it alleviated. This social friction led to new iterations of racial animus, the additional entrenchment of corporate exploitation, and economic inequality, and it exposed our own deep-seated antipathy toward ethnic and national enemies abroad and at home. In these patterns, World War II was indeed total, one in which society on the home front mimicked state militancy abroad, resulting in permanent cleavages in American society that we have yet to reconcile in our national consciousness.

Nor were American citizens in World War II encouraged, or even allowed, to discuss this rending of social institutions freely or openly. Rather, for the duration of World War II and for some time after, the mainstream news media provided Americans with a stylized image of the war and all of its associated activities. Picking up where the CPI left off in World War I, the Office of Censorship, a federal department established by the Roosevelt administration immediately after the American entry into World War II, was charged with the production of state propaganda in order to ensure that the American citizenry would remain supportive of the war and sufficiently dedicated to the destruction of Germany, Italy, and Japan for the duration of the fighting. Contradictory texts were censored, and visual imagery was monitored for the promotion of a pro-war narrative. In this, the press became an arm of the state, promoting unquestioned support of the war effort and eliminating opposition to military activity: "Reduced to its essence, the message of wartime propaganda was that Americans lived in a well-ordered society that was threatened by Axis aggression."[4] The tendrils of the Office of Censorship reached into distant corners of American society and governed the rules of international as well as domestic communications, along with retaining a special remit to control

Photo 4 A U.S. Marine position at the Battle of Guadalcanal, an offensive in the Pacific Theater of the war lasting from August of 1942 until February of 1943.

"information originating from military installations and certain industrial plants with military contracts."[5]

And like its predecessor in World War I, the CPI, it was an effective arm of state propaganda, creating a picture of the most precise and moral army fighting abroad while portraying nothing but racial cooperation and social bliss at home: "Released photographs created the impression that American bombs, bullets, and artillery shells killed only [...] soldiers. Pictures of young, elderly, and female victims always ended up in the file of censored images [while] wartime imagery urged blacks and whites to work harmoniously in the common cause."[6] In creating and funding the Office of Censorship through the war, the Roosevelt administration demonstrated its desire to construct for the public a discourse surrounding the events during World War II while simultaneously controlling the distribution of information describing the social relations between communities within the country as well. There can be little doubt then that the government of the United States deemed the control of information to be critical to its overall success in the war and applied its influence in the authoritative press to secure the control of information provided to the American people. The Office of Censorship was designed for just such a purpose; the public discourse created during the war itself was its product. Given these characteristic traits of society in the United States on the eve of and during the greatest global conflict the world has ever known, a deeper investigation of American society and social practice during World War II, along with an examination of the discourse around that society and its values, is in order here.

The New War Economy

The Japanese bombing of Pearl Harbor Naval Station on December 7, 1941, resulted in the deaths of more than 2,300 soldiers and civilians and all but crippled the U.S. naval capacity in the Pacific.[7] This event, famously labeled by then President Franklin D. Roosevelt as "a day which will live in infamy," instantly catalyzed America's martial sensibility and kneejerk, patriotic fervor. After Pearl Harbor, a public groundswell propelled the U.S. headlong into the international fray, resulting in the American declaration of war on Japan on December 8, 1941, and on their Axis ally Germany[8] three days after that. Like the attacks on the World Trade Center in New York that would occur some 60 years later, politicians, pundits, and professional journalists exploited Pearl Harbor, using the event as a driver of anti-Japanese sentiment and feverish pro-war trumpeting alike. The aforementioned Office of Censorship was at the center of these efforts.

The U.S. declarations of war on Japan and Germany in December of 1941 had widespread consequences both abroad and at home. In the short term, over the course of the next four years, the added American military capacity quite naturally swung the tide of the war in the Allies' favor. By 1944, the German Wehrmacht was in retreat in Europe, and a previously unbreakable system of island fortifications held by Japan in the Pacific had begun to crumble. In short, upon entry into the fray, later than their allies, as in World War I a quarter of a century earlier, the U.S. military was the difference maker on the field of battle. But in the long view, examining the development of the international economy and the power structure of American capitalism, U.S. participation in World War II had wider-ranging social and economic impacts.

U.S. involvement in the war came to be defined by the concept of total war, an all-encompassing political, military, and economic endeavor wherein all productive capacities and industrial efforts focused success in the ongoing military campaign: "It was total in that it affected every segment of society and economy: the worker and the farmer were enlisted, the scholar and the scientist, women as well as men."[9] In order to fight this war, a complete commitment was undertaken by the government of the United States, compelling a redesign of the national economy from the top down and impacting all phases of economic production, from the commanding heights to the assembly line worker and all points in between. As it happened, this substantial economic narrowing was successful: "in the end it was the sheer weight of American production that turned the tide in the war."[10] Such a thorough and dramatic shift in the capacities and priorities of a country as large and diverse as the United States could not occur, however, without profound and long-term consequences.

While soldiers and sailors were fighting and dying in distant lands on behalf of noble ideals like freedom and democracy, "behind the headlines in battles and bombings, American diplomats and businessmen worked hard to make sure that when the war ended, American economic power would be second to none in the world."[11] This was done by vesting money and power in the largest producers of military materiel and ancillary war products in the country. Those firms began to consolidate during the war years to the extent that by "1941 three-fourths of the value of military contracts were handled by fifty-six large corporations" with state investment shifting more than "$400 million [...] to ten large corporations."[12] State countenance for, even sustenance of, private business changed the economic future of the United States by creating a permanent economic sector for war-related industries and their subordinate subcontractors. We recognize these businesses today as the so-called defense contractors who continue to exact huge amounts of investment from state coffers in Washington year on year, demanding increasingly exorbitant sums in each and every federal budget. These economic relationships, now the established norm within the American political system, have their origins in decisions made by the Washington consensus[13] during World War II:

> The war [...] created the mixed marriage of government and private enterprise that is with us still: a huge and diverse manufacturing sector dedicated to serving one customer—the Department of Defense. It includes thousands of small and medium-sized firms and a handful of mammoth corporations that are prime contractors. All are deeply dependent on politics to fill their order books.[14]

So entrenched is this structure of government, business, and hyper-militarization that it rarely receives attention, let alone criticism, within the United States. Unthinking patriotism and ubiquitous, uncritical pro-military symbolism within contemporary culture encourages rote acceptance of these structures while simultaneously discouraging or punishing organized dissent. In the words of one of the few critics of these political and economic priorities: "Objections that this [...] is sowing future conflict rather than peace are brushed aside."[15]

The ramifications of these policy decisions were profound and long-lasting. During World War II, a small group of business elites began reaping huge rewards from ventures producing war materiel, with corporate profits skyrocketing "from $6.4 billion in 1940 to $10.8 billion in 1944."[16] For the public majority, though, these spiking revenues were of no use. Instead of war profits and a climate of animosity promised by the encroaching Cold War, evidence suggests that public sentiment largely favored a focus on domestic affairs and the public good. But despite widespread public agreement that the American economy should return to root manufacturing and agricultural industries while beginning a significant global demilitarization, the Truman administration, with Harry Truman ascending to the office of the president upon the death of his predecessor Franklin D. Roosevelt on April 12, 1945, pursued the opposite course. Truman and other political leaders doubled down on belligerent economic pursuits. In order to justify this move against popular sentiment in the country after the war, Truman and the national leadership of the United States grossly exaggerated the specter of communism, authoritarianism, and Bolshevism to continue to expand war industries. Progressive historian Howard Zinn explains that: "In a series of moves abroad and at home, [Truman] established a climate of fear—a hysteria about Communism—which would steeply escalate the military budget and stimulate the economy with war-related orders. This combination of policies would permit more aggressive actions abroad, more repressive actions at home."[17] As such, a war-weary American public would get no reprieve. Instead, they were manipulated by the government and media and maintained in a state of quiescence and fear. Later, they would be satiated by the creation of a prolific consumer economy that "promised Americans a cornucopia of consumer goods—everything from nylon stockings to suburban homes—to sustain their slumping patriotism."[18]

The explosion of industry and the innovation of American consumer culture are processes that are typically evaluated as universally positive by historians and economists alike. And while huge segments of America were still locked out of this financial windfall (blacks, Native Americans, women, and landless, hand-to-mouth whites, to name a few), by all standard statistical measures, the American economy did improve dramatically during the decade of the 1940s, bringing unprecedented purchasing power and an overall increase in quality of life for millions of Americans in the postwar era. But it is the type of economy that developed during this period that was of crucial import to the direction of America in the second half of the twentieth century. These decisions by a conglomeration of business leaders, military commanders, and policymakers in the months that followed American victories in both European and Asian theaters reified existing economic priorities, skimping on badly needed social programs and promoting yet more military expenditures. Nor were these decisions the same as those undertaken in other allied states upon the war's conclusion. Author Naomi Klein explains that the United States was quite alone in its decision-making around economic priorities among Allied nations after the war: "the world came together to try to create conditions that would prevent genocidal logic from ever again taking hold. It was this, combined with significant pressure from below, that formed the rationale for generous social programs throughout Europe."[19]

Architects of American policy and economic priorities in the postwar era clearly chose a different path, though. Instead of taking advantage of the country's pristine landscape and infrastructure that survived unscathed throughout the entirety of the war in order to lead greener, more peaceable economic priorities, business elites and political leadership invested heavily in those government departments and private agencies that sought to profit from the war. After World War II then, the structure was set to fix a huge section of the American economy into a permanently bellicose engine.

Fighting for Jim Crow

In addition to decision-making that would extend economic inequality and promote unending American militarism, another element that has largely been lost in popular narratives about American involvement in World War II is an appreciation of the hypocrisy inherent in the American military's mission during the war. From the Roosevelt administration's support of the Allied war effort during the Lend Lease Act through to the bloody battles in Europe and Asia, mainstream notions about America in World War II tell us that the U.S. participation in the war served to liberate oppressed peoples around the world. These herculean efforts made the world safe for democracy and paved the way for global equality by eliminating authoritarian tyrants in Germany, Italy, and Japan and by bracing the world against a similar form of collectivism and oppression manifested by nefarious actors in the Soviet Union after the conclusion of the war. This, in sum, encapsulates a schoolyard history of the war from the perspective of mainstream America. Good triumphed over evil. Democracy defeated collectivism and fascism. The United States heroically won the war. The architects of this victory were members of the Greatest Generation in American history.

Few mainstream narratives of this period in American history include details about the social system in place in the United States during this period of time, details that might remove a measure of the gloss from the self-congratulatory discourse surrounding American participation in World War II. Fewer still would assert that the American war effort, understood as a monumental martial and industrial feat organized to make the world a safer and more equal place, actually served to entrench racism, segregation, and inequality within its own borders while ostensibly combating these practices in nations abroad. A closer examination of these popular narratives, though, will identify the fact that the differentiation of the rule of law according to racial classification existed on the streets of the hometowns of the soldiers fighting ostensibly to end racist oppression during the war. Further, these racist policies carried over from American social practice and enforced legal statues at home to the ranks of the military itself, structuring the manner of interaction between American soldiers throughout the fighting. In this enforced segregation, the architects of the American war effort not only normalized racism within the ranks of the American military during World War II, they also modeled oppressive and segregationist practices for Americans back home as well.

Among the handful of scholars to investigate this characteristic of society in the United States during World War II, author Kenneth Rose informs that segregation in the military during the war effort was as regulated and as inviolable within the ranks as it was on the streets of towns and cities in America. The U.S. military in World War II rigidly enforced racial segregation[20] operating under the fallacy of "separate but equal" facilities for black and white soldiers. And like that flimsy standard in the United States itself, "black troops found that facilities were certainly separate but definitely not equal."[21] Rose goes on to inform that, despite the preponderance of uncritical views of the U.S. military in World War II, "Black troops were typically assigned to menial positions with few opportunities for promotion."[22] This was accomplished through the establishment of segregated units within each of the branches of the armed forces, with the most difficult and most dangerous forms of wartime labor being the exclusive purview of the black units. A member of one of these segregated units later recounted, "That's where most of us were put. We serviced the service. We handled food, clothing, equipage. We loaded ammunition, too. We were really stevedores and servants."[23] With few notable exceptions, this manner of segregation in the military during the war was widely endorsed by military leadership as well as frontline soldiers within the field: "Army segregation [...] not only was official policy but also was overwhelmingly endorsed by white soldiers."[24] This relegation of black soldiers to positions of servitude also affected their ability to receive promotion[25] or pay increases. As a result, there were no black officers in any branch of the military except the army until nearly the end of the war, with mess duty or labor details defining a career in the military for the vast majority of African American soldiers in World War II.[26]

Nor were menial duties or dangerous jobs the limit of the perils faced by black soldiers in the U.S. military in World War II. Being stationed in the South[27] for training or education could get black soldiers harassed, harmed, or even killed as a result of exposure to the violent racism that had become commonplace in America in the 1940s: "In April 1941, a black private stationed at Fort Benning, Georgia, was found in a nearby woods handing from a tree with his hands tied behind his back. Post officials suggested that it was suicide."[28] Black soldiers deployed abroad could not be guaranteed fair treatment under the law either. The racist system of military justice, both formal and informal, carried over to U.S. encampments in Europe and Asia, as well as making life for black soldiers in the American armed forces as dangerous abroad as at home. One firsthand account recalls violence enacted by American soldiers in England in the name of patently racist values held to be sacrosanct at home: "If a young black fellow, eighteen years old, would get together with a British girl, sixteen, that girl would be encouraged to say she was raped. We had a number of young black soldiers who were hanged. We had one in our outfit who was hanged."[29]

Clearly, whether by exhaustion or overwork in menial conditions, because of white supremacy and racist violence in the American South during periods of training, or as a result of the violations of racist American norms while abroad, the status of black soldiers in the American armed forces during World War II was precarious in the extreme. But these facts represent a decidedly unflattering and, therefore, inconvenient part of the American story in retellings of the U.S. role in World War II. As such, they are routinely omitted from mainstream histories of the period, and they are certainly not a component of news media discourse describing the actions of the U.S. military in the war during training or deployment. Omissions such as these result in the creation of only a partial history of the military and/or the war effort in descriptions of American exploits in World War II.

Bleak as the status of African American troops was within the armed forces during the war, the situation on the home front for black Americans was even harsher. Segregation and discrimination at work and in public venues persisted even while the United States was ostensibly committed to ending racial oppression abroad, and although the soldiers that fought in World War II are now famously known as the Greatest Generation for their accomplishments on the battlefield, "it was also a generation that maintained a Jim Crow system in both military and civilian life."[30] As such, racism defined the political, social, and economic experience of African Americans during the war years, with the workplace being among the key institutions where these racist policies were either formally or informally enacted. Very often, employment was denied to African Americans as managers and factory owners enforced unwritten quotas that prohibited the hiring of black workers. When African Americans did find work in the civilian sector of the wartime economy, they were met with spite and derision: "A labor leader in Portland, Oregon, noted that when a local shipyard hired a black worker, 'so many wrenches and hammers fell off decks around him he quit within twenty-four hours'."[31]

If outright abuse did not maintain a segregated workplace, racist white workers took to organizing industrial action to demonstrate their discontent with either the hiring or the promotion of black workers. Philadelphia, Portland, and San Francisco all saw such demonstrations take place during the war. In the South, these actions resulted in violence: "In Mobile, [Alabama], white shipyard workers staged a full-fledged riot after several black welders were promoted. Eleven black workers were seriously injured in the Mobile fracas."[32] White supremacist violence would go on to injure hundreds and cause millions in property damage in Detroit, Los Angeles, and New York in 1943, the height of the U.S. fight against injustice and racial oppression around the globe.[33]

Nor did the war's end did bring with it an end to racism in America, far from it. When millions of veterans returned home and began looking for work, black Americans who had held gainful employment during the war were fired en masse, and their positions were handed over to the newly returned white workers. Those African Americans who did continue to work went on to earn far less than whites following the end of World War II, and in 1947, 60 percent of black families in America lived in poverty compared with only 23 percent of their white counterparts.[34] Hoping to clear a path for education and self-promotion for returning veterans, on June 22, 1944, President Roosevelt signed the Servicemen's Readjustment Act into law, well known by now by its oft-referred-to nickname, the G.I. Bill. The bill included within it a provision for low-interest, zero-dollar-down home loans for wartime veterans, with the loans backed by federal guarantees. But of the 67,000 mortgages that were insured under the G.I. Bill in New York and New Jersey immediately following the war, fewer than 100 were granted to black veterans. In the State of Mississippi in the year 1947, two out of 3,200 federally-backed loans were given to black borrowers. Following educational opportunities granted to veterans by

Photo 5 U.S. Marines at the Battle of Saipan, June 1944.

the Servicemen's Readjustment Act, by 1947, half of all college students in the U.S. were veterans. But in the decade of the 1940s, fewer than 5 percent of those college students were African American.[35]

The opportunities afforded to soldiers returning to the United States after the war allowed many veterans to transition into the middle class and secure economic stability. The fact that these opportunities were denied to African Americans and other veterans representing minority groups within the United States was consistent with social and political practices both in the ranks of the military and throughout the country before and during the American prosecution of the war. These economic disparities had profound effects on the character and structure of American society throughout the twentieth century and would impact the social dynamics of the country up through the present day. In view of these conditions and of the staid and wholly oppressive nature of racial attitudes in postwar America, as one scholar concluded, "blacks looking at [ongoing] anti-Semitism in Germany, might not see their own situation in the U.S. as much different."[36]

The Destruction of Japan

Upon entering the war against Germany and Japan in the days after the bombing of Pearl Harbor, the U.S. government, military, and, as demonstrated, its economy focused substantial effort and ample resources on the project of defeating Germany and bringing a swift end to the war in Europe. This mission was generally considered to be a priority over and above the war effort in Asia that would target the aggressors at

Pearl Harbor and the dominant military power in the eastern hemisphere, the Japanese Empire. A number of practicable reasons, both political and military, fed into this prioritization within Washington:

> Washington's pre-war focus had been on Europe rather than the Pacific. The outbreak of war did not immediately change this. Germany and Italy—as well as Japan—had declared war on America. America's British allies also stressed Europe, despite the disaster to their empire in the Far East. In the background was the need to keep Russia in the war.[37]

But, while deliberate decision-making and the practical elements of prosecuting war may have marked the American undertaking in Europe, in Asia the pillars of American policy and militarism likely had a different purpose in mind.

Rather than simply defeating the Japanese, abundant commentary and imagery from the period indicates that the American war effort against Japan had a much different object, one that was motivated in equal parts by a desire for vengeance against the perpetrators of Pearl Harbor and by a profound racial hatred pervasive within American culture. As it was explained by one soldier in the Pacific Theater of the war, this ubiquitous American racism influenced the U.S. military too, meaning that the average G.I. arrived in Asia with preconceived notions about the nature of their enemy: "We had been fed tales of these yellow thugs [...] with teeth that resembled fangs. If a hundred thousand Japs were killed, so much the better. Two hundred thousand, even better."[38] Indeed, while it was common for American soldiers and sailors to perceive Germans as militant and malicious, conceptions of the Japanese within American culture during World War II portrayed them as monstrous and evil, as a race that was something other than human: "The Japanese were subhuman. They were little men, inferior to white Westerners in every physical, moral, and intellectual way. They were collectively primitive, childish, and mad—overlapping concepts that could [...] also received 'empirical' endorsement from social scientists and old Japan hands."[39] American soldiers' stereotypes about the Japanese were informed by cultural products from within the United States, which in turn informed their attitudes and actions during the fighting in the Pacific Theater of the war.

Nor were these perceptions limited to men and women active in the military during the time. Popular imagery in the mainstream media hammered home representations of the Japanese as dastardly and inhuman creatures that were barbarous and cruel and unique among the combatant nations in their rejection of civilized warfare: "The Japanese were vermin [...] they were apes, monkeys, 'jaundiced baboons'."[40] Once reports of fighting from the Pacific Theatre began to filter back to the American public, they were seized upon in order to confirm the worst of American preconceptions about the Japanese. Images of desperate fighting and an enemy who refused to surrender penetrated the American consciousness and reaffirmed the beastly nature of the Japanese: "The straits of island warfare in the Pacific led U.S. marines and GIs to descend to the lowest levels. Few Japanese prisoners were taken and not because they would never submit."[41] Portrayals like this one, confirmed by reports of the fighting in Asia, landed dramatically in the popular imagination in the United States, aligning with the worst of the American soldiers' experiences and the most entrenched racist assumptions present within the public as a whole. No battlefield throughout the war was predictable or rational, but on Asian battlefields, a new level of war fever was reached.

In the spring of 1942, news from the Pacific fighting turned for the worse when Major General Edward P. King Jr. surrendered at Bataan, marking what is still today "the biggest mass surrender in American history—12,000 Americans and 66,000 Filipinos."[42] Tensions were heightened then, not just among the soldiers doing the fighting but also among the attendant public absorbing information about the Pacific War. An unforgiving terrain meshed with a pitiless enemy and strategic setbacks to construct the war in Asia in the national consciousness as a torturous and bleak environment foisted upon earnest American soldiers by the duplicitous Japanese themselves. From this volatile intellectual mix, violations of the rules of war became understandable, even acceptable in the face of such a vicious enemy: "There were especially routine violations of applicable rules about the treatment of the dead [in the Pacific], skull collections were especially popular, alongside necklaces of harvested gold teeth."[43] Though these and other atrocities committed by the U.S. military and its allies were largely hidden from public view thanks to the diligent efforts of the Office of Censorship, they were known to be a feature of fighting against the Japanese and therefore marked a profound difference in attitudes and behaviors between soldiers fighting in Europe as compared to those fighting in Asia. Following on from this mutilation and macabre assemblage of war trophies, a limited number of reports of American soldiers killing civilians in Asia would soon follow, contributing to a different public sensibility about the Japanese enemy as compared to their European allies.

In February of 1942, seizing upon this public animus, President Roosevelt signed into law Executive Order 9066, a federal writ authorizing the forcible relocation of Japanese Americans to inland "relocation centers" where they would be tracked and monitored for the duration of the American effort during the war.[44] The passage of this legislation resulted in the forcible removal of more than 100,000 Japanese Americans from their homes and the forcible sale or direct requisition of their property and businesses in the western United States. The relocation centers themselves were akin to prison camps; cots, tents, and temporary dwellings characterized the centers, and limited use of shared facilities was commonplace throughout. In addition, each of the camps was surrounded by barbed wire, and all of the detainees were under armed guard day and night. Entry and exit to and from the camps were controlled by the armed military personnel stationed at the gates.

The detention of Japanese Americans ensured that this community would specifically be identified as an enemy within the borders of the United States. Executive Order 9066 affected the internment of a whole community of U.S. citizens and legal residents classifying them as dangerous saboteurs or fifth column agents living in the country. No similar orders were authorized by the federal government targeting Germans or Italian Americans, and no such legislation was seriously considered in the offices of government during this time. Rather, it was the specific lot of Japanese Americans, among the other national groups with origins from enemy states living in the United States during World War II, to be targeted for discrimination, dispossession, and relocation by the government of the United States. The detention of Japanese Americans would last until March of 1946 (months after the end of the Pacific War), but the release of these citizens brought fresh hardships given that they were left destitute and humiliated by this unprecedented process. The United States would not offer a formal apology for this treatment of Japanese Americans until the Reagan administration, some 40 years after the episode had concluded.

Clearly, as evidenced by practices of dehumanization common to U.S. soldiers fighting in the Pacific, as well as the state-mandated identification of Japanese Americans as internal enemies, the United States had a distinct hatred for Japan during the war. Motivated by this hatred and possessed of an ethos of revenge for the bombing of Pearl Harbor, from Washington's vantage point, there was only one suitable enemy target for the deployment of a new, terrible weapon that had been developed by military personnel and some of the world's leading chemists, scientists, and engineers working in secret at Los Alamos Laboratory. The product of this malevolent collaboration, known as the Manhattan Project, was three devices: Gadget, Little Boy, and Fat Man. They were the world's first nuclear bombs, and after the detonation of Gadget on July 16, 1945, at Trinity Test Site in the New Mexico desert, the U.S. government was in possession of a new weapon with unprecedented destructive power, one that would alter the course of the war and, with it, would accomplish no less than changing the course of human history.[45]

The remaining two bombs were dropped on Hiroshima and Nagasaki, Japan, to devastatingly punctuate the conclusion of the war in the Pacific, and since their unprecedented use on virtually all civilian targets during wartime,[46] much controversy has surrounded their construction and their deployment. Much more will be said about both these catastrophic weapons and the manner in which they were discussed in the authoritative news media in the section in this chapter subtitled "The Good Bomb," but suffice it to say here that these bombings mark the sole use of nuclear weaponry against a human enemy in the entire history of mankind. These bombs caused instant death to hundreds of thousands of Japanese civilians in August of 1945 and would go on to produce devastating long-term consequences among the populations and in the natural environments of these Japanese cities. And though the number of nuclear nations has disturbingly increased since 1945, with combined nuclear arsenals topping more than 13,000 active devices at the time of this writing, the depravity of the human destruction caused by the United States at Hiroshima and Nagasaki has thankfully not been repeated on the same scale by any national military against any other people in the intervening years since 1945. It is of critical importance, though, that history continues to commemorate August 6th and August 9th of 1945 as a potent reminder of the human capacity for callousness, for racist indifference, and for militant revenge perpetrated by the United States against a despised, sworn enemy.

With this alternative history of the American war effort in World War II now recorded, this chapter will turn to an examination of certain key elements within the public discourse on the U.S. military's participation in World War II. Critically, this examination will frame the actions of the U.S. military as the war drew to a close, culminating in the obliteration of two Japanese cities by nuclear explosion. Considerations throughout this section of the chapter will be framed by the ever-present conception within the authoritative media of the era framing World War II as "The Good War," a trope that continues to mark discussions of World War II in both public and private spheres of inquiry in the United States. This case study chapter, then, intends to proffer alternative views of the U.S. military during this conflict by cataloging popular media discourse and collective public bias surrounding this perceived goodness of the war as well as surrounding the role of the United States in the geopolitical realm in the aftermath of the war and throughout the second half of the twentieth century.

Discourse and Knowledge: Frames of Representation in Print News Media Coverage of World War II

This narrative history of alternative perspectives brought to bear on the defining global conflagration of the twentieth century began with the proposition that the vastness of this war, the people it subsumed, the locations over which it trafficked, and the lives it irrevocably impacted or simply erased for perpetuity cannot be overstated. Depictions of World War II come to students of history as a behemoth, an all-encompassing political, industrial, and military engagement that represented the culmination of all human history that had come before as much as it informed them about the directions that history was going. If this descriptive scope is remotely accurate, then a study in the language brought to bear in describing these monumental events from sites of authoritative discourse distribution is destined to fail. No singular work, no matter how exhaustive, could come close to an authoritative presentation of functional discourses applied and disseminated during this period of time, given the immensity of the volume of news, knowledge, and information that was levied in the attempt to describe these unprecedented events. The volume of text materials applied in this endeavor alone would render such an activity prohibitive at best and foolhardy at worst.

And while the scope of World War II is accurately depicted as immense, even incomprehensible to those few still alive who can remember it, the function of lines of discourse within a given public and/or news media community can still be made discernible in outline, given a suitably robust approach to an assessment of language brought to bear during the war itself. As such, what follows does not purport to be a description of the definitive news discourse of World War II or even a definitive accounting of that discourse within the United States. As mentioned earlier, the circumscription of such an analysis is rendered all but impossible given the scope and scale of the history in question here. Rather, what is given below is a circumscription of prominent frames of representation that were to be found, if not in their ubiquity, certainly with great frequency over specific periods of time in news media descriptions of the war produced in the United States. This relatively short description is, while informative and influential in future news media discourse surrounding war and the U.S. military, necessarily incomplete given the breadth of the history and the dynamism of the intellectual structures herein described. Nevertheless, the text analysis to follow below presents certain key elements that were prevalent within the authoritative news media's presentation of wartime events distributed during this period of time and, as such, constitute a discourse on certain aspects of World War II crafted for an attendant American audience. Speculative conclusions as to the specific impact of this discourse and its particular frames of representation on the intellectual environment of the United States during this era, as well as its impacts on ongoing conceptions of American identity crafted within the country during wartime, follow this textual analysis.

The Good Bomb

From the first moments the decision to use nuclear weapons against Japan was taken, the government showed a vested interest in controlling the narrative about the reasons for their use and the effects that came from their deployment: "President Truman, at the suggestion of General Groves, sent an unusual request, 'in confidence,' to American editors and broadcasters. Truman, in the interest of 'the highest national security,' asked the media not to publish information on a wide range of matters related to the bomb, including its 'operational use,' 'without first consulting with the War Department'."[47] Given this imperative from the highest office in the American government, after the horrific destruction wrought by the deployment of two nuclear devices by American forces on Hiroshima and Nagasaki in August of 1945, the authoritative print news media of the era was at great pains to assure their readership in the United States that nothing especially untoward had occurred. Instead, in hundreds of articles that appeared between August and December of that year, established newspapers and periodicals published news pieces that substantially mitigated the grotesque destructive force of the American nuclear arsenal while also minimizing the long-term damage it was to cause the people of Japan. In some cases, that degree of mitigation extended to outright praise of the bombings, lauding, as numerous articles did, the swift end of the war or perhaps even more commonly, the benefits to be derived from nuclear militancy. This decidedly optimistic narrative of the nuclear destruction of two Japanese cities focused upon multiple, complimentary intellectual constructions repeated within the authoritative publications of the day. Among these narrative tropes were assertions that no radiation poisoning attended the unleashing of the explosions at Hiroshima and Nagasaki, that Japanese propaganda from their national news agency had exaggerated the effects of the bombings, and ultimately that the nuclear destruction of Hiroshima and Nagasaki was an act in service of the greater good of humanity. At best, these oft-repeated text representations in late 1945 underreported the sheer destruction that came with the nuclear annihilation of two Japanese cities, an act that remains to this day a singular action in world history. At worst, these frames of representation praised the United States and its military for an act of unique and wanton devastation, the likes of which have never been seen since. The specific form these representations took and the potential intellectual consequences they produced among a riveted and news-obsessed public attending to the final stages of American involvement in World War II are investigated next.

One prominent journalistic element applied in news media presentations of the nuclear ruins of Hiroshima and Nagasaki was the idea that the destruction of the two Japanese cities occurred via only conventional explosive force and was not accompanied by massive amounts of nuclear radiation. Patently false as this assertion is—and was known to be at the time—this frame nevertheless appeared again and again in news media coverage of these uniquely destructive bombings. Typical examples of this frame were included in a *Washington Post* article entitled "Radioactivity From Hiroshima Discounted" that quoted a reputed American nuclear expert, Brigadier General Thomas Farrell, who declared unequivocally that the "bomb dropped on Hiroshima destroyed or damaged 68,000 buildings but left 'no measurable radioactivity' after the explosion."[48] The article went on to guarantee that "no evidence had been found that the bomb would cause deaths through radioactivity after a long period of time."[49] Other publications followed suit with this narrative, covering still larger areas of the American media market in the aftermath of the war. One *Los Angeles Times* piece similarly reassured readers that radiation would not be an issue in Japan as a result of the bombings: "An American atomic bomb expert on August 8 [...] said that there was no reason to believe there was any appreciable radioactivity on the ground at Hiroshima, or that its effects lingered."[50] The expert referenced here was also Farrell, who had been the deputy commanding general and chief of field operations of the Manhattan Project, effectively number two to the project's military commander, General Leslie Groves. These assessments were universally printed without question or criticism, even though Farrell's objectivity as regards the destruction wrought by the American nuclear arsenal upon Japan was far from a foregone conclusion.

In point of fact, a significant percentage of reporting about the damage caused by the bombing of Hiroshima and Nagasaki either directly quoted Major General Thomas Farrell or else made reference to his reports and his public declarations denying the existence of radiation in Japan as a result of the American use of nuclear bombs. Ubiquitous though these references were in the period press, there are multiple reasons to doubt Farrell's honesty in his evaluation of the bombs and their aftereffects. Farrell's highly political role as representative of the head of the Manhattan Project, General Leslie Groves, in postwar Japan was well known to journalists on the ground in Japan during Farrell's fact-finding mission. Authors Robert Jay Lifton and Greg Mitchell specifically call Farrell's objectivity into question in their extensively researched book released on the 50th anniversary year of the bombings entitled *Hiroshima in America: Fifty Years of Denial:* "How objectively did Farrell approach his inquiry? A member of the research team later revealed that Farrell had instructed him that 'our mission was to prove that there was no radioactivity from the bomb'."[51] This dubious approach to scientific inquiry was never made public, though, and was never revealed by officials within the authoritative news media who knew of Farrell's intentions and yet continued to quote him in the period press unreservedly. This failing of journalistic investigation (or perhaps journalistic integrity) allowed Farrell's declarations concerning the limited damage caused by the bombings of Hiroshima and Nagasaki to be carried by publications across the United States as if they were the unvarnished truth of the matter.

The *New York Times,* for its part, also contributed to this widespread narrative with their coverage of the nuclear bombings, asserting after the fact that "At the rate the radiations [sic] have diminished during the past two months, it was pointed out, the entire area will be free of them within a relatively short time."[52] Readers were likewise informed that all of these rational assessments were to be trusted given that they were based upon "careful scientific studies of the effects of the atomic bombing of Hiroshima and Nagasaki" which confirmed "that no prolonged dangerous radioactivity lingers after the blast."[53] These and many other examples of news reports during this period of time provide a narrative of mitigation, informing readers that the damage done by these powerful devices was not all that bad and was certainly not attended by massive doses of radiation that would beset the populations of Hiroshima and Nagasaki for generations. Sober, scientific, and military analysis informed these conclusions, and the officials drawing these conclusions were likewise forthright and trustworthy. In short, the fantastical vision of non-nuclear nuclear weapons causing conventional destruction was, if not ubiquitous, then decidedly prevalent in news coverage of the Hiroshima and Nagasaki bombings immediately after the war. Readers of this coverage would have been hard-pressed to find a countervailing narrative with equivalent discursive impact in authoritative news coverage throughout this period.[54]

Though if they did discern a more damaging, more long-lasting, and/or more grue-some punitive element present in the nuclear destruction of Hiroshima and Nagasaki beyond simple, conventional harm, likely it was a result of misinformation spread by the Japanese themselves and their compromised, propagandistic national news agency known as the *Domei*. In keeping with racist tropes within news media coverage dur-ing World War II that attached particularly nefarious and underhanded motivations to the Japanese during the war,[55] this frame of representation asserts that the Japanese national news agency spread false propaganda about the impacts of American nuclear bombs in Hiroshima and Nagasaki, namely that radiation poisoning was killing hun-dreds of Japanese civilians weeks after the detonations. The print news media in the United States was quick to refute such a claim, stating, for example, that "American experts on Japanese propaganda suggested that the Japanese may be attempting to capitalize on the horror of atomic bombing in an effort to win sympathy from their conquerors and to play on the possibly divided opinion among the Allies."[56] The crux of the claim in this article was twofold. Firstly, the Japanese were exaggerating the death toll at Hiroshima and Nagasaki; civilian deaths as a result of radiation poisoning were not occurring en masse in Japan in late 1945. Secondly, this lie was a devious ploy of the Japanese media institution applied in order to win sympathy from global observers in the aftermath of the war.

Attributing base and duplicitous to the Japanese citizenry and government, the arti-cle further explains that the country as a whole was attempting to "shorten the Allied occupation and lessen reparations and other war costs [...] converting an abstract hor-ror theory into allegations that they count upon to arouse humanitarian reactions."[57] Additional headlines asserting this argument are: "Fantastic Atomic Bomb Horror Deaths Described";[58] "U.S. Atom Bomb Site Belies Tokyo Tales";[59] and "Foe's Radiation Stories Denied At Hiroshima."[60] In sum, these news pieces and many others like them published in the aftermath of the U.S. nuclear strikes on Japan paint a clear picture for American readers of the deceitful nature of the annihilated enemy, one in which the radiation poisoning endured by generations of subject Japanese civilians is remade as a plot to garner false sympathy. The resultant narrative within the news media further emphasizes ideas of Japanese villainy and American righteousness by substantially modifying the truly terrifying impacts of nuclear radiation in the Japanese countryside. Years would pass before the news media as an institution ever acknowledged the long-lasting impacts of Hiroshima and Nagasaki and the generational imprint of American war upon the Japanese populace.

A final, macabre pillar in the broad narrative justifying the use of nuclear weapons upon Japanese civilians entails the proclamation that nuclear weapons are, in fact, a global good and that their prescient deployment by military planners in the United States in 1945 served to advance human history in an altogether positive forward direction. As such, the United States military and political institutions were owed a debt of gratitude by citizens throughout the world, now set to experience a utopian, nuclear future. One such article, unironically entitled "Atomic Bomb Viewed As Aiding Cause of World News Freedom" praised the new era of open communication and global cooperation heralded by the U.S. military's use of nuclear weapons: "Whatever other effects the detonation of an atomic bomb over Hiroshima, Japan, may have had, it advanced the cause of honest dissemination of news between nations by many years and ushered in a new era of international understanding between peoples."[61] The "other effects" not mentioned in this article included the deaths of tens of thousands of Japanese civilians and the poisoning of the city grounds for years. These effects constituted a small price to pay, if this line of argument is followed, for the abstract promise of "international understanding between peoples," which, in any case, has quite obviously never materialized.

Other news pieces promised the end of the war and the proliferation of peace thanks to the use of nuclear devices, with bold assertions casting the United States as the harbinger of a new global era of peace and understanding, with grandiose reports promising that "the atomic bomb makes peace imperative by making war impossible"[62] and that "the last half of the century could produce a world-wide flowering of the human spirit such as we have not known since the Renaissance."[63] Naturally, these two narrative elements work in tandem as complimentary pillars in the new, peaceable global order. Together, they constitute a powerful argument in praise of America's use of nuclear weapons: "This devastating weapon [is] a potent argument for a freer flow of news between peoples in order that there shall be less cause for misunderstanding and world conflict in the future."[64] In short, the entire world was greatly improved by the use of atomic weapons, and the United States, as the sole country responsible for the deployment of this weaponry, has shown the community of nations the way forward into a glistening, technological future. In other words, according to an article published in the *Los Angeles Times* a day after the August 9th bombing of Nagasaki, these weapons "may well lead into a bright new world in which man shares a common brotherhood."[65] Needless to say, these utopian visions of the strictly beneficial potential of nuclear weapons have proven to be as fantastical as they were inhumane when they were first put to print. It also bears mention that these paeans to the devastating weaponry that symbolized the nuclear age were disseminated in authoritative print publications that rarely, if ever, offered an accounting of the damage done or of the lives lost as a result of the American deployment of nuclear bombs in Japan. Further conclusions to be drawn from the discursive and intellectual consequences of these, and the other ever-present discursive tropes cast about during news coverage of American participation in World War II follow below.

The American Military Identity

In the aftermath of World War II, the United States was ascendant. The U.S. military had been victorious in multiple theaters of harrowing warfare, each landscape and each foe more wicked and brutal than the last. With the destruction of Hiroshima and Nagasaki, American participation in the second global war within the span of three decades was at an end, and the United States could begin, once again, to think about the future. From this vantage point, and with an eye on the second half of the twentieth century, the United States was already in possession of a number of key geopolitical advantages. In the first place, the infrastructure of the United States was completely intact and unspoiled. Unlike our European allies, no battles took place in our fields or within our cities. The landscape of the United States in 1945 was, therefore, pristine, leaving open enumerable possibilities for growth, development, and economic prosperity on a scale unachievable by our European counterparts. Furthermore, the United States was on the cusp of a substantial population increase, the so-called Baby Boom, which would outfit the country with a sizable labor force and a diverse social fabric in the decades of the 1950s, 1960s, and 1970s. Our political processes, though partial and available to only a segment of the population, were stable and capable of administering to a growing and diversifying population. Finally, the United States in 1945 enjoyed global goodwill after having again fought and bled for the causes of freedom, democracy, and liberty around the globe.

In assessing this collection of positive national attributes following the war, the print news media within the United States was at great pains to identify a key component in the American story whose necessity in the coming years would be beyond dispute: the U.S. military. In article after article published in reputable publications across the country, both staff writers and editorial contributors alike spoke to the moral imperative of maintaining, indeed expanding, the power and prestige of the U.S. military. These articles warn against complacency in the postwar world, arguing that the end of the fighting in Europe and the Pacific should not lead to a movement for demobilization. Quite the opposite in fact, soldiers, bullets, and bombs were in more dire need at the conclusion of the war than ever before, considering the proliferation of new enemies, both at home and abroad, to be faced by the United States in the near future. Routinely, this narrative advocating for increased military production, an expansion of the armed forces, and even calling for universal male military training was a staple component of news articles and think pieces considering the position of the United States during peacetime. Taken together, these texts create a powerful strain of militarism in the popular discourse considering World War II and the position of the United States upon its conclusion as they circumscribe the stark boundaries of American identity, inclusive of aggression, jingoism, and military prowess over and above other collective considerations of the national consciousness for generations to come.

One popular narrative trope that conveyed the indelible connection between American national identity and ongoing state militarism entailed protestations and dire warnings concerning the inevitable processes of demobilization of American forces that were taking place around the globe at the end of the war. This trope begins with overt praise of U.S. military power with declarations like, "The United States now has a fighting strength greater than at any other time in our history. It is greater than that of any other nation in the world"[66] and "American military strength [is] now reaching its apex."[67] Descriptions of U.S. demobilization then follow: "For two months the mightiest nation on earth has been disarming itself at great speed. The rate of self-disarmament is accelerating. Within a few months the United States might not be the mightiest nation on earth in terms of mobilized military power."[68] More common are the reports that directly criticize decampment and/or a reduction in troop numbers: "The armed power of the United States, so mighty a force for victory and peace only a few months ago, is disintegrating at an alarming rate. It is alarming because the disintegration is taking place so rapidly and without plan."[69] Many equated normal processes of limited disarmament following the war with weakness promising grim consequences for continuing this policy with embedded article subheadings like "Peril in U.S. Weakness"[70] and "Might Will Help Keep Peace."[71]

A final, possibly predictive pillar of the broader narrative tying American identity with expanded militarism in the postwar world tellingly pointed to the futility of reliance upon supranational organizations like the United Nations in order to avoid future conflicts: "All who have faith in the United Nations, all who see it as the hope of the world must wish for strength of the United States as an imperative requisite for fulfilling its promise."[72] The Atlantic Charter was also condemned as ephemeral and vague within this narrative trope, too: "The Atlantic Charter is a statement of ideals, far off and general."[73] Taken as a whole, these commentaries portray the United States as a nation of unmatched military prowess, beating its swords into plowshares to its own detriment. America was made strong by its military, and only by its military will it continue to oversee the course of global events into the future. A strong case is made to connect the public understanding of American identity and American consciousness as connected irrevocably to military superiority. And indeed, the American century to come would bear out these powerful, intellectual associations established at the end of World War II, on a massively destructive, global scale.

For many observers, the obvious solution to the problem of demobilization was to be found in a national program of universal military training (often referred to in publications as UMT), a compulsory commitment to instruction and drill akin to military boot camp but falling short of fully-fledged active duty. This UMT was first considered by President Wilson in World War I but ultimately rejected in favor of the more euphemistically named Selective Service Act of 1917. Now reinvigorated by growing calls for an overt American military identity, UMT returned as a proposal by Franklin D. Roosevelt in January of 1945, becoming a policy priority for President Truman, who introduced it before a joint session of Congress on October 23, 1945. Its provisions included mandatory training for the period of a year by all male citizens aged 18 to 20, followed by a six-year stint in a general military reserve system.[74] As a policy initiative, it ultimately failed, as did subsequent measures in the 1950s forcing compulsory military enrollment during peacetime. But while this proposal remained a viable domestic policy potentially to be enacted by the Truman administration, discussions concerning UMT proliferated on the pages of authoritative national newspapers. Predictably, these deliberations were substantially positive about the proposal, suggesting that UMT provided the answer to demobilization and to the presumed flagging patriotism that came with it. Naturally, these widely read perspectives contributed markedly to widespread narrative tropes connecting America's future and the ongoing construction of the American identity to the militarism embodied by the U.S. armed forces.

One *Washington Post* article puts forward the cause for UMT very plainly: "universal military training, in the widest and most modern sense of the phase [*sic*], is more than ever essential to the security of the United States."[75] This clearly argues for the preeminence of security as a national priority after World War II and links this supposed urgency for an expansion of the national defense to an increase in the available armed forces through military protocols such as the UMT. The piece goes on to place the same arguments in the mouths of respected policymakers and military officials, trusting their legitimacy to carry the weight of this frame of representation among a reading public attending to news about the U.S. military in the aftermath of global war: "In outlining the essentials of a military policy for the United States, [U.S. Army Chief of Staff] General Marshall puts great emphasis on universal military training."[76] Advocacy for this policy, then, is not purely an editorial stance but rather is in keeping with the opinions of the most venerable and trusted voices on these matters within the country.

Not to be outdone, the *New York Times* opined in agreement with the *Washington Post* in describing UMT as a logical and essential step in U.S. policy in a postwar world that would indeed be shaped by American political and military supremacy: "United States political influence should be positive and commensurate with our military strength, or we shall have allowed the mere waging of a war to dominate policy, instead of using war as an instrument of policy."[77] Another tactic in the construction of this discursive narrative was to identify a delay in UMT and immediate military expansion with a form of betrayal to the American mission in the world and/or the overarching American military identity: "Let us not by a short-sighted neglect of our national security betray those who come after us."[78] The message here is clear: to reject the implementation of UMT, effectively a compulsory draft of all American young men, would be a betrayal to future generations and a curse on the American soul itself, reaping misfortune in the decades to come. These news articles, along with many other reports advocating for an expansive, militaristic policy in the same vein as the examples earlier, formed a powerful discursive element connecting military expansion and predicted future wars indelibly to the American identity in the postwar world.

A final telling element within this frame of representation establishing an immense and dominant U.S. military as inherent in the American national consciousness involved denying the inevitable result of UMT within the American populace. In advocating for UMT, an expansive piece published the day after Truman's October 1945 address to Congress suggests that the implementation of this training regime would not create an armed and militant citizenry, stating that this predictable consequence of compulsory military expansion did not constitute a laudable policy goal: "We want no nation of sol-diers."[79] Nevertheless, delaying UMT and concomitant nationwide conscription would leave the United States in a vulnerable military position vis-à-vis suspected external military threats, thus leaving the United States with no option but to draft all able-bodied men and to expand U.S. military fortifications: "anything less than a nation of trained citizenry able to defend our country, would be a deplorable weakening of the position and influence we have gained in the world and an invitation to aggression."[80] The use of the term "defend" is a consequential editorial choice within this narrative frame. In addition, the assertion that the United States does not *want* to implement UMT training but rather is *forced* to do so through no fault of our own overlaps con-siderably with previously prevalent discursive frames applied in news coverage of the U.S. military during World War I (see Chapter 3, "World War I: American Service," in the section entitled "American Bravery, American Humility"). The American iden-tity is then remade not only as a militant one but as possessive of a decidedly reluctant militancy and a chagrined aggression in oft-repeated discursive constructions of the American self in the authoritative print news media.

Conclusions: The American War and the American Self

World War II is framed within the discussions in this chapter as a "Good War," one in which the noblest of efforts and purest of intents within American militancy and policy were on display for the world to see. And undoubtedly, the United States won a substan-tial amount of cultural and political capital for joining the fight in Europe and Asia in 1941 and for helping to bring about an end to fascist, racist, and imperialist regimes on two continents. But the manner in which the authoritative press constructed a discourse around the U.S. war effort for readership on the home front both during and after the war itself informs dynamic and ongoing reifications of American identity constructed substantially as it was then, and as it is now, connected to the dominance of the U.S. military. Within those discursive frames were recognizable elements of duty, honor, and sacrifice, which accompany all state-sustaining commentaries considering U.S. military engagement. But further to those elements were also narrative tropes praising horrific nuclear destruction in Japan, denying the true consequences of the American choice to unleash nuclear weaponry upon the globe, and possibly predictably, convincing the reading public that the American self is irrevocably connected to the military for gen-erations of citizens to come.

With the exception of the discursive elements analyzed herein connected specifically to the American bombings at Hiroshima and Nagasaki, these tropes describing the American military imperative all the while explaining the United States as a reluctant warrior state are not unique. Instead, they connect readily with intellectual conceptions of warfare, military, statehood, and self that had been distributed by the same authori-tative press outlets in previous iterations of American military conflicts decades earlier. As such, the weight of this information and the connections of these channels of knowl-edge become resonant lines of discursive memory absorbed, reified, and replicated in their own way by the recipients of that authoritative discourse themselves. Through this process, a broader, more massive intellectual construction becomes discernible. State, society, the military, and our own conceptions of these functional elements in the American story will move into the second half of the twentieth century and toward ever more bloodshed and more war in the name of sacrosanct American values and of the sanctified American self.

Notes

1 Samuel Hynes, *The Soldiers' Tale Bearing Witness to Modern War* (New York: The Penguin Press, 1997), xii.
2 Some scholars dispute these dates as the beginning and ending points of the war. These specific dates are applied here according to slightly more recent historical work done by Evan Mawdsley in his *World War II: A New History* (Cambridge: Cambridge University Press, 2009).
3 American military participation in this war followed its financial intervention in the growing global conflagration in the early 1940s, which primarily took the form of military aid dispatched to American allies: "in March 1941 Congress passed the Lend-Lease Act, which in effect allowed the transfer of weapons and supplies to Britain and other friendly states without direct payment" (Ibid., 202).
4 George H. Roeder, Jr., "Censoring Disorder: American Visual Imagery of World War II," in Lewis A. Erenberg and Susan B. Hirsch (eds.), *The War in American Culture: Society and Consciousness during World War II* (Chicago: University of Chicago Press, 1996), 59.
5 Ibid., 48.
6 Ibid., 51–56.
7 It is perhaps less well known that this attack did not actually constitute an enemy military operation on sovereign American soil, being that Hawaii was not a state in the United States and would not become so until August 21, 1959. Equally, it is lesser known that official records later released by the U.S. government revealed that "a White House conference two weeks before Pearl Harbor anticipated a war and discussed how it should be justified" (Howard Zinn, *A People's History of the United States* (New York: HarperCollins, 2003 [1980]), 411).
8 Japan, Germany, and Italy signed the Tripartite Pact formalizing a military alliance between the three states on September 27, 1940.
9 Henry Steel Commager and Richard B. Morris, "Introduction," in Russel A. Buchanan, *The United States and World War II: Volume I* (New York: Harper & Row Publishers, 1946), xiv.
10 Ibid., xv.
11 Zinn, *A People's History of the United States*, 413.
12 Ibid., 417.
13 This term originated in critiques written by Noam Chomsky and his analyses of the economic structure of the United States after World War II. He describes the Washington consensus as: "masters of the private economy, mainly huge corporations that control much of the international economy and have the means the dominate policy formation as well as the structuring of thought and opinion" (Noam Chomsky, *Profit Over People: Neoliberalism and Global Order* (New York: Seven Stories Press, 1999), 20).
14 William Greider, *Fortress America: The American Military and the Consequence of Peace* (New York: Public Affairs, 1998), 52.
15 Ibid., 54.
16 Zinn, *A People's History of the United States*, 425.
17 Ibid.
18 Gary Gerstel, "The Working Class Goes to War," in Lewis A. Erenberg and Susan B. Hirsch (eds.), *The War in American Culture: Society and Consciousness during World War II* (Chicago: University of Chicago Press, 1996), 105.
19 Naomi Klein, *No is Not Enough: Resisting Trump's Shock Politics and Winning the World We Need* (Chicago: Haymarket Books, 2017), 97.
20 Segregation in the military was so strictly enforced, in fact, that captured German prisoners were given preferential access to military facilities over and above African American soldiers because of the color of their skin. In one incident recorded by black soldiers traveling by train

during this period in Texas "black troops were fed behind a curtain at one end of the dining car, while German prisoners dined with whites in the main section" (Kenneth D. Rose, *Myth and the Greatest Generation: A Social History of Americans in World War II* (New York: Routledge, Taylor & Francis Group, 2008), 136).

21 Ibid., 135.

22 Ibid., 4.

23 Studs Terkel, *The Good War: An Oral History of World War Two* (New York: Pantheon Books, 1984), 11.

24 Rose, *Myth and the Greatest Generation*, 137.

25 In fact, press censorship and other machinations of the Office of Censorship saw to it that even those few black officers or non-commissioned officers among the ranks in World War II remained unknown to the public even after the end of the war: "Refusal to publish pictures of African American soldiers in leadership positions sustained postwar assumptions of white supremacy" (Roeder, Jr., "Censoring Disorder: American Visual Imagery of World War II," 64).

26 Ibid.

27 As in World War I, black American soldiers from the industrial North who were sent south for training prior to deployment were often horrified by the blatant display of racist violence that tended to be more commonplace in the Jim Crow South than in their own Northern communities. As well, the likelihood of their exposure to these dangerous and disturbing conditions was extraordinarily high given that "a preponderance of army training camps during the Second World War were located in the South" (Rose, *Myth and the Greatest Generation*, 135).

28 Ibid., 138–39.

29 Terkel, *The Good War*, 279.

30 Rose, *Myth and the Greatest Generation*, 4.

31 Ibid., 133.

32 Ibid.

33 Edward J. Escobar, "Zoot-Suiters and Cops: Chicano youth and the Los Angeles Police Department during World War II," in Lewis A. Erenberg and Susan B. Hirsch (eds.), *The War in American Culture: Society and Consciousness during World War II* (Chicago: University of Chicago Press), 284.

34 Though the overall economic prosperity of the American family would improve as time went on, the connection between poverty statistics and racial categorization within the United States has remained a disturbing constant. In 1968, 23 percent of black families lived in poverty, compared with 9 percent of white families. In 2021, 31 percent of black children lived, below the national poverty line while 11 percent of white children were in that same economic category (See "Kids Count Data Center" for a clarification of these statistics: https://data-center.kidscount.org/data/tables/44-children-in-poverty-by-race-and-ethnicity#detailed/1/any/false/2048,1729,37,871,870,573,869,36,868,867/ 10,11,9,12,1,185,13/324,323).

35 Erin Blakemore, "How the GI Bill's Promise Was Denied to a Million Black WWII Veterans," History.Com. Last modified April 20, 2021. https://www.history.com/news/gi-bill-black-wwii-veterans-benefits.

36 Zinn, *A People's History of the United States*, 409.

37 Mawdsley, *World War II: A New History*, 216.

38 Terkel, *The Good War*, 67.

39 John W. Dower, "Race, Language, and War in Two Cultures: World War II in Asia," in Lewis A. Erenberg and Susan B. Hirsch (eds.), *The War in American Culture: Society and Consciousness during World War II* (Chicago: University of Chicago Press, 1996), 173.

40 Ibid., 174.

41 Samuel Moyn, *Humane: How the United States Abandoned Peace and Reinvented War* (New York: Farrar, Straus and Giroux, 2021), 136.

42 Mawdsley, *World War II: A New History*, 209.

43 Ibid.

44 "Executive Order 9066: Resulting in Japanese-American Incarceration (1942)," *National Archives*. https://www.archives.gov/milestone-documents/executive-order-9066.

45 Mawdsley, *World War II: A New History*, 412.

46 Press reports attempted to justify the bombing of Hiroshima because it contained a Japanese military base and communications center, and while this was technically true, the base was

largely empty of military personnel in the final stages of the war. Authors Robert Jay Lifton and Greg Mitchell noted in their 1995 book *Hiroshima in America: Fifty Years of Denial*, that in the Hiroshima bombing, "of the more than one hundred thousand dead in the city, only about two hundred and fifty were Japanese military personnel—the same number of prisoners of war killed or injured by the blast" (Lifton and Mitchell, *Hiroshima in America: Fifty Years of Denial* (New York: Putnam Books, 1995), 163).

47 Ibid., 55.
48 "Radioactivity at Hiroshima Discounted," *The Washington Post*, September 13, 1945, 2.
49 Ibid.
50 "30,000 Died of Burns in 2 Weeks after Attack: People Entering Area after Blast Became Ill; Some Begged for Death Rays," *The Washington Post*, August 25, 1945, 1.
51 Lifton and Mitchell, *Hiroshima in America*, 53.
52 William L. Laurence, "U.S. Atom Bomb Site Belies Tokyo Tales: Tests on New Mexico Range Confirm That Blast, and Not Radiation, Took Toll," *New York Times*, September 12, 1945, 1.
53 "Prolonged Radioactivity Peril of A-Bomb Denied: Gen. Farrell Reports on Studies in Japan; Rep. Luce Calls for U.S. Underground Plants," *Los Angeles Times*, August 21, 1945, 12.
54 Some reports pointing out the obvious inconsistencies between the American expert evaluation of the effects of the bombs and the facts on the ground in Hiroshima and Nagasaki came in the obscure *New Journal and Guide*, which reported dramatically that "it now appears that life will be just about impossible in an area hit by the atomic bomb for 75 or more years!" Still, extensive research into the authoritative news media during this period of time uncovered very few examples of this narrative within news media discourse ("Atomic Bomb Found More Deadly than First Believed," *New Journal and Guide*, September 8, 1945, A9).
55 Racial epithets were commonplace in press coverage of the Pacific Theater of the war and were particularly prevalent around discussions of the bombings of Hiroshima and Nagasaki. Typical coverage can be found in an example from the *Los Angeles Times*, which unapologetically declared that it was "the Nip propagandists who say the use of the new weapon is 'sufficient to brand the enemy for ages to come as the destroyed of mankind'." (Hanson W. Baldwin, "Howls of Jap Anguish Betray Heavy Bomb Damage," *Los Angeles Times*, August 8, 1945, A4).
56 "Japanese Stress 'Horror': Atomic-Bomb 'Radioactivity' Killed 30,000, Says Tokyo—Sympathy Effort Seen. Such Effect Denied Here. Enemy Radio Talks of Toll Still Mounting From 'Burns' Caused by 'Rays' in Area Japanese Propaganda Aim Noted Tokyo Builds Up Details," *New York Times*, August 25, 1945, 3.
57 Ibid.
58 Russell Brines, "Fantastic Atomic Bomb Horror Deaths Described: Russian Witness Tells of Effects Wrought on Japanese People by Hiroshima Blast," *Los Angeles Times*, November 4, 1945, 2.
59 Laurence, "U.S. Atom Bomb Site Belies Tokyo Tales," *New York Times*, September 12, 1945, 1.
60 Homer Bigart, "Foe's Radiation Stories Denied At Hiroshima: Gen. Farrell, Atomic Bomb Expert, Says All Victims Were Hit by Initial Blast," *New York Herald Tribune*, September 13, 1945, 2.
61 Wilbur Forrest, "Atomic Bomb Viewed As Aiding Cause of World News Freedom: Hiroshima Demonstration of Future War's Horror Called Potent Argument for Better International Relationships Based on Better Information," *New York Herald Tribune*, August 14, 1945, 21A.
62 Anne O. McCormick, "Abroad: The Promethean Role of the United States Not Launched Lightly Power to Shape the Future," *New York Herald Tribune*, August 8, 1945, 22.
63 Raymond Fosdick, "The Challenge: One World or None: 'We Are in a Race with Our Technologies; with Our Mounting Capacity to Destroy'. One World or None One World or None," *New York Times*, September 2, 1945, 69.
64 Wilbur, "Atomic Bomb Viewed As Aiding Cause of World News Freedom," *New York Herald Tribune*, August 14, 1945, 21A.
65 Hanson W. Baldwin, "Atom Bomb Wins Victory, but Sows Whirlwind: Newly Discovered Force May Lead to World Brotherhood or Obliterate Civilization," *Los Angeles Times*, August 10, 1945, 2.

66 Raymond Fosdick, "Truman's Address Urging Military Training for All Boys Between 18 and 20: President Says Only Might can Assure Peace Asserts Plan Will Implement U. N. O. and Calls Big Army Sole Alternative," *New York Herald Tribune*, October 14, 1945, 16A.

67 Hanson W. Baldwin, "U.S. Effort Mounting: Battles of Ardennes Bulge and Luzon Point to Peak of Our Military Power The Political-Military Link The Army Nurse Problem," *New York Times*, January 10, 1945, 6.

68 Ernst Lindley, "U.S. Won't Be Mightiest Much Longer," *The Washington Post*, October 10, 1945, B5.

69 George F. Elliot, "Armed Forces' Demobilization Is Called Hasty and Disorderly: Qualitative Reduction Is Deplored; Retention of Draft Is Urged Until Volunteers Fill Gaps and a Policy Is Set on Universal Training," *New York Herald Tribune*, December 24, 1945, 13.

70 Mark Sullivan, "Military Training Held Needed To Make United Nations Work: Mark Sullivan Says a Strong U. S., Equal to Russia in Might, Is Required to Prevent Fatal Flaw in Constructing World Peace Organization," *New York Herald Tribune*, November 21, 1945, 21A.

71 George F. Elliot, "Atomic Bomb Seen Increasing Necessity for Military Training: Truman's Position Defended, and Argument That Cosmic Weapon's Effectiveness Makes Defense Moves Futile Is Called Dangerous Foolishness," *New York Herald Tribune*, October 26, 1945, 25.

72 Sullivan, "Military Training Held Needed To Make United Nations Work," *New York Herald Tribune*, November 21, 1945, 21A.

73 Baldwin, "U.S. Effort Mounting," *New York Times*, January 10, 1945, 6.

74 Frank D. Cunningham, "Harry S. Truman and Universal Military Training, 1945," *The Historian* 46, no. 3 (1984): 397–415. http://www.jstor.org/stable/24445419.

75 Ernst Lindley, "U.S. Military Training: Marshall Believes It Essential," *The Washington Post*, October 10, 1945, 10.

76 Ibid.

77 Baldwin, "U.S. Effort Mounting," *New York Times*, January 10, 1945, 6.

78 Fosdick, "Truman's Address Urging Military Training for All Boys Between 18 and 20," *New York Herald Tribune*, October 14, 1945, 16A.

79 "Training for All," *The Washington Post*, October 24, 1945, 6.

80 Ibid.

Chapter Five

AMERICA IN VIETNAM

War strips away our civilized adornments and reveals our nakedness.[1].

—*Michael Walzer, 1977*

Colonialism and Nationalism in Vietnam: 1858–1954

By the middle of the nineteenth century, European colonial powers had long cultivated an avaricious interest in Southeast Asia. In 1858, a joint Franco-Spanish military expedition arrived there using the suppression of the Catholic Vietnamese minority[2] to justify a full-scale military invasion: "When the Vietnamese emperors persecuted the missionaries and their converts as a subversive foreign sect, France used the pretext of 'freedom of religion' to justify military intervention."[3] In September of that year, European navies besieged the Vietnamese city of Da Nang (called "Tourane" by the French), engaging in a punitive war against Emperor Tu Duc. The Franco-Spanish effort sought to lay European claim to the rich ports and productive hinterland of Southeast Asia and to extract those resources (particularly rubber)[4] for European gain with or without the consent of the majority Buddhist population. The Siege of Tourane, as the French destruction of Da Nang came to be known, resulted in a bloody, 22-month occupation of the port city. Vietnamese nationalists counterattacked and besieged the city, resulting in hundreds of European casualties from attrition and disease, particularly cholera. The European army decamped in March of 1860, but by 1862, France and its allies had regained the upper hand. In suing for peace, Emperor Tu Duc was forced to relinquish three of his southern provinces, Bien Hoa, Gia Dinh, and Dinh Tuong. With their capital at Saigon (now Ho Chi Minh City), the French established the state of Cochinchina, beginning a repressive colonial rule in Vietnam that would last for a century.[5]

The French governance of Vietnam was cruel and detached. Successive French Governors General lived in a luxurious palace in Hanoi, the largest city in the northern provinces, and maintained their rule by virtue of a sprawling administration within Vietnamese cities. Most French officials spoke no Tieng Viet, ruling instead through a series of French-speaking Vietnamese bureaucrats who were willing to carry out the will of the French overseers in exchange for a position of privilege within colonial society. Known as Mandarins, these bureaucrats would constitute a fledgling middle class in a country that quickly became riven with poverty and want thanks to the effete French administration and their abusive colonial policies. The Mandarin officials, many of whom were members of the minority Catholic community within Vietnam, would see their fortunes rise and fall with the French colonial experience: "Vietnamese converts to Catholicism had been used by the French as a fifth column to penetrate precolonial Vietnam and then had been rewarded by the colonizer for their collaboration."[6] Their descendants would come to play a major role in the future of Vietnam through the American military venture in the region that would begin the country during World War II and extend until 1975 and beyond.

In 1941, invading armies of the Japanese Empire took possession of the country and began administering the Asian nation via puppet governments headed by French politicos who collaborated with the Axis Powers. Some Vietnamese nationalists hoped to be granted a measure of autonomy under Japanese occupation. One emerging leader of the Vietnamese people knew better. A determined nationalist who adopted more than 70 aliases during his lifetime, Ho Chi Minh had no faith that the Japanese would bestow independence upon Vietnam. Instead, he made contacts with the American wartime agency responsible for clandestine operations and espionage, the Office of Security Services (OSS), the precursor agency to the CIA. The OSS parachuted a team of operatives into Ho's camp and began to train the Vietnamese in the use of small arms and other guerilla tactics. Ho, a one-time resident of the United States, thought highly of the Americans who advised him. He believed that the United States represented a third way, a potential alternative path to national sovereignty independent from either European colonialism or Japanese expansionism: "Ho Chi Minh began to call his followers 'the Viet American Army' and praised the United States as a champion of democracy that would surely help them end colonial rule."[7] The OSS officials encamped with him apparently had high hopes for Ho, too. When the Japanese retreated, Ho was encouraged to officially end the colonial period in Vietnam's history by declaring the nation both unified and independent. He agreed and celebrated the occasion with a public speech on September 2, 1945. With an OSS officer close by his side, "Ho read the Vietnamese declaration of independence and proclaimed the establishment of the Democratic Republic of Vietnam to a crowd of 500,000 people assembled in Ba Dinh Square in Hanoi. He began with the words from the declaration Jefferson had written for the Thirteen Colonies: 'All men are created equal [...]'."[8]

But the French would not be put off so easily. Fresh from liberation from Nazi occupation and suffering colonial humiliations in North Africa and the Middle East, in the mid-1940s, French planners moved to reassert colonial control over Vietnam. The movement for a unified Vietnam had coalesced under Ho Chi Minh as a centralized, socialist political movement, and by 1950, communist militias in North Vietnam, known as the Viet Minh, had begun to receive support from the Soviet Union and the People's Republic of China. Under the obsessive objective of containing communist expansion that would preoccupy Washington for the remainder of the century,[9] the United States opted to abandon their erstwhile ally Ho Chi Minh and to fund his colonizing enemies instead: "The first stage of American involvement [in Vietnam] began during French rule when President Harry Truman offered financial assistance for the war against the Viet Minh. Under President Dwight Eisenhower, America's financial aid increased, ultimately to the point of paying 80 percent of France's war costs."[10] But even these massive sums would not be enough to quash the Viet Minh. In 1954 in a valley called Dien Bien Phu, five Viet Minh divisions led by General Vo Nguyen Giap besieged the army of the French Union for months. By the spring of that year, French forces were exhausted, outgunned, and undersupplied, and on the May 7th, their garrison was overrun by Viet Minh forces. The French surrendered. 11,000 French soldiers were taken prisoner by Vietnamese nationalists, and by July of that year, French forces would leave Southeast Asia for good. French colonialism in Indochina had come to a bloody end: "In its misbegotten eight-year-war, France lost a staggering 44,967 dead and another 79,560 wounded."[11]

After the French defeat at Dien Bien Phu, peace talks in Geneva created a wholly artificial divide within Vietnam along the 17th parallel. Communist political and military forces reorganized under Ho Chi Minh and established an infrastructure north of this line, all the while maintaining a substantial amount of support and sympathy south of the 17th parallel as well. Diplomatic relations between the newly created North Vietnam and sympathetic backers in the Soviet Union and China deepened. Meanwhile, the fabricated entity that was South Vietnam became a client state of the United States under Ngo Dinh Diem, a pliable member of the Catholic minority descended from a Mandarin family line. There was one caveat to this arrangement: nationwide elections to determine the fate of a unified Vietnam would be held within two years. It was plain to all observers that Ho and the communists would have won these elections in a landslide, but Diem, with backing from the United States, refused to participate in nationwide elections, arguing that "his regime was not a party to the Geneva Accords."[12] American regional ambitions effectively parroted by Diem thereby insured that Vietnam would remain divided. To press the issue of unification under a communist government, in December 1960, a revolutionary new guerilla group formed

Photo 6 U.S. soldiers running for a helicopter in a specified landing zone during the Vietnam War.

Photo 7 U.S. soldiers during Operation Hastings conducted near the so-called Demilitarized Zone located at the 17th Parallel near the Quang Tri province in July of 1966.

in North Vietnam, calling itself the National Liberation Front (NLF). Using the NLF as frontline cadres, the North Vietnamese Communist Party approved a people's war on Diem's government in the United States-backed South and opened the Ho Chi Minh Trail, a supply line running food, medicine, and war materiel to Ho's supporters below the 17th parallel. Between 1961 and 1963, roughly 40,000 communist soldiers filtered into South Vietnam, having as their stated goal the withdrawal of American advisers from Southeast Asia and the unification of a divided Vietnam. Collectively, they became known to American military personnel by two letters, a simple abbreviation that identified their status as Vietnamese communist fighters; they were the V. C., the Vietcong.

America in Vietnam: 1962–1965

1962 marked a precipitous increase in the American presence in Southeast Asia as the United States steadily began to shift its remit in South Vietnam from that of adviser to that of patron, working feverishly to sustain the corrupt and unpopular Diem government in Saigon. In that year, "the president was to nearly quadruple the number of American military men in South Vietnam [...] from 3,200 at the beginning of 1962 to 11,300 by Christmas."[13] Ostensibly, this U.S. military and industrial commitment was in service of democratic governance in Vietnam, a noble human right that would have been brutally quashed had Ho and the communists in the North been allowed to overrun the Army of the Republic of Vietnam (ARVN) in the South. A robust and visible U.S. military presence in the country, it was argued, would serve to offset the myriad of logistical and tactical problems hampering the ARVN, a force that on its own was ill-equipped and ill-prepared to face the committed communist forces from the North.

From the vantage point of Washington insiders, therefore, an increased U.S. military commitment would prove a deterrent to communist forces from the North, who were growing increasingly impatient about the stalled initiatives toward national unification.

But the ARVN served an elitist and unpopular government under Diem, who was placed in a position of power as much for his pliability as for his political acumen: "Diem was the American surrogate. Lacking a popular base, plucked from a religious group that represented only 10 percent of his country's population, surrounded by a venal family and uninterested in the daily work of government, he was chosen because no one else fit American requirements."[14] Diem's shortcomings and his government's incompetence meant that without a large American presence in the region to sup-plant the role the French colonizers had assumed for the previous century, a popular revolt could erupt in South Vietnam, which would invite communist advances from the North. Diem himself was so unpopular and ineffective, in fact, that his backers in Washington soon began looking for his replacement. They were too slow. In 1963, internal rivals assassinated Diem and his brother and seized control of the implements of governmental power in Saigon. Political instability then became the order of the day in the South as one government after another was supported by the United States only to fall to internal political rivals within weeks or months: "a parade of generals, paid and commanded by the United States, play[ed] a seemingly endless game of musical chairs to succeed Diem."[15] This perpetually rotating political support came along with huge sums of American aid for South Vietnam, mostly in the form of military or security financing, making South Vietnam one of the largest recipients of American largesse by the beginning of the 1960s.[16]

By late 1963, though, U.S. president John F. Kennedy had proven reluctant to increase troop levels more dramatically and had privately expressed reservations about the ongoing U.S. military and advisory mission in Vietnam. With his shocking assas-sination in November of 1963 (less than a month after Diem's killing), the presidency of the United States abruptly shifted to Lyndon B. Johnson, a career politician rumored to have been much closer with Pentagon officials and much more willing to commit American forces en masse than the younger, more idealistic Kennedy had been.[17] Whatever their differences, in 1964, Johnson still needed a clear *casus belli* in order to win public and congressional remit to unleash the full force of the American mili-tary against the communists in Vietnam. That event seemed to come on August 4th of that year, when North Vietnamese gunboats allegedly opened fire on an American vessel in the Gulf of Tonkin in the South China Sea. And while there had been a brief engagement wherein U.S. Navy vessels fired upon North Vietnamese torpedo boats from Vietnam two days prior, the attack on the 4th of August was, in fact, a pub-lic relations narrative that Defense Secretary Robert McNamara later admitted had never taken place.[18] Misinformed by vague, inaccurate, or in some cases, patently false reports of these incidents within the authoritative press, the American public began to incline toward Washington's view supporting a much larger U.S. military presence in Southeast Asia: "On virtually every important point, the reporting of the two Gulf of Tonkin incidents [...] was either misleading or simply false."[19] On August 7, 1964, the Gulf of Tonkin Resolution passed through Congress with only two dissenting votes. It immediately provided Johnson with the power to conduct extensive military operations in Southeast Asia without the hindrance of having to officially declare war. In effect, according to author H. Bruce Franklin, "President Lyndon B. Johnson's administration had concocted naval battles in the Gulf of Tonkin to legitimize air attacks on North Vietnam and to stampede Congress into signing a blank check to make war."[20]

With the swift and easy passage of the Gulf of Tonkin Resolution, the Gulf of Tonkin Incident, as the phantom gunboat attack came to be known, had served its purpose admirably. Johnson immediately expanded the U.S. role in Vietnam, a massive commitment of the American war machine that would, at its peak, involve "more than 540,000 American troops [...] plus some 100,000 to 200,000 U.S. troops participating in the effort from outside the country."[21] With near-complete congressional approval, Johnson, McNamara, and the remainder of the administration set about prosecuting an expansive war on land, in the air, and at sea throughout Southeast Asia, sometimes confining their theater of operations to Vietnam proper, other times invading across international borders into Laos or Cambodia. McNamara, with a professional background as a corporate executive, would conduct the war as a businessman might balance his books, analyzing and quantifying every conceivable aspect of the war in an attempt to wrest some slight advantage out of a political and military morass.[22] He would become the primary architect of a decade of highly technical, impossibly expensive, and indescribably grisly war, all ostensibly in aid of supporting a democratic South Vietnam that was anything but, and on the pretense of a defensive posture after an attack by an enemy navy that never actually occurred. And once it had begun, the U.S. war in Vietnam would not end until well over a million people were dead, thousands of villages

Photo 8 A U.S. soldier passes by a burnt out village in Vietnam.

were destroyed, countless acres were in ruin, and more than $168 billion was spent, all of which resulted in a thorough American military and political failure.[23]

American Atrocities: 1965–1975

Shortly after the full-scale American commitment to the war in Vietnam was duplicitously arranged by the Johnson administration, collective punishments, indiscriminate killings, and other war crimes began to be undertaken. In part, this was due to the detached, industrial nature of the American war in Vietnam and the indiscriminate tools applied by the U.S. military in that effort. Facing an enemy adept at using small arms and employing guerilla tactics in jungle terrain that they knew much better than the American soldiers, the decision was made at the Pentagon to bomb North Vietnam into submission. This tactic would employ dominant U.S. air power, an element of the war that would become a trademark of the American destruction of the country. To that end, in March of 1965, the Johnson administration unleashed Operation Rolling Thunder, an extensive bombing campaign designed to cripple the military and industrial capacity of North Vietnam while simultaneously preventing them from bolstering the growing communist insurgency in the South. The massive bombing campaign would last until November of 1968 and would include both military targets and logistical ones intended to destroy North to South supply lines and transportation networks (inside and outside of Vietnam). Predictably, thousands of civilians would perish in this extensive campaign, bombed, burned, or blown up by technologically advanced American planes flying thousands of feet above the catastrophic destruction that they wrought. By some estimates, as many as 180,000 civilian Vietnamese were killed in Operation Rolling Thunder, a scale of human destruction that received little attention in the earliest phases of what would become a decade-long American war.[24]

But these were far from the only civilian casualties that resulted from American bombing campaigns in Vietnam. Operation Menu was a covert bombing campaign conducted exclusively against targets in Cambodia, intended to destroy North Vietnamese supply lines and sympathetic communist forces in that country. Officially, only 4,000 Cambodians died in that campaign lasting from March 1969 to May 1970, but more civilian deaths were to come. In the summer of 1972, Operation Linebacker targeted industrial areas of North Vietnam, dropping more than 20,000 tons of explosives onto military and civilian areas; almost 2,000 civilians were killed in that campaign. Operation Freedom Deal would return to targets in Cambodia but would last for three years and kill at least 50,000 noncombatants, though some have argued it killed many more. This particular bombing campaign was so extensive as to inspire U.S. Secretary of State Henry Kissinger to interpret President Nixon's conception of the plans for the air campaign as "a massive bombing campaign in Cambodia. Anything that flies on anything that moves."[25]

The payload from these practically indistinct aerial bombing campaigns conducted over more than a decade of warfare in Vietnam was only a portion of the total amount of conventional bombs that were dropped in Southeast Asia by the United States between 1965 and 1975, a number exceeding seven million tons of bombs, more than three times the amount deployed in all of World War II.[26] In sum, U.S. air power obliterated the Cambodian, Vietnamese, and Laotian countryside, dropping "the equivalent of five Hiroshimas."[27] on Cambodian towns and villages from 1969 to 1973. Those civilians who did not flee during the near ceaseless bombing of the region were left behind to gather the corpses of dead family members and to try to reorganize shattered homes and shattered lives. Of that monumental tonnage, two million tons were dropped on Laos alone, officially a non-belligerent in the U.S. fight against Vietnamese communism. Of those bombs, some 80 million bombs or bomblets failed to explode. Today, roughly 50 Laotians are killed every year when these bombs are discovered or are accidentally discharged. The vast majority of the victims of these campaigns were, in fact, guilty of nothing more than unfortunate proximity to an official U.S. military objective.[28]

Other crimes committed by U.S. soldiers in Vietnam were much more intimate than the ubiquitous death from above that characterized the U.S. air war against the Southeast Asian peninsula. News crews embedded with U.S. soldiers in fact caught some of these indiscriminate assaults on camera and heard stories of many others during their deployment as journalists in the war zone: "The first Vietnamese peasant homes to be burned by U.S. troops were put to the torch by the Marines in several hamlets near Da Nang on August 3, 1965. Morley Safer of CBS filmed the burning and shocked millions of Americans who watched the network's evening news."[29] Collective punishments such as this one, the complete destruction of a Vietnamese village by American soldiers, came to be commonplace during the U.S. military commitment in Vietnam, despite official protestations to the contrary. They were given a particular name: "Zippo jobs" in reference to the brand of lighter often used to ignite the thatched wood homes that characterized rural dwellings throughout Vietnam. By the war's end, evidence of this practice had become common knowledge both in the military and among attendant audiences at home, so much so that the initial shock that beset Americans upon first exposure to these war crimes had largely worn off by the end of the war: "'Zippo jobs' on Vietnamese hamlets by American soldiers had become so common that television audiences in the United States were no longer scandalized by them."[30]

But these incidents were far from the only instances of American abuse of Vietnamese civilians during the war. In what is by now an infamous attack, in March of 1968, a U.S. Army platoon under the leadership of Lieutenant William Calley and Captain Ernest Medina marched into a series of connected hamlets in the village of My Lai and went on a macabre rampage, resulting in the massacre of more than 500[31] innocent men, women, and children:

> The American soldiers and junior officers shot old men, women, boys, girls, and babies. One soldier missed a baby lying on the ground twice with a .45 pistol as his comrade laughed at his marksmanship. He stood over the child and fired a third time. The soldiers beat women with rifle butts and raped some and sodomized others before shooting them. They shot the water buffalos, the pigs, and the chickens. They threw the dead animals into the wells to poison the water. They tossed satchel charges into the bomb shelters under the houses. A lot of the inhabitants had fled into the shelters. Those who leaped out to escape the explosives were gunned down. All of the houses were put to the torch.[32]

The slaughter lasted hours; the American soldiers even stopped for lunch before continuing the massacre. Searches after the fact discovered no Vietcong soldiers in hiding and located no enemy weaponry throughout the village complex. In short, the mass murder at My Lai had no military value for the American mission in Vietnam at all. The story of the slaughter was eventually leaked to investigative journalist Seymour Hersh, who published his findings of the crime widely along with graphic photographs taken at the scene by ex-army photographer Ron Haeberle. Later, "Charlie Company's Paul Meadlo appeared in a CBS television interview with Mike Wallace, confessing his crimes. He admitted that the troops had rounded up and shot hundreds of men, women, and children. 'And babies?' Wallace asked repeatedly. 'And babies,' Meadlo replied."[33] As a result of the media's attention to this incident, 26 U.S. soldiers were charged with a crime connected to My Lai. Only the company commander, Lieutenant William Calley, would be convicted of murder, though, and sentenced to life in prison. He actually served only three and a half years under house arrest before his sentence was commuted by President Richard Nixon.

My Lai was an American atrocity, the largest publicly known American massacre of innocents recorded in the twentieth century, but it was far from unique. On the same day as the My Lai Massacre, U.S. troops in the nearby village of My Khe killed an additional 60 to 155 civilians, similar to the brutality carried out at My Lai. Later, at Truong Khanh 2, 63 civilians were massacred by U.S. troops. And during the same period of time, at least 100 civilians were killed in sweeps by "Tiger Force," "an elite squad of the 101st Airborne [division]."[34] Vietnam was utterly brutal, and it was clearly made more so by the commonplace disregard for human life demonstrated by American soldiers. Frustrated, frightened, far from home, and present in an increasingly impossible military scenario, American soldiers committed unspeakable acts against a civilian populace that they casually dehumanized with the ubiquitous use of the racial epithet "gook." As in the Philippine war at the turn of the twentieth century (discussed in Chapter 2 of this work), American troops were comfortably distanced from even those Vietnamese that the U.S. presence was ostensibly designed to help. These crimes were shocking for their intimate nature and the cruelty that they revealed to be endemic within American military personnel, but they were no more disturbing than the human damage caused by a decade of U.S. bombing campaigns conducted over the same period of time. According to one critic of the U.S. war in Vietnam "had [the soldiers] killed just as many over a larger area in a longer period of time and killed impersonally with bombs, shells, rockets, white phosphorus, and napalm, they would have been following the normal pattern of American military conduct."[35]

The War at Home

Scandals like the My Lai Massacre created considerable dissent among the American public as regards the U.S. prosecution of the war in Vietnam. But public opinion had already begun to turn against the war as early as 1967. It was in that year that General William Westmoreland, commander of all U.S. forces in Vietnam, prematurely predicted victory. In November of 1967, he significantly qualified this prediction in a speech at the National Press Club by saying the war had reached a point "where the end comes into view." In January of 1968, in the middle of the traditional Tet New Year's cease-fire, the North Vietnamese Army and the Vietcong launched a coordinated attack throughout Vietnam with the explicit hope of sparking a national uprising against the South Vietnamese government. 100 cities were attacked by 85,000 communist troops; General Westmoreland's headquarters were assaulted, as was the U.S. Embassy in Saigon. In Saigon during this offensive, 1,000 Vietcong fighters held off 11,000 U.S. and ARVN troops for three weeks. In all, 1,100 Americans, 2,000 ARVN soldiers, and more than 30,000 communist forces were killed. Despite assurances of political and military leadership in the United States, then, whatever the war was in the spring of 1968, the end had most definitely not come into view.

Tet marked a turning point for the United States in Vietnam and proved the death blow to the Johnson presidency. Public support for the war waned precipitously as a clear American victory against North Vietnam and the Vietcong seemed increasingly remote. Opposition to the Vietnam War spread across diverse groups opposed to U.S. militarism including the New Left, Students for a Democratic Society, the Black Panther Party, the Catholic Worker Movement, and the vaguely described counterculture as a whole. In August of 1968, at the Democratic National Convention in Chicago, anti-war protesters were charged by thousands of police with billy clubs, initiating a full-scale riot and severely injuring untold hundreds. In May of 1970, anti-war students protesting Nixon's expansion of the U.S. war into Cambodia at Kent State University in Ohio were fired upon by National Guard soldiers. Four students were killed, and nine were seriously wounded. Also in May of 1970, police opened fire on a nighttime anti-war demonstration at Jackson State College in Mississippi. One Jackson State student, Phillip Lafayette Gibbs, and one young passerby, James Earl Green, were killed. Twelve more Jackson State students were wounded.[36] In all, though from diverse backgrounds and with sometimes contradictory agendas, American protesters as a whole were united about the brutality of the American war in Vietnam and the corporatist, militant, and neoliberal nature of U.S. foreign policy during the Cold War in general: "The protest movements also raised as never before the charge of American imperialism, of violent mistreatment of third world peoples for the pursuit of corporate interests (rather than virtuous anticommunism). This caused a disruption of the Cold War consensus and has been a point of political contention ever since."[37] By 1970, an estimated two-thirds of Americans believed that the United States had made a mistake by sending troops to Vietnam. The Nixon administration struggled to maintain social cohesion while continuing the brutal prosecution of a war that cost hundreds of lives and millions of dollars a day to maintain.

Beyond accusations of military brutality and outright imperialism, both valid criticisms of U.S. foreign policy in the early 1970s, one of the most controversial policies connected to the U.S. war in Vietnam causing public opposition and social disruption was the military draft, a forced conscription of men of fighting age pressed into the armed forces in order to fight in Vietnam. While a substantial majority of U.S.

soldiers in Vietnam were volunteers, through the application of the Selective Training and Service Act of 1940, which itself was an extension of the first Selective Service Act signed by Woodrow Wilson in 1917 (see Chapter 3 of this work), more than two million men were drafted for the U.S. military between 1964 and 1973, approximately 25 percent of the military personnel during that period.[38] Being drafted did not condemn a citizen to a position on the front line, though. Draftees could pursue deferments for college enrollment, a lack of medical fitness real or feigned, or a career in an area of "vital national interest," such as engineering. These potential caveats in the draft system provided a significant advantage to young men with the means to attend college or call in a favor with a local doctor. This meant that poor men and/or men of color were disproportionately represented among the soldiers drafted for the Vietnam War, a fact that exacerbated racial tensions in the country at the height of the Civil Rights Movement. Other draftees avoided the military by fleeing to Canada or burning their government-issued draft cards, preferring a jail sentence to a tour on the frontlines in Vietnam. In the end, even while increasing troop numbers for the war in Vietnam, "the draft had made American conflicts [...] endemically controversial."[39] It may also have fueled the resistance to the war in the country, rendering this policy, at best, a double-edged sword for Washington policymakers.

In January of 1973, Richard Nixon announced a suspension of offensive action against North Vietnam, signing the Paris Peace Accords on the 27th of that month.[40] This agreement between the warring parties guaranteed the territorial integrity of Vietnam and provided a sixty-day period for the total withdrawal of U.S. forces from the country. The ARVN continued their fight against communist forces in the North, but without the massive U.S. military presence that had been positioned in the region for more than a decade, they quickly lost ground. On April 29, 1975, communist forces conquered Saigon, and the last American personnel left the city. All of Vietnam was united under a communist government with close ties to both China and the Soviet Union. The United States had failed in its objective to prevent this unification and had suffered terribly in the effort: "From 1955 to 1975, the United States lost more than 58,000 military personnel in Southeast Asia. Its troops were wounded around 304,000 times, with 153,000 cases serious enough to require hospitalization, and 75,000 veterans left severely disabled."[41] But these numbers are but a fraction of the damage wrought upon the combatant and civilian populations of Southeast Asia during the American war: "the U.S.-allied Republic of Vietnam reportedly lost more than 252,000 killed and more than 783,000 wounded. And the casualties of the [communist] revolutionary forces were evidently far graver—perhaps 1.7 million including 1 million killed in battle."[42] In the aftermath of the U.S. evacuation, a Senate subcommittee speculated that as many as 1.4 million South Vietnamese civilians were killed or wounded as a direct result of U.S. actions in the country, figures in keeping with the statistics-obsessed U.S. Secretary of State Robert McNamara, who "estimated total war dead at 2,358,000."[43] Likely, an additional 300,000 Cambodians and 62,000 Laotians died in the course of the war, as well as becoming international victims of U.S. operational targets during the war. In total, possibly as many as 3,800,000 people died because of the U.S. war in

Vietnam, though this number, like much about the war and its legacy, remains "mired in embittered controversy."[44]

The Print News Media and the Vietnam War

More than a decade of the U.S. diplomatic, political, and military presence in Southeast Asia between roughly 1963 and 1975 brought with it a predictably voluminous amount of news media attention within the United States. Traditional sources of news coverage filtered into American homes in the form of newspapers and radio broadcasts covering the rise in military action involving American personnel, as well as political developments in South Vietnam during that country's fraught and fragile alliance with its wealthy patron, the United States. Increasingly, though, Americans began to drift to nightly news coverage on television, trusting stable and presumably stalwart voices like Walter Cronkite's to bring news of the war and of the young men and women in the U.S. military to families and homes across America. Journalists were embedded with U.S. troops, and combat footage was available on the nightly news, depicting graphic images of combat with up-to-the-minute commentary from soldiers, sailors, and commanders. Some, including officials at the White House and the Pentagon across multiple presidential administrations during this period, felt that these journalists showed an attendant American public far too much of the death and destruction inherent in the U.S. mission in Vietnam, leading to direct and often public disagreements between journalists and the White House.[45] In any case, by most quantitative estimates, the Vietnam era marked the period in American history during which most of the country engaged with the news and turned on the television for information rather than picking up the newspaper for the first time ever. This led to some analysts and social scientists dubbing Vietnam "Television's War."[46] As described by one media scholar: "Television news came of age on the eve of Vietnam. The CBS and NBC evening news broadcasts took their present form in September 1963, expanding from fifteen minutes to half an hour [...] Two years later American troops went to war under the glare of the television spotlight."[47]

Not discounting the growing influence of television news on the Vietnam generation, as in previous chapters, the media analysis to follow will focus on textual representations of the prosecution of the Vietnam War and its surrounding social and political dynamics as they appeared in major newspaper publications across the country. This analysis will identify and elucidate prevalent strands of the broader news discourse on the war in Vietnam from within the authoritative news media establishment in the United States during the period of substantial American military and political presence in Southeast Asia. This examination does not intend to supplant media studies focusing on television news coverage, nor does it intend to assert the following discursive elements as unitary or singular within news coverage of the war. Indeed, the expansive nature of news coverage of an American war as controversial and as long-lasting as the American war in Vietnam renders such blanket assertions anathema within either discourse analysis or media studies. Instead, what follows is intended to bring into focus certain prominent narrative elements within ostensibly intellectually neutral news coverage of the longest American war to date. It is to that discursive analysis that this case study now turns.

Troop Morale and American Optimism

Among the cacophony of voices purporting to inform American audiences about military outcomes during the Vietnam War, a steady stream of assessments from the print news media regularly informed as to the consistently high levels of troop morale among American soldiers. Despite mounting casualties, perilous tactical positions, and increasing calls for peace from the American public, within this discursive thread, the authoritative news media assured the readership that American soldiers were in good spirits and were prepared to fight on, no matter the hardship they might be enduring. From this perspective, military successes were enumerable, and the war, overall, was imminently winnable. Even though contradictory reports had begun to reach American audiences from both international and more critical domestic news sources, elements within the journalistic establishment of the United States persisted in optimistic assessments of the war, typically centered on the notion that American G.I.s remained positive in their outlook and steadfast in their mission.

A typical example from within this frame of representation during the Vietnam War characterizes the mindset of American soldiers in the spring of 1968, several months after the coordinated Tet Offensive initiated by North Vietnam signaled to Washington and the rest of the world the strength and determination of the North Vietnamese. Despite this substantial military setback, one that would later be recognized as the beginning of the end for the American military in Southeast Asia, journalists continued to underline the excellent morale and undying fighting spirit of the American soldier: "For three years of intensifying warfare in Vietnam, the morale of the American fighting man has never flagged."[48] Tet was a jolt to American planners; it would lead directly or indirectly to a shifting war strategy under President Richard Nixon (the so-called Vietnamization of the war) as well as to the reassertion of forced military service for American citizens in the form of the draft discussed previously. Yet, judging by a number of prominent news articles during this period, Tet and other offensives by the North Vietnamese did not have a significant impact on U.S. morale: "The Communist offensive in February which wrought so much damage had only a peripheral effect on the spirit of U.S. troops." [49] Seemingly impervious to tactical setbacks and unfazed by increasing casualties, the American soldier endured, even flourished. In fact, according to one prominent headline, the Vietnamese communist offensive actually improved American morale rather than dampening it: "Reds' Tet Offensive Improved Spirit in Many Cases."[50] Far beyond daunted, then, increasing adversity in the field actually resulted in a more positive outlook among U.S. troops. Such was the clarity and capacity of the average American fighting man in the war.

The U.S. Marines at Khe Sanh likewise had only positive assessments of the progress of their war and their role in it, despite their increasingly desperate situation. The Marines in question were fearless and relentlessly positive, literally smiling as they attempted to fortify their position against incoming enemy artillery rounds: "Now in the bunkers and trenches and holes and ditches of Khe Sanh, that gesture [a thumb's up, was] accompanied by a fleeting smile."[51] According to these reports, the Marines at Khe Sanh were confident, resolute, and even happy in their work adding sandbags to existing mud fences in an attempt to defend against enemy bombardment: "In Khe Sanh, happiness is a well-constructed, properly sandbagged bunker."[52] Reports from the front in Vietnam went to great lengths to equate this unyielding positivity prevalent among our GIs to an overall American sensibility identifying resilience, courage, and pluck as American traits in the service of American goals: "But morale is very high. 'You take away a man's morale and you haven't got an American any longer,' said Bill Trottno, 33, of Oxnard, Calif."[53] The resultant tone of these articles is one of confidence and positivity, as attendant audiences on the home front were reassured that progress was being made and America was winning the day. Clinical assessments were also employed to highlight this truism, informing that "psychiatrists feel that there are no serious morale problems among the troops in Vietnam."[54] Morale was high, the troops were happy, and we were winning the war.

Government officials concurred with this evaluation, and the printed news media was quick to recognize this convergence of opinion: "A House armed services subcommittee reported that morale of American troops in Vietnam is 'extremely high from the highest general to the lowest private'."[55] The resolve of the average American soldier was rated to be exceptional, and a number of factors were proffered by way of explanation of what might seem to be an unexpected scenario: "The group [in the House of Representatives] noted that men serving in Vietnam receive, in addition to combat pay, tax-free mail and tax exemptions of all pay for enlisted men for the first $500 of monthly pay for officers during the time they serve."[56] A typical American motivation is identified here: pay. In doing battle with a communist enemy, American freedom and largesse, specifically a generous pay package, were overwhelming the communist, nationalist oeuvre. American troop morale is high because America pays its soldiers well and provides incentives in the form of benefits or bonuses, such as "tax-free mail." The connection between contented soldiers and the superiority of the American system is made plain, all the while reinforcing the value of the prosecution of the war in Vietnam to counteract the communist ethos. This self-congratulatory assessment, proffered by elements within the U.S. Congress and dutifully reported by the established news media, completes the conceptual circle of interdependent American institutions.

Additional reporting in the print news media during the U.S. war in Vietnam reified established tropes of American optimism among senior officers and policymakers while confirming soaring troop morale among the G.I.s fighting on the ground. Period headlines insisted: "GI Morale Called High In Vietnam";[57] "Troop Morale In Vietnam Is High";[58] and "Viet Situation Getting Better."[59] Tellingly perhaps, the latter headline titled a lengthy piece penned by General Maxwell Taylor that appeared in a number of national news publications during the spring of 1968. Taylor was a much-decorated army officer and senior Pentagon official appointed as the chairman of the joint chiefs of staff and later as ambassador to South Vietnam during the Kennedy administration. In the widely distributed article in question, Taylor assures his readers that the United States is winning the war and that troop morale is, as reported, high: "air action against the north has had a very clear effect in improving the military morale."[60] That Taylor was not a regular contributor to the period press does not diminish the intellectual weight of his assessment of the American position in Vietnam. On the contrary, along with the president and other instantly recognizable White House officials, Taylor was presented by the news media establishment as a trusted expert in matters to do with Vietnam, especially in the early phases of the American war. The overwhelming message carried forward by this lengthy commentary from Taylor, then, as well as many of the professional journalists evaluating the U.S. war in the printed media, is to take heart in the eventual and inevitable success of the American military.

A final noteworthy element adding to the overall optimism in media coverage of the long-running U.S. war in Vietnam concerns the extensive social benefits the military's presence in Vietnam was bound to have upon the social fabric of the United States itself. It was there, on the home front, where institutional racism and de facto segregation continued to thrive, threatening the integrity of Lyndon Johnson's ambitious domestic social program, the so-called Great Society. According to print coverage of the war in Vietnam, though, one potential remedy for persistent racism in America was participation in the Vietnam War: "Fourteen weeks of interviews with black and white American serving here reveal that Vietnam is like a speeded-up film of recent racial progress at home."[61] In this conception, the boundless positivity of the American soldier in Vietnam extends to the fraught race relations of the 1960s while promising a model for social progress and racial harmony back home: "During the battle for Hue in February, a knot of white and Negro marines stood knee deep in the mean red mud beside their tank."[62] The comradeship and loyalty of the American soldiers in Vietnam cut across standard American racial divides. The subtext in these representations is that the American experience in Vietnam is actually a force for good promising social reform and domestic repair as well as the defeat of the looming specter of international communism. Though more specific and less prevalent in period news discourse than more general positive assessments and reports of high troop morale, this particular discursive trope expresses the lengths to which print reporting during the Vietnam era went to heap praise on the military establishment and the Vietnam War writ large. And while subsequent media coverage began to reflect a more nuanced view of the American position in Southeast Asia as the war dragged on, a dedicated expression of positivity and good feeling in the military would remain discernible within the news media establishment long after the dire consequences of the American prosecution of war in Vietnam were widely known.

American Competence, Enemy Inferiority

According to news media narratives of the era, it stood to reason that troop morale was high and policymakers were optimistic during even the darkest phases of the American war in Vietnam, given the toughness, grit, and determination of the average U.S. soldier.[63] This trope extends and complements print news media conceptions of the American military as perpetually sanguine by providing a functional context for that buoyancy: the toughness and stick-to-itiveness of America and its soldiers. With this news media frame of toughness likewise comes the anticipated ability to accomplish any task set for them. Likewise, within this discursive construction, existing news reports of high American morale are complimented by predictions of success in the face of hardship and difficulty. American soldiers were tough, agile, and able, and reports from the front informed the readership back home of the "tough, supple and resilient"[64] Marines at Khe Sanh, a bloody and protracted siege that cost at least 274 Americans their lives and possibly as many as ten times that with serious injury. That article, entitled "Tough, Resilient: Marines Thumb Noses at Death at Khe Sanh," goes on to describe the almost callous nature with which American soldiers view death, claiming a supernatural American ability to exist beyond fear in clearly perilous circumstances. The story continues by assuring readers that even though the American Marines face "death at any hour of the day or night," they are impervious to such concerns. They remain optimistic and bright: "The marines at Khe Sanh are confident they can hold out."[65] This narrative context begins to construct a discourse of the American soldier as superhuman, beyond fear of death or pain, and able to achieve masterful victory despite the odds stacked against him. He is an underdog but, indubitably, a successful one, emanating confidence and self-assurance while performing his difficult and dangerous job admirably.

Other narratives complementing this perspective include physical descriptions of the soldiers fighting in Vietnam as gruff, strong, and determined. American soldiers "were grimy-faced, beard-stubbled, and grease-spattered,"[66] clearly descriptors intended to convey an image of toughness, grit, and stereotypical masculinity to audiences back home. In the same vein, soldiers' work was described in some detail, conveying an image of Americans as soldier-laborers equally adept with an M-16 or with a plow: "everyone agrees that morale gets higher the deeper in the ground you dig"; and "Now in the bunkers and trenches and holes and ditches of Khe Sanh."[67] The focus of these narrative tropes is on the work ethic of the American soldier and the lengths he will go to on behalf of duty or fealty toward his country. Readers reviewing this coverage are presented with robust, masculine imagery, including supreme physical strength and facets of the American experience in Vietnam, intended to provoke a sense of reassurance for attendant audiences. The message is conveyed that the task of the military is in the hands of strong, able men, all of whom were virile representations of the American self. In their hands, a certainty of accomplishment is conveyed as attendant American audiences understand that the job of winning the war will soon be done. American sweat, American blood, and American work will see us through to an inevitable victory.

Other representations were still more overt, lauding the U.S. Army in Vietnam and all but guaranteeing an eventual U.S. victory. Within this frame of discursive representation, readers at home are implored to remain patient while holding the line, to believe in the American cause, and to castigate those who did otherwise. One example from this theme promises victory on the basis of past military success, declaring that "it would be hard for any serious student of American history to believe that the United States will fail to carry out its purpose."[68] Competence, clarity of purpose, and eventual success were always traits associated with U.S. military missions, according to this narrative, and it would be folly to presume any other result would be forthcoming in Southeast Asia. More than that, according to reports from this period, the U.S. Army in Vietnam was better than previous iterations of the U.S. Army. Indeed, it was "the best prepared army, the most skilled army, the most compassionate army"[69] anywhere to be found. Textual examples such as these contribute to the pervasive narrative of confidence and high morale discussed in the previous section of this study. They also serve to underscore the toughness and determination inherent in the U.S. military mission. The U.S. military is the best in the world; it has always been successful and it will be successful here, too. Or, by some valuations, as early as 1968, it already had succeeded. Speaking to the positive impact of the U.S. military and diplomatic mission in Southeast Asia, one report asserted that "the United States mission here has succeeded in helping to set up the forms of democracy for the first time."[70] A series of military coups and strongman dictatorships in South Vietnam belie this glowing assessment while simultaneously ignoring the prolific negative impacts in terms of loss of human life and destruction of agriculture and infrastructure caused by American forces. Nevertheless, this narrative of eminent success or success already achieved persisted throughout print news reports, emphasizing the competence of the American soldier and the unstoppable power of the American will on every occasion.

As with previous American wars discussed at length in preceding chapters, a final, standard frame of representation to be mentioned in conjunction with American competence, determination, and optimism about a swift and complete victory included lengthy considerations of enemy incompetence and overall inferiority in the face of the might of the U.S. Army. This trope is especially visible in print media coverage of the 1968 Tet Offensive, which was, as discussed, a bold and shocking maneuver by communist forces that signaled to policymakers and military leaders the strength and resolve of enemy forces. The establishment press was quick to condemn this series of attacks as a failure, though, and/or to point to the inevitable American victory that would soon follow: "While saying that the Vietcong had failed to capture almost all of their military objectives in the attacks, General Weyland conceded that the Vietcong had concentrated on 'remunerative' objectives of political and psychological warfare. This is the point of the new strategy, he said."[71]

In this consideration, the North Vietnamese Army and its allies not only failed in their military objectives, but they have been diminished in the eyes of U.S. military leadership (voiced here by General Frederick Weyland, the last American commander in Vietnam) to the extent that their main goals now consist of "psychological warfare" and other petty or political objectives. This damning assessment undercuts the military prowess of America's enemies while recasting them as lesser foes, unable and unworthy of consideration as a legitimate military enemy. Various forms of this narrative were repeated throughout the print media in response to the communist Tet Offensive: "The over-all [sic] strategy of the enemy, as interpreted by the Pentagon, is aimed primarily at political and psychological objectives. The terrorist attacks in Saigon and elsewhere were intended as 'headline-grabbers,' as one officer put it, 'to make us look silly'."[72] The constructed discourse remakes North Vietnam and the Vietcong not as worthy opponents of a massive American military venture but rather as amateurs and novices unable to compete with the United States on a level playing field. They engage in political or military tricks simply to grab headlines and in aid of questionable motives. Chicanery and underhandedness are on their side; honesty and righteousness are on ours.

Other assessments concur with this view and continue to diminish the military capacity and/or political organization of the communist North Vietnamese: "United States officials say that the Vietcong miscalculated in the current phase of their offensive and failed to achieve their maximum objectives."[73] Yet the objectives in question here were defined in the same news article incredibly narrowly so as to only be able to conclude that the enemy offensive was a profound failure: "overthrowing the South Vietnamese Government and establishing control in many of the major cities."[74] Indeed, the results of Tet were shocking to political and military leadership in the United States, prompting a reassessment of the broader U.S. strategy and a sea change in political power in the United States from Lyndon B. Johnson to Richard Nixon. Publicly, though, the news media remained positive in their assessments of enemy failure and impending American successes: "the costs to the enemy were very high, with most of his highly trained special action units and many local guerilla units believed to have been wiped out."[75] The order of the day, then, from the view of the print media was an emphasis on the American will and a concomitant focus on the denuded and dilapidated condition of the enemy. Presented much less often in news articles during this period was the idea of the Tet Offensive as a defeat of the American military or their South Vietnamese allies. Though when it was, it was likewise recontextualized as a U.S. victory waiting to happen: "Most officers in Washington are said to be confident that the enemy cannot repeat such a victory against American forces."[76] As the new Nixon administration shifted, then, to an official policy of Vietnamization, placing the bulk of the military operations against the communist forces into the hands of the Army of South Vietnam, an attendant public would have had every reason for optimism and confidence in this strategy and importantly, in an eventual American victory throughout the whole of the war. In sum, according to the establishment print media and applying near Orwellian levels of official doublespeak, major U.S. military setbacks in Vietnam were wholly beneficial to the U.S. mission in the country: "There is hardly an American here who doesn't view this all as encouraging."[77]

Rewriting My Lai

Significant effort and determination were required on the part of investigative journalist Seymour Hersh and army photographer Ron Haeberle to publish the story and accompanying photographs depicting the massacre at My Lai at the hands of U.S. soldiers in the spring of 1968. Collectively, the news media institutions in the U.S. wanted to avoid public depictions of American soldiers as unrestrained killers and held the general but consistent editorial line that civilian casualties are the unintended consequence of the legitimate use of force by well-trained American soldiers. The fact that this frame of public discourse around the military has been held constant in subsequent U.S. wars of the twentieth and twenty-first centuries will be a topic for further exploration in the coming chapters of this work. Suffice it to say here that in the months after the grisly attack on Vietnamese civilians by Charlie Company in the My Lai/Songmy village complex, a concerted effort was made by military leadership to cover up or, at the very least, overlook these potential crimes.[78] Once the rumors of widespread crimes against civilians committed by American soldiers in Vietnam became too numerous to ignore, the story of the My Lai Massacre was run in dozens of publications around the country: "On November 13, Hersh's article ran in thirty five newspapers, including the *Chicago Sun-Times, St. Louis Post-Dispatch,* and *Milwaukee Journal.* Within a couple of weeks, the *Cleveland Plain Dealer* and *Life* had both published grisly photographs of the massacre taken by Ron Haeberle, including a heap of civilian bodies with children clearly among them."[79] Once released into the public domain, the story of My Lai spread rapidly. Issues connected to U.S. troop conduct, the pressures and exigencies of the American war in Vietnam, and the righteousness, or lack thereof, of the American war effort began to consume a substantial amount of column inches within the print news media discussions of the ongoing U.S. war. And while it is beyond the scope of this work to analyze all of the print coverage of this discursive element within media considerations of the broader war, nevertheless, discernible patterns of discourse construction around My Lai are evident within the print news and are therefore available for analysis here.

Among the prominent elements within news media presentations of the My Lai Massacre for attendant American audiences is the simple assertion that the American war in Vietnam was violent, that American soldiers were suffering high numbers of casualties, and that, if they had inadvertently killed Vietnamese civilians (a fact of the My Lai Massacre scarcely admitted in press coverage during this period), it was an understandable mistake given the dangers and stresses of the war. According to an article ostensibly covering the My Lai Massacre, the period of early 1968 "was one of the bloodiest periods of the Vietnam war [*sic*]. Before dawn, Jan. 31, 1968, enemy forces had unleashed the savage Lunar New Year, or Tet, attacks on Saigon and more than a score of other cities and bases."[80] Putting a finer point on it, the article enumerates American losses across Vietnam during this period of time: "American combat losses for the week ended March 2 were 542 killed, 2,191 wounded; for the week ended March 9,509 killed and 2,766 wounded; for the week ended March 16, 336 killed and 1,916 wounded."[81] Another article followed suit, numbering the Americans killed in Vietnam in the weeks just before the massacre took place: "March 1,453 American soldiers were killed, the high for the year."[82] The assertion here in articles purporting to cover the American atrocity at My Lai is that American forces were under undue stress in early 1968. The soldiers were harried, fearful, and likely to have known of or been witness to the deaths of their comrades; they were angry and emotional as well. In this concise narrative framing emphasizing the damage done to American troops and the danger that they were in during the period before the massacre, empathy is created. The attendant public reading these accounts becomes deeply concerned with and invested in the fates of the U.S. soldiers, thereby constructing a powerful sense of understanding between the American soldiers who committed the crimes, and the American readership of news publications on the home front.

An additional layer to the discursive subtext lessening or even excusing American atrocities consists of journalists pointing to the village or the specific region in which the massacre took place as being particularly violent and dangerous in the context of an already violent and dangerous war: "The war in Sontinh District of Quangntai Province is tough and frustrating."[83] Within this discourse, peaceful villagers are recast as Vietcong soldiers, representing life-threatening danger to troopers on patrol for Charlie Company in March of 1968: "Two or three times [...] patrols went near the village, which they called Pinkville, and 'harassed it with gunfire,' he said. Each time, he added, they were shot at and men were wounded, while others fell to mines and booby traps."[84] News reports such as this one emphasized the clear and present danger to the American soldiers embodied by the farmers of My Lai. The thrust of these descriptions leads readers to the conclusion that hostility on the part of the Americans was rational, not malevolent, and that violence was endemic in the area rather than a product of the American military presence in the region. Sources go on to note that "the Songmy area was a 'free-fire zone.' In such a zone, the local authorities warn the inhabitants that anyone moving outdoors after certain hours will be assumed to be hostile—and a target."[85] Reference to a "free-fire zone" indicates to readers the presence of hostile forces, thereby further contextualizing and even softening uber-violent American actions when encountering a village full of farmers and their families. The inclusion of this declaration further serves to blame the victims of the massacre themselves for being in a combat area (their homes, as it happened) at a time when the U.S. military deemed the environment unsafe. After all, if "The Marines are certain that the villagers were and are Vietcong,"[86] surely that characterization is sufficiently reassuring to readers back home in their efforts to obtain a clear picture of the event in question.

Other purported explanations for My Lai diverted from making excuses for the U.S. army altogether and instead pointed the finger at the Vietcong in order to justify American brutality: "the Vietcong had committed atrocities";[87] "evidence showed Vietnamese customarily regard life lightly and treat their enemies brutally."[88] These reported allegations against communist forces were put forward adjacent to or instead of discussions of My Lai within period-printed news pieces ostensibly covering My Lai. The subtext in this approach is to take the eye of the American reader off of U.S. crimes and condemn, instead, the true enemies of the United States and of the American soldier: the communist Vietnamese. Further depictions of these events continued to heap the blame for the murdered villagers onto the Vietcong, calling out their tactics in the context of a violent and asymmetrical war: "The enemy [...] fights from ambush, he hits and runs, he mines and boobytraps. Bomb and shell the enemy's villages and strongholds, and he digs in to re-emerge after the barrage."[89] This construction not only foists responsibility for the killings at My Lai onto the massacred themselves; it simultaneously blames the Vietcong and associated communist forces for fighting the war and for doing so effectively. Under these conditions, this robust rationalization continues, and the frustration felt by the upstanding American soldier is at the least understandable, if not excusable: "Sometimes frustration and fury combine into outbursts of impotent cruelty motivated, perhaps, by the need to reduce an insoluble problem to a comprehensible ultimate. Something like this must have happened on March 16, 1968 in the village of Songmy in the Sontinh District."[90]

The text examples provided here are but a few of the hundreds of period news articles that went to great lengths to qualify American brutality in My Lai, proffering rumors of Vietcong presence in the village, describing generic wartime violence, or using the effective asymmetrical tactics of the American enemy as excuses to justify U.S. soldiers shelling, shooting, raping, and slaughtering more than 500 Vietnamese villagers in March of 1968. As individual strategies within period discourse, each of these narrative layers was asserted in an effort to condition, qualify, or contextualize the crimes of American soldiers in My Lai. In sum, this coverage can be classified as conservative at best: "My Lai coverage was usually cautious and dispassionate, a great deal of it focused in legal issues [...] rather than on the massacre itself, which of course became an 'alleged massacre' once changers were filed."[91] Further conditioning the public response to the atrocity at My Lai, the print news media went on to assert en masse that, in fact, it was the operatives of the Vietcong and their North Vietnamese patrons who were the ones most responsible for careless civilian death in the Vietnam War and not, as critics of the war like Hersh and Haeberle might have it, the American soldiers. Further, Hersh and Haeberle themselves were the targets of slander in the press, being accused, among other things, of taking unjustified payments for their story on My Lai: "A former combat photographer who took pictures of victims of the alleged massacre has sold them for an estimated $40,000, although he originally sought $100,000."[92] And even those publications that eventually began to accept the full scope of the brutality visited upon the population of the Songmy hamlets by American soldiers typically qualified the atrocity as aberrant or "wholly unrepresentative."[93] In so doing, print news media discourse in the coverage of the My Lai Massacre fully embraced the "bad apple" argument as discussed in this study's introductory chapter and as it would be applied, among other wartime contexts, to the criminal behavior of American soldiers in Iraq some 35 years after My Lai.

Conclusions: Constructing the Vietnam War

The decade-long American war in Southeast Asia resulted in massive civilian deaths and virtually unfathomable injuries to the population and the landscape of Vietnam, Cambodia, and Laos. And though "the whole Pentagon strategy centered on portraying My Lai as a one-off aberration,"[94] troves of evidence have come to the fore in the years since the American decampment from Saigon depicting intentional civilian killing on a large scale throughout the U.S. war. Typical print news coverage of the war did not focus on these war crimes, though, or if they did, qualified and conditioned them to such an extent as to render them thoroughly acceptable within the intellectual considerations of the U.S. military in Vietnam. Importantly, though, in considering these American actions, the print news media didn't ignore American war crimes altogether or simply neglect to report on civilian casualties. Rather, as described earlier, a common tactic among the authoritative press was to eventually come to terms with the specifics of civilian killings while ultimately qualifying them in such a way as to minimize or possibly entirely negate the dire nature of these actions. As a result of this consistent media conditioning, during the Vietnam War, it was as if:

civilian suffering was everywhere and yet nowhere in the American media. News reports described thousands of incidents that violated the laws of war, but usually skipped blithely past the implications, neither labelling nor acknowledging the crimes. And for every war crime that was mentioned in a newspaper or magazine, a mass of other evidence was covered up in the field or kept secret at higher command levels.[95]

In the end, these conditioned or otherwise excusable atrocities lined up within the print news media discourse next to conceptions of American competence and toughness, which reassured attendant audiences at home of the honesty and bravery of the men in the fight as much as they convinced that readership of an inevitable American victory. That forthcoming victory justified the exceptionally high morale that was evident, and oft-reported-upon, among the American troops in Vietnam, particularly in the earlier phases of the U.S. war. Mixed in with these discursive tropes were familiar condemnations of the American enemy. While the U.S. soldier had superhuman perseverance and determination, the Vietcong soldier was a sneak, play-acting at war for headlines or for some other duplicitous aim. Imbibing the morally bankrupt philosophy of communism, enemy forces were inferior objects and worthy of scorn. According to prominent news media conceptions, toughness, honesty, and ultimately, righteousness remained firmly situated on the American side of the conflict line.

Overall, during a preponderance of the Vietnam War, the print news media remained faithful to long-held narrative tropes concerning the U.S. soldier individually and the U.S. military as a collective, regardless of the mass of evidence available to contradict those conceptions. Across multiple presidential administrations and spanning years of brutal and costly warfare, the news media institution held firm to the solemnity of the American soldier and worked diligently to highlight his attributes, all the while justifying, contextualizing, or minimizing his crimes. These threads of discourse on the U.S. military align with previously established tropes created during former iterations of American warfare and, in so doing, create recurrent and powerful public conceptions of what has been constructed as arguably America's most untouched, uncriticized institution. American military ventures in the post-Vietnam era would extend that discursive consideration in the print news media even further and would likewise inculcate subsequent generations of American media consumers in these powerful and intellectually impactful news narratives well into the twenty-first century.

Notes

1 Michael Walzer, *Just and Unjust Wars: A Moral Argument with Historical Illustrations* (New York: Basic Books, 1977), 4.
2 Christian missionaries began proselytizing in the region as early as 1524. A fraught relationship between these missionaries and indigenous political powers had ensued, and eventually, official Vietnamese tolerance of the Catholic missionaries, whose remit included political activities as well as matters of the spirit, waned. After Catholic participation in a three-year-long revolt against Emperor Minh Mang, six Catholic missionaries were executed, and tens of thousands of Vietnamese Catholics were persecuted because of their fealty to the religion.
3 Neil Sheehan, *A Bright Shining Lie: John Paul Vann and America in Vietnam* (New York: Vintage Books, 1988), 175.
4 Rubber was key to the French occupation of Vietnam. Author Nick Turse informs: "French rubber production in Vietnam yielded such riches for the colonizers that the latex oozing from rubber trees became known as 'white gold.' The ill-paid Vietnamese workers, laboring on the plantations in harsh conditions, called it by a different name: 'white blood'" (Nick

Turse, *Kill Anything that Moves: The Real American War in Vietnam* (New York: Picador Press, 2013), 6–7).

5 John F. Cady, "The Beginnings of French Imperialism in the Pacific Orient," *The Journal of Modern History* 14, no. 1 (1942): 71–87. Accessed March 20, 2023. https://doi.org/10.1086/236591.

6 Sheehan, *A Bright Shining Lie*, 143

7 Geoffrey C. Ward, Ken Burns, and Lynn Novick, directors. *The Vietnam War* (PBS, 2017), 18 hr. https://www.dailymotion.com/video/x6yjy69.

8 Sheehan, *A Bright Shining Lie*, 148.

9 In his critical assessment of CIA activity throughout the world in the twentieth century, analyst Stephen Kinzer elucidates the folly of this paranoiac worldview: "This narrative of encirclement and imminent danger that Americans were fed was distant from reality, but it seized hearts in Washington and had profound effects. It allowed the CIA to convince itself that it was waging a purely defensive war. In its collective mind-set, nothing it did was aggressive. It justified all of its projects, even those that caused immense pain to individuals and nations, as necessary to block Communism's relentless expansion. Nowhere was this obsessive and destructive American agenda on fuller display than during the long years of American war in Vietnam" (Stephen Kinzer, *Poisoner in Chief: Sidney Gottlieb and the CIA Search for Mind Control* (New York: Henry Holt and Company, 2019), 82).

10 Robert P. Saldin, *War, the American State, and Politics since 1898* (Cambridge: Cambridge University Press, 2011), 191.

11 Stephen Kinzer, *Overthrow: America's Century of Regime Change from Hawaii to Iraq* (New York: Times Books, 2006), 151.

12 Saldin, *War, the American State, and Politics since 1891*, 191.

13 The president in question in 1962 was, of course, John F. Kennedy (Sheehan, *A Bright Shining Lie*, 38).

14 Kinzer, *Overthrow*, 155

15 H. Bruce Franklin, *M.I.A. or Mythmaking in America: How and Why Belief in Live POWs Has Possessed a Nation* (Brooklyn: Lawrence Hill Books, 1992), 41.

16 U.S. military aid to South Vietnam topped $1.65 billion for the years 1955 to 1961 alone (Sheehan, *A Bright Shining Lie*, 55).

17 A great deal of debate revolves around speculation of what Kennedy might have done in Vietnam had he survived his presidency. Scholar and author John Tirman sums this debate up neatly by analyzing Kennedy's record in Vietnam before he was assassinated: "The question of whether Kennedy would have expanded the war as Lyndon Johnson did is hotly debated to this day, but whatever Kennedy *might* have done, what he *did* do was to deeply involve the United States in Vietnam: the counterinsurgency effort, the growing numbers of special forces, the covert operations, the raids in Laos, and, most decisively, the insistence that Vietnam was a momentous arena of the Cold War. All of this made possible the programs were resulting in sizable human costs and creating a trajectory toward the colossal carnage that was soon to come" (John Tirman, *The Deaths of Others: The Fate of Civilians in America's Wars* (New York: Oxford University Press, 2011), 140).

18 Over the course of extensive interviews for the documentary film *Fog of War* released in 2003, former Secretary of Defense McNamara admitted to lying about the Gulf of Tonkin incident in order to allow for more freedom for the U.S. military in Vietnam. An undated NSA memo from 2005 confirmed McNamara's revised account.

19 Daniel C. Hallin, *The "Uncensored War": The Media and Vietnam* (London: The University of California Press, 1986), 16.

20 Franklin, *M.I.A. or Mythmaking in America*, 41.

21 Turse, *Kill Anything that Moves*, 9.

22 It is perhaps telling, if not surprising, that among the enumerable calculations that McNamara and his aids conducted as part and parcel of the prosecution of war in Vietnam, non-combatant casualties were never among these statistics: "While the U.S. military attempted to quantify almost every other aspect of the conflict—from the number of helicopter sorties flown to the number of propaganda leaflets dispersed—it quite deliberately never conducted a comprehensive study of Vietnamese noncombatant casualties" (Turse, *Kill Anything that Moves*, 12).

23 Seymour Melman, *Pentagon Capitalism: The Political Economy of War* (New York: McGraw-Hill Book Company, 1970).

24 Ronald B. Frankum, Jr., *Like Rolling Thunder: The Air War in Vietnam, 1965–1975* (Washington, DC: Rowman & Littlefield Publishers, 2005).

25 John Pilger, "From Pol Pot to ISIS—'Anything that Flies on Everything that Moves'," *Green Left Weekly* 1029 (2014): 14–15. https://search.informit.org/doi/10.3316/informit .692653257186934.

26 The United States also used napalm extensively during its bombing campaigns in Vietnam. Napalm, a gelatinous defoliant and anti-personnel weapon designed to stick to human skin, devastated the civilian populations of Southeast Asia. From 1963 to 1973, the United States dropped over 388,000 tons of napalm in Vietnam, causing widespread and indiscriminate death and/or gruesome injury throughout the Vietnamese countryside (Marine Guillaume, "Napalm in US Bombing Doctrine and Practice, 1942–1975," *The Asia-Pacific Journal* no. 5 (2016). Article ID 4983. Accessed March 13, 2023. https://apjjf.org/2016/23/Guillaume.html).

27 Pilger, "From Pol Pot to ISIS," 14–15.

28 Erin Blakemore, "Why the U.S. Is Pledging Millions to Clean Up Bombs in Laos Decades Later, a Once-secret War Still Threatens Laotians," *Smithsonian Magazine*, September 8, 2016. https://www.smithsonianmag.com/smart-news/why-us-pledging-millions-clean-bombs -laos-180960351/.

29 Sheehan, *A Bright Shining Lie*, 589.

30 Ibid.

31 The U.S. Army puts the number of civilians killed at My Lai/Son My at 347. The Vietnamese government puts the number at 504.

32 Sheehan, *A Bright Shining Lie*, 689.

33 Turse, *Kill Anything that Moves*, 227–28.

34 Ibid., 155.

35 Sheehan, *A Bright Shining Lie*, 690.

36 In keeping with America's pervasive racial bias, though, the Jackson State shooting received much less media attention and a far smaller collective cry for justice than the killing and maiming of the white students at Kent State.

37 Tirman, *The Deaths of Others*, 180.

38 George Q. Flynn, *The Draft: 1940-1973* (Lawrence: University of Kansas Press, 1993), 166.

39 Samuel Moyn, *Humane: How the United States Abandoned Peace and Reinvented War* (New York: Farrar, Straus and Giroux, 2021), 207.

40 Nixon's signature on the Paris Peace Accords did not, in fact, stop aggressive U.S. military action against North Vietnam and Cambodia, and the United States would go on to conduct a substantial bombing campaign in 1973 after the signing of the accords. This violation of the Paris Peace Accords led to congressional action in Washington, and with the passage of the War Powers Resolution of 1973, the independence of the U.S. president to conduct unilateral military campaigns was curtailed. Much of that presidential power has subsequently been recovered by successive administrations in Washington, though, and the president's ability to wage war independent of congressional approval remains substantially intact in the twenty-first century.

41 Turse, *Kill Anything that Moves*, 11.

42 Ibid.

43 Tirman, *The Deaths of Others*, 168.

44 Ibid.

45 These and other disputes between journalists and policymakers resulted in much more stringent control of the flow of news and imagery back to U.S. audiences during subsequent American wars, a control that was enforced by Pentagon spokespersons in Washington as well as military personnel in the war zones themselves. This strict oversight was particularly evident during the First Gulf War, an American military intervention examined in Chapter 6 of this study.

46 Michael J. Arlen, "Television's War," *The New Yorker* (New York), May 20, 1967.

47 Hallin, *The "Uncensored War"*, 105.

48 George McArthur, "U.S. Troop Morale in Vietnam Held Still High: Reds' Tet Offensive Improved Spirit in Many Cases, Field Survey Shows," *Los Angeles Times*, March 20, 1968, A16.

49 Ibid.
50 Ibid.
51 William Tuohy, "Tough, Resilient: Marines Thumb Noses at Death at Khe Sanh," *New York Times*, February 14, 1968, 1.
52 Ibid.
53 Ibid.
54 George McArthur, "U.S. Troop Morale in Vietnam Held Still High: Reds' Tet Offensive Improved Spirit in Many Cases, Field Survey Shows," 1.
55 "Troop Morale in Vietnam Is High, House Unit Says: Troop Morale," *The Los Angeles Times*, May 8, 1968, 1.
56 Ibid.
57 *The Washington Post*, May 8, 1968, A8.
58 *The Los Angeles Times*, May 8, 1968, 1.
59 *The Los Angeles Times*, May 18, 1965, 13.
60 Ibid.
61 Thomas A. Johnson, Special to the *New York Times*. "The U.S. Negro in Vietnam: The Negro in Vietnam: Strides Toward Partnership Contrast With Lag at Home Military Career A Road to Dignity But Cost in Lives Is High—Many Civilians Attracted Abroad by Premium Pay," *The New York Times*, April 29, 1968, 1.
62 Ibid.
63 This frame of representation widely present in print news media coverage of the American war in Vietnam complements similar news media tropes describing U.S. military action in wars both before, and since, the American war in Southeast Asia.
64 Tuohy, "Tough, Resilient," *New York Times*, February 14, 1968, 1.
65 Ibid.
66 Johnson, "The U.S. Negro in Vietnam," *The New York Times*, April 29, 1968, 1.
67 Tuohy, "Tough, Resilient," *New York Times*, February 14, 1968, 1.
68 Maxwell D. Taylor, Jr., "General Taylor Says—The Cause in Vietnam Is Being Won," *New York Times*, October 15, 1967, 251.
69 Max Frankel, "President Visits G.I.'s [sic] in Vietnam in Surprise Trip: Spends 2 Hours at Base at Camranh Bay, Greeting Men And-Praising Them, Presents Decorations. He Jests And-Shakes Hands—After Return to Manila, He Flies On to Thailand The President Salutes American Fighting Men in Person on Secret Trip to Vietnam," *New York Times*, October 27, 1966, 1.
70 Bernard Weintraub, Special to the *New York Times*. "Americans' Impact on Vietnam Is Profound: American Impact on Vietnam's Economy, Politics and Culture Is Profound," *The New York Times*, July 6, 1968, 1.
71 Charles Mohr, Special to the *New York Times*. "Street Clashes Go On in Vietnam, Foe Still Holds Parts of Cities: Enemy Toll Soars: 'Offensive is Running Out of Steam,' Says Westmoreland Street Clashes Continue in South Vietnam; Enemy Still Controls Parts of Cities. Letup Is Foreseen by Westmoreland but He Expects an Assault on Marines at Khesanh," *New York Times*, February 2, 1968, 1.
72 Hanson Baldwin, "News Analysis: Public Opinion in U.S. and South Vietnam Is Viewed as Main Target of New Offensive by Vietcong," *New York Times*, February 1, 1968, 12.
73 Hanson W. Baldwin, Special to the *New York Times*. "Washington Feels Vietcong Offensive Failed to Gain Maximum Objectives," *The New York Times*, February 17, 1968, 2.
74 Ibid.
75 Baldwin, "News Analysis," *New York Times*, February 1, 1968, 12.
76 Ibid.
77 Robert Keatley and Peter R. Kann, "Faltering Under Fire: Americans Say Attack during Tet Underscored Saigon Regime's Defects Heroic Acts Overshadowed By Bickering, Indecision, Exploitation of Citizens Glimmers of Reform Again Faltering Under Fire: Critics Say Tet Attack Showed Regime's Flaws," *The Wall Street Journal*, March 5, 1968, 1.
78 Among the architects of this cover up was future Secretary of State highly regarded public figure, Colin Powell (Kelsey D. Atherton, "There's Nothing Honorable or Decent about Colin Powell's Long List of War Crimes," *Jacobin Magazine*, October 19, 2021. https://jacobin .com/2021/10/colin-powell-war-crimes-iraq-my-lai-massacre-iran-contra).

79 Turse, *Kill Anything that Moves*, 227–28.
80 Pete R. Kihss, "A 'Real Tight' Company and Its Test at Songmy: A 'Real Tight' Company of American Soldiers and Its Test at the Village of Songmy A Seargeant [*sic*]] Says Men Were Angry, Notes Losses Before Attack at Site of Alleged Killing of Vietnamese Civilians," *New York Times*, November 30, 1969, 1.
81 Ibid.
82 "Vietnam U.S. Began Withdrawal from War," *Los Angeles Times*, December 28, 1969, H7.
83 Henry Kamm, "Songmy 2: The Toll of Frustration and Fury," *New York Times*, November 23, 1969, E2.
84 Kihss, "A 'Real Tight' Company and Its Test at Songmy," *New York Times*, November 30, 1969, 1.
85 Ibid.
86 David Hoffman, *Washington Post* Foreign Service, "Cemetery Is Mylai's Reminder: There Are No Flowers to Mark the Graves of Mylai No Provocation Fortified Pits U.S. Protection Immediate Response Hamlet's Name," *The Washington Post*, November 30, 1969, 1.
87 Robert Smith, Special to the *New York Times*. "Army Will Review Study of '68 on Alleged Killings," *New York Times*, November 25, 1969, 16.
88 Jack Nelson, "Vietnamese Atrocities 'Accepted,' Court Told: Witness for Levy Reports Saigon Troops With U.S. Forces Beat, Killed Prisoners," *Los Angeles Times*, May 25, 1967, 5.
89 Kamm, "Songmy 2," *New York Times*, November 30, 1969, E2.
90 Ibid.
91 Hallin, *The "Uncensored War"*, 180.
92 Albin Krebs, "Some Reap Financial Returns from Alleged Massacre at Songmy," *New York Times*, November 29, 1969, 15.
93 "My Lai Slides 'Sicken' Senators," *Newsday*, November 28, 1969, 3.
94 Turse, *Kill Anything that Moves*, 230.
95 Ibid., 222.

Chapter Six

IRAQ PART I: SANITIZED WAR, UBIQUITOUS PATRIOTISM

The actual historical record of the war belies the popular view gained via the media that this was a clean, sanitized conflict fought out largely with "smart weaponry" in which death and destruction were noticeable by their absence.[1]

—*Phillip M. Taylor, 1998*

Saddam Hussein: American Client

By the 1950s, the masters of the American regime and its exploding military-industrial complex were growing in their interest in Southwest Asia alongside their increasing interventionist stance in the Southeastern corridor of that continent. In Iraq, the U.S. intelligence community bullied its way into a direct role in the internal politics of the state. There, in the summer of 1958, a military dictatorship arose under the leadership of 'Abd al-Kareem Qassim, an army general who assumed power by overthrowing the Hashemite monarchy in Iraq, one of the few remaining regional governments established by British colonial policies during the interwar years. Assuming control in what came to be called the July Revolution, in one grisly stroke at the Royal Palace in Baghdad on July 14, 1958, Qassim loyalist Abdul Sattar Sabaa Al-Ibousi murdered King Faisal II, Crown Price 'Abd al-Ilah (the king's first cousin once removed), several members of the Crown Prince's family, and the king's prime minister, Nuri as-Said. A number of valets and servants attendant to the royal family were killed too, serving notice to those in the country who still maintained loyalty to the Hashemite monarchy or to the old order of the Iraqi state.[2] By the end of the month, Qassim assumed the position of prime minister, claiming publicly that he had been elected to the post. In order to maintain strict control over the military, the very institution that promoted him to political power, he also assumed the post of Iraqi defense minister. Promised constitutional and social welfare reforms were few and far between, though, as Qassim's government quickly descended into autocracy.

In fulfillment of his nationalist promises, Qassim quickly moved to seize control over Iraqi oil revenues, which had been consigned primarily to American and British interests vis-à-vis the foreign-owned Iraq Petroleum Company (IPC). Qassim's Public Law 80 immediately limited the operational purview of the IPC while at the same time restoring a number of previously shared oil fields to exclusive state control. In effect, this canceled the IPC's international concessions altogether and was one of the most significant early steps leading later to the creation of the International Organization of Petroleum-Exporting Countries, or OPEC, the organization of oil-rich states that came to formalize indigenous control of regional resources in Baghdad in September of 1960.[3] Along with these domestic developments, Qassim's foreign policy agenda was equally worrying to Kennedy administration officials in Washington. Within a year of seizing power, he removed Iraq from the Baghdad Pact, a U.S.-centric defense partnership agreed to as part of Middle Eastern Cold War dynamics during the Hashemite regime. He also ended the ban on the Iraqi Communist Party as part of a shift in policy orientation toward the Soviet Union, with whom he engaged in formal talks for economic and military aid in 1959. Qassim also threatened regional expansion by declaring Kuwait's sovereignty to be null and void and speaking publicly about the injustice of Arab-speaking minorities residing within Iranian territory, both issues that would not soon fade from Iraq's regional political considerations.[4] More generally, Qassim's vocal criticism of the United States, along with his public plaudits for anti-colonial movements in Palestine and Algeria, very quickly rendered him a persona non grata within the allegedly liberal-minded Kennedy administration. A plan was formulated to mitigate the troubling policies emanating from Baghdad.

Utilizing the CIA, the Kennedy administration turned to proxy politics by engaging the predominantly anti-communist Ba'ath Party in their efforts to redirect nationalist sentiment in Iraq away from Qassim's pro-Soviet regime. Increasingly, Ba'ath Party leadership came to believe that the only way to stop the momentum of Qassim and his communist supporters was to assassinate the general and stage their own 1958-style coup to replace his government. Among these leaders was a Ba'athist lieutenant and party enforcer named Saddam Hussein, who, though young during this period, soon grew in the estimation of senior party members through his sheer ruthlessness and commitment. Ever eager to show his worth to the party, Saddam was set up close to Qassim's primary office in Baghdad and soon became the point man for an early Ba'ath assassination attempt on Qassim in October of 1959. Rushing the prime minister's car with his coconspirators, Saddam is reported to have spoiled the attempt with a premature volley of bullets: "One former CIA official said that the 22-year-old Saddam lost his nerve and began firing too soon, killing Qasim's driver and only wounding Qasim in the shoulder and arm."[5] Qassim survived this attempt on his life, but his hold on political power in Iraq would not last much longer. Invigorated by outside support and the growing distaste for Qassim within the region, the Ba'ath Party officially ousted Qassim and began a purge of his communist backers in February 1963. Qassim was given a show trial on national radio, found guilty of crimes against the country, and was then summarily shot. Scholars differ on the extent of the role of the CIA in this successful overthrow of another Middle Eastern government (they toppled populist nationalist Mohammed Mossadeq in Iran in 1953), but at the very least, it is agreed that the Kennedy administration knew of this plot and sanctioned the assassination and overthrow of Qassim.[6]

The new Ba'athist regime was overseen by President Abdul Salam Arif, with Ahmed Hassan al-Bakr serving as prime minister after the February coup. An internal purge in 1968 would elevate al-Bakr, though, with Saddam Hussein playing a prominent role in securing his power base by brutally eliminating party opponents, whether communists or rival Ba'athists. Al-Bakr oversaw the party's expansion from some 5,000 members to more than a million, while Saddam operated as an ultra-violent party enforcer through-out the decade. By 1979, Saddam was in a position to assume control of the party apparatus in his own right and, through it, the whole of the country. Wisely perhaps, Al-Bakr stepped aside as Saddam began eliminating potential rivals via imprisonment or assassination. Once assured of his domestic stability, Saddam turned his gaze toward Iran, the populous Shi'a state to his east that, in early 1979, had just undergone a desta-bilizing revolution. Iran's revolution meant a shift from secular dictatorship to expressly Shi'a governance next door to Iraq, a state that Saddam and the Ba'athists positioned as secular but that trended heavily Sunni given Saddam's Sunni background and his desire to control the Iraqi Shi'a majority. Beyond religious differences, there was also the matter of the oil-rich territory along the border between Iraq and Iran that Saddam had long coveted. Saddam had the solution:

> Assuming that the Islamic Revolution had left Iran militarily weak and therefore vulner-able, Saddam Hussein spied a chance to help himself to some easy pickings [...] Saddam [also] coveted [...] Iran's oil-rich Khuzestan Province, just across Iraq's eastern border. He also wanted to assert unquestioned Iraqi control of the Shatt al-Arab waterway, formed by the confluence of the Tigris and Euphrates Rivers.[7]

If Saddam's calculations were correct, his unilateral invasion of Iran in September of 1980 could benefit Iraq both politically and economically, and it could bring the kind of prestige and international leverage to the Arab leader not seen within regional politics since Egypt's Gamal Abdel Nasser in the 1960s.

But Saddam had miscalculated. Weakened and disorganized, though they were in the immediate aftermath of the Islamic revolution, Iran was still a formidable military opponent. Though surprised by the initial ferocity of the Iraqi assault, Iran regrouped, and the fighting between the two armies developed into a bloody stalemate involving both conventional and chemical weapons, wherein civilians were routinely targeted, especially by Saddam's Iraqi forces. The fighting would last eight long years, costing possibly as many as a million lives and setting the economies and infrastructure of both states back significantly.[8] From the view of the Reagan administration in Washington, though, this fight was an opportunity to gain an upper hand on a hated political enemy: "Bitterly anti-American militants had recently seized power in Iran, and President Reagan was eager to ensure that they did not win this war. That meant helping Saddam, which Reagan did in several ways."[9] These methods included many of the usual forms of state-to-state assistance common for close allies, including intelligence sharing, finan-cial assistance, and the donation of military equipment:

> American intelligence agencies began sending Saddam reports about Iranian troop move-ments that allowed him to fend off what might have been abject defeat. Over the next seven years, the United States sold Saddam $200 million worth of weaponry, as well as a fleet of helicopters that were supposedly for civilian use but were immediately turned over to the Iraqi army. Washington also gave him $5 billion in agricultural credits and a $684 million loan to build an oil pipeline to Jordan, a project he awarded to the California-based Bechtel Corporation.[10]

The remarkable thing about this generous military and economic largesse, though, was that the United States and Iraq were not, in fact, allies. Before the Iran-Iraq War, in fact, Washington maintained strenuously that Iraq was a state sponsor of terror. Indeed, the two states had not had official diplomatic relations since Iraq decamped from its embassy in Washington in 1967 in protest of American support for Israel during the June 1967 War.[11] So committed was the United States to preventing an Iranian victory in this conflict, though, that these policies were all quietly reversed in order to recreate Saddam Hussein as a dutiful American client. Gone were the accusations of thuggery and terroristic intent. Replacing those were "friendly messages from Secretary of State Shultz to his Iraqi counterpart emphasiz[ing] the 'very important common interests' shared by the two countries."[12] This sudden about-face in policy and procedure was not discussed publicly by Reagan administration officials. Instead, this complete reversal was treated as an age-old practice in commentary emanating from the Reagan administration.

To seal this new, diplomatically intimate relationship between the two states, in 1982, the Reagan administration dispatched "former (and future) defense secretary Donald Rumsfeld, acting as Ronald Reagan's personal representative."[13] Rumsfeld was assigned the role of Middle East Envoy and was dispatched to the Iraqi capital to assure Saddam of the sustained support he would receive from the United States during his war with Iran: "Rumsfeld assured Saddam that any resolution of the ongoing war 'which weakens Iraq's role or enhances [the] interests and ambitions of Iran' was not going to find favor in Washington. Along those lines, the United States was

Photo 9 Coalition jets fly in formation during the First Gulf War.

'encouraging others not to sell weapons to Iran' and would continue to do so."[14] The two politicos, looking very much like old friends, were recorded on video shaking hands and smiling, sealing for posterity the American largesse to and protection for Saddam's Iraq. And for his part, Rumsfeld was true to his word. Money, intelligence, and weapons flowed into accounts, offices, and bases in Iraq. Business between the two countries boomed: "Between 1983 and 1989, annual trade between the two countries grew from £571 million to $3.6 billion."[15] Saddam also won a moral imprimatur through this arrangement using America's good standing on the international stage to cover for some of the most egregious violence perpetrated on the Iranian populace. Saddam was roundly known to be a butcher and a thug, but he was our thug, so the thinking went within the halls of power in Washington, and we therefore supported him unreservedly throughout the Iran-Iraq War. For his part, ever the dutiful client, Saddam carried out the policy wishes of his patron, the United States, by punishing the government and the people of Iran for their turn toward Islamic governance. When an armistice was finally reached, both states remained viable, if badly damaged, and a stalemate was confirmed by United Resolution 598. Surprisingly, though, friendly relations between Washington and Baghdad would not last.

The Invasion of Kuwait and Operation Desert Storm

After eight years of exhaustive warfare with Iran, Iraq's infrastructure was damaged, its military morale was low, and, critically, its economy was miserably depressed. In addition to extensive support from the United States, Saddam had leveraged the Arab and Sunni nature of his state in order to borrow exorbitant sums from similarly constituted neighbors during his fight with Iran. This strategy resulted in Iraqi state debts of more than $80 billion owed to Saudi Arabia and Kuwait, amounts that could not have been repaid even if Saddam had wanted to act as a good-faith borrower; he didn't. In addition, Saddam convinced himself that Iraq had not simply been fighting Iran for its own glory but rather for the safety and longevity of all Arabs and all Sunnis. As such, it was unthinkable that the Kuwaiti ruling family, the al-Sabahs, would demand repayment of war debts accrued in the great Iraqi battle against the Iranian Shi'a heretics: "since Iraq had been fighting on Kuwait's behalf (and by extension on behalf of all Arabs and all Sunni Muslims), Saddam thought it only appropriated that the al-Sabahs should forgive Iraq its debt and even provide an additional line of credit to help Iraq's recovery from its exertions."[16] Kuwait, more than Saudi Arabia in this case, antagonized Saddam in other ways, too. The Iraqi leader charged Kuwait with "encroachments into claimed Iraqi territory, including the extraction of oil from the al-Rumaila oil field. The 'stolen' oil, it was claimed, was worth $2.4 billion."[17] What gives some measure of credence to this specific claim of theft is the fact that the al-Sabahs were known to doctor the books in their oil production portfolios, frequently incurring the ire of Iraq and other OPEC members, too: "Saddam charged Kuwait with violating OPEC production quotas, which drove down world oil prices [and] had the effect of hurting the already-ailing Iraqi economy."[18] And, since Kuwaiti independence in 1961, Iraq had resisted the idea of Kuwaiti sovereignty and, from Qassim to Saddam, had claimed the wealthy emirate as its own territory, asserting regularly, often publicly, that Kuwait was nothing more than the nineteenth province of Iraq. Battered and bruised though the Iraqi Army was, Saddam was certain that all of these problems could be solved militarily.

As a client state in good standing in Washington, as these financial and diplomatic issues were coming to a head in the summer of 1990, Saddam reached out through the proper channels to engage the U.S. Ambassador to Iraq, April Glaspie. Glaspie had been in that critical position within Middle Eastern politics and dynamics emanating from Washington since 1987, though this was reportedly the first time she sat down face-to-face with Saddam.[19] Still, she knew the company line well, and when Saddam railed against the injustice being done to him both regionally and internationally, Glaspie went out of her way to reassure him of the good intentions of the H. W. Bush administration, the U.S. presidential administration that replaced Ronald Reagan after the election of 1988: "The ambassador went out of her way to insist that the United States sought friendly relations [and] sympathized with his hurt at attacks on his character from the American media."[20] Communicating what Saddam could only presume to be the official line from Washington as she was the top American representative in Iraq, she went on to guarantee Saddam that "we have no opinion on the Arab-Arab conflicts, like your border disagreement with Kuwait."[21] Saddam came away from this meeting with the green light he needed to invade Kuwait. And while it is true that President Bush cabled Saddam a few days later to clarify the U.S. position and strongly urge the dictator not to use force against Kuwait,[22] the die had already been cast. Saddam began to regroup his forces and move them into position along the border with Kuwait. On August 2, 1990, Iraq invaded Kuwait and annexed the emirate, officially renaming it as the nineteenth province of Iraq. Saddam believed his financial troubles would soon be over, and he thought, with good reason, that he had been given the go-ahead for this military resolution from the United States itself.

By August 3rd, Kuwait City and most of the ports and centers for oil production throughout the small emirate were firmly in the hands of the Iraqi Army. The American about-face targeting Saddam for these aggressive actions was swift and severe. Working through the United Nations Security Council (UNSC), the Bush administration in Washington moved definitively to protect their ally in the Persian Gulf, turning their back on decade-long client Iraq and coming to the aid of the al-Sabahs in Kuwait. The UNSC passed resolutions 660 and 661 in early August, calling Iraq to surrender its positions in Kuwait and imposing strict economic sanctions against Iraq in order to compel an Iraqi withdrawal. Thanks to hasty negotiations between Washington and Riyadh, permission was given by Saudi King Fahd to billet large numbers of American troops in Saudi Arabia beginning in the same month, and by mid-September of 1990: "over 150,000 U.S. troops and their equipment had been deployed in Saud Arabia."[23] These were the frontline soldiers in what became a broad-based coalition of support- ive states, which included the contributions of some 39 governments, including Arab partners like Egypt and Syria. This show of force pushed Saddam into a corner, and he was compelled to offer a meek acceptance of UNSC Resolution 660, though only in the context of a counteroffer that could not be taken seriously. Iraq "announced its willingness to withdraw from Kuwait in compliance with Resolution 660, but [only if]

Iraq's historical territorial claims be guaranteed; that a new form of government be considered for Kuwait; that Coalition nations pay war reparations to Iraq; and that all Iraq's foreign debts to Western and Gulf countries be forgiven."[24] Saddam also threw in the caveat that Israel decamps from all occupied Palestinian territories as a further condition of his compliance with UNSC 660. Predictably, these conditions were quickly rejected by the United Nations. War was coming.

The UNSC Resolution 678 in November of 1990 gave Iraq a withdrawal deadline of January 15, 1991, and allowed "all necessary means" to enforce each and every resolution aimed at Iraq since Saddam's invasion of Kuwait. When Saddam predictably ignored this deadline, the fighting commenced with aerial bombardments of Iraqi positions. Iraq responded with surface-to-surface missile launches against coalition, Saudi, and Israeli targets using SCUD missiles, but these resulted in minimal casualties and had little, if any, military effect. On February 24, 1991, the ground assault against Iraq began forcing widespread desertions in the Iraqi ranks, driving whole units back toward Baghdad. During their retreat, a column of 1,400 Iraqi vehicles and an attendant number of soldiers stretching out more than 60 kilometers along a highway moving from Kuwait to Iraq were identified by U.S. air communications and attacked. The incident, which came to be known as "The Highway of Death," killed between 500 and 600 retreating Iraqi soldiers and caused momentary media criticism of what was otherwise perceived to be a highly specialized, highly sanitized military performance by the U.S. and its coalition partners. And while the substance of that media coverage will be discussed in some detail in the pages to follow, it was obvious to observers both within the region and internationally that Iraq's defeat at the hands of the coalition was as thorough as it was decisive. Within three days of the beginning of the ground offensive, a cease-fire was declared. As abruptly as it began, the Gulf War ended.

Operation Desert Storm, the official military nomenclature for the attack against Iraq in 1991, proved that the United States and its military broadsword would go to great lengths to secure the global oil supply, even to the extent of reversing course on a close ally in the Middle East in order to stabilize access to that most precious of global resources: "Oil was indeed the key factor in the crisis, the one responsible for sparking it. For the West, it was the extraction of oil and its unrestricted exportation that made the Gulf a vital zone."[25] Seen through this lens, the military operation against Saddam was an unmitigated success: "The dual goal of Western powers to liberate Kuwait and to regain control of oil resources is clearly illustrated by the fall in the price of oil, from an average of $33 per barrel in October 1990 to $19 in March 1991 and even through 1992 and 1993."[26] But there was yet another, unspoken American interest served by military operations in the Persian Gulf in 1990 and 1991. U.S. military expert and Middle East historian Andrew Bacevich adeptly described the implicit purpose behind the deployment of massive numbers of American soldiers to the Middle East during the First Gulf War: "On August 7 [1990], the implementation of OPLAN 1002-90, Defense of the Arabian Peninsula, commenced. In reality [...] U.S. troops were never going to 'go home.' From this point forward, U.S. military engagement in the Greater Middle East became permanent and sustained, rather than occasional and episodic."[27] Indeed, though major combat operations ended in the region with Saddam Hussein's defeat, large numbers of American troops would continue to occupy bases and outposts in the Middle East continually through to a subsequent iteration of the Gulf War and continuing through to the present day. Perhaps predictably, though, this convenient byproduct of a war intended to sustain the American Empire received no mention within the authoritative news media in either the buildup or the aftermath of military operations against Saddam's Iraq. In fact, in arguing for the merits of this military action in the late summer and fall of 1990, a very different story was related to the American people regarding the reasons for massive military action against Saddam Hussein and the Iraqi Army.

Nayirah and American Propaganda

As the Bush administration inched closer to military intervention ostensibly on behalf of Kuwait but truthfully on behalf of American oil interests, the population of the United States as a whole was decidedly lukewarm about the prospects of another large-scale military commitment overseas for an indeterminate period of time. Public opinion polls reflected this reluctance and put the hawkish Bush administration in an increasingly difficult scenario: go forward with the desired military intervention in Kuwait against the wishes of a reluctant populous, or demure, in the face of Saddam Hussein's invasion of Kuwait and risk losing face in the Middle East. Bush, who had already endured years of criticism and mockery on television and in cartoon strips for being wimpy and weak, could not personally tolerate the latter decision. But as a politician looking to extend the Republican stronghold on the White House even longer than the 12-year period the party was enjoying, and with a career of espionage and working around the political rules firmly under Bush's belt, he could likewise not tolerate the former option. Enter the Citizens for a Free Kuwait.

In 1990, Citizens for a Free Kuwait was a small special interest group made up of expatriate Kuwaitis living in the United States who wanted to advocate on behalf of their home country, now occupied and controlled by Saddam Hussein and the Iraqi military. While the Bush administration appeared content to wait for United Nations censure and resolutions against Iraq to run their course, Citizens for a Free Kuwait began campaigning within the United States to gather funds and raise awareness about the harsh reality of life in Kuwait under Iraqi rule. A massive injection of cash allowed the group to hire Hill and Knowlton, a high-priced, highly-touted public relations firm based in Washington DC, who were engaged in order to present the case for Kuwaiti to the American people. As a Hill and Knowlton representative had it at the time, their purpose was simply to "get Kuwait's story out."[28] In fact, the true purposes behind the machinations of Citizens for a Free Kuwait were much more elaborate. As it happened, the massive cash deposit into their coffers came directly from the government of Kuwait itself, with donation entries in the accounts of the group citing a nearly $12 million contribution from "The State of Kuwait." On investigation, this huge contribution stood out considerably against donations of $1.50 or even $100 that came in from concerned citizens around the United States. In effect, this rendered the Citizens for a Free Kuwait much more than simply a special interest group. They were, in fact, a wing of another sovereign state operating to manipulate U.S. policy from within the United States itself. To quote Morley Safer, the host of the January 1991 CBS news program "60 Minutes" that helped to break the true story behind the subterfuge created by Hill and Knowlton: "That funding had one purpose: to get a lethargic American public to support intervention and a war against Iraq."[29]

But funds alone would not be enough to accomplish this task. As such, Hill and Knowlton went to work lobbying members of Congress and making direct contact with high-ranking Bush administration officials who were already preparing a resolution to go to war in the Persian Gulf should the United Nations resolutions demanding Iraqi withdrawal from Kuwait go unheeded by Saddam (predictably, they did). Hill and Knowlton went further, still. Using their existing, strong connections to the Bush administration (the president of the agency, Craig Fuller, was formerly chief of staff for George H. W. Bush during his tenure as vice president),[30] the fast-paced PR firm was able to arrange public hearings with the Congressional Human Rights Caucus on behalf of Citizens for a Free Kuwait. The hearings took place in October of 1990 and were used by Hill and Knowlton to make the strongest possible case advocating for war against Saddam Hussein and Iraq in order to liberate the victimized population of Kuwait. The firm was characteristically thorough in their preparations for the public hearings, which were designed to elicit the maximum possible sympathy for the Kuwaiti people on one of the grandest stages available in the country, the Senate floor:

> The hearing had been arranged by the Hill and Knowlton public relations firm on behalf of [...] Citizens for a Free Kuwait [...] Hill and Knowlton's Washington, DC office [...] provided witnesses for the hearing, coached them, wrote testimony, produced videotapes detailing the alleged atrocities and ensured that the room was filled with reporters and television cameras.[31]

For these efforts in arranging these highly public and exceedingly official hearings and, in so doing, behaving as de facto agents for Kuwaiti policy intent upon influencing American opinion in the direction of the war against Saddam Hussein, "Hill and Knowlton had received $10.7 million from Citizens for a Free Kuwait."[32]

Still, in order for the message to be truly unforgettable, Hill and Knowlton needed the spokesperson for that message to connect deeply with an American audience hearing a truly harrowing tale of Iraqi atrocity. And they had it. Easily the most memorable witness of the October 20, 1990, Senate hearings was Nayirah, an intelligent and articulate teenage girl, who told the gathered and esteemed congressional committee members a truly terrible story. Her story was that she was a Kuwaiti national who happened to be living in the United States. She had been home for a summer visit to Kuwait in 1990 and decided to volunteer at her local hospital. At that point, tragedy struck. The Iraqis invaded, and marauding soldiers quickly made their way to their high-value military and political targets, one of which was apparently the maternity ward of the hospital where Nayirah was volunteering. In their haste to denude Kuwait of its riches and resources, Nayirah claimed that Iraqi soldiers set about systematically removing babies from their incubators, leaving them to die miserably on the cold floor while absconding back to Iraq with their war booty (in this case, baby incubators). Nayirah's voice quivered, and her tears flowed while she testified. Brief though her statement was, a more compelling witness could scarcely have been imagined by the working group at Hill and Knowlton. The case for war against Iraq now was stronger than ever in the minds of the American public.

The impact of Nayirah's testimony was undeniable, and its effects were felt throughout the country. More critically, perhaps, it was also distinctly felt by policymakers, especially members of Congress who narrowly voted to approve the resolution for the United States to go to war against Iraq on January 12, 1991. Their voting record reflects the pivotal nature of the hearings of the Congressional Human Rights Caucus arranged by Hill and Knowlton, and specifically, the pivotal nature of Nayirah's eyewitness testimony to the Iraqi atrocity: "The decision to go was a close one. In the Senate, the war resolution passed by five votes. And incidentally, six Senators referred to the baby incubator story as a reason to go to war."[33] But Nayirah, who claimed to be operating under an assumed name to protect her family in Kuwait (she was not), was not who she seemed. Nor, in fact, was her shocking testimony all that it seemed to be either. Shortly after the passage of the war resolution, hailed as the most decisive congressional action in favor of military intervention since the Gulf of Tonkin Resolution (see the previous chapter in this work), disquieting rumors about Nayirah's true identity and the role of the Citizens for a Free Kuwait began to circulate in Washington. Within the year, months after a military route of Saddam's forces in Kuwait, clandestine threads of collusion between the Kuwaiti government, the Kuwaiti ambassador to the United States, and an unscrupulous public relations firm, Hill and Knowlton, began to surface:

It was Hill and Knowlton that gave to the group [of witnesses] the story of Iraqi soldiers pulling newborns from their incubators so that these machines could be removed to Iraq [...] the story also made an appearance on Capitol Hill, where a young woman named Nayirah told a hearing of the Congressional Human Rights Caucus, chaired by Representative Tom Lantos, that she had witnessed this event firsthand. After John R. MacArthur, publisher of *Harper's Magazine*, revealed in a *New York Times* op-ed piece the fact that Nayirah was, in fact, the daughter of the Kuwaiti ambassador to the U.S., it was also disclosed that Hill and Knowlton had helped to prepare her testimony, which she had rehearsed before video cameras in the firm's Washington headquarters.[34]

Nayirah, as it happened, was not the coincidental eyewitness she claimed to be, but was in fact the daughter of the Kuwaiti ambassador to the United States at the time, Sheikh Saud Nassir al-Sabah. Furthermore, and as previously indicated, the name al-Sabah carries significant influence inside Kuwait, given that it is the name of the ruling family of that particular hereditary monarchy. This fact makes Nayirah a Kuwaiti princess, a member of that emirate's ruling family. She was not, in fact, someone who had ever volunteered at any hospital, and she had never borne witness to the by now trite and overused images of marauding soldiers brutalizing babies that have become common tropes in condemnations of national enemies, real or perceived. Officially, "according to Kuwaiti doctors and other prospective witnesses interviewed by Middle East Watch, a human-rights group, the incident never occurred."[35]

These carefully crafted lies had substantial influence here in the United States as well as in coalition countries abroad. Nayirah's story was repeated throughout the authoritative news media and was rarely questioned for its veracity. The president himself used it as a case study in the sinister nature of the Iraqis, repeating the story publicly "at least ten times in the following weeks"[36] after the congressional hearings. Undeniably then, with a presidential imprimatur and with all the hallmarks of a compelling narrative drama, Nayirah's testimony, coached by Hill and Knowlton, paid for by the Kuwaiti government, and facilitated by an eager and hawkish Bush administration, paved the way for another American war: "The stories of Iraqi atrocities helped gain public and congressional support for military action."[37] Some scholars have concluded that the Gulf War of 1991 would have occurred anyway, whether sooner or later, given Saddam Hussein's intransigence juxtaposed with Bush's obsession with his own wimpy public image. Even if this were true, though, this conclusion does not excuse the collusion, manipulation, or outright prevarication practiced by the Bush administration, the Kuwaiti government, or the public relations firm of Hill and Knowlton during this time. The entire episode remains among the most disturbing in the annals of recent American policy and diplomacy. In the words of Morley Safer, the news anchor for "60 Minutes," who broke the Nayirah story to the country a year after we had all been duped by it, "The troubling part of the story is [...] that with enough access, enough money, and knowing which buttons to push, war can be marketed just like soft drinks and tooth paste."[38]

Photo 10 General Norman Schwarzkopf gives a briefing to the assembled press corps during the First Gulf War. U.S. military leadership was intent upon the control of information related to the war throughout the conflict.

Print Media Coverage of Gulf War I

The discussion in the pages that follow examines newspaper coverage of the Gulf War and, as with the print news media analysis conducted in previous chapters, examines text language, story selection, and narrative construction, among other discursive strategies, to uncover elements within the news media discourse surrounding Gulf War I within the United States. While video, audio, and general news imagery were prevalent in the news coverage of this war, this approach follows on from the discourse analyses in previous chapters as it retains the primacy of the written word in information distribution in a given society. This methodology further establishes period newspapers, particularly de facto papers of record among American readership such as the *New York Times*, *Washington Post*, and the *Los Angeles Times*, as especially influential sources of domestic news, period culture, and foreign policy commentary for the attendant American audience. This approach reaffirms that, regardless of the era in which an American war takes places and regardless of the technological advancements that have subsumed American society since the last war fought, information in American wars belongs substantially to the United States military and to the political leadership of the country, not to the press agencies themselves, and less so to the American people. As media scholar Phillip Taylor established: "Although the Gulf War will undoubtedly be remembered as CNN's war or television's war, it was no such thing. The conflict belonged to the coalition's armed forces, and to the victors went the spoils of the information war."[39] It is to the information war in America during the Gulf War crisis of 1990 and 1991 that this study now turns.

Modern Technology, Sanitized War, and Artful Consequence

The most common frames of representation embedded within news media narratives produced during and after the First Gulf War include the idea that the war being fought by coalition armies, particularly by the Army and Air Force of the United States, constituted an exact, precise, and clinical military effort. This frame of representation consists of complimentary discursive components. In one, the print news media was at great pains to lionize the technological capacities of the American military. In aid of this narrative construction, adjectives such as "laser-guided," "smart," and "targeted" abounded in descriptions of the American arsenal during the print coverage of the Gulf War. These descriptions and others like them amounted to a kind of weapons worship, a form of collective journalistic fawning over some of the most deadly and destructive implements ever employed in warfare. Along with this narrative line, a second component within this frame constructed the military leadership of the coalition, and especially the American forces, as careful and restrained, likening their war effort not to a destructive oeuvre designed to obliterate an opposing army but rather as a surgical procedure designed to meticulously and precisely dissect the opposition with little to no human damage as a consequence. Together, these complementary narrative frames asserted within the print news media portray the United States military as obsessively precise, utterly restrained, and ultimately totally moral in their actions. In news pieces contradicting this overarching discursive frame, for example, coverage of the February 13th destruction of a civilian air raid shelter by "precision" bombs,[40] was minimized in reporting of the combat operations carried out during the Gulf War. The collective effect of this institutional approach to the distribution of news information about the Gulf War was to portray fighting in the Persian Gulf as an antiseptic affair, one that was highly technical, thoroughly precise, and altogether accurate, having been conducted by the most moral army anywhere in the world.

Technology serves as the focal point of news descriptions espousing this narrative frame, all but excluding the human beings who are responsible for the design and implementation of this weaponry as well as those who are grievously affected by its deployment in war. One such description praises shiny, new American weaponry as if describing the latest offerings from high-end automobile manufacturers at an exotic car show: "That distinction is likely to belong instead to the younger, flashier, higher-tech weapons that-with their smarts and precision-have dazzled military experts and the admiring public."[41] Even "military experts" are awed by this machinery, which is attributed not only with efficiency and effectiveness but also with something akin to physical beauty being "younger" and "flashier" than previous iterations of the military technology with which this journalist is evidently enamored. Later in the same news piece, readers are informed via elements of literary personification that there are "eyes" operating this fancy new tech, although human beings themselves remain distinctly outside of the causal reality of these wondrous, modern objects: "Directing the punch of many of these high-tech weapons are some amazingly high-tech eyes, notably the seven spy satellites launched from NASA space shuttles into orbits 300 to 500 miles above the conflict."[42] The picture presented here is one of astounding technological capabilities that are awesome and ultra-modern in their inception and implementation. Mention of the human cost that unleashing this brand-new technology will perpetrate on captive populations is conspicuous for its absence in these discursive constructions constituting unending praise for American weaponry and its destructive power. In this discourse, war itself is remade not as a lived, human experience perpetrated upon a subject population and often harming civilians, but rather as a futuristic contest of high-tech wizardry free from human agency or human casualties. No wonder, then, that journalists were so anxious to declare technology the winner in this war before the dust from the fighting had even settled: "If there is a champion to emerge from the Persian Gulf War thus far, it appears to be American high technology."[43]

Naturally, the thrust of discussions emphasizing America's high-tech implements of war is to assure an attendant American public reading war coverage that our armies are advanced and that, above all, our military is moral. This connection between technology and morality, between military precision and sanitized war, is implicit throughout the enumerable column inches devoted to discussions of advanced weaponry during period-war coverage. It was also made explicit by a media institution that wanted to guarantee its readership that their military was righteous in its intent and morals and in its impact during the war in the Persian Gulf. In an example of this narrative frame, a news piece from the nation's capital lauds the American discovery of "clean war," as if such a concept can be said to exist: "It has laser-guided this and radar-guided that, weapons of such precision that military targets can be detected, isolated and killed almost without collateral civilian damage [...] If there is such a thing as a 'clean war,' Operation Desert Storm appears to have discovered it."[44] Cleanliness and precision then become catchwords utilized regularly to describe U.S. military operations during the war and deployed within authoritative news discourse to comfort, console, and reassure the readership at home of the righteousness and U.S. military action. Exceptional efforts, above and beyond what is required by the rules of war, are the result: "the extraordinary effort now being made to avoid civilian casualties by using only precision weapons is leaving Baghdad intact."[45] It may be said to be curious as to how a bombing campaign constituting hundreds of sorties into Iraq and destroying huge swaths of both military and civilian infrastructure can be said to be "leaving Baghdad intact." Nevertheless, the central message in these descriptive narratives is abundantly clear: American soldiers do not kill civilians. And now, thanks to incredibly new military technologies, we have the equipment readily available to secure our position as the most righteous, most careful, and most decent military on the planet.

The net effect of the deployment of this cutting-edge technology and this moralistic deployment of destructive force is the unmitigated military success in the waging of what seemed like a totally precise and nearly bloodless war. These successes are so thorough as to have been unanticipated by military planners, all of whom were considered "experts" in their respective fields of martial authority: "Military experts say the computerized weapons of the international force in the Persian Gulf war seem to be working much better than expected [...] computers big and small have clearly endowed the equipment with vast new powers of precision and coordination."[46] Again, the focus in these news pieces is the equipment and not the personnel, certainly not the Iraqi soldiers or civilians on the receiving side of these highly technical killing machines. In fact, these frames of representation would have it that the Iraqi Army, stilted, old, and technically inferior as it was, is actually fighting computerized forces as much as they are fighting the soldiers and sailors of the American-led coalition: "Large computers are now synchronizing the forces arrayed against Iraq and churning out detailed battle plans [...] smart weapons with tiny computer 'brains' are zeroing in on targets with deadly precision."[47] Smart weapons with their own brains are doing the fighting, then, and in so doing, they are removing American soldiers from harm's way while ostensibly making perfectly rational and militarily moral decisions. Indeed, this coverage seldom, if ever, mentioned the potential for technical failure or the possibility of unintended consequences when operating new technologies first deployed in the field. Rather, in the examples provided here and in many other period news pieces, the journalists reporting on these wondrous pieces of equipment took it on faith that these new, praiseworthy weapons always performed as they were intended to and that they never failed to accomplish their assigned task. Discerning readers seeking information outside of the authoritative news discourse on the Gulf War would then be within their rights to question the events surrounding the February 13, 1991, U.S. bombing of a civilian shelter at Amiriyah, which resulted in at least 500 Iraqi casualties. Was there a flaw in the implementation of sparkling, new, unfailingly precise technology? Or were these particular "smart bombs" intended to destroy a civilian shelter?[48]

Finally, the American war in the Persian Gulf was not only highly technical, precise, moral, and dutiful, but it was also rendered artful and beautiful thanks to wondrous new technologies unveiled by the architects of American wars. Flags fly, guns blaze, and bombs glisten in the Middle Eastern sunlight. Attendant audiences to these descriptions are meant to be enraptured by war's beauty while they are encouraged to forget about the true consequences of war as they are felt daily by civilian populations living within the theater of war itself: "The long awaited air war that opened Operation Desert Storm had all the precision of an aerial ballet, choreographing the lethal work of 24 types of aircraft from four fiercely independent U.S. military services and four allies' air forces."[49] In this reporting, the emphasis is on spectacle over substance, art ahead of consequence, as if the air war in the Persian Gulf was being conducted for the viewing pleasure of American audiences. The cynicism of these and many similar news media descriptions emphasizing the beauty of a war that is denuding infrastructure and killing thousands is patently evident. This glib discourse within the mainstream print news media in the United States encapsulates the celebration of war as technical, precise, clinical, and even beautiful as audiences view the military spectacle from the comfortable distance of a home living room, "shown on our TV screens for an unprecedented look at war from the missile's own point of view."[50] Recreating war as compelling entertainment, then, these descriptions from the print news media present for attendant audiences a new and uniquely macabre American experience.

Restoring Vietnam: Catharsis and Celebration in the Coverage of the Gulf War

Beyond the overt celebration of the technological and/or the remaking of warfare as a viewing spectacle, it is clear from the print news coverage of the First Gulf War that the American military defeat in Vietnam loomed large in the minds of the journalists and editors crafting the wartime narrative for recipient audiences in the United States. This perspective called forth memories of a longer, bloodier, and much more socially fraught conflict than the one at hand and gave news media professionals the opportunity to exorcise the demons of defeat that still lingered in the American psyche in the early 1990s. Simultaneously, the news media as an institution used the opportunity provided by the swift and thorough victory in the Persian Gulf to heap additional praise on soldiers from previous conflicts while at the same time celebrating the newfound glory of an unmitigated victory attended by robust displays of overt and hyper-masculine patriotism. One common method through which Vietnam was recalled in the construction of the discourse on the First Gulf War in the print news media was the insertion of interviews and quoted material from soldiers who had fought and lost in Vietnam. In one article unabashedly entitled "Flying Symbols of Patriotism," the narrative of the news story ostensibly speaking to current events in the Persian Gulf focuses upon the father of a deployed soldier detailing his experiences in Vietnam, informing: "[The] father, Air Force Col. Gary Wright Sr., had been shot down near Hanoi and was listed as missing in action."[51] Since that moment, readers are told, the family has had a troubled relationship with the American government and the military establishment as well, and they have "quarreled with the government over the treatment of soldiers missing in action and their families, and [...] had disagreements on other military issues, too."[52] The narrative neatly ties the two conflicts together, though, through the trials and tribulations of one military family as it reassures readers that the family's issues with the country during the Vietnam era have not "stopped [them] from supporting the country or its troops in the Persian Gulf." As such, we are informed that they will uncritically support military action in the Middle East. The conclusion here speaks to the family's resolution to not only provide unquestioned support to the country and to the military but also to forgive transgressions of the Vietnam era and to move on from the painful memories of the past.

The theme of resolving past wrongs committed by the state and society against soldiers from the Vietnam era was on full display during print news coverage of the Gulf War in another period article entitled "200,000 Cheer Troops in O.C. Victory Parade Celebration." That news item openly condemns the country's treatment of soldiers returning from Vietnam,[53] placing this broad criticism in the testimony of one of the reported 200,000 who attended a Los Angeles parade uncritically celebrating the military and its most recent war: "I think the country is very ashamed of the way it treated the Vietnam vets," said Carla White.[54] Once again, the news item provides interviews and quotations speaking specifically to Vietnam and antagonizing the state and society for its supposed poor treatment of soldiers who fought in that war. In this case, as with many similar news items from the Gulf War-era, the implication is that the unashamed, unmitigated celebration of the military and of the soldiers is the remedy to that ailment, a way to right the embarrassing wrongs of the past that have hung over the citizenry since the time they were committed. Ms. White is allowed further commentary to inform of her fear that "I was just afraid today's soldiers might get the same treatment as during Vietnam."[55] Once again, the specter of Vietnam looms large for the attendant readership approaching this news piece covering the aftermath of the First Gulf War. This article goes on to provide a repeat of the narrative resolve, the conclusion that though we, as a nation, wronged our soldiers in the past, we will not be committing those same mistakes again. Through these discursive constructions, the print news ably informs readers of the import of raucous celebration for, during, and after war, for it is only through this kind of full-throated merriment and uncritical patriotism that the evils of a muted past and the allegedly disdainful treatment of a once defeated army can be rectified.

Still, other news pieces overtly established the connection between the military that had fought and won in the Persian Gulf and those who had fought in the past, especially the defeated army of the Vietnam era. In one print article, the former commander of all American armed forces in Vietnam, General William Westmoreland, was announced as having attended a post-Gulf War reception. The news piece allowed his commentary to heap praise upon the Gulf War army and, in so doing, to restore a measure of his own gravitas and credibility that was so badly damaged when he was in command in Vietnam: "Gen. William C. Westmoreland, who commanded U.S. forces in Vietnam, was among the dignitaries in the reception room. 'Any time I can be with the troops it's an exhilarating experience,' he said."[56] The status and experience of a former soldier like

Westmoreland, defeated and controversial though he was in his own time, are intended in this piece to add to the connections between past national trauma and the current martial catharsis. Westmoreland goes on in the article to praise the bonds of fellowship between fighting men and to stand as an individual symbol of the new era of military success free from the memory of past defeats or misdeeds: "'There's lots of camaraderie.' The controversial general, blamed by some for deepening the U.S. involvement in Vietnam, received rousing hoorays along with other Vietnam veterans."[57] The "rousing hoorays" reported here represent a critical step forward in the national mood, considering the military and its behavior in war. Within this news piece and within the print news media more broadly, the U.S. Army of the Gulf War is free from the burden of defeat, having quickly and decisively beaten a challenging foe. More crucial still, there was scant report of any crime or human rights violation committed by the soldiers of the Gulf War-era military, while the same could not be said, of course, for the U.S. Army in Vietnam. Importantly, in this and other similar articles from authoritative coverage of the Gulf War, Westmoreland, by his presence and commentary, becomes a symbol of something wrong put right, of the restoration of American character and accountability in a new, modern era of military glory. Fresh from its resounding victory, according to these frames of news media representation, the American military identity is victorious, and therefore whole, once again.

In addition to expurgating the American record in Vietnam, other references in coverage of Gulf War I cast readers back to the Korean Conflict and World War II, using nostalgia and emotive imagery to create a tone of resolution, unity, and finality in news coverage of the postwar celebrations following the American victory in Kuwait. Ecstatic crowds were described as whooping and cheering as soldiers from previous wars marched in celebration of an uncomplicated war won handily: "Big cheers also greeted veterans of World War I, World War II, Korea and Vietnam who marched in the parade."[58] The raucous mood of celebration extended to those soldiers as well, according to the print news narrative, as the end of a successful war marked a moment of collective victory for all soldiers past and present. Still, the truly redeemed, and those marked out for special attention, remained the Vietnam veterans, purged as they now were from the guilt and shame of criminal action, or possibly worse, defeat: "The response was especially sweet for Vietnam veterans, who had come home not to fanfare but to a nation torn by the controversial war."[59] Further extending the performative theater of the moment, coverage also pointed to the ceremonial reenlistment of some soldiers who were discharged after the end of the war only to be re-enlisted in a public demonstration accompanied by great fanfare. In one such ceremony, the presiding marshal was Hollywood royalty, and, it was emphasized that he himself was a former soldier: "A re-enlistment ceremony was staged before the parade for three Army reservists who served in the war. Actor Jimmy Stewart, who served as a bomber pilot in World War II and rose to the rank of brigadier general in the reserves, performed the ceremony."[60] The celebrity, longevity, and measured reliability of Old Hollywood in the personage of Jimmy Stewart sufficiently convey a sense of tradition and nostalgia to the postwar celebrations herein described. America has scored a badly needed win in a far-off theater of war and, in so doing, has ameliorated the transgressions of the past while paving a gilded road toward our own, military future.

The collective effect of these reminiscences in print coverage of the Gulf War and the postwar period is to create positive historical associations between the most recent military performance in the Persian Gulf and all military endeavors of the past in order to lionize the victors and wipe clean the slates of the vanquished. A special focus is paid to the legacy of Vietnam, which, in association with other, more successful, and uncontroversial American wars, casts a net of redemption over the soldiers and sailors whose military experience occurred during that much longer, much less popular, and much more psychically traumatizing war for the nation. Indeed, according to these frames of representation, the Gulf War effectively vanquished the memory of Vietnam and "has pulled America up and out of its post-Vietnam depression."[61] Descriptions of huge crowds and fawning celebrities remind us that this catharsis is indeed a national endeavor where average citizens rub shoulders with cultural elites in an ecstatic mélange of communal festivity. Past misdeeds are washed away by present successes, while similar military dominance is indicated for wars yet to come. As all the bunting, singing, chanting, and cheering give way to citizen testimony, the readership is plainly told exactly what all of the performative celebration of war and ceremonial merriment is supposed to mean: "It makes me proud to be an American."[62]

Yellow Ribbons: Imposed Sentimentality, Compulsory Unity

A number of distinct, and occasionally competing, historical narratives within American folklore have established yellow sashes, banners, and particularly ribbons as emblems of an overt display of patriotism in the country. One element of this tradition traces the custom back to the American Civil War and represents the color as a symbol of homecoming for soldiers returning from the front, or conversely, as a symbol of mourning for those who did not. A 1949 film starring John Wayne and Joanne Dru entitled *Round Her Neck She Wore A Yellow Ribbon* confirms that historical link, though evidence from the Civil War period itself is less readily available. In May of 1973, the song "Tie a Yellow Ribbon Round the Ole Oak Tree" by plop duo Tony Orlando and Dawn sold three million records in under a month, seemingly tapping into a war-weary public's desire for homecomings for American soldiers still deployed in large numbers in Vietnam. This song inspired, or at least extended, the practice of displaying yellow ribbons on homes or in storefronts across the country, an overt display of pro-military sentiment that lasted throughout the 1980s.[63] By the end of that decade and with the United States on the brink of war in the Persian Gulf, the practice of displaying yellow ribbons became ubiquitous, reflecting a public in lockstep with the country's military and political leadership throughout the American war in the Persian Gulf.[64]

This public demonstration of militarism and patriotism was likewise the focus of thousands of news articles during the Gulf War period. According to prominent discursive frames within that coverage, the yellow ribbon was simultaneously a symbol of the sentimental national mood, an emblem of support or approval of the American martial character, and/or a necessary commitment to the American military, the absence of which was viewed as conspicuous if not suspicious. Commonly, a distinct element of wistfulness accompanied news stories featuring discussions of yellow ribbons, as in one description: "Yellow ribbons, wrapped around trees, telephone polls [sic], satellite dishes, pinned to lapels, or fluttering from car radio antennas, mail boxes and shopping carts, have blossomed into a national reminder of combat in the gulf."[65] The article adeptly applies florid language in the depictions of flags "fluttering" and national emblems "blossoming" in an effort to communicate not a physical act of decoration but rather an emotional ornamentation evoking the purest elements of wistful Americana. Another period news piece, rife with sentimentality, was simply but evocatively entitled "A Father's Pride, A Yellow Ribbon." It described the Gulf War not through a description of tactics or military strategy but rather through the eyes of a proud father describing his son's deployment: "A few weeks ago, Glenn Ogdon, a 23-year-old Marine reservist [...] was called up. His father Donald, a retired psychology professor, was proud to see Glenn go. He recalls wishing him well and saying 'War is a terrible thing, but we've got to stop Hussein'."[66] Here, the love of country guides the son while the father, a professor and therefore a member of the country's intellectual elite, sets aside intellectual criticism in favor of emotionality and ultimately conformity, confessing: "We've got to stop Hussein." This particular piece of patriotic drama ends with the ultimate act of acquiescence on the part of the professorial father as he manifests his contrition physically: "Then the professor went out and tied a yellow ribbon around a tree in the front yard." This tight, dramatic narrative soothingly provides readers with a brief conflict, and then ultimately, with a comforting resolution. The son goes to war; the father supports the military; and a yellow ribbon flies proudly in the front yard.

The narrative hook of familial emotion and patriotic sentimentality abounds in news descriptions of a specific family from East Los Angeles. Within this print news media narrative, willing participation in the U.S. military and the latest American war effort is presented as a salve to emotional barriers and family tensions of the kind experienced by American families in the early 1990s. Beyond resolving troublesome family dynamics, war is remade as a salve for racism and poverty, too, if discursive frames within descriptions of the family are to be thoroughly absorbed. Indeed, an entire neighborhood reaps the benefits of American militarism as five residents of La Verne Avenue are deployed to the Persian Gulf: "And now there are five. Ramon Sandoval Jr., 23, a lance corporal in the Marine Corps has become the fifth son that La Verne Avenue has sent to the Persian Gulf."[67] Readers are informed that this is not just any American neighborhood but rather a hard-scrabble neighborhood populated by primarily Hispanic families full of pride for their contribution to the country's war effort: "In this corner of East Los Angeles—a barrio of working-class folks wedged between Whittier and Olympic boulevards-the discovery of yet another boy from La Verne in the war zone is a source of great pride."[68]

Situated in challenging economic circumstances though they were, readers are assured old that the families of La Verne Avenue generally, and the Sandoval family in particular, were normal, honorable, and traditional American families: "An outgoing athlete who excelled at football and baseball at Nogales High School in La Puente, Sandoval initially was overlooked in the neighborhood nose-counting of Gulf participants because his father [...] usually is away during the week, working at a sea-food exporting business."[69] Participating, even excelling in typical American pastimes like football and baseball, situates this narrative's protagonist in the in-group, a typical American prepared to serve the country in that most laudable of ways, to join the U.S. military during their war effort. The patriarch of the family is likewise bestowed with traditional, honorable, and stereotypically American character traits, according to media representations, being that he is an exceptionally hard worker and therefore "away during the week." Finally, readers are provided with a satisfying conclusion to what is ostensibly a news desk piece published during ongoing military action in the Gulf War: "'Don't worry,' said Reyes [a Sandoval neighbor]. 'You're now one of us'."[70] The ultimate reward for this conspicuous service and sacrifice, readers are informed, is acceptance, belonging, and membership within the national military tribe. This emotive, dramatic, and ultimately satisfying family and community narrative was published under the overtly sentimental title "Field of Yellow Ribbons Waves as Street Sends 5th Son to Gulf."

The symbol of the yellow ribbon was not confined to overt displays of emotional or patriotic sentimentality, though. At the conclusion of the war, authoritative news media discourse converted the yellow ribbon from a symbol of wistful Americana into an emblem of robust, hyper-masculine patriotism as journalists joined with military and political leadership on a victory lap of the country. These narratives were notable for their overt championing of all things military while they simultaneously omitted or otherwise self selected stories critical of the war or the hyper-militant national mood. Through them all, the yellow ribbon featured prominently as a symbol of pride, of boastful victory, and of an overt form of militant nationalism. One article glibly entitled "Yellow Fever" loudly promoted that the national mood was one of "celebration" and of what "many Americans seem to consider as a national rejuvenation."[71] This jubilant mood was ubiquitous according to this narrative, a unity of purpose that was, in fact, driven by war itself: "Once combat started [...] the doubts of all but a small minority seemed to have been instantly resolved."[72] This article and dozens of other similarly ecstatic news pieces published in the aftermath of the coalition victory informed the readership of the triumphant nature of this war and of the myriad of benefits it brought back with it to the home front. Of course, a critical component central to receiving these benefits is the concept of victory. America won; Iraq lost. The distance between our army and their army, recast as the moral and intellectual distance between us and them, remains vast. Gleefully recalling Theodore Roosevelt's quip about the Spanish-American War (see Chapter 2 in this book), this author finishes his narrative with a paean to the American war and to victory itself: "Above all, this war, from its first day, was *victorious* [...] it was a war quickly finished, too quickly for battlefield attrition or home-front second thoughts—'a splendid little war' indeed"[73] (emphasis in the original).

Other examples from period news discourse proclaimed the ubiquity of the yellow ribbons and held aloft this uncritical support of American war as a marker of national strength and a laudable, unquestioning loyalty to the state. Typically, period pieces were presented as uncritical descriptions of rallies and marches that were held around the country in the weeks and months after the war's end: "Carrying American flags, sporting yellow ribbons and occasionally chanting 'USA! USA!' about 500 people marched and rallied yesterday in Northwest Washington in a Persian Gulf victory celebration."[74] Other descriptions quantified these patriotic symbols in an unusual form of wartime one-upmanship wherein various parts of the country possibly attempted to outdo one another in overt displays of national pride, as in: "More than 1,000 yards of yellow ribbon were tied to the trees in front of the Corona Civic Center on Wednesday to show the city employees' support for troops in the Persian Gulf";[75] or "Across the Washington area thousands of houses, cars and mailboxes are decorated with yellow ribbons, flags and other tributes to show support of the soldiers serving in the Persian Gulf."[76] Other news pieces simply embraced the ubiquity of this wartime symbol, fully committing to the paroxysm of unquestioning patriotism that gripped the country throughout the Gulf War period: "Yellow ribbons, banners and U.S. flags are popping up everywhere around the San Gabriel Valley, and marches and rallies supporting U.S. troops in the Persian Gulf are planned."[77]

In sum, authoritative print news media descriptions of overt displays of yellow ribbons during the First Gulf War uncritically extended the militant patriotism of the American public to attendant readership, constructing paeans to the United States armed forces, to our collective national identity, and to the political leadership that called forward these militant policies in the first place. In this way, the print press played its own, crucial role in the war by extending pro-military and pro-state narratives and by imbuing national symbols like the yellow ribbon with exceptional levels of nostalgia, emotion, loyalty, and/or sentimentality. Through these discursive strategies, the print news media aided substantially in the dissemination of full-throated expressions of patriotism and self-satisfying celebrations of Americana before, during, and certainly after the conclusion of the brief but consequential Persian Gulf War.

Conclusions: Duplicitous Policy, Ubiquitous Patriotism

The American entry into the politics and social dynamics of Iraq in the early 1980s was predicated upon the U.S. desire to cooperate with a brutal dictator on the premise of the ancient edict cum staple political policymaking: "the enemy of my enemy is my friend." At the point in time when that friend, Iraq, funded and sustained through nearly a decade of close diplomatic support from the United States, sought retribution for perceived wrongs against another regional ally, Kuwait, the U.S. abruptly reversed course. Having assured Saddam Hussein of American apathy toward Arab-Arab conflicts, the first Bush White House changed its mind and worked through diplomatic channels to deter Saddam while loudly and frequently condemning the man himself as the incarnation of evil (public comparisons between Saddam and Hitler from U.S. government officials were not uncommon). The logical question to ask as this geopolitical dynamic unfolded on the global stage was, "If he was evil now, why had the United States been working so closely with him before? It was hard to claim that some essential flaw in Saddam's character had only just been revealed, having been previously masked."[78] The print news media analysis provided in this chapter amply demonstrates that this vital institution within the American social fabric was profoundly uninterested in asking this question on the eve of another American war. Rather, the news media institutions generally and print news media organs specifically began to rally around pro-state and pro-military symbolism and messaging in the United States, helping to pave the way toward another large-scale American military commitment on foreign soil.

As it happened, that commitment was swift and successful, unlike the drawn-out, costly, and unpopular American military experience in Vietnam (which was assessed for its media coverage in the previous chapter). As evidenced by the prolific referencing to the Vietnam War that occurred during the 1991 war in the Persian Gulf, the media were cognizant of the deep fractures their coverage of Vietnam precipitated within the American public and were collectively determined not to stage a repeat of their critical output of that era: "The extent to which the perceived lessons of Vietnam were adapted by the Pentagon [...] ensure[d] that a desired media perspective was being taken [...] of the information war in the Gulf."[79] As a result, embedded within the complex reality of wartime coverage was a series of patterns, a constructed discourse asserted through the creation and distribution of frames of news media representation.[80] These frames consistently emphasized particular narrative tropes, among them the precision and technical competence of the new U.S. Army; the extent to which the clean victory in the Gulf erased the record of dirty defeat in Vietnam; and, as indicated, the ubiquity of the either nostalgic or hyper-aggressive patriotism of the public at large in their all but unanimous support of the military during the Gulf War. The consequences of these frames of representation substantially contributed to the construction of a new, refreshed, and repackaged American perception of war in the post-Vietnam era. The following, and final, case study chapter will explore the extent to which this reanimated public perception held true during yet another American war of choice in the Middle East, this one also launched against erstwhile American ally Saddam Hussein, though instigated in the years just after the dawn of the twenty-first century.

Notes

1 Phillip M. Taylor, *War and the Media: Propaganda and Persuasion in the Gulf War* (Manchester: Manchester University Press, 1998), xv–xvi.

2 Jean Shaoul, "The Bombing of Iraq: An Old Tradition in the Anglo-American Alliance," *The Greanville Post*, 2003, May 31. https://www.greanvillepost.com/2014/10/06/the-bombing-of-iraq-an-old-tradition-on-the-west/.

3 Kathleen M. Langley, "Iraq: Some Aspects of the Economic Scene," *Middle East Journal* 18, no. 2 (1964): 180–88. http://www.jstor.org/stable/4323702.

4 These complaints of the Qassim regime recalled old grievances between Iraq and Kuwait that dated back to the birth of these nation-states, and even before: "The Uqair agreements of 1922–1923 specified Kuwait's northern borders with Iraq, following the lines of those defined in the U.S.-Ottoman convention of 1913—a convention that had never been ratified. The 1923 borders were favorable to Kuwait, since they gave it the islands of Bubiyan and Warba. The emirate's northwestern and western borders were specified in the Iraqi-Kuwaiti convention of 1932, after Iraq had become an independent state. Despite its formal recognition of Kuwait in 1963, Iraq continued to request modifications of the borders, particularly with respect to the islands" (Alberto Bin, Richard Hill, and Archer Jones, *Desert Storm: A Forgotten War* (Westport: Praeger Publishers, 1998), 13).

5 R. Sale, "Saddam-CIA links (1959-1990)," *Peace Research* 35, no. 1 (2003): 17–20. https://www.proquest.com/scholarly-journals/saddam-cia-links-1959-1990/docview/213485200/se-2.

6 At least one high-ranking government official from the Cold War-era has spoken publicly of the link between the Kennedy administration and the Ba'ath Party overthrow of Qassim: "[Former National Security Council staffer Roger] Morris claimed recently that the CIA was behind the coup, which was sanctioned by President John F. Kennedy" (Ibid).

7 Andrew Bacevich, *America's War for the Greater Middle East: A Military History* (New York: Random House, 2016), 88–89.

8 Ian Black, "Iran and Iraq Remember War that Cost More than a Million Lives," *The Guardian*, September 23, 2010 (Manchester). https://www.theguardian.com/world/2010/sep /23/iran-iraq-war-anniversary.

9 Stephen Kinzer, *Overthrow: America's Century of Regime Change from Hawaii to Iraq* (New York: Times Books, 2006), 286.

10 Ibid., 286–87.

11 Lawrence Freedman, *A Choice of Enemies: America Confronts the Middle East* (New York: Public Affairs, 2009), 157.

12 Bacevich, *America's War for the Greater Middle East*, 91.

13 Ibid.

14 Ibid.

15 Freedman, *A Choice of Enemies*, 166.

16 Bacevich, *America's War for the Greater Middle East*, 111.

17 Freedman, *A Choice of Enemies*, 216.

18 Bacevich, *America's War for the Greater Middle East*, 111.

19 Freedman, *A Choice of Enemies*, 219.

20 Ibid., 220.

21 Ibid.

22 Bin, Hill, and Jones. *Desert Storm*, 13.

23 Ibid., 67.

24 Ibid., 140.

25 Ibid., 5.

26 Ibid., 211.

27 Bacevich, *America's War for the Greater Middle East*, 112.

28 Arthur Bloom (Dir), Morley Safer, Presenter, "*Nayirah*," *CBS News*, 1992, January 19, 15 min., 25 sec. https://www.youtube.com/watch?v=vdjsT1oDrss.

29 Ibid.

30 Hill and Knowlton President Craig Fuller was interviewed for the groundbreaking "60 Minutes" story in January of 1991 that revealed the double dealings of Hill and Knowlton, Nayirah, and the Bush administration, and openly boasted of the hand-in-glove relationship shared between his public relations firm and the presidential administration for whom he had recently worked: "Almost spontaneously, as the Kuwaitis were talking to us, we were also talking to the people in the [Bush] administration to find out how we could be supportive with respect to the president's program" (Ibid).

31 James E. Grunig, "Public Relations and International Affairs: Effects, Ethics and Responsibility," *Journal of International Affairs* 47, no. 1 (1993): 137. http://www.jstor.org/stable /24357090.

32 Ibid.

33 Bloom (Dir), Morley Safer, Presenter. "*Nayirah*," *CBS News*.

34 Jarol B. Manheim, "Strategic Public Diplomacy: Managing Kuwait's Image during the Gulf Conflict," in W. Lance Bennet and David L. Paletz (eds.), *Taken by Storm: The Media, Public Opinion, and U.S. Foreign Policy in the Gulf War* (Chicago: The University of Chicago Press, 1994), 140.

35 Manheim, "Strategic Public Diplomacy," 140.

36 Bloom (Dir), Morley Safer, Presenter, "*Nayirah*," *CBS News*.

37 Freedman, *A Choice of Enemies*, 230–31.

38 Bloom (Dir), Morley Safer, Presenter, "*Nayirah*," *CBS News*.

39 Ibid., 278.

40 Analyst Phillip M. Taylor describes the February 13, 1991, destruction of a civilian shelter as follows: "At about 04:30 (Iraqi time) two allied bombs, some reports said several minutes apart, shattered the roof of a facility apparently containing civilians, mainly women and

children. The Iraqis lifted all censorship restrictions as daylight revealed the sheer extent of the horror now available to their propagandists in and around the Amiriya instillation [*sic*]. According to early reports, possibly 500 or even 1,000 were said to have been killed." Though belying the collective narrative of a clean or precise war, these Iraqi civilian deaths did nothing to remove the gloss from the U.S. military victory in the Persian Gulf and had no effect on the public approval rating of either the military or the Bush administration during this period (Taylor, *War and the Media*, 188).

41 Charles Leroux, "Smart' Weapons at Head of Class," *Chicago Tribune*, January 20, 1991, 1.
42 Ibid.
43 Evelyn Richards, "Lowdown on High-Tech Weapons in Gulf War: Systems Could Be Better if Pentagon Kept Pace With Advances in Electronics, Experts Say," *Washington Post*, January 27, 1991, A9.
44 Guy Gugliotta, "High-Flying War May Next Come Down to Earth; Ground Must Still Be Won," *The Washington Post*, January 20, 1991, A27.
45 Edward N. Luttwak, "Splendid Sorties, Tangential Targets War: Big Air Statistics Suggest Much Is Being Accomplished. But Little of that Reduces the Need for a Ground Offensive," *Los Angeles Times*, January 30, 1991, 7.
46 William J. Broad, "War in the Gulf: High Tech: War Hero Status Possible for the Computer Chip," *Chicago Tribune*, January 21, 1991, A8.
47 Ibid.
48 Taylor, *War and the Media*, 188.
49 Melissa Healy, "Radar Choreographed the Allies' Aerial Ballet: Tactics: An Elaborate Network Coordinated 24 Types of Aircraft from Five Nations during Iraq Raids," *Los Angeles Times*, January 18, 1991, A7.
50 Luttwak, "Splendid Sorties," *Los Angeles Times*, January 30, 1991, 7.
51 Jane Seaberry, "Flying Symbols of Patriotism; Home Decorations Show Support for Troops in Gulf," *The Washington Post*, February 27, 1991, D01.
52 Ibid.
53 Among the many important works that have deconstructed the myths surrounding the rumored ill-treatment of Vietnam veterans returning to the United States, this work has relied upon H. Bruce Franklin's critical 1992 publication *M.I.A. or Mythmaking in America: How and Why Belief in Live POWs Has Possessed a Nation*.
54 Eric Bailey, "200,000 Cheer Troops in O.C. Victory Parade Celebration: Gulf Veterans Get a Warm Welcome Home. Spectators View Military Might on Land and in Air," *Los Angeles Times*, May 19, 1991, 1.
55 Ibid.
56 Scott Harris and Josh Meyer, "Gulf Troops Welcomed With Hollywood Flair Parade: Hundreds of Thousands Watch Them March in Festive Display. Veterans of All Conflicts Are Honored," *Los Angeles Times*, May 20, 1991, 1.
57 Ibid.
58 Ibid.
59 Ibid.
60 Ibid.
61 Ellen Goodman, "Ties that Bind Behind Ribbons, War Enthusiasm Reflects Yearning for Community," *Chicago Tribune*, May 3, 1991, 8.
62 Harris and Meyer, "Gulf Troops Welcomed With Hollywood Flair Parade," *Los Angeles Times*, May 20, 1991, 1.
63 The display of a yellow ribbon was also given perhaps an unnatural longevity once it was recreated as a symbol of national solidarity with the American hostages captured by revolutionaries in Iran and held in captivity there for 444 days. According to one news source: "The yellow ribbon, inspired by a 1973 song and popularized during the Iran hostage crisis that ended in January 1981" Iran Alessandra Stanley, "War in the Gulf: Home Front; War's Ribbons Are Yellow with Meaning of Many Hues," *New York Times*, February 3, 1991, A1.
64 Gerald E. Parsons, "How the Yellow Ribbon Became a National Folk Symbol," *Folklife News* XIII, no. Summer 1991 (1991): 9–11. Accessed April 26, 2023. https://www.loc.gov/folklife/ribbons/ribbons.html.
65 Stanley, "War in the Gulf," *New York Times*, February 3, 1991, A1.

66 "A Father's Pride, A Yellow Ribbon," *New York Times*, January 9, 1991, A8.
67 George Ramos, "Field of Yellow Ribbons Waves as Street Sends 5th Son to Gulf: On La Verne: A War Diary: Five U.S. Servicemen in the Middle East Hail from a Single East Los Angeles Street," *Los Angeles Times*, February 11, 1991, 9.
68 Ibid.
69 Ibid.
70 Ibid.
71 Tom Wicker, "Yellow Fever," *The New York Times*, February 27, 1991, A27.
72 Ibid.
73 Ibid.
74 Eric Charles, "Gulf Victory Celebration Draws 500 to District: Marchers Express Firm Support for Veterans," *The Washington Post*, March 10, 1991, A26.
75 Ted Johnson, "Corona Shows Its True Colors Support: The Civic Center Is Awash in Yellow Ribbons as Employees Pay Tribute to Troops," *The Washington Post*, January 31, 1991, 11.
76 Seaberry, "Flying Symbols of Patriotism," *The Washington Post*, February 27, 1991, D01.
77 Franki V. Ransom, "Rallies Planned Throughout the Valley to Support Troops," *Los Angeles Times*, January 31, 1991, 2.
78 Freedman, *A Choice of Enemies*, 231.
79 Taylor, *War and the Media*, 272.
80 Patrick O'Heffernan, "A Mutual Exploitation Model of Media Influence in U.S. Foreign Policy," in W. Lance Bennet and David L. Paletz (eds.), *Taken By Storm: The Media, Public Opinion, and U.S. Foreign Policy in the Gulf War* (Chicago: The University of Chicago Press, 1994), 243.

Chapter Seven

IRAQ PART II: INVASION, OCCUPATION, AND IMPERIAL OVERREACH

The two wars that the United States launched preemptively were the pet projects of special interest groups that used the attacks of 9/11 as a cover to hijack American foreign policy and implement their private agendas. These interest groups include the military-industrial complex and the professional armed forces [...] and neoconservative enthusiasts for the creation of an American empire.[1]

—*Chalmers Johnson, 2004*

Destination Imperium: Iraq 2003

By any standard of military measure, the U.S. war against Saddam Hussein after his ill-fated invasion of Kuwait was a massive success. The U.S. military, along with their coalition partners, acting at the behest of international opinion as rendered by the United Nations, destroyed a substantial amount of the dictator's military capability and forced his hasty retreat to Baghdad. There, though still in power, Saddam became increasingly isolated as he and his regime were the targets of a series of UN sanctions intended to further restrict his martial reach while also potentially fomenting domestic rebellion against his autocratic regime. This rebellion was meant to explode from the heartland of Kurdistan, an ethnically distinct region of northern Iraq frequently mentioned by U.S. president George H. W. Bush throughout the Gulf War period as being prepared for and worthy of independence. Indeed, in the aftermath of the 1991 war, the Kurds were encouraged by Bush and other U.S. officials to rise up against Saddam and wrest control of the northern Kurdish regions of Iraq away from Baghdad. Commitments of funding and general support were offered by American officials to political and military leadership in Kurdistan, encouraging this action. Kurdish leadership kept their part of the bargain and, in the aftermath of the U.S. military defeat of Iraq, took up arms against the central government of Iraq in an attempt to create an independent Kurdistan in its region of ethnic dominance within Iraq. But the H. W. Bush administration reneged on their promise. The resulting fight between lightly armed Kurdish nationalists and heavily equipped Iraqi Army regulars was a slaughter:

> Saddam responded with pitiless repression [...] Thousands were killed. Many hundreds of thousands more fled. In the United States and elsewhere in the West, images of forlorn Kurdish refugees, huddled in the desolate Turkish outback without food, water, or shelter, led nightly news programs [...] Meanwhile, the forces under Schwarzkopf's command, still occupying southern Iraq as they prepared to redeploy, did nothing. The result was an epic humanitarian disaster and a huge embarrassment for the United States[2].

It is doubtful whether the deaths of thousands of Kurds (and thousands more Iraqi Shi'a) at the hands of an unrestrained Saddam Hussein caused President Bush or anyone else in his administration any "embarrassment," despite their frequent encouragement of armed Kurdish rebellion against postwar Iraq. Quite the contrary, Washington insiders seemed content to treat Saddam's slaughter of those led into the fight by the Bush administration as business as usual. Administration representatives typically did not even count this mass death among the direct consequences of U.S. operations in the Middle East during the Persian Gulf War.

But that doesn't mean that military and political managers in the United States became unconcerned with Iraq or Saddam Hussein after 1991. In many ways, Saddam Hussein's Iraq became an obsession of the remainder of the H. W. Bush administration and remained so in Bill Clinton's administration beginning in 1992. In fact, between 1990 and 2002, no fewer than 49 U.S.-backed UN resolutions were passed targeting Saddam Hussein and his regime.[3] A number of these resolutions focused on his military capacity and the potential threat of a long-distance chemical or biological weapons program, the infrastructure of which was irrevocably damaged as a result of bombing during the Gulf War. The more punitive of these resolutions, though, and those with much more sinister outcomes targeted the transmission of civilian goods and supplies, including foodstuffs and medicine, into Iraq. Partially enforced by a joint U.S.-U.K no-fly zone over Iraq during this period, the outcomes of these restrictive sanctions, ostensibly designed to encourage more domestic discontent among the Iraqi people, in fact had the effect, well known at the time, of killing civilians, especially the most vulnerable among the Iraqi populous. Debate still circulates around the intent and impact of these U.S.-backed international measures, but a conservative estimate published by Columbia University in the year 2000 acknowledged that over 200,000 Iraqi children below the age of five died during this period in excess of expected child mortality in the region.[4] It is widely accepted that these, and other deaths, are directly attributable to the international imposition of U.S. policy goals in Iraq in the 1990s.

But the H. W. Bush administration did not stop to dwell on inconveniences like mass civilian casualties or the most recent betrayal of the Kurdish national oeuvre.[5] The American defeat of Saddam Hussein in Gulf War I, coupled with the end of the Cold War in the wake of the collapse of the Soviet Union, had brought the United States to a position of global *hyperpuissance*. George H. W. Bush rode these momentous historical events to a domestic approval rating of over 90 percent, while the United States likewise enjoyed a measure of respectability both within the Middle East and internationally. Still, Saddam Hussein remained in power. From the purview of Washington, though, he was a useful heel, safely contained within Iraq and unable to threaten regional stability. Though within his own borders his power was absolute, as evidenced by his retribution against the Kurds and the Shi'a in 1991, he was a known quantity, brash and boastful, but ultimately internationally insignificant. Saddam was left in power, then, to reap what damage he might against his own populations but sufficiently cowed so as not to antagonize U.S. allies in the region like Saudi Arabia and Israel. Moving through the 1990s, the Washington elite was content with that policy decision, too, as expressed in 1994 by future vice president to the second Bush administration, Dick Cheney:[6]

If we would have gone into Baghdad, we would have been all alone. There wouldn't have been anybody else with us. It would have been a U.S. occupation of Iraq, and none of the Arab forces that were willing to fight with us in Kuwait were willing to invade Iraq. Once you got to Iraq and took it over and took down Saddam's government, then what are you going to put in its place? That's a very volatile part of the world and if you take down the central government in Iraq, you can easily end up seeing pieces of Iraq fly off. Part of it the Syrians would like to have to the West. Part of eastern Iraq, the Iranians would like to claim [...] If the Kurds spin loose and join with the Kurds in Turkey then you threaten the territorial integrity of Turkey. It's a quagmire if you go that far and try to take over Iraq.[7]

This creditable assessment of the manifest reasons not to invade Iraq, topple Saddam's government, and attempt to rebuild it in an American image surprisingly enough came from the mouth of the man who would preside over precisely those policy maneuvers in the second Bush administration, that of George H. W. Bush's son, George W. Bush. His presidency began ignominiously in 2001, years after this prescient analysis was uttered. Until then, this off-the-cuff policy brief from future vice president Dick Cheney effectively encapsulated the American position vis-à-vis Saddam Hussein throughout the decade of the 1990s. Then, apparently, everything changed.

On September 11, 2001, 19 hijackers hailing from various points of origin throughout the Middle East (15 of them Saudi) seized four commercial planes in the United States and flew them into various buildings along the Eastern Sea Board of the United States. The most destructive of these kamikaze raids hit the two towers comprising the World Trade Center in downtown New York City early on a Tuesday morning, sending enough fuel, flame, detritus, and destruction throughout those buildings to bring them both to the ground. 2,977 American civilians died during that attack, as well as the 19 hijackers. The attack was the masterstroke of the senior leadership of Al-Qaeda, Arabic for "The Base," a shadowy group then operating off the grid primarily in the frontier areas between Pakistan and Afghanistan and determined to foist an arch-conservative, millenarian vision of Islam onto both the Muslim and Western worlds. The attack was as shocking to the American system as it was to the rest of the world. After that shock wore off and the criminal masterminds behind the attacks were identified, the United States invaded Afghanistan in early October of 2001 in order to punish the Taliban government[8] there for harboring Al-Qaeda leadership, particularly the most public face of the organization, the disgraced heir of a multimillion dollar Saudi construction firm, Osama Bin Laden. Quickly seizing the initiative in a country already denuded by war, foreign occupation, and protracted civil strife, the United States established a foreign military occupation in Afghanistan under the auspices of self-defense that lasted until May of 2021: the longest war in American history.

But Iraq was never far from the minds of the senior leadership of the second Bush administration, the so-called Neoconservatives, whose stark view of human society postulated America and its allies in the camp of good, viewed Islam and the East as evil, and emphasized military resolutions over diplomacy in most political scenarios. This insular clique, with such familiar names as Dick Cheney, Condoleezza Rice, Donald Rumsfeld, and Paul Wolfowitz, became fixated upon Iraq as the next country to, once again, be subject to American military might. Despite the fact that "no credible evidence [existed] that Iraq had anything to do with the terrorist attacks against the World Trade Center and the Pentagon or more generally that Iraq is collaborating with al Qaeda,"[9] the Neocons and their Beltway allies began circulating rumors that Saddam Hussein was attempting to buy yellowcake uranium from Niger, a necessary precursor for the construction of a nuclear weapon. In February 2002, after having been dispatched to Niger to investigate the veracity of this rumor, diplomat Joseph Wilson published an op-ed in the *New York Times* identifying these claims as utterly false.[10] Ignoring the inconvenient facts of the matter, on February 5, 2003, Bush's secretary of state Colin Powell was dispatched to address the UN Security Council and to press the case for military intervention in Iraq on the basis of the yellowcake uranium lie. Fearing more bloodshed in the Middle East, during the weekend of February 15, 2003, as many as ten million citizens in 60 countries took to the streets to protest the impending U.S. war in Iraq. It was the largest civil protest against a single political action in world history.[11] That mass movement, along with the March 2003 report from UN weapons inspector Hans Blix that inspections in Iraq were progressing satisfactorily, gave many international peace activists hope that another American-made Middle Eastern war could be avoided. In the end, though, they did not stave off America's next war of choice. In March 2003, the Bush administration announced that diplomacy had failed and international weapons inspectors were advised to leave Iraq. By March 20th of that year, in a maneuver all too familiar to observers around the world, the U.S. invasion of Iraq began.

Photo 11 The results of a U.S. bombing campaign in Iraq during the American invasion in 2003.

War and Insurgency: The Iraq War Debacle

The U.S. invasion and occupation of Iraq was packaged and sold to the American public as a necessary police action set in motion to remove a dangerous and volatile dictator. Promised as a swift and inexpensive military exercise, the American people were told that the region and its peoples—a myriad of established and diverse confessional and ethnic communities that senior Bush administration officials clearly neither valued nor understood—would welcome the United States and Allied forces as "liberators."[12] Further, repeated messages from the Bush administration assured the American people and a large international audience as well that the U.S. invasion and occupation of Iraq was necessary for two primary reasons: first, Saddam Hussein was in possession of weapons of mass destruction and he was looking to acquire more, possibly even nuclear weapons, as the debunked yellowcake uranium story was meant to indicate. Secondly, Saddam himself was partnered with nefarious global actors like Al-Qaeda who intend to spread destruction all across the world, particularly in places where Americans or American interests are located.[13] Each of these justifications for still more American war in the Middle East was touted often by administration officials and pro-war spokespeople from the intelligence services and the defense industry, but it was the second element, Saddam's alleged connection to global terrorist networks, that gave this iteration of American war against Iraq both its Orwellian name and its timeless and nebulous purpose:

> We were sold the war in Iraq as part of the "war on terror." This was a war that would supposedly make the world safer in the wake of 9/11. Iraq was supporting terrorism and Saddam's "weapons of mass destruction" were an immediate threat they might either be deployed directly or passed to terrorists. Spreading democracy would itself promote security—if only on the logic that democratic countries are less likely to go to war.[14]

According to this framing by administration officials, the American war against Iraq in 2003 was not one with a limited scope or short-term objectives. The war in Iraq would be but a piece in a large puzzle, the design of which posits a global American military presence in any country deemed a threat to American interests, whether in the Middle East or elsewhere. Put another way: "The 'war on terror' represents the new application of an old doctrine: the doctrine of endless war."[15]

Having laid the groundwork for another Middle Eastern war despite a significant domestic opposition and broadscale international resistance at both the state and street level, the Bush administration pushed ahead unilaterally having lost virtually all of the support from coalition partners that marked the 1991 Gulf War against Saddam years earlier (one notable exception, Tony Blair's Britain, seemed to be in lockstep with the American Neocon's binary vision of twenty-first century geopolitics). On March 20, 2003, the invasion of Iraq began with a simultaneous aerial assault and coordinated ground attack. On April 9, 2003, U.S. forces captured and occupied the Iraqi capital, Baghdad. News footage showed what seemed to be spontaneous, effusive celebration coming from thousands of joyous Iraq nationals. To celebrate the occasions, U.S. forces joined with the Iraqis to desecrate a potent symbol of Saddam Hussein's power and authority, apparently undertaking this joint project on a whim. But all was not as it seemed:

US marines and a group of apparently jubilant Iraqis tore down the giant bronze statue of Saddam in Firdos Square in central Baghdad. Portrayed to the world as the spontaneous actions of a people's liberation, the scene was in fact carefully choreographed by the US Psychological Operations Unit, designed to serve the twin purposes of a mass media spectacle and to promote the legitimacy of the war across a sceptical globe.[16]

That deception successfully achieved and splashed across all major media outlets in the United States, U.S. forces moved on to Tikrit, Iraq, Saddam Hussein's hometown. That city fell to U.S. hands on April 13, and while easy military successes were stacking up for the American air and ground units in this war, casualties on the Iraqi side in the early stages of the war were disturbingly high "with numbers of military dead normally put at over 9,000 and civilian dead at over 7,000."[17]

Clearly, this was related to the hyper-aggressive tactics that defined the early military operations undertaken and executed by exuberant U.S. forces: "Methods employed by U.S. forces invited comparison with the tactics of intimidation that Israeli troops used in policing the West Bank. These included the destruction of homes belonging to families of anyone suspected of being an insurgent."[18] As casualties mounted and questions were raised about U.S. military methods that included free-fire zones in civilian areas and collective arrests of whole neighborhoods of fighting-aged men on a whim, Bush administration officials continued to refute eyewitness reports of U.S. military excess in Iraq. More disturbing still to critics of U.S. war policy and military tactics in Iraq was what these tactics indicated for the long term of U.S. military and political involvement in the Middle East. Clearly, the stated aims of the Bush administration—to topple Saddam and root out terrorist networks in the region—belied unspoken desires to occupy Iraq and remain there long into the future. Comparisons between the U.S. posture in Iraq and the ongoing Israeli occupation of Palestine were, therefore, obvious: "Parallel methods suggested parallel aims. The 'get tough' posture of Israeli Defense Forces reflected an Israeli determination to maintain a permanent grip on the West Bank. That U.S. forces were taking a similar approach raised the specter of the United States maintaining permanent control of Iraq, Washington's insistence to the contrary notwithstanding."[19] The U.S. military was not just a seek-and-destroy force in Iraq in the spring and summer of 2003. They were a shock troop laying the groundwork for a long, drawn-out military occupation of another sovereign state. To administer that long occupation, Washington needed a government entity in Baghdad to carry out the military and economic priorities of the Bush administration.

The Coalition Provisional Authority (CPA) was established in Baghdad in April 2003 under Jay Garner in order to serve as Iraq's de facto government once Saddam's Ba'athist, socialist state had been thoroughly destroyed. Garner intended on using the CPA to reconstruct Iraq in earnest and to provide as many necessary state functions for the Iraqi people as possible. After a month, he was unceremoniously fired in a phone call from U.S. defense secretary Donald Rumsfeld. His replacement, L. Paul "Jerry" Bremer, was hand-picked by George W. Bush and would operate the CPA until the end of its remit in July of 2004. The headquarters for the CPA and for the entire American presence within Iraq was inside Baghdad's Green Zone, a heavily fortified base of operations in the center of the city, outside of which Bremer and his administration rarely ventured. As head of the only functional government in the country, Bremer became the de facto ruler of Iraq and began remaking the country into a free-market paradise, authoring a radical, top-down economic transformation of the country in order to facilitate Western access to Iraqi oil wealth quite apart from any interest in, or concern for, the needs of the Iraqi people themselves:

> From deep inside his Green Zone fortress, Bremer issued decree after decree about how Iraq should be remade into a model free-market economy [...] Bremer ordered, for instance, that Iraq should have a 15 percent flat tax [...] and that government should be dramatically down-sized [...] Bremer, with an eye on the fossil fuel fields of Iraq and beyond, was determined to get his country makeover done before Iraqis went to the polls and had any kind of say in what their "liberated" future would look like.[20]

Bremer did not stop there. As head of the CPA, he also issued decrees that dismantled the Iraqi Army and fired any former soldiers who fought for Saddam immediately. He also fired all Ba'ath Party members from positions throughout the country with no regard for the fact that most held only nominal party membership since it was required for professional advancement in a myriad of industries throughout Iraq during the period of Ba'ath Party rule. Bremer and the CPA also made sectarianism worse in the country by marginalizing the Sunnis in the country for fear of their continued allegiance to Saddam, thereby establishing a highly sectarian federal system that remains in many tangible ways to this day. Bremer also never thought to protect ancient Iraqi antiquities, which were looted wholesale under the CPA watch, nor did he ever provide for a civil police force in the country during his time in power. In short, Bremer's emphasis on market economics over and above civil, social, or political reconstruction or rehabilitation was, predictably, a disaster for Iraq, one that led to untold violence and destruction that will take generations to resolve.

The failures of the CPA administration under Bremer combined with the unnecessarily brutal tactics of the U.S. soldiers in Iraq during the early stages of the American occupation left hundreds of thousands of Iraqis without jobs and without safety or security, but with a great deal of understandable anger about the current state of affairs in their country. And many of them, especially recently fired former soldiers, were "very well-armed and well-trained members of the military and security apparatus—without an adequate source of income."[21] Predictably, shortly after the American overthrow of Saddam Hussein, an organized insurgency began to assert itself within the country. After a series of calculated sectarian attacks by politically savvy and self-interested ethno-military forces, Iraq was riven into three: the Sunni Kurdish north, the Sunni Arab west, and the Shi'a Arab southeast, the majority ethnic group under whose leadership the new Iraq was meant to be reconstituted. Throughout 2004, U.S. casualties climbed, reaching a peak of 1,431 soldiers wounded in November of that year.[22] Iraqi deaths soared, too, most often during this period from Iraqi-on-Iraq violence resulting from sectarian attacks in a dangerously unstable political landscape. Iraq, the former bastion of sectarian cooperation where the distinction between Sunni and Shi'a used to be difficult to

Photo 12 A prisoner of U.S. forces in Iraq.

distinguish because of generations of comingling and cohabitation, began to look more like an internecine nightmare-scape, a land of seemingly interminable civil despair that would persist for more than a decade after the heinous protestation of an American military "Mission Accomplished."[23] And punctuating this escalating violence and profound social instability, in April of 2004, photos began to circulate among major international news organizations showing American soldiers abusing Iraqi prisoners at a location that would become infamous in the rehashing of this gruesome story: Abu Ghraib.

Abu Ghraib: The American Legacy in Iraq

As part and parcel of military control of the country, U.S. forces in Iraq operated the prison system there, focusing these operational resources in particular on any Iraqi civilian suspected of being part of the burgeoning armed resistance to U.S. forces. Among the facilities U.S. forces occupied during this phase of the war was the prison at Abu Ghraib, a sprawling, remote edifice employed by Saddam Hussein to house and torment some of the most detestable criminals in Iraq, alongside not a few of Saddam's personal and political rivals. For U.S. forces, though, Abu Ghraib became a catch-all site housing thousands of detainees (including families and children), many or most of whom were arbitrarily arrested in massive, neighborhood-wide sweeps that became the stock and trade of U.S. soldiers on patrol throughout Iraq after the collapse of the Saddam government. For the U.S. soldiers deployed to Abu Ghraib as prison guards, weeks on end without contact with their supervisors was compounded by an already unclear chain of command. Occasionally, plain-clothed officers without identification would show up at Abu Ghraib, demanding access to certain individuals. Other times officers, some CIA field agents, others uniform military, would demand a particular prisoner be "softened up" before questioning. According to the International Committee of the Red Cross, these "softening" tactics included: "insults and verbal violence during transfer; sleep deprivation due to loud music or lights kept on in the cell at night; walking in the corridors handcuffed and naked except for female underwear over the head; and handcuffing either to the upper bed bars or doors of the cell for three to four hours at a time."[24] In short, U.S. Army personnel at Abu Ghraib abused and tormented thousands of Iraqi prisoners being held without due process at Abu Ghraib.

In this environment, several American soldiers took photos of the Iraqi prisoners they chose to abuse. These photographs depict images of U.S. soldiers piling up detainees on top of each other naked, terrorizing them with dogs, connecting their genitals to car batteries, and forcing them to simulate sex acts with one another. According to a report filed by Major General Antonio Taguba, after an internal military investigation, these degradations do not tell the whole story of the Abu Ghraib torture sessions conducted by American soldiers either:

> The report detailed incidents including sodomising of prisoners with a chemical light and broomstick, threatening detainees with loaded weapons, breaking chemical lights and pouring the phosphoric liquid on people, sexual humiliation that included forced nudity, prisoners being threatened with rape [...] the use of military working dogs to bite and terrify those detained, beatings with broomsticks and other implements, pouring cold water on naked detainees and hitting prisoners.[25]

The Taguba Report detailed incidents of repeated humiliation, torture, and rape conducted by U.S. soldiers placed in positions of authority at Abu Ghraib. The photos taken by the soldiers engaging in some of these practices do not depict the full extent of these heinous criminal activities, but their leak to the public months after they had been discovered caused a moment of self-reflection among military and civilian officials in the Bush administration. As one, the news media institutions in the United States became instantly interested in evidence of systemic abuse carried out by U.S. military personnel in Iraq.

Beyond the press reaction, when these photographs were leaked to the American public in April of 2004, there was an outcry: shock and dismay circulated throughout the country. Such a crisis of faith in the heroism and altruism of the American soldier provided an opportunity for the United States to reflect upon the U.S. invasion of Iraq and, indeed, on all U.S. military interventions, their efficacy, their costs, and the masters who are served by the ubiquity of the American Armed Forces deployed aggressively around the globe. These legitimate concerns and collective probing questions were quickly derailed, however, by an administration that seemed unconcerned with the bigger picture. Speaking to reporters shortly after the revelation of the photographs of soldiers abusing mostly innocent (or uncharged) Iraqi young men, President Bush assured the country that the United States remains a "nation of laws," and using that tested, highly successful, palliative analogy, that the abuse at Abu Ghraib was the work of "a few bad apples," and nothing more.[26] While detaching these crimes from the institution of the military generally and the system of protocols in place during the U.S. occupation of Iraq more specifically, the Bush administration appeared content to scapegoat the soldiers at Abu Ghraib while also attempting to justify their criminal actions to an impatient public: "the atrocities were blamed on 'a few bad apples', while at the same time the higher echelons of the Bush administration engaged in debates to legally justify the use of 'enhanced interrogation techniques' as acceptable and necessary to protect the public."[27]

While clearly a myriad of institutional, procedural, and moral issues were to blame for the degrading abuses inflicted upon captive Iraqis beyond simply the whims of a handful of sadistic American soldiers, Bush's main task in the aftermath of the Abu Ghraib scandal was the swift, public, and repeated acquittal of the military-industrial behemoth that brought the young and untested American soldiers to Iraq under demonstrably false pretenses in the first place. The Bush administration needed to remind the observing public that disgusting and brutal though the acts of the foot soldiers at Abu Ghraib may have been, they were not, in and of themselves, cause to question the integrity of the American military system. Rather, they were the result of a few misguided individuals working under pressurized conditions who made bad decisions, nothing more.[28] Neither did later reports of more torture conducted by U.S. soldiers affect this assessment of the Abu Ghraib incident during the presidency of Barack Obama. As such, when "[i]n 2010, WikiLeaks released the Iraq War Logs, which contained classified military documents citing hundreds of cases of systematic torture, rape and murder in Iraq,"[29] Obama administration officials demurred but did not cast institutional aspersions onto the military nor onto the civilian federal officials overseeing it. The print news media analysis of the U.S. invasion of Iraq in 2003 that follows this discussion will include a more in-depth investigation into the national and international dismay surrounding the abuses at Abu Ghraib and will consider the extent to which the news media either embraced or rejected the "bad apple" justification espoused by the Bush White House.

The 2003 American invasion of Iraq decimated the physical, cultural, and historical integrity of the country. Many hundreds of thousands of Iraqis have died by violence since 2003, with conservative estimates identifying 400,000 civilian deaths directly resulting from U.S. military violence. In addition, "an untold and unimaginable number have been injured. The war has also created approximately 2.7 million internally displaced people, 2 million refugees and countless migrants who have understandably chosen to leave Iraq since 2003."[30] The war was catastrophic for American soldiers, too, with over 4,400 losing their lives in Iraq (along with 16,000 Iraqi police and U.S. partners) and more than 30,000 post-9/11 U.S. soldiers having committed suicide as a result of unresolved trauma absorbed and internalized during American wars of choice.[31] These devastating human costs say nothing of the loss of irreplaceable antiquities that were destroyed as a result of CPA oversight, or perhaps more accurately, as a result of their callousness. Furthermore, estimates put the total cost of the latest American war in Iraq at close to $6 trillion dollars. But while it was public monies that were used to destroy Iraq, private firms and their individual owners have been the sole beneficiaries of its reconstruction, mostly via no-bid, American-only sweetheart deals diverting still more state funds into the hands of private industry. The business of war in Iraq, then, and the playbook for the U.S. military-industrial complex in the twenty-first century was to destroy with the publicly funded military what privately held American corporations could then rebuild:

> The biggest contract for reconstruction in Iraq—potentially worth US$680 million [...] went to the Bechtel conglomerate, which has close ties to the Bush administration and makes substantial donations to the Republican Party and its candidates. Halliburton, headed from 1995 to August 2000 by Cheney (who retains stock options), was awarded the main contract for restoring Iraq's oil industry; the contract was awarded without competitive tendering and Halliburton's Iraq contracts up until October 2004 were worth US$9 billion.[32]

Tax monies feed into the military that creates the destruction; private corporations collect the largesse of reconstruction contracts coordinated by the same architects of war policy who hold seats in the federal government. The engineers on both sides of this macabre, self-sustaining coin are the same few individuals. Through this process and in the birthplace of civilization, the inseparable union between the publicly funded American military imperium and privately held, self-serving corporate interests was made complete.

None of the stated military or political objectives espoused frequently by Bush administration officials before the war were brought to fruition either, since the U.S. military "failed not only to find WMDs or links to al-Qaeda, but also to deliver on their promise of a democratic, peaceful and prosperous Iraq."[33] Quite the opposite, in fact; the U.S. invasion of Iraq created the political and social instability that led directly to the proliferation of violent, fundamentalist groups that still hold sway in large sections of the country. Arguably the most known and most violent among them, the so-called Islamic State, continues at the time of this writing to hold territory along the border of Iraq and Syria using that base for the export of arch-conservative, fundamentalist forms of Wahhabi Islamist doctrine.[34] As such, while "there was no credible al-Qaeda presence in Iraq before the Coalition forces staged the intervention [...] today large swathes of the country are held by one of its more nefarious offshoots."[35] These assessments say nothing of the complete dissolution of international sympathy for the United States felt by citizens or governments around the world in the wake of the attacks on September 11th, a withdrawal of understanding that coincided with the U.S. war of choice in Iraq and the routine abuse of civilians and captives perpetrated by U.S. soldiers that was endemic to the war itself. In short, the U.S. invasion and occupation of Iraq was a costly and unmitigated failure the consequences of which will continue to be borne by generations of Iraqis for decades to come.

Print News Coverage of Iraq II: Context and Conditioning in Service of the State

To suggest that the authoritative media, print, audio, or television, was in lockstep with the Bush administration in its war in Iraq in 2003 would plainly be false. A number of journalists working within large media conglomerates and/or for national publications of the kind that have already been reviewed for discursive content in previous pages of this work doubted the veracity of the Bush administration's arguments for war in Iraq. The news media as an authoritative institution contributing to the intellectual sphere within the country then allowed those doubts to find voice in many of the national news desk articles and television commentaries that were published in the run-up to the U.S. invasion of Iraq in March of 2003. In keeping with their oft-purported role as the mouthpiece for the *vox populi*, this somewhat countervailing posture from the media institution opposing another war of choice in the Middle East during the Bush presidency concurred with the views of a substantial subset of the American population during the country's approach to war (roughly one-quarter of the country according to polling conducted by the Pew Research Center during this period).[36] Amid the broad spectrum of militarism and patriotism in the news media inherent to any American war, then, it would be possible to author an investigation into print news media coverage of the second Iraq War, pointing to institutional criticism of the Bush administration and, in the main, questioning the legitimacy of the impending invasion and occupation of Saddam Hussein's Iraq in 2003.

Still, according to data reviewed for this study, in the run-up to war and throughout the eight years of military occupation that characterized the primary phase of the American invasion of Iraq at the turn of the twenty-first century, the print news media constructed a discourse around the presence of the United States in that country that would be considered broadly supportive of the role the United States was playing in the Middle East while at the same time remaining unwilling to criticize the institution of the U.S. military as a whole. From within this general discourse, certain key narrative elements emerged that can themselves be cataloged as frames of representation, extending that broad discourse into the intellectual environment of the attendant public reading news articles about the war. The news media analyses to follow then purport to dissect a number of these frames of representation within the broader discourse during this period of time that sought to sustain America's role in geopolitics while also applauding the military establishment of the country. The argument to follow does not contend that these frames of representation represent the sole manner of news construction during this period of time, far from it. The volume of authoritative news media publications over the near decade-long span of the U.S. military presence in Iraq prohibits such categorical declarations. Rather, the news analysis to follow highlights frames of representation within news coverage of the U.S. war in Iraq that were present and prevalent during the period of coverage examined herein. Alternative, potentially even contrary elements within the discourse on the United States and Iraq during this period might likewise be discerned in period news coverage, but it is the frames of coverage adumbrated below that were determined to be both prominent within news coverage and also influential in establishing the discourse on the American war of choice in Iraq in the early twenty-first century. It is to this examination that this chapter now turns.

A Beneficent Invasion

Key to the ongoing print news discourse surrounding the U.S. invasion and occupation of Iraq throughout the decade of the 2000s was that the United States, as a military institution and as a body politic, was doing good and, more importantly, doing good for Iraq. Central within this particular discursive construction imparted via text to American readers keeping up with the most recent American war in the Middle East was the notion that Iraq before the U.S. invasion was a violent wasteland. By comparison, what was being instituted in its place would be judged as a significant improvement. Proponents of this view within the media establishment deemed the counterarguments to this assertion, including widespread insurgent violence, a significant drop in the standard of living, and the total absence of national or regional services, as simply defeatist. And in Iraq, readers were told: "the defeatist [media] images beamed into American living rooms must not force America to back down, as it did in Vietnam and Somalia."[37] The messaging, according to this broadly distributed frame of representation within the authoritative news coverage of the second American war in Iraq, was then fixated on the many positives being visited upon the people of Iraq thanks to American largesse juxtaposed with the enumerable negatives visited upon those people by Saddam Hussein and his government, which the Americans had very wisely displaced. The Iraqi future was bright, and it was the American state, and specifically the American military, who were the architects of that optimistic destiny.

Within this frame of representation, journalists emphasized the dysfunction of the Iraqi state under Saddam Hussein and described, sometimes in graphic detail, the violence, trauma, and decay that were endemic in the country during the years of Ba'athist rule. In one pointed example of a description of the horrors of Iraq under Saddam, one journalist described a visit to Iraq before the U.S. invasion: "I had visited a village where 33 men and boys, virtually all the males in the village, had been lined up, shot and killed by Hussein's soldiers as part of the genocidal Anfal campaign against the Kurds."[38] No doubt such a visit did take place, but it might be remembered that the genocidal Anfal campaign against Kurdish Iraq occurred in late 1988, 15 years before the U.S. war then under examination in this particular news piece. As such, the U.S. war in Iraq was hardly an immediate, moralistic intervention to stop a brutal dictator, despite the causal relationship between the events suggested in this news narrative.

The piece goes on to detail more dread in Saddam's Iraq: "In the hospitals, babies died of malnutrition, and a perpetual shortage of antibiotics meant many deaths that could have been prevented."[39] Whether these descriptions are accurate or embellished, the main thrust of this and other similar news pieces was the conveyance in vivid detail of the want and depredation experienced by Iraqis under Saddam. Logically, what follows within this conceptual construction is that the American replacement of that brutal system will be a substantial improvement over what came before. And in a news piece subtitled "Most People Are Better Off," that message is neither subtly rendered nor easily ignored by a readership aspiring to believe in the good being done by Americans in the Middle East.

Nor did the attendant audience in the United States have to sift carefully through news coverage of the U.S. war in Iraq to find examples of feel-good stories of the American military or American bureaucratic personnel performing good deeds across occupied Iraq. Much of the news coverage in the early phases of the U.S. invasion confirmed, in fact, what had been reported by a number of Bush administration officials in their justifications of the war: that the American soldiers would be greeted as liberators throughout the land and would be thanked for their removal of a pitiless dictator. Iraqi children featured heavily in those descriptions, cheering and smiling all the while American Humvees and Armoured Personnel Carriers rolled down their streets: "The children were jubilant, crowding the soldiers and calling out 'zain,' or 'good.' One shouted that Hussein was 'vile'."[40] Iraqis throughout the country tore down or defaced the emblems of the old regime, heaping glory on the beneficent American forces in the process. These easy American victories promised a "New Day in [an] Ancient Land," as one featured news article was entitled, declaring that "In Baghdad and other cities now controlled by U.S. [...] forces, Iraqi mobs removed, defaced and destroyed pictures and statues of Hussein. The successes in the capital after three weeks of war are a tribute to the generals who planned the campaign and the sergeants who executed it."[41] Other news pieces were quick to describe the calm after the storm that visited Iraq after early military successes. For American audiences, this was portrayed through scenes of citizens returning to work and establishing a stable economy, soothing touchstones of normality for the heavily work-oriented American public: "imams in the city's many mosques had urged worshipers to return to their jobs. And many government employees did so Saturday"; and "both the traffic police in their blue trousers and the green-uniformed Interior Ministry police were visible in downtown Baghdad."[42] Taken together, the unifying message of these news media narratives was one of unmitigated praise for American military successes. These, readers were told, should be ample evidence to silence the critics of the Bush administration or of the U.S. military: "Whether or not one supported the U.S. decision to go to war, there is no question that Iraq now has the opportunity to become a much better place than it was."[43]

According to this framing, the accomplishments of the U.S. military in its invasion of Iraq and the subsequent administration of the country under the auspices of the CPA were utterly praiseworthy: "The U.S. accomplishments [...] were impressive: 1,260 schools renovated and reopened in time for the beginning of the term in October, 90% of the health clinics reopened, 12,000 tons of pharmaceuticals brought into the country, $300 million worth of jobs created." And lest readership forget, despite profuse protestations from Bush administration officials that their ongoing war of choice in Iraq was not about manipulation of the global oil supply, "Oil production is up to a rate of 1.9 billion barrels per year."[44] Within this news narrative, the print news media was substantially aligned with the White House and were adept, as a collective, in repackaging and redistributing the official Washington line to a readership at home who were keen to learn about American success. This frame was also conveyed on the micro level, though, with stories of small projects and individual American soldiers demonstrating conspicuous kindness and generosity amid the hostile environs of war (neglecting to mention, of course, that this particular war was entirely of American making). Through these micro-narratives, American beneficence overall is displayed through the actions of a few who are propped up within the news media discourse to serve as shining examples of the whole. In one such story, a military family raised funds to donate school supplies to Iraqi children: "One thousand, four hundred and forty pencils, painted red with a white and blue Bank of America logo, are headed to Iraq."[45] In what unfolds as a typical heart-warming story for the American audience, readers are told about the great lengths one soldier's brother went to in order to raise money for Iraqi schools gathering pencils as well as "8,000 notebooks, 350 boxes of crayons and 40 hand-crank metal pencil sharpeners" to send to "Iraqi schoolchildren in a town called Laylan, near the city of Kirkuk."[46] Throughout this anecdotal narrative, readers were encouraged to embrace the benevolent nature of this military family and, through them, understand the desire to do good that was central to the U.S. war in Iraq from its inception and throughout the brutal military campaign.

The argument put forth here in descriptions of this frame of representation is not that Saddam Hussein was a good leader or a decent man. By the time of the second U.S. invasion of Iraq, his brutality was already legendary, as it has been described both in this chapter and in the previous case study examining the first American Gulf War. Nor is it the contention of this author that there were no American soldiers or politicians who wanted to perform good works once they arrived in Iraq. No doubt, there were. Rather, the assertion here points to the selection of a particular kind of story by the print news media falling closely in line with official descriptions of wartime events and political goals. As this analysis intends to show, far from being the moralist oppositional force it is sometimes credited with being during the U.S. war in Iraq, the authoritative print media commonly fell into officially acceptable patterns of reportage using nakedly pro-military, pro-American, or otherwise sentimental or overtly emotive narrative frames to convey the beneficence of the U.S. invasion of Iraq to American audiences. As further evidence will show, this protective trend in coverage of sacred American institutions like the U.S. military remained a staple feature of the print news media to a greater or lesser extent for the duration of the decade-long American military occupation of Iraq.

Americans in Three Dimensions, Iraqis in the Background

For print media journalists covering American wars within the media institution of the United States, certain discursive structures come to be relied upon as standard pillars through which to relay information and disseminate perspectives to American audiences. Embedded among these staple frames of representation is the provision of a measure of depth and detail when it comes to descriptions of American actors in theaters of war, namely U.S. soldiers, and a distinct lack of reciprocation of that depth or detail when it comes to describing actors on the opposite side of the combat line, in this case, the indigenous inhabitants of Iraq. This general bias toward approaching militarism and war within the authoritative news media establishment in the United States can be traced throughout the coverage of American wars since the inception of the news media as a contemporary institution. Yet, with American wars of choice in the Middle East in the post-9/11 geopolitical environment, the depth of characterization and contextualization of American actors as compared to the lack of detail provided to actors in Muslim-majority areas who are subject to the whims of American military operations has arguably reached new heights. When embedded within news narratives purporting to cover American wars, and in particular in the coverage of the American invasion and occupation of Iraq in 2003, as often as not, details about Iraqis, their motivations, and/ or their political goals were simply absent.

American readers of print news coverage of the U.S. war in Iraq came to understand this detail and depth of portrayal as it was associated with American soldiers, their backgrounds, and/or their hopes for the future early on in the coverage of the war. Typical coverage providing this meaningful context connecting American soldiers to readership in the U.S. on an emotional level read: "Some [soldiers] were saving money for college; some had left jobs at home doing things like resealing driveways."[47] In this description, politics and military action are quite beside the central point of the narrative provided. Rather, readers are informed about the life of a young man before his entry into the military. He was a hard worker, humble, and ambitious. He advanced himself and improved his future opportunities through odd jobs and manual labor. Each of these elements within this news text purporting to inform audiences about the war in Iraq serves as touchstones of emotional connectivity, propelling American audiences to identify and sympathize with this earnest American soldier. Other examples of this specific frame of representation included descriptions of the backgrounds of American soldiers to include the names of their hometowns, their hobbies, and their personality traits: "[He] grew up in Telford, Pa., a small town about 25 miles northwest of Philadelphia. He graduated from Souderton Area High School in 1988, where he had been a center on the basketball team and a class leader."[48] Through this narrative frame, backgrounds are established for American soldiers, providing them with a depth of personality as well as a complex emotional life. Readers are introduced to their families, their schools, possibly their teachers, and/or their significant others. Emotional narratives such as these were exceedingly common in the early phases of the American war in Iraq and belied notions of objective or fact-based reporting on troop locations, tactical decisions, or other purely military notions that one would think would be more evident in news coverage during war.

Even soldiers who were roundly criticized for their participation in the abuse of Iraqi prisoners at the Abu Ghraib prison facility (the news coverage of which is described in some detail below) were given back stories and personal histories so as to contextualize them in their full humanity within the broader picture of American war: "Pfc. Lynndie R. England was married and divorced before she was 21, worked at a chicken-processing plant in West Virginia and wanted to attend college to become a storm-chasing meteorologist"[49] and "And Staff Sgt. Ivan Frederick, another prison guard, planned to quit the Army Reserve this year to spend more time fishing near his rural home in central Virginia."[50] The picture presented in these descriptions is one of full-fledged individuals, human beings with hopes, dreams, hobbies, and frailties. They were sociable and kind ("To friends, a gentle man");[51] they were young, patriotic, and brave ("Kids join as soon as they leave high school [...] because they're proud of their country and they want to help").[52] Coverage within this frame of representation was at pains to indicate the appearance, manner, and/or personalities of American personnel (including the "delicate-looking"[53] Jessica Lynch, a prisoner of war for a brief period of time), as well as pointing specifically to the goodness inherent in the average American soldier, and by extension, Americans themselves. Benchmarks of traditional Americana, including work ethic, rural backgrounds, quiet hobbies, and respectable professions, proliferated in these elaborate presentations of the humanity and depth of character of American soldiers in Iraq.

By contrast, Iraqi citizens, for whom this war was being conducted according to official justifications, were presented with context, depth, and multi-dimensionality much less frequently. In fact, much of the coverage of the Iraqi point of view was not even voiced by Iraqis themselves but was rather described by American officials or journalists whose accurate assessment of the Iraqi perspective was presented as a foregone conclusion: "They will begin the task of stabilizing Iraq and reconstituting it as a sovereign, democratic nation."[54] The "they" in this example is not precisely identified, but the journalist in this case could mean a smattering of ruling elites just as well as they could mean a country of tens of millions. Typical in these representations is the implicit notion that Iraqis are not fully constructed as individuals; in fact, they were not individuals at all. Instead, they were a collective, often portrayed as an amorphous mass with common characteristics but certainly not with the uniqueness or depth that was provided for the American soldiers within these news representations: "[Iraqis] swarmed toward the visiting journalists"[55] and "[officials were] visibly surprised"[56] by the crush of people, as examples. On other occasions, news representations pitted the American military not against an Iraqi enemy at all but rather against the whole of the Muslim world: "foreign fighters encompass[ing] anti-American Al Qaeda-type characters from Syria and Jordan, among other nations"[57]

The collective effect of these and many other similar characterizations was to render Iraqis specifically and Muslims generally, given the geography of the second Iraq War, as a collective force without any individual depth or quality. Americans in print news media coverage of the Iraq War, by contrast, were given a background, depth of personality, aspirations, and, above all, individuality. Little wonder, then, given this narrative depth and dimensionality of American actors, that American soldiers, who were themselves fed upon these same news media narratives of individualized U.S. soldiers and sailors in news coverage of previous wars, landed in Iraq in the full confidence that they would be warmly welcomed by the mass of the indigenous populace: "'They love us,' concluded Ratledge, the medic."[58]

Obscuring Systematic Torture: Case Study, Abu Ghraib

In considering the systematic torture and humiliation of prisoners held at the prison complex at Abu Ghraib in central Iraq, which was revealed to the public in April 2004, the print news media constructed a variety of influential narratives and discursive constructions. Upon the revelation of torture and viewing of the dozens of photographs that were taken by U.S. soldiers conducting the abuse, a number of news media reports were instantly critical of the actions of these few individuals. Others went so far as to assert that a form of collective psychosis had descended upon the troops stationed at Abu Ghraib or that it was the indescribable stress and isolation brought on by the war generally, and by this posting specifically, that led to this abusive behavior. For other journalists, these soldiers were just bad actors. They had intended to do harm, and they did so, but luckily for the American public reading these considerations, they were in a very small minority of American soldiers then deployed to Iraq. This particular narrative closely aligned with official protestations from the Bush administration at the time and from the president himself, who famously labeled the Abu Ghraib scandal as the product of a handful of "bad apples." This oblique defense of these misdeeds assures attendant audiences that these actions are neither systemic nor institutional but rather squarely the responsibility of a handful of individuals out of a collective U.S. military presence in Iraq numbering in the hundreds of thousands. But while media criticism over the conduct at Abu Ghraib was swift and prolific during this period of time, it stopped well short of impugning American systems, political, military, or otherwise. As such, and as the textual analysis below will indicate, print news media criticism of Abu Ghraib was constructed within acceptable discursive parameters and rarely, if ever, breached the walls of those boundaries to impugn the military as an institution or the administration as a whole for their highly problematic war of choice in Iraq.

Critical to recasting the horrific abuses at Abu Ghraib for the American public was a narrative emphasis on the horrors of war, the stress of combat, and/or the generally harsh conditions under which U.S. soldiers generally, and the soldiers and military police at Abu Ghraib specifically, were working. That these harsh conditions, challenging though they no doubt were, existed as a consequence of the U.S. decision to engage in a war of choice in Iraq was not included within this news media frame. With this context removed, and with the victims utterly nameless in these news narratives, the authoritative print media in the United States appeared blithely to justify the torture and humiliation of hundreds of Iraqi prisoners at Abu Ghraib as a function of the hardships endured by the torturers themselves. This discursive repositioning effectively rendered the abusers as the victims and amorphous actors like the war, the country of Iraq, or possibly the collection of detainees themselves, as the ones responsible for the torture. In an example of this frame of representation, overcrowding at Abu Ghraib became an important culprit in the abuses conducted by U.S. soldiers there: "About 450 MPs [military police] were supervising close to 7,000 inmates, many of them crowded into cells, many more kept in tents hastily arranged on dirt fields within the razor-wired walls of the compound. Around the perimeter, GIs kept wary eyes on Iraqi guards of questionable loyalty."[59] A number of influential narrative elements come to the fore in this news item, which emphasizes the crowdedness and chaos of the prison complex. First, this narrative frame adeptly recasts the victimizers as victims given how outnumbered they were when committing and photographing the torture of these inmates. Also, the specific mention of the "questionable loyalty" of the Iraqi nationalists coopted by the U.S. Army to assist as prison guards at Abu Ghraib adds a further narrative complex, placing the American soldiers under potential threat, and thereby adding a measure of justification to their heinous deeds. Each of these dramatic elements presented to the readership in the United States constructs a distinct moral environment in which fear, anxiety, and unease were clearly on the side of the U.S. military occupiers rather than being endured by the 7,000 prisoners themselves, the vast majority of whom were imprisoned as collective punishment without having been charged with a crime.

Indeed, details of the difficult conditions at Abu Ghraib and their impact upon the psyche and/or disposition of the American soldiers stationed there were rife in news coverage during this period: "Divided into dusty camps ringed by razor wire, Abu Ghraib is a tense world of seemingly frustrated Iraqis";[60] "For U.S. military police officers in Baghdad, the Abu Ghraib prison was particularly hellish";[61] and "all described Abu Ghraib as remarkably chaotic and dangerous."[62] This frame of representation proliferated precisely because of the context it provided for readers to invest in the lives of the American soldiers guarding the prison camp. The continued provision of this context served to humanize the U.S. soldiers and connect readers with their decision-making processes, even if their eventual choice to torture and humiliate captive, innocent Iraqis may not be fully understood. In effect, readers were encouraged by these narratives to internalize the idea that monstrous conditions create monstrous acts: "extreme conditions can bring to the fore irascible tendencies common to some young adults, and the mission in war—to get the job done—might at times cause a certain degree of sadism."[63] In the end, it was not the nature of the American soldier nor the U.S. decision to go to war in Iraq that caused harm. Rather, it was a particular set of circumstances informed by a particular set of stressors at a given moment that led to these horrific abuses. The moral compass of the U.S. military, the American body politic, and indeed, the soul of the American self, was sufficiently cleansed by this highly forgiving narrative context.

If the extant conditions of Abu Ghraib and deployment to Iraq were contextually telling as the scandal of prisoner abuse broke across the United States, this conditioning was only extended in print news media discourse by repeated references to the stakes of the military operations being conducted at the prison facility. Within this element of the discursive recontextualizing of Abu Ghraib, news stories reported U.S. soldiers who were not only working in a harsh environment but who were also placed under enormous pressure to extract information from the prison population in their charge. Specifically, according to this telling, the lives of U.S. soldiers in Iraq were dependent upon the results of interrogations conducted at Abu Ghraib. The provision of this added layer of discursive setting in the print news media served to further condition the actions of the soldiers cum abusers located, as they were, in a harsh setting and under extraordinary pressure to extract information. One news narrative stated this connection quite plainly: "Much of the alleged abuse began last October, when the military was under mounting pressure to collect information regarding [...] potential threats to

U.S. forces."[64] According to investigative records, the idea that there were any prisoners at Abu Ghraib who possessed information that could potentially save American lives is, at best, highly debatable. Nevertheless, in this article, this vague potentiality is accepted as fact and portrayed as such to the readership in the U.S. Other news pieces adopted the same narrative position: "Teams of interrogators and translators working under the 205th Military Intelligence Brigade were responsible for extracting information from those prisoners that battlefield commanders could use to thwart attacks and save U.S. troops' lives."[65] According to another article, this responsibility brought with it an "unrelenting pressure to ramp up the number of interrogations and intelligence reports."[66] Iterations of the gravest possible consequences of failure at Abu Ghraib, the death of more Americans, served to expand the narrative context in which the abusive soldiers were operating. The immediacy of this narrative trope added yet another gripping and ultimately justifying layer to the news media discourse covering the abuse of Iraqis at the hands of American soldiers. Through this multilayered contextualization, the soldier-abusers were narratively connected to attendant audiences within the United States who were given ample opportunity to process, understand, and forgive their misdeeds.

Another method employed within the print news discourse to recontextualize the narrative frames surrounding the soldier abuse scandal involved assurances from the print news that the U.S. military was a benevolent institution and that its soldiers were utterly moral actors. In some instances, this trope was conveyed in the praise of the soldier who reported the habitual abuse at the Iraqi prison site. In other examples, this moral righteousness was communicated via text descriptions of the Army's decisive corrective actions performed in the wake of the revelations of the abuse: "the entire detention process in Iraq is being revamped, with an emphasis on a quick release for prisoners not deemed threats or of intelligence value"[67] and "[General] Miller has modified interrogation techniques, banning controversial practices such as placing hoods on prisoners and subjecting them to sleep deprivation and painful 'stress positions.' Visiting rights are being expanded and detainees are now getting two hot meals a day, instead of packaged meals ready to eat."[68] One might well question why hooding and tormenting of prisoners by denying them basic human functions such as sleep would require an internal investigation and a system overhaul before being banned, but the answer to this question was not forthcoming in the print news sample reviewed for this study. In any case, by describing revisions to the criminal code employed by the Army, journalists reassured their readers of the virtue and respectability of the military and its personnel, previous lapses in honor notwithstanding. And though a number of samples from the print news media in this period were generally critical of the soldiers who abused prisoners at Abu Ghraib, even in criticizing these actions, an underlying praise for the military and its pervasive morality still encroached into the reporting: "the military hierarchy is not one of unquestioning obedience and clear orders."[69] In the final accounting, the tremendously moral nature of the U.S. military and its constituent membership pervaded news coverage of the Abu Ghraib scandal. Readership at home in the United States was thereby dutifully assured of the average "GI's 'Sharp Moral Compass'"[70] even while ostensibly being informed of the utter lack of American morality within the confines of Iraq's most notorious prison.

It is conceivable that audiences reading up on news about the Abu Ghraib prisoner abuse scandal would have internalized several foundational lessons about the entire sordid episode, none of which had to do with the cruelty of U.S. soldiers left to their own devices to dehumanize Iraqi civilians in any macabre manner they saw fit. According to print news media narratives, the abuse was the fault of the environment in which it took place, or the fault of the high stakes of fighting a war and aggressively pursuing information underneath a ticking clock. If those explanations failed to satisfy, readers could always lean on assurances that the U.S. military and everyone in it were a beneficent, moral actors regardless of the voluminous evidence to the contrary. At the end of the day, a comforting message was at the heart of official narratives about the scandal, too: it was simply the fault of "a few bad apples." In embedding this discourse within reportage covering the Abu Ghraib scandal, the print news media substantially conformed to the official narrative espoused by the Bush administration as well, confirming that "people in Baghdad are freer"[71] now than they have ever been, all thanks to the U.S. military.

Conclusions: Media War and Discursive Agendas

The U.S. invasion of Iraq in 2003 was controversial, as much in the domestic media within the United States as in media produced abroad. Unlike the first American military venture in Iraq just over a decade earlier, there was no invitation by a regional power for a massive U.S. military commitment in the Middle East. Likewise, there was no international consensus that military assault, invasion, and subsequent occupation were advisable policy options from the international community writ large. Finally and most egregiously, very much like the story of the blood-soaked and politically futile American military presence in Southeast Asia in the 1960s and 1970s (and as with the origins of the Spanish-American War), the American people and the rest of the world were told fabrications as to the compelling *casus belli* that precipitated the U.S. invasion of Iraq. Outraged at the brazenness of these flimsy justifications, millions across the globe marched in protest of the war in the spring of 2003, though to no avail. Thousands of lives and uncountable sums of money and materiel later, Iraq remains a shadow of the society it was promised to be on the back of heroic American military intervention authored by a detached and hubristic cabal of politicos and planners in place at the highest levels of American government.

For its part, the news media, as is its wont, largely supported Bush administration plans in Iraq, ill-conceived and nebulous though they surely were. Some outlets proudly trumpeted pro-war messaging and were well compensated as a result: "Rupert Murdoch exploited and fueled the war-fever over Iraq with pro-war editorial positions. His 140 tabloid newspapers around the world were selling 40 million a week. Murdoch's hyperpatriotic Fox news channel showed bombers heading for Baghdad to the accompaniment of the US national anthem."[72] Though this kind of full-throated patriotism might be expected by media outlets on the right-most edge of the American political spectrum, even traditional left-leaning publications and news outlets maintained a healthy support for the state and its military in the early phases of America's war of choice. The military was sustained as a moral force, while the stated objectives of the war were portrayed as beneficial and laudable. The American soldier was an actor in three dimensions and, though occasionally fallible, was always striving to do the right thing in service of his or her country. Criticisms of the war and of policy authored in Washington began to rise along with American casualties, but there were bounds beyond which these media criticisms did not stray. As in all other wars reviewed in this study, the print news media maintained that the military was ethical, the country's intentions were good, and our aims were praiseworthy. In the final retelling, the consistency of these narrative frames and their diligent repetition within the confines of news media coverage of American wars have consequences upon both the cultural and intellectual environments as they continue to operate within the United States in the twenty-first century. Those consequences and the results of more than a century of discursive protection of the U.S. military as an institution will serve as the focal point of the concluding chapter in this study.

Notes

1 Chalmers Johnson, *Blowback: The Costs and Consequences of American Empire* (New York: Owl Books, 2004), xviii.

2 Andrew Bacevich, *America's War for the Greater Middle East: A Military History* (New York: Random House, 2016), 131.

3 Lawrence Freedman, *A Choice of Enemies: America Confronts the Middle East* (New York: Public Affairs, 2009), 417.

4 Andrew Mack and Asif Khan, "The Efficacy of UN Sanctions," *Security Dialogue 31*, no. 3 (2000): 279–92. Accessed May 4, 2023.

5 Since World War I, the United States has dangled autonomy and/or independence in front of Kurdish leaders in order to foster American policy goals in Iraq and the broader Middle East, only to betray those promises and fail to deliver Kurdish independence approximately eight times (J. Schwarz, "The U.S. is Now Betraying the Kurds for the Eighth Time," *The Intercept*, October 7, 2019.) https://theintercept.com/2019/10/07/kurds-syria-turkey-trump -betrayal/?fbclid=IwAR3gsRTmUQUrkWwGpLD1ZKDTQmpnxWmgLWIPM2c6ciYE0 CBHnBg8hVB5HyU.

6 Dick Cheney's career in government and the private sector is extensive. He was a White House staff member for both the Nixon and Ford administrations in the 1970s before becoming chief of staff of the White House in 1975. He was a U.S. Representative from Wyoming from 1979 to 1989 and was nominated as the Secretary of Defense for the George H. W. Bush administration, fomenting and overseeing the First Gulf War in his capacity in that post. Before effectively nominating himself to be George W. Bush's vice president in 2000, he was the chairman and CEO of logistics firm Haliburton from 1995 to 2000, leaving that position under a buyout clause worth a reported $34 million. Then, once firmly entrenched as one of the most powerful vice presidents in this country's history, he oversaw no-bid contract deals extended from the federal government to his old company, Halliburton, during the reconstruction phase of Gulf War II. The total amount of those monies funneled back to Halliburton coffers from this White House largesse totaled more than $39 billion (Conor Friedersdorf, "Remembering Why Americans Loathe Dick Cheney," *The Atlantic*, August 30, 2011. https://www.theatlantic.com/politics/archive/2011/08/remembering-why-americans -loathe-dick-cheney/244306/. See also Naomi Klein, *No is Not Enough: Resisting Trump's Shock Politics and Winning the World We Need* (Chicago: Haymarket Books, 2017)).

7 "1994 Clip of a C-SPAN Interview with Dick Cheney," C-SPAN, August 15, 2007. Video, 00:01:14. https://www.youtube.com/watch?v=w75ctsv2oPU.

8 "Taliban" translates as "Student Party" and is a fundamentalist Islamist movement founded by a cadre of young, motivated exiles from the decade-long Soviet occupation of Afghanistan who were based in refugee camps in neighboring Pakistan. Historian Lawrence Freedman

explains: "in 1994 a group of students (Talibs) raised in the refugee camps and outraged by the depravity of mujahideen rule presented themselves as a new, idealistic, and disciplined force." Promising to replace the decentralized mujahideen forces that rose during the Soviet occupation, they moved en masse into Afghanistan and collected an increasing number of followers, growing from a few hundred in number to an army of more than 20,000 dedicated followers. By 1996, they were the largest and most stable military and political force in the country (Freedman, *A Choice of Enemies*, 354).

9 John J. Mearsheimer, and Stephen M. Walt, "An Unnecessary War," *Foreign Policy*, November 3, 2009. Accessed May 4, 2023. https://foreignpolicy.com/2009/11/03/an-unnecessary-war-2/.

10 For his disloyalty to the Bush administration and the Neocon regime, Wilson's wife, Valerie Plame was publicly identified as an undercover CIA operative on international assignment via government leak, an information dump that jeopardized her life. Though she escaped her field assignment unharmed, she was never able to hold a position in field operations for the CIA again. It was later confirmed that the leak was deliberately released by Vice President Dick Cheney's Chief of Staff, Scott "Scooter" Libby. Libby resigned from his post in disgrace and was charged with five criminal counts including obstruction of justice and perjury. He was found guilty on four of the five counts and was sentenced to 30 months in prison and fined $250,000. Shortly after this conviction, President Bush commuted this prison sentence. He was later pardoned of all crimes by Donald Trump.

11 This author was one of those 10 million.

12 A number of Bush administration officials made this claim publicly, perhaps most notable among them Deputy Secretary of Defense Paul Wolfowitz and Vice President Dick Cheney.

13 Historian and policy analyst Andrew Bacevich has succinctly stated three actual goals of the Bush administration in the Second Gulf War having dismissed the weak, rhetorical justifications offered in the run-up to the March 2003 invasion: "First, the United States was intent on establishing the efficacy of preventive war. Second, it was going to assert the prerogative, permitted to no other country, of removing regimes that Washington deemed odious. And finally, it was seeking to reverse the practice of exempting the Islamic world from neoliberal standards, demonstrating [...] what Condoleezza Rice called 'the paradigm of progress'—democracy, limited government, market economics, and respect for human (and especially women's) rights [...] Here in concrete and specific terms was a strategy to 'change the way they live'" (Bacevich, *America's War for the Greater Middle East*, 240).

14 David Keen, *Endless War? The Hidden Functions of the War on Terror* (London: Pluto Press, 2006), 11.

15 Ibid., 68.

16 Benjamin Isakhan, "Introduction: The Iraq Legacies—Intervention, Occupation, Withdrawal and Beyond," in Benjamin Isakhan (ed.), *The Legacy of Iraq From the 2003 War to the 'Islamic State'*, 1–20 (Edinburgh: Edinburgh University Press, 2015), 5.

17 Freedman, *A Choice of Enemies*, 426.

18 Bacevich, *America's War for the Greater Middle East*, 263–64.

19 Ibid., 265.

20 Klein, *No is Not Enough*, 132–33.

21 Isakhan, "Introduction: The Iraq Legacies—Intervention, Occupation, Withdrawal and Beyond," 6.

22 Bacevich, *America's War for the Greater Middle East*, 267.

23 Joseph Stepansky, "The US 'War on Terror', 20 Years after 'Mission Accomplished' Experts Say 'Lack of Democratic Accountability', Transparency Continue to Define US Operations against 'Terror' Threats," *Al-Jazeera*, May 1, 2023. https://www.aljazeera.com/news/2023/5/1/the-us-war-on-terror-20-years-after-mission-accomplished.

24 Aloysia Brooks, "Torture at Abu Ghraib: Non-disclosure and Impunity," in Benjamin Isakhan (ed.), *The Legacy of Iraq From the 2003 War to the 'Islamic State'* (Edinburgh: Edinburgh University Press, 2015), 52.

25 Ibid., 52–53.

26 "Just a Few Bad Apples?" *The Economist, 2005.* Accessed May 12, 2023. https://www.economist.com/united-states/2005/01/20/just-a-few-bad-apples.

27 Brooks, "Torture at Abu Ghraib: Non-disclosure and Impunity," 59.

28 Of those culpable individuals, only a few were punished at all for their roles in the Abu Ghraib torture. Human Rights scholar Aloysia Brooks informs that "Some of the lower-level US troops who directly participated in the torture at Abu Ghraib were brought before a court martial and served prison time [...] [Lance Corporal] Graner was convicted of conspiracy, assault, maltreating prisoners, dereliction of duty and committing indecent acts. In 2005 he was sentenced to ten years [...] but was released early in August 2012 for good behavior [...] Some of the commissioned and noncommissioned officers involved were handed 'punitive letters', fined or relieved of their duties" (Ibid., 54).

29 Ibid.

30 Isakhan, "Introduction: The Iraq Legacies—Intervention, Occupation, Withdrawal and Beyond," 11–12.

31 "U.S. and Allied Killed," *Watson Institute of International & Public Affairs at Brown University*, *2023*. Accessed May 12, 2023. https://watson.brown.edu/costsofwar/costs/human/military /killed.

32 Keen, *Endless War?* 69.

33 Isakhan, "Introduction: The Iraq Legacies—Intervention, Occupation, Withdrawal and Beyond," 1.

34 Wahhabism is a fundamentalist form of Islamic thought and practice innovated by Muhhamad Ibn Abd al-Wahab during the eighteenth century. It is known for its highly restrictive and unfailingly conservative forms of worship and social practice and is the foundational philosophy for a number of fundamentalist Islamist organizations throughout the world, including Al-Qaeda and the so-called Islamic State.

35 Ibid., 12.

36 Carroll Doherty and Jocelyn Kiley, "A Look Back at How Fear and False Beliefs Bolstered U.S. Public Support for War in Iraq," *Pew Research Center*, March 14, 2023. Accessed May 17, 2023. https://www.pewresearch.org/politics/2023/03/14/a-look-back-at-how-fear-and-false -beliefs-bolstered-u-s-public-support-for-war-in-iraq/.

37 Nicholas Goldberg, "Iraq: Place the Fate of Iraq above U.S. Politics; The Truth Is a Mixed Bag: Most People Are Better Off, but Crime and Chaos Have Risen," *Los Angeles Times*, November 9, 2003, M1.

38 Ibid.

39 Ibid.

40 Thomas E. Ricks and Anthony Shadid, "A Tale of Two Baghdads; As U.S. Soldiers Perceive Warm Welcome, Residents Express Anger," *The Washington Post*, June 2, 2003, A01.

41 "New Day in Ancient Land," *Los Angeles Times*, April 10, 2003, B14.

42 John Daniszewski, "After the War: A Battered Baghdad Showing New Life; Workers Are Returning to Their Jobs and Shops Are Reopening. Iraqi Police Hand the Former Finance Minister over to the Americans," *Los Angeles Times*, April 20, 2003, A3.

43 Goldberg, "Iraq: Place the Fate of Iraq above U.S. Politics," *Los Angeles Times*, November 9, 2003, M1.

44 Ibid.

45 Cynthia Schreiber, "Soldier's Brother Gets Donations to Help Supply Some Iraq Schools," *Wall Street Journal*, October 29, 2003, B4.

46 Ibid.

47 Richard Serrano and Greg Miller, "Iraq Prison Scandal; A Combustible Mix at Iraq Prison; At the Abu Ghraib Facility, the Combination of MPs' Poor Training and Heavy Demands on Interrogators Resulted in a Disregard for Rules," *Los Angeles Times*, May 8, 2004, A10.

48 Joel Brinkley, "9/11 Set Army Contractor on Path to Abu Ghraib: The Struggle for Iraq: A Civilian Interrogator, and the Karbala Tangle," *The New York Times*, May 19, 2004, A13.

49 James Dao, Paul V. Zielbauer, and Fox Butterfield, "Abuse Charges Bring Anguish in Unit's Home," *New York Times*, May 6, 2004, A1.

50 Ibid.

51 Brinkley, "9/11 Set Army Contractor on Path to Abu Ghraib," *The New York Times*, May 19, 2004, A13.

52 Elizabeth Williamson, "Hostile Mission for Recruiters; Prison Scandal Discourages Enlistment in 372nd MP Unit," *The Washington Post*, July 8, 2004, A01.

53 Associated Press, "Home at Last: Jessica Lynch, Months after Being Injured in Iraq, Returns to West Virginia," *Chicago Tribune*, July 23, 2003, 3.

54 Daniszewski, "After the War: A Battered Baghdad Showing New Life," *Los Angeles Times*, April 20, 2003, A3.

55 Sewell Chan, "Rage Is on Display During Prison Tour: General Touts Reforms, New Facilities," *The Washington Post*, May 6, 2004, A19.

56 Ibid.

57 Alissa J. Rubin, "The World; U.S. Finds War in Iraq Is Far From Finished; Guerrilla- Style Attacks Are Growing. A Military Official Vows to Stay the Course in Quelling Resistance and Rebuilding the Nation," *Los Angeles Times*, June 29, 2003, A1.

58 Ricks and Shadid, "A Tale of Two Baghdads," *The Washington Post*, June 2, 2003, A01.

59 Scott Higham, Josh White, and Christian Davenport, "The Struggle For Iraq: Prisoner; Iraqi Tells of U.S. Abuse, From Ridicule to Rape Threat," *The Washington Post*, May 9, 2004, 9.

60 Evan Osnos, "Military Gives Media Tour of Infamous Jail; U.S. Tries to Block Fallout of Scandal," *Chicago Tribune*, May 6, 2004, 17.

61 Higham, White, and Davenport, "The Struggle for Iraq," *The Washington Post*, May 9, 2004, 9.

62 Serrano and Miller, "Iraq Prison Scandal; A Combustible Mix at Iraq Prison," *Los Angeles Times*, May 8, 2004, A10.

63 G. J. McDonald, "Why Are They Smiling? The Stresses of War Can Distort Morality and Draw Out the Worst in Human Nature, Psychologists Say, but Sadistic Behavior Is Not Inevitable," *The Christian Science Monitor*, May 26, 2004, 15.

64 Richard A. Serrano and Greg Miller, "The Conflict in Iraq: Documents Provide New Details of Abuse; Army Investigators Heard Accounts from Inmates of Abu Ghraib and Intelligence Officers," *Los Angeles Times*, May 23, 2004, A1.

65 Thomas E. Ricks, "In Iraq's Guerrilla War, Army Intelligence Faces a Tough Job," *The Washington Post*, August 26, 2004, A18.

66 Christopher Cooper and Greg Jaffe, "Under Fire: At Abu Ghraib, Soldiers Faced Pressure to Produce Intelligence; Analysts, Interrogators Say Many Were Ill-Prepared; Quotas, Unsafe Conditions; In a Tent, as the Shells Flew," *Wall Street Journal*, June 1, 2004, A1.

67 Patrick J. McDonnell, "New Chief of Prisons Defends His Role in Iraq; Maj. Gen. Miller Headed a Team that Suggested Last Summer that U.S. Guards at Abu Ghraib Take a More Active Role in Interrogations," *Los Angeles Times*, May 9, 2004, A1.

68 Ibid.

69 Peter Grier and Faye Bowers, "Military Denies Pattern," *The Christian Science Monitor*, May 20, 2004, 01.

70 "GI's 'Sharp Moral Compass'," *The Christian Science Monitor*, August 26, 2004, 08.

71 Goldberg, "Iraq: Place the Fate of Iraq above U.S. Politics," *Los Angeles Times*, November 9, 2003, M1.

72 Keen, *Endless War?* 71.

Chapter Eight

SELLING THE DRAMA: CULTURE, MEDIA, THE MILITARY, AND THE AMERICAN SELF[1]

War is an American tradition.[2]

—*Daniel Hallin, 1986*

The Media and the Military: Sustaining American Empire

Each of the preceding case study chapters has sought to produce two distinct but complementary and mutually reinforcing intellectual outcomes. In the first place, each of the preceding chapters suggested a historical narrative of an American war conducted over the course of the last 125 years that is definitively outside the mode of the mainstream, broadly accepted, conspicuous public histories that are produced within standard institutions of the American state, society, and culture today. These histories proffered alternative views of the American state and the American military in either their ideological positioning, conduct, motives, and/or affected outcomes in the context of the political world in which a given war—of which there have, of course, been many—was conducted. The second element of these case study chapters contained an analysis of print news language as it was constructed and disseminated to American audiences in order to convey information about the military and the wars that were conducted in a given social context during the time period of the war itself. This investigative element, as it was framed and predicated by the theoretical discussion in the introductory chapter to this work, situates itself firmly in the academic history of CDA, which begins with the premise that language encodes meaning both beyond and within the superficial or the semiotic. CDA also asserts that large, public, or state-sustaining institutions like the authoritative print news media wield power in the construction of language and assert substantial influence in their ability to access huge audiences in order to disseminate that language and power. As indicated, then, and as has been referenced frequently throughout this work thus far, this study engages language and discourse, which are in turn crucial intellectual components in the construction of knowledge and information about the observable world. Also, and perhaps in a more immediate sense, this study argues that language, discourse, and the associated knowledge that comes with these intellectual components are disseminated in a given culture and inform considerably about the political and social worlds beyond the immediately accessible or verifiable.

Though somewhat dated in relation to available information technology in the digital age, media scholar Gaye Tuchman's foundational work *Making News: A Study in the Social Construction of Reality* offers a framework for interpolating the connections between news language and the information it carries with the construction of a lived and experienced social reality for the recipients of that news information in a given media community: "News is a window on the world. Through its frame, Americans learn of themselves and others, of their own institutions, leaders, and life styles, and those of other nations and their peoples [...] the news aims to tell us what we want to know, need to know, and should know."[3] Tuchman's view of the news here coincides with both the structure and influence of what has been referred to throughout this study as the print news media, the authoritative news media institution, or more simply, printed news. Yet, Tuchman's perspective here does not incorporate the hyper-focus and emotive connection of the news audience in the United States when approaching news media texts concerning American wars. Given this added urgency in both attending to and valuing information disseminated by national news desks during war, it is evident that ubiquitous narrative elements within the institution of journalism default to sustaining state narratives while at the same time reconstructing the news media as an institution sufficiently as "an ally of legitimated institutions."[4] If these tendencies are present and verifiable during routinized news coverage of domestic or international events within a given news media community, this study has attempted to show that they are only heightened within news coverage of war within the contemporary United States. As such, while "public journalism proclaims itself to be about invigorating democracy [and] simultaneously positions itself as non-partisan,"[5] as evidenced in the extensive examinations of the news media as a cultural product produced during wartime here in this work, there are discernible limits to the democratic and/or independent nature of journalism produced in the United States during the war. Rather than democratizing the public sphere as media is often proclaimed to do, wartime journalism much more regularly "confirms the legitimacy of the state"[6] and, in so doing, limits itself in the degree to which it will, as an institution, question the war in progress, criticize the architects of war policy, and/or challenge the prevailing establishment in their preferred view of the international political order.

This is a particularly salient point in criticisms of the ongoing products of the news media institutions in the United States, given American policy decisions in the twenty-first century envisioning a permanent state of war against a vaguely defined and wholly subjective concept, the so-called War on Terror. It is also a relevant criticism of news media production in the United States, given the ubiquity of American military presence around the globe. Each of these political phenomena respectively portends unending war, police action, and/or military intervention in a variety of global theaters into the far future:

We have entered an age of constant conflict [...]. There will be no peace. At any given moment for the rest of our lifetimes, there will be multiple conflicts in mutating forms around the globe. Violent conflict will dominate the headlines [...]. The de facto role of the US armed forces will be to keep the world safe for our economy and open to our cultural assault. To those ends, we will do a fair amount of killing.[7]

This simple fact of aggressive posturing and avowed policy priority means that, in effect, all news media products of our time and those to come forth in successive generations are, and will be, media products of a country at war. News media discourse, then, can be expected to bend decidedly in the direction of the state narrative given the parameters of the news media institution that are active and functional in the contemporary United States, namely that it "moves complacently within the historically established parameters of liberal democracy and separates [itself] from radical projects for change."[8] Situated within this public space and subject to these structures of media discourse creation, movements calling for substantial change in the existing state-corporate-military structure that dominates American political life cannot expect to find a voice within the establishment news media. Rather, those voices advocating for structural change must contend with limited access to the mainstream reading, listening, and viewing public while also facing overwhelming competition from standardized and conventional media outlets, given that "those who hold recognized reins of legitimated power clearly have more access to the media than those who do not."[9] The structure of these social relations can be expected to define news media coverage of the U.S. military and the tendency toward justification from American imperial ambitions well into the twenty-first century.

Nor is this matter a partisan issue whereby the political right overwhelms the political left in the United States, accessing the channels of the news media and trumpeting their view much more loudly and vigorously than their opponents across a narrowly constructed ideological aisle. Instead, a substantial conformity exists across both mega-parties within the contemporary United States, championing more funding, more recruiting, and more freedom of action for the U.S. military. As such, the already astronomical U.S. military budget continues to grow so much so that an expression of shock at previous growth of the military budget within the country now seems quaint by comparison: "From 1960 to 1970, the budget of the Department of Defense has been enlarged by 80%—from $45 to $83 billion."[10] Today, the all-inclusive annual expenditure of the Department of Defense has risen into the trillions. The United States spends 12 cents of every federal dollar allocated to the military as a function of its mandatory spending. This number rises sharply, though, to 50 cents on the dollar, or fully half of the federal budget, when considering discretionary monies spent by the government on the U.S. military. All told, "The United States spends more on national defense than China, Russia, India, Saudi Arabia, United Kingdom, Germany, France, South Korea, Japan, and Ukraine—combined [...] the United States has also historically devoted a larger share of its economy to defense than many of its key allies."[11]

The fact that the occupant in the White House at the time of this writing responsible for overseeing this staggering military bloat happens to be from the center-left party within U.S. partisan dynamics makes no difference to the foregone approval of these budget increases. Indeed, in an age of significant partisan discord and disagreement on even basic facts about state and society, the expansion of the U.S. military year on year remains one of the few policies within government spending and debate that regularly finds bipartisan consensus. This cooperation within the executive and legislative processes of government in the country on issues related to military spending and operations leads plainly to the conclusion that "the [...] prevailing dogma of our time is aggressive militarism, of which the new policy of pre-emptive strike against potential enemies is but an extension."[12] Without a robust public institution to advocate the other side to this debate, such as the mainstream press, a voice for change in the new dogma of aggressive American militarism around the world remains absent. And since "Democracy depends, in large part, on a free and frank press willing to speak painful truths to the public about our society,"[13] the absence of any systematic or institutional movement among press agencies to challenge the growth or expanse of the American military as an institution reveals a dysfunction of the democratic process within the United States. In the absence of a sea change in news media coverage of the military, this dysfunction can only be expected to grow and fester in successive generations of citizens. Or, as reasoned by activist and scholar Cornel West: "There can be no democratic *paideia*—the critical cultivation of an active citizenry—without democratic *parrhesia*—a bold and courageous press willing to speak against the misinformation and mendacities of elites."[14]

Perhaps uncreatively, writing in the late 1990s, military analyst Ralph Peters called the oncoming twenty-first century the "new American century." He anticipated a fraught and conflictual era wherein creature comforts and overall ease of existence for the average American citizen would expand exponentially while simultaneously war, hardship, and forcible cultural and political change would be foisted upon those unfortunate populations subject to U.S. militarism around the globe. At the heart of the conflict between those two dichotomous visions, he argued, was access to legitimate information: "Information is at once our core commodity and the most destabilizing factor of our time."[15] In this argument, he appears prescient. The structuring, repackaging, and dissemination of information, especially information constructed as news items informing a recipient public, has revealed itself to be among the most challenged and challenging aspects of American political discourse in the twenty-first century. And with the advent and alarming rate of advance and sophistication of programs and products containing artificial intelligence and self-generating programming, the contest over legitimate and legitimated forms of information promises to loom even larger in the growing cacophony of political, cultural, and social deliberations in the decades to come. Without a significant shift in the paradigm of news coverage and institutional sustenance of the U.S. military, though, this institution will continue to proliferate and dominate both spending and policy priorities within the operations of the U.S. government, but even more critically, subject populations in areas of interest for the military institution around the globe. Without this change, news media discourse that serves to condition and support the U.S. military while sustaining the expansive reach of the American Empire will not cease. In addition, the consequences of these political and discursive realities on cultural products outside of the news, and indeed, on our vision of ourselves from inside the American imperium, likewise provide fertile ground for the embrace of militarism and the sustenance of empire for many years to come.

The U.S. Military in Contemporary American Culture: In Praise of Killing

As indicated, the authoritative print news media has constructed distinct discourses through the articulation of a variety of frames of representation throughout the long history of American wars. Within the bounds of this discourse, criticism of the state and society including the actions or inactions of the U.S. military, is, in fact, permissible as this study has demonstrated. However, the boundaries protecting the institution of the military from wholesale censure or existential critique are likewise firm. As such, when criticism of policy or military action occurs, it is approached in a guarded fashion and most commonly surrounded by narrative context and discursive detail reassuring readership in the righteousness of the institution overall, and in the morality of American military action wherever it might be conducted. The persistence of this form of news media discourse across generations and through dozens of U.S. wars, conflicts, interventions, and police actions speaks to its stability within the American cultural milieu. This, the concluding chapter of this study, will refer to this discourse as a stable force within the intellectual environment of the contemporary United States. But it does not exist, nor act upon a recipient audience, alone or in isolation. As such, remarks in this chapter consider this constructed and disseminated print media discourse in conjunction with other media forms such as film in assessments of the potential consequences of these collective intellectual phenomena as they exist and act upon the consumers of that media culture. Remarks to this end will consider the relationship between these cultural products, the ongoing discourse on the U.S. military as it exists in the printed news, and conceptions of the American self as a constructed identity, designed and disseminated within the country by select agents of cultural power.

In approaching a unified definition of a given state or community's media culture, author and cultural studies scholar Douglas Kellner has come to describe the connection between the cultural products manufactured in a given social environment and the formation of individual and collective identities as a result of the conspicuous consumption of those products:

A media culture has emerged in which images, sounds, and spectacles help produce the fabric of everyday life, dominating leisure time, sharing political views and social behavior, and providing the materials out of which people forge their very identities [...] Media culture helps shape the prevalent view of the world and deepest values: it defines what is good or bad, positive or negative, moral or evil.[16]

Interpreted in this manner, the existence of a distinct media culture in a given country gives rise to constructed identities within that country at both the micro and macro levels. To this point in the current narrative, the most critical element of that media culture under examination in the United States has been those products of the printed news media and its constructed discourse surrounding considerations of the U.S. military, the wars it has fought, and the connected policy decisions emanating from Washington deploying that institutional juggernaut around the world. Truly though, while foundational in the establishment of a specific kind of intellectual environment over the course of the last century of American history and more, this particular cultural product is only one part of the whole when it comes to considerations of an American media culture. The remaining elements within that media culture, like radio, television, film, and the internet, likewise contribute highly influential components of the cultural landscape as it pertains to internalized conceptions of the military within the United States. It is to those additional elements of the media landscape, especially considerations of popular films, that this concluding chapter in this broader work now turns.

Hollywood's contributions to contemporary American culture have a profound influence on the moral and ethical value systems of both individuals and groups within the contemporary United States. And from its earliest days, the film industry has been fixated upon the U.S. military and American wars repackaging and dramatizing American military activity for successive generations of audiences. This obsession with the military on the part of the film industry has only grown during the ubiquitous U.S. military operations in the context of the so-called War on Terror as they have lionized and dramatized the lives of soldiers in combat as well as at home for audiences number-ing well into the millions of viewers: "From its inception, the motion picture industry has been fascinated with warfare not only as entertainment but also as a vital part of the country's deeply patriotic legacy—a phenomenon that has taken on new meaning since the end of the cold war and, more emphatically, since the events of September 11, 2001."[17] Beyond simply entertainment for entertainment's sake, this perspective on contemporary films and filmmaking suggests that there are discernible agendas being set and relayed in the creation of these cultural products, particularly those that deal with the military as a central component to the plotline of a film. Like the news, then, films have the capacity to create a discourse that itself communicates values, morals, and even pillars of identity to attending audiences. As such, movies retain a significant influence within a given culture and can impart, reify, design, or otherwise construct the acceptable boundaries of social normativity, moral values, ethical practice, and, crucially, military and political aims, as well as the acceptable means through which to achieve them.

The last 20 to 30 years have seen a proliferation of Hollywood films, among other national and cultural products, whose net effect, if not their express and ultimate pur-pose, is to compel the viewing audience to accept, to agree with, and ultimately to publicly and overtly support the political and military agenda of the United States as a hegemonic actor in the international political arena. In recent years, several specific movies, including *The Hurt Locker, The Green Zone, Lone Survivor, Zero Dark Thirty, American Sniper, Yellow Birds, and Top Gun II*, to name only a few, have effectively and expertly served U.S. military and political interests by performing as vehicles of state propa-ganda, driving large segments of the American populace toward identifying with the justifications for and missions inherent to U.S. wars of choice in Iraq and Afghanistan. As functions of media culture in the contemporary United States, then, these films adequately fill the role of manicured cultural products carefully designed with spe-cific political goals in mind: "Media culture has evolved into a propaganda appara-tus, especially in the realm of international concerns where corporate and Pentagon interests are able to create their own version of 'reality' for an American public already inclined to follow the prevailing discourses."[18] Specifically, these films combine three-dimensional character development with narrative depth, a highly evocative musical score, punchy dialogue, impressive cinematography, and gritty portrayals of soldiers and U.S. intelligence personnel. The dramatization of American war recasts soldiers as uber-cool action-adventure heroes involved in gripping international sagas. These sagas are beautifully, compellingly, and expertly packaged for the viewing audience. They come replete with car chases, gun fights, near-miss explosions, love affairs, passionate romance, and thrilling, high-tech espionage. The audience is drawn into an ahistorical and de-contextualized world in which the mission at hand is immediate, critical, and, most importantly, moral and righteous. This myopic value system unfolds for viewing audiences using a subject and minimizes indigenous society as set-props and backdrops only, little more than staging material set in place to tell a one-sided story: the story of American do-goodery, of ethnic and religious supremacy, of American moral and political rectitude.

In this genre of film—action-adventure, military-politico dramas—the audience knows, at best, one-half of a narrative. Only the American protagonist and his/her allies are provided with more than two-dimensional character depth. The hero is reflective and thoughtful, intelligent and responsible. The protagonist has a family, a personal history, and is presented as a complete person with hopes and dreams equivalent to those of the viewing audience. The protagonist makes difficult but ultimately righteous decisions involving life and death. In every situation, the life of the American protagonist and/or his comrades is infused with moral and religious rectitude: "U.S. military forces are innately driven by noble ends, an assumption so embedded in movie images and narratives that it rarely demands much over articulation within the script."[19] The lives of the non-white, typically non-Christian antagonists, however, are expendable and dispensable. In fact, a particular characteristic of this genre of film fictionalizes the manner in which the antagonists themselves callously disregard their own lives and the lives of their families and/or political allies. Choosing death and destruction over life and lawfulness, non-white, non-Christian antagonists embrace the cult of the martyr and prefer death and destruction to life and liberty: "Enemy forces are routinely shown as primitive and barbaric [...] a cinematic portrait often infused with strong elements of racism and national chauvinism [...] Like Indians of Western movie lore, opposition to U.S. military power is seen as the work of cartoonish, one-dimensional male warriors whose very mission is to visit evil on the world."[20]

This obvious distinction of action and intent dramatizing the villain's psychopathic embrace of death and active pursuit of violent martyrdom provides verification for American viewing audiences that the non-white, antagonist, Other[21] has less objective human value than the white protagonist and his/her comrades. This differentiation in form, function, and, crucially, motivation between the American hero and the non-American villain provides the audience with a video record of racial and cultural stratification. This stratification is reified and sustained based upon an active, conceptual vocabulary that contributes to the construction of subjective frames of collective association and deflective dissociation comprising the Us and Them of contemporary ideological parlance. Predictably, there are very real consequences for the rote absorption of these frames of presentation within the fantasy-fiction of contemporary war films: "The repetitive fantasies, illusions, myths, images, and story lines of Hollywood moves can be expected to influence mass audiences in predictable ways [...] One popular response to the flood of violent combat [...] films is a stronger readiness to support U.S. military operations, which, in a patriotically charged milieu, will require little justification."[22] This dichotomous conceptual framing further allows for the construction of deterministic knowledge identifying non-white, non-American groups as Other or Alien, among the lowest rungs of the racial and cultural ladder.

In the parlance of psychologist Phillip Zimbardo, these films substantially contribute to the construction of a "hostile imagination," a key weapon in the psychology of a soldier that effectively constitutes his or her ability to identify an enemy and to act upon that enemy with extreme prejudice and without hesitation:

> What does it take for the citizens of one society to hate the citizens of another society to the degree that they want to segregate them, torment them, even kill them? It requires a "hostile imagination," a psychological construction embedded deeply in their minds by propaganda that transforms those others into "The Enemy" [...] It is all done with words and images [...] The process begins with creating stereotyped conceptions of the other, dehumanized perceptions of the other, the other as worthless, the other as all-powerful, the other as a fundamental threat to our cherished values and beliefs. With public fear notched up and the enemy threat imminent, reasonable people act irrationally, independent people act in mindless conformity, and peaceful people act as warriors. *Dramatic visual images of the enemy on posters, television, magazine covers, movies, and the Internet imprint on the recesses of the limbic system, the primitive brain, with the powerful emotions of fear and hate.*[23] (my emphasis)

On the basis of this concept, it is entirely conceivable that the limbic system, or "primitive brain," as identified here by Zimbardo, is in a near-permanent state of activity, even overactivity, on the basis of the ubiquitous and highly militarized cultural products present within the culture of the contemporary United States. Within those products, simplistic and often binary constructions derive from formatted, deterministic knowledge of the Other as decidedly unlike Us. They are an Other motivated by extremes of action, and a profound disregard for humanity the likes of which we cannot fathom. As such, their death and their communal destruction, their social and civil obliteration, and their prolonged and inhumane torture at our hands can be white-washed, contextualized, conditioned, justified, even lauded in the defense of our political, civil, and military legitimacy. That is to say, the death and destruction of the Other causes us no pause in our construction of our own vision of ourselves. We remain righteous and virtuous. We embrace life. Our way of life remains, in our own minds, ultimately moral. Our wars are righteous. Our fight is right:

> The culture of war banishes the capacity for pity. It glorifies self-sacrifice and death. It sees pain, ritual humiliation and violence as part of an initiation into manhood [...]. The culture of war idealizes only the warrior. It belittles those who do not exhibit the warrior's "manly" virtues. It places a premium on obedience and loyalty. It punishes those who engage in independent thought and demands total conformity. It elevates cruelty and killing to a virtue. This culture, once it infects wider society, destroys all that makes the heights of human civilization and democracy possible. The capacity for empathy, the cultivation of wisdom and understanding, the tolerance and respect for difference and even love are ruthlessly crushed.[24]

The capacity of films, then, to contribute to banal forms of nationalism or patriotism[25] within the contemporary American culture, to endorse war, to preserve the military institution, and to suspend criticism of unjust wars of choice in aid of corporate, military, and political elites, then, is profound. In short, "Hollywood is preparing the battlefield"[26] for both ongoing and future American wars abroad. Taken together with elements of news discourse already discussed in this chapter and detailed extensively in previous chapters in this work, the added element of film discourse within excessively pro-military dramas serves to expand militarism within American culture while at the same time paving the way for future wars and expansive military operations around the globe in generations yet to come.

Discourse, Culture, and National Identity: Constructing the American Self

Taken together, these compelling media constructions, both the printed news that has been extensively investigated in this work, and the cultural products of the film industry lionizing the U.S. military as exclusively righteous and honorable, contribute significantly to the ongoing formation of a unifying American identity within the contemporary political and social realms. This is a function of the fact that discourse has a profound effect on the creation of national identities. In conjunction with other cultural products such as music and television, an ongoing, normative discourse of support and sustenance for the imperial oeuvre within the United States itself creates standards of conception and modes of thought when it comes to American considerations of self. Following these lines of inquiry and theorizing the complexity of the dynamic construction of national identities, author Ruth Wodak has argued that "national identity is a complex of common or similar *beliefs or opinions* internalized in the course of socialization [...] and of common or similar *emotional attitudes* with regard to these aspects and outgroups, as well common or similar *behavioral dispositions*, including inclusive, solidarity-oriented and exclusive, distinguishing dispositions"[27] (emphasis in the original).

This offering thereby renders national identities as both dynamic and mutable, wherein groups within the designated national space devise and reify their own self-conceptions regarding collective identity.[28] It follows that there would be normative identities forming foundational or mainstream social elements within a national space as well as outgroup or fringe identity constructions posed in common by minority groups. These minority or outgroup conceptions inevitably prove ineffectual in authoring wholesale change to in-group, normative identity formations. Or if they are able to serve as the agents of change for mainstream, normative identity groupings, the process of change itself is typically sluggish and fraught. It has been argued throughout this work, then, that overt identification with and support of the military within the designated national space that is the United States is constructed as a normative, mainstream aspect of identity while opposition to this rote sustenance for military endeavors remains an outgroup or minority proposition within the American intellectual space. As indicated earlier in this chapter, and given that Wodak et al. propose the discursive construction of national identity to be a dynamic process, I have argued here that cultural products such as the traditional American war film along with daily produced products of the print news media are deployed in order to reify and reestablish this foundational aspect of the American identity within the contemporary and popular culture.

Nor do print media and film retain exclusive influence in the construction of a militaristic American identity within the contemporary United States. Sports, both collegiate and professional, have also begun to contribute to these conceptual linkages through highly dramatized presentations of military personnel, technology, and collective performance before, during, and after athletic contests. These sensationalized demonstrations, which can include spectacular Air Force flyovers before professional football games;[29] performative displays of national flags carried by active duty military before contests; the presentation of soldiers stationed abroad in live cameos during commercial breaks; and/or simply the routine playing of the American national anthem before any athletic activity in the United States, collectively create an overt and powerful link for the audience between American sports culture and the American military. This forced relationship between sports and the military is both a recent development as well as a highly contingent one, having come about only after the deliberate negotiation between U.S. military representatives and the numerous leagues and athletic associations built up over years of closed-door conversations. In fact, in at least one well-known case, the agreement to use sporting contests as a vehicle through which to thrust military propaganda in front of spectators came to pass only after the offer of substantial sums of money by the military establishment to the league in question.[30] Today, this conditional connectivity between militarism and athletics remains a staple feature of Americana, targeting sports viewers with highly choreographed, polished images of the U.S. military, its personnel, and its technology in all of its glory. These efforts inform sports fans of the foundational nature of the military in the contemporary American milieu: "These meticulously crafted and coordinated [...] ceremonies across various broadcasting channels and geographic sites create an extremely persuasive vehicle for sustaining and extending a culture of militarism, desperately garnering support for [...] failed wars, and reasserting national identity through excessive displays of patriotism and hegemonic masculinity."[31] This military pageantry endemic to the viewing of sporting events across the country largely escapes the attention of the majority of sports viewers throughout the United States and is perceived as normal and/or necessary background staging for American sporting contests.

Nor does the cultural penetration of the pervasive pro-military ethos predominant in contemporary American culture stop at sports. Given the highly technical, video-oriented nature of the contemporary U.S. military, recruiters and marketing personnel attempting to drive often vulnerable or marginalized members of the country's youth[32] into the military have specifically sought toy manufacturers and the gaming industry for the dissemination and inculcation of the military product within their merchandising. Video games now commonly feature true-to-life military scenarios that package the death and destruction inherent in war as a fun pastime, one in which quick decision-making and skillful hand-eye coordination are incredibly beneficial to the completion of realistic, three-dimensional, and/or real-time missions. And as with the film industry, which is very often beholden to U.S. military approval for scripts, stories, and imaging,[33] the gaming industry now works hand in glove with the military to ensure that their products are both visually slick as well as hyperrealistic. Military coordinators, for their part, are repaid in this partnership via the conditioning of hundreds of thousands of daily video game players who interpolate the images, missions, and motivations of the U.S. military, all while developing the technical skills and physical coordination considered to be valuable to military recruiters:

> Today, the military, toy, and gaming worlds are completely entangled, and the future promises only more [...] with the U.S. toy industry registering $22 billion annually, annual video game software and hardware sales in the U.S. topping $12.5 billion, and U.S. sales of PC games reaching over $1 billion each year; with an over-stretched, all-volunteer military, multiple, unpopular wars abroad, a Global War on Terror in full swing, and [...] the militarization of popular culture—who knows what the future holds?[34]

Undoubtedly, this lucrative and mutually beneficial arrangement between the U.S. military and U.S.-based gaming manufacturers will only continue to deepen and expand as the militarization of American culture continues to reify the centrality of its military identity through discourse and ongoing cultural productions. And while "the process of an encroaching militarization of public space and our everyday culture"[35] has clearly been an evolving process for a generation or more, the types of symbiotic corporate and ideological relationships described here indicate the likely persistence of these processes for generations still to come.

Militarism, empire, power, and prestige, then, become conceptual elements that are foundational to a broad-based national imagining of the constituent components of American identity. Returning briefly to Wodak et al. in their assessment of the connectedness between discourse, national identity, and media culture, her research group suggests that:

> If a nation is an imagined community and at the same time a mental construct, an imaginary complex of ideas containing at least the defining elements of collective unity and equality, of boundaries and autonomy, then this image is real to the extent that one is convinced of it, believes in it and identifies with it emotionally.[36]

Borrowing from Benedict Anderson's by now well-known notion of nations existing as "imagined communities," the theoretical frame provided here suggests that these elements of media text, film product, and cultural attachment all serving to frame the U.S. military in a highly supportive, highly sympathetic light only achieve their intellectual aims if the recipient nation (i.e., the attendant public) subscribes to these notional constructions en masse. It is on the basis of these notions of belief and emotional engagement from the recipient audience that the emblems of military support proffered within the culture in otherwise unnecessary or incongruous segments of cultural production are so effective in relaying messages of military support. Sports, toys, and games are all standard American pastimes, leisure activities involving commitment to a team, a character, or a cause that elicit an emotional response and/or an overt connection to the object at hand. These are at once activities of no measurable consequence, fun, and free from danger, while at the same time being highly emotionally charged and commitment-inducing, often over the course of lifetimes or generations, as is common in sports fandom.

Emblems of military support are inserted here, at the moment of emotional commitment: "By co-opting the civilian 'culture of cool,' the military-corporate complex is able to create positive associations with the armed forces, immerse the young in an alluring, militarized world of fun, and make interaction with the military second nature to today's Americans."[37] Through this highly suggestive insinuation, audience connectivity and fully expressed emotionality are realized. In this pivotal moment of identity formation, repeated across all national regions and throughout all demographic categories: "military discourses in reality become fully integrated into the vast framework of ideological hegemony."[38] Said another way, the nation becomes fully imagined and robustly connected on an emotional level when military symbolism is enfolded around and within evocative pastimes and popular leisure activities. The identity of the United States is formed, reified, and disseminated in these spaces, where those elements of emotional response inform constituent members of the national community to pay homage to the military and to be awestruck by its performative power.

Through text, image, film, and cultural product, "the United States has produced a culture of militarism in which the themes of warfare, combat, and patriotism have resonated across the entire society."[39] In the internalization of this culture, with overt enthusiasm or through subtle recognition, hundreds of millions of individuals come to embrace their collective membership in a nebulous national community, one replete with internal dispute and dissidence, and into which none of them, none of us, chose to be born. This imagined community, the United States of America, compels with equal fervor the misremembering of history as it invites the claim of credit for accomplishments its current membership had nothing to do with. It is a membership that demands ritualized performance at home, at school, at work, and at worship, and that demands loyalty over logic in impelling a boundless faith in utterly flawed institutions. "In this context protofascist tendencies within American society—militarism, authoritarianism, xenophobia, racism, the weapons cult—can be assimilated into a rationalized state."[40] This is the contemporary United States, a violent, power-hungry entity. It is draped in honor of action and legitimacy of purpose, hung with banners, billboards, bunting, and flags, and it is meant to tell us, all of its constituent membership, about who we are, where we have been, and where we are going. It is the bloat, the waste, the aggression, and the patriarchy, the masculinity, the intolerance, and the elitism of the contemporary American experience. It is the U.S. military at home and abroad. It is us.

Constant Conflict: The Consequences of Contemporary Discourse

And while this discussion may situate the ongoing conversation around discourse, nationality, identity, and the military in a theoretical or otherwise groundless space, the real-world consequences of the manifestations of these concepts are anything but theoretical. The United States of America bestrides the known political world with a military presence, or with the threat of military intervention should the architects of the military-political structures deem it warranted. The budget afforded the U.S. military by complicit politicos in both mega parties in the country dwarfs other military budgets in the world today, topping the next 10 to 12 largest competitors combined, depending on the source, and these amounts (\$2 trillion in 2023),[41] only measure publicly disclosed spending.[42] The existence, indeed, of the proliferation of black projects and dark money running through the U.S. Department of Defense is by now legendary and likely remains the primary reason that there has never been a successful audit conducted of the U.S. Pentagon. There has likewise never been a significant investigation into the annual national financial waste sacrificed to the altar of the American military. By any measure, these facts rank the United States as the most military-oriented state and society in the history of humankind. But the economic opportunity costs that result from this orientation domestically are legion. Escalating healthcare and education costs, for example, are starved of the kind of federal funding that is uncritically bestowed upon the U.S. military without hesitation. In fact, a common positioning in debates surrounding both student debt and medical debt is that the debtor ought to join the military, a career pathway that pays for both healthcare and higher education expenses. Herein lies the foundational underpinning of the military-imperial structure of the contemporary United States. Should the citizens desire secure access to basic human needs like medical attention and education, the military will provide it in exchange for a contribution to the construction of the American Empire. Seek an alternative pathway, and American citizens are left to their own devices. And yet, while clearly "a shift in federal activity from defense to non-defense activities would, in itself, contribute toward a relative improvement in the economic activity,"[43] such a shift remains unattainable, if not unimaginable, in the contemporary United States.

We are left with a choice between a risky venture in a cruel and callous open market or the personal security of membership in the state's most protected institution. For scores of thousands, the choice of security is too precious to forego, even in the midst of a ceaseless war. As a result, a military of millions of activity duty, reserve, contracted, or support personnel are currently stationed in one of 800 bases across 80 countries the world over.[44] This gargantuan global presence serves as a guardian to a complex and multifaceted twenty-first century American Empire, and "like every hegemonic power in history—Persian, Greek, Roman, Chinese, Spanish, Ottoman, British, French, and Soviet, among others—America's global power was forged by the sword and the cannon."[45] The U.S. military retains its expansive remit to man the posts of the American Empire, then, and will continue to do so into the foreseeable future, presuming the continued protected status of the military as an institution as is daily constructed and reified in contemporary discourse and cultural production. For this reason, and as has been established in the case study chapters in this work, the producers and arbiters of contemporary national discourse are careful not to attack the military or their political managers from the position of an institutional or existential critique. This critical, intellectual assault from the mainstream architects of discourse would potentially damage the prevailing political status quo. This would be anathema when the preservation of the status quo preserves America's overall imperial structure. In essence, this omission is an act of conservation and is therefore championed by the minority of elites who wield enough power in outlets of news and cultural production to persuade the majority of the people that their best interests lie in the preservation of that system, too. These persistent patterns of social and cultural production reveal that the "wide panorama of militarized images and narratives, visible across several decades, has contributed deeply to the legitimation of empire"[46] within domestic rationale here in the United States.

But the domestic consequences of these theoretical structures, while informative and compelling, likely pale in comparison to the damage that is done by the American military in its imperial oeuvre overseas. American wars have wrought incalculable damage throughout the nineteenth, twentieth, and twenty-first centuries to communities across disparate locations, most often, as has been rendered here in previous chapters, in aid of highly dubious or ultimately self-serving political goals: "The deadly effects of armed [American] intervention include widespread human casualties, population displacements, a drain on material resources, and environmental ruin—not to mention the subversion of international law along with heightened attacks on domestic rights and freedoms."[47] And though it is true that "all wars produce atrocities"[48] and that quite obviously, not all wars in human history have been American ones, the particular dominance of the American state in the center of its modern empire has likewise contributed to its dominance in the production of war, death, and misery through the vehicle of the U.S. military for many decades. America and Americans, therefore, remain peculiar in our unrestrained praise of the warrior class and its leadership, continuing to freely contribute, as we do, increasing proportions of blood and treasure to its cause and the cause of the empire it sustains, year after year. Ours is, in short "a culture and ideology of militarism [...] so far-reaching, so sophisticated, and yet so illusory, dependent upon powerful myths."[49] These are myths of the news media's making, myths of the cultural elite's making, and ultimately, myths of our own making in the consumption of culture and the reification of conspicuous examples of our ongoing, normative, militant nationalism. Through these networks, and with the media ensconced in its role as arbiter of national culture and distributor of national identity, the locus of the dynamic American self is produced and daily reified in service to the military establishment now and into our foreseeable future.

Notes

1 This chapter title takes its name from the title of a chart-topping song written by the band Live and released as their debut single on the album *Throwing Copper* on April 26, 1994 (MCA Records).

2 Daniel Hallin, *The "Uncensored War": The Media and Vietnam* (London: The University of California Press, 1986), 142.

3 Gaye Tuchman, *Making News: A Study in the Social Construction of Reality* (New York: Free Press, 1978), 1.

4 Ibid., 4.

5 Simon Cottle, *Mediatized Conflict: Developments in Media and Conflict Studies* (New York: The Open University Press, 2006), 112.

6 Tuchman, *Making News*, 210.

7 Ralph Peters, "Constant Conflict," *Parameters* 27, no. 2 (Summer 1997): 4–14. (US Army War College Quarterly: US Army War College Press), 5–7.

8 Cottle, *Mediatized Conflict*, 112.

9 Tuchman, *Making News*, 134.
10 Seymour Melman, *Pentagon Capitalism: The Political Economy of War* (New York: McGraw-Hill Book Company, 1970), 20.
11 "U.S. Defense Spending Compared to Other Countries," *Peter G. Peterson Foundation.* Accessed June 2, 2023. https://www.pgpf.org/chart-archive/0053_defense-comparison#:~ :text=Defense%20spending%20accounts%20for%2012,of%20the%20annual%20federal %20budget.
12 Cornel West, *Democracy Matters: Winning the Fight against Imperialism* (New York: Penguin Books, 2004), 5.
13 Ibid., 39.
14 Ibid.
15 Peters, "Constant Conflict," 5.
16 Douglas Kellner, *Media Culture: Cultural Studies, Identity and Politics between the Modern and Postmodern* (London: Routledge, 1995), 1.
17 Carl Boggs and Tom Pollard, *The Hollywood War Machine: U.S. Militarism and Popular Culture* (Boulder: Paradigm Publishers, 2007), ix.
18 Ibid., 180.
19 Ibid., 13.
20 Ibid.
21 The concept of the enemy "Other," was established and utilized as a theoretical construction applied via discourse in order to construct and reaffirm in-group and out-group identities within a given cultural milieu by Edward Said, referred to in the introductory chapter of this study, among other prominent scholars and philosophers. See his work on this matter, *Culture and Imperialism* (New York: Vintage Books, 1994).
22 Boggs and Pollard, *The Hollywood War Machine*, 11.
23 Phillip Zimbardo, *The Lucifer Effect: How Good People Turn Evil* (Rider: London, 2007), 11.
24 Chris Hedges, "Killing Ragheads for Jesus," *Truthdig*, January 26, 2015. https://www.truth-dig.com/articles/killing-ragheads-for-jesus.
25 Michael Billig, *Banal Nationalism: Theory, Culture, and Society* (London: SAGE Publications, 1995).
26 Ralph Peters, "Constant Conflict," 11.
27 Ruth Wodak, et al. *The Discursive Construction of National Identity* (Edinburgh: Edinburgh University Press, 1999), 28.
28 Ibid., 186.
29 During one NFL contest between the Green Bay Packers and Tampa Bay Buccaneers in October of 2020, the in-game announcer team of Troy Aikman and Joe Buck were caught, seemingly unaware, uttering on-mic criticisms of the financial waste inherent in the U.S. military flyovers that take place before many NFL games throughout the season. They were met with significant public censure and even calls for their removal from their broadcast duties as a result (Allen Kim, "Broadcasters Joe Buck and Troy Aikman Caught on Hot Mic Appearing to Mock Military Flyovers as Wasteful," *CNN*, October 21, 2020. https://www .cnn.com/2020/10/20/us/troy-aikman-joe-buck-flyover-trnd/index.html).
30 Peter Swope, "Gridiron Imperialism: How the NFL Propagandizes for the US Military," *The Brown Political Review*, November 22, 2021 (Brown University). https://brownpoliticalreview .org/2021/11/gridiron-imperialism-how-the-nfl-propagandizes-for-the-us-military/.
31 Mia Fischer, "Commemorating 9/11 NFL-Style: Insights into America's Culture of Militarism," *Journal of Sport and Social Issues* 38, no. 3 (2014): 208.
32 In describing the predatory nature of the American military establishment as it regards poor and minority youth in America, theorist Cornel West noted: "This new doctrine of U.S. foreign policy goes far beyond our former doctrine of preventive war. It green-lights politi-cal elites to sacrifice U.S. soldiers—who are disproportionately working class and youth of color—in adventurous crusades" (West, *Democracy Matters*, 5).
33 Author David L. Robb has conducted extensive research into the close, advisory relationship that exists between the military and the movie industry, which includes the presence of a film office within the Pentagon building itself: "And that's what moviemaking is all about for the Pentagon—putting positive images of the military on the screen so that kids will like what

they see and join up one day" (David L. Robb, *Operation Hollywood: How the Pentagon Shapes and Censors the Movies* (New York: Prometheus Books, 2004), 178).

34 Nick Turse, *Complex: How the Military Invades Our Everyday Lives* (New York: Metropolitan Books, 2008), 139–40.

35 Fischer, "Commemorating 9/11 NFL-Style," 218.

36 Wodak, et al. *The Discursive Construction of National Identity*, 22.

37 Turse, *Complex*, 100–1.

38 Boggs and Pollard, *The Hollywood War Machine*, 21.

39 Ibid., ix.

40 Ibid., 36–7.

41 Agency Profile, "Department of Defense." Accessed May 25, 2023. https://www.usaspending.gov/agency/department-of-defense?fy=2023.

42 The staggering size of this expenditure may well be more of a function of domestic strategy than international need. According to analyst Seymour Melman, who studied the exponential increase of the U.S. military and its federal bureaucracy in the 1960s, "the state management, drawing on its unique capital resource—an annual portion of the nation's product—applies this directly to increasing either the scope or the intensity of its decision-power." Following this assessment, the more the military spends, the bigger its share of national policy, and the more funding that will be available to it in the future. Fifty years after this valuation, it is difficult to argue with the trend Melman predicted (*Pentagon Capitalism*, 23).

43 Ibid., 171.

44 This figure does not include the so-called Black Sites where the U.S. intelligence community secretly detains and interrogates prisoners in locations throughout the world (Amy Goodman and David Vine, "The U.S. Has 750 Overseas Military Bases, and Continues to Build More to Encircle China," *Democracy Now!* February 14, 2023. https://www.democracynow.org/2023/2/14/david_vine_us_bases_china_philippines).

45 John Tirman, *The Deaths of Others: The Fate of Civilians in America's Wars* (New York: Oxford University Press, 2011), 52.

46 Boggs and Pollard, *The Hollywood War Machine*, 15.

47 Ibid., 224.

48 Tirman, *The Deaths of Others*, 286.

49 Boggs and Pollard, *The Hollywood War Machine*, 20.

APPENDIX A: PRINT NEWS MEDIA ARTICLES ANALYZED IN CHAPTER TWO, *FIN DE SIÈCLE*: THE BEGINNINGS OF AMERICAN EMPIRE

Note to the Reader

The articles cited represent a sampling of the articles analyzed in the construction of Chapter 2 of this book entitled "*Fin de Siècle*: The Beginnings of American Empire." These articles were selected because of their presence within authoritative or otherwise mainstream news sources covering events connected to the Spanish-American War during the latter years of the nineteenth and the earliest years of the twenty-first centuries. These news products were selected using archive and database searches that selected keywords connected to the war such as "Manila + Soldiers" or "Cuba + Fighting," applied in a series of distinct but related searches performed over the course of research conducted for this project. Many thousands of articles were hit during the aforementioned keyword searches, and as such they are not all represented in the list to follow here. Instead, what is presented within this Appendix and throughout the Appendices of this book are those articles that are representative examples of the kind of articles uncovered during this research process and then subsequently analyzed for the critical, discursive perspective contained therein. Major publications reaching a total audience of millions were included in this sampling, though, to include news articles from the *Los Angeles Times*, the *New York Times*, and the *Washington Post* among other authoritative news sources.

A final note regarding the sample to follow here: it was common practice during the period of the Spanish-American War for news articles to be identified using an extended article title (sometimes dozens of words long) and a publication name, date, and location. But specific journalists, editors, or authors were rarely identified in the archival examples of the original publications reviewed for the creation of this chapter. As such, the citations to follow below do not typically identify the author but rather point only to the often extended title of the news item and its publication information only.

Print News Articles

"Action Close At Hand: Land and Naval Forces of the United States Engaged in Important Movements. Cube to Be Invaded Early Next Week. Report of a Battle at Manila between Dewey's Fleet and the Spanish Forces Hourly Expected. A Portion of the Cape Verde Fleet Sails and May Be on the Way to This Country." (1898, April 30). *New York Times*, 1.

"Active Hostilities Continue: Reports of Battles Reach Manila." (1901, March 14). *New York Times*, 1.

"Administration Is Mystified: But Strongly of the Opinion that the Disaster Was Accidental. Naval Officers Not Easily Convinced. They Firmly Combat All Theories as to a Mishap Aboard the Ship. A Day of Suppressed Excitement in Official Circles, Pending More Definite Reports Touching the Origin of the Explosion—White House Festivities Abandoned—No Warship to Be Sent to Havana. The President's Opinion Stated. Excitement at the Navy Department." (1898, February 17). *The Washington Post*, 1.

"Admiral Dewey Testifies: The Real History of the Surrender of Manila. Resistance All a Sham. Governor General Gave Up the City When the Spanish Fleet Was Sunk—Dealings with Aguinaldo." (1902, June 27). *New York Times*, 8.

"Alarmists Rebuked Again: No Extraordinary War Preparations on Foot. Both Secretary Long and Secretary Alger Authorize an Emphatic Denial Of Sensational Rumors—'Public Judgement Should Be Suspended' Still the Administration's Watchword. Military and Naval Activity Explained. Things Looking Better, Mr. Long Says. Confidence in The Court of Inquiry. Senator Proctor in Havana [...] Denies That He Is There. No Public Business. A Talk With Admiral Sicard. Movements of the Fleet Explained." (1898, February 27). *New-York Tribune*, 1.

"All-Day Battle With Filipinos: Gen. Lawton, With 3,000 Men, in The Hardest Fight of the War. Loss on Both Sides. Heavy American Casualties Sixty and Those of the Enemy Unknown. Desperate Struggle at a Bridge over the Zapote River—The Navy Assists the Army." (1899, June 14). *New York Times*, 3.

"Almost Stunned by the Catastrophe. Rumors of Foul Play Not Credited. The President and Members of the Cabinet Regard the Disaster as Due to Some Mysterious Accident—This Country's Naval Strength Now Inferior to That of Spain—Prompt Measures Take for Relief of the Injured. The Administration's View." (1898, February 17). *New-York Tribune*, 1.

"American Discipline." (1899, April 26). *New York Times*, 6.

"American Forces Capture Malolos: Filipinos Leave the City Burning and Flee. Aguinaldo Not There. The Enemy Now in Full Retreat to the North. A Desperate Battle, Rebels Resisted MacArthur's Advance to the Last, Losing a Great Number of Men." (1899, March 31). *New York Times*, 1.

"American Patriotism and Patriotic Americanism." (1989, May 1). *Los Angeles Times*, 2.

"Americans Hold Manila Securely: Lines Extended Nine Miles to the North and South. No Fear of Water Famine. The Works Captured and Missing Machinery Recovered. Natives Put To Rout. One-third of the Hostile Body of Filipinos Incapacitated and the Survivors in Full Retreat." (1899, February 8). *New York Times*, 1.

"Americans Take Calamba: After a Hard Fight Lasting Two Hours the Rebels Retreat. Battle in The Swamps. Gen. Hall Led the Expedition and His Losses Were Four Killed and Twelve Wounded." (1899, July 28). *New York Times*, 6.

"Another Fight at Samar: Ninth Infantry Company Again Does Battle with the Insurgents." (1901, November 18). *New York Times*, 3.

"Army Life around Manila: Regulations for the Bivouac after the Fighting of the Day—Outposts Detailed—Health Precautions." (1899, October 20). *New York Times*, 5.

"As Major Generals: Four Officers of the Regular Army Have Been Selected to Direct Campaign In Cuba. They Are Veteran Fighters and Hare Excellent Records. Shafter, Otis, Merriman, and Wade." (1898, April 30). *The Washington Post*, 1.

"Autonomy Failure: Insurgents Will Accept No Terms not Based on Independence." (1898, February 27). *Los Angeles Times*, A3.

"The Battle of El Caney: Description by a Spanish Officer, Aide on Gen. Vara del Rey's Staff. Americans Fought Like Lions. Were Mowed Down by Hundreds, but Never Fell Back an Inch—Only Five Hundred and Fourteen Spaniards Engaged." (1898, August 14). *New York Times*, 3.

"The Battle of Manila: Gen. Greely Issues a Map of Operations of Last August." (1899, March 3). *New York Times*, 7.

"Battle in Philippines: Moro Jikiri and Band Exterminated -Our Loss 1 Dead, 23 Wounded." (1909, July 6). *New York Times*, 1.

"Battle-Ship Vizcaya Coming: A More Powerful Fighter Than the Maine to Visit American Ports." (1898, January 27). *The Washington Post*, 1.

"A Battle With Filipinos: Americans Triumph After Having 3 Killed and 13 Wounded. The Fight Was Near Manila. San Mateo Taken after Considerable Resistance—Twenty-three Rebels Known to Have Been Killed." (1899, August 14). *New York Times*, 3.

"A Battle With Filipinos: Sanguinary Engagement Within Seven Miles of Manila." (1903, February 10). *New York Times*, 1.

"Brave Work of Marines: Full Story of the Fighting at Guantanamo Camp. In Fancied Security the Midnight Surprise Second Night's Fighting Cubans on Skirmish Duty. Final Rout of The Spanish." (1898, June 27). *New-York Tribune*, 3.

"The Campaign at Manila: Details of Events That Succeeded the First Pitched Battle." (1899, March 23). *New York Times*, 5.

"Canalejas Letter Admitted. State Department Acts Promptly. Assistant Secretary Day Calls the Offending Diplomat to Account—Senor De Lome's Resignation Sent to Madrid—His Sentiments Will Be Disavowed by the Spanish Government. The Minister Resigns. Gravity of the Offence, Previous Affairs of the Kind. The Rule of Action, Dismissal of Lord Sackville West." (1898, February 10). *New-York Tribune*, 1.

"Cannot Trust The Cubans: Gen. Young Says It Would Be Folly to Give Them the Island. His Estimate of Their Character Based Upon His Experience at Santiago—Praises the Conduct of Maj. Gen. Joe Wheeler." (1898, August 6). *The Washington Post*, 4.

"Capt. Dyer's Anger Roused: Former Commander of the Baltimore Denounces The Secretary of the Anti-Imperialist League." (1899, July. 12). *New York Times*, 4.

"Cheer For Roosevelt: Republicans Have an Enthusiastic Ratification Meeting. A Fashionable Assemblage. Men and Women Applaud the Candidate in Carnegie Hall. Col. Roosevelt, Gen. Woodford, Seth Low, Joseph H. Choate, and Lieut. Gov. Woodruff Speak." (1898, October 6). *New York Times*, 1.

"Chief Aguinaldo Means To Rule: Asks for an American Protectorate for the Philippines." (1898, June 8). *New York Times*, 2.

"Conditions In Manila: Pessimistic View of a Correspondent in the City—Negros Delegates Communicated with Aguinaldo Secretly." (1899, March 18). *New York Times*, 1.

"Congress and the Cubans: Two Resolutions Asking for Information Passed, One in the Senate and One in the House. Reliable Knowledge Wanted. Desire Expressed for Statements That Shall Show the Conditions in Cuba and Our Relations with the Island." (1898, February 15). *New York Times*, 3.

"A Crisis Imminent: Cuban Complications Threaten Immediate War With Spain. President McKinley's Patience Almost Exhausted—Inexplicable Delay of the Foreign Relations Committee—Additions to the Spanish Navy." (1898, February 6). *Los Angeles Times*, 6.

"The Cuban Insurgents' Victory: Home Rule as Conceded by Spain the Result of Their Long Fight." (1898, January 14). *New York Tribune*, 2.

"Cubans Are Dying of Hunger: Charles W. Russell Says 200,000 Reconcentrados Are Living in Dire Distress. Should Have $20,000 a Day. Measures of Relief Already Taken Wholly Inadequate to Check the Ravages of Disease and Death—Soldiers Ill Fed." (1898, January 2). *New York Times*, 4.

"Cubans Cheer the Rebels: The Third Anniversary of the Beginning of Their War Celebrated. A Wildly Enthusiastic Meeting in Chickering Hall—Flags Draped with Black Displayed, and Resolution of Sympathy Over The Loss of the Maine, Passed Suffering in Cuba. Miss Barton Almost Prostrated at the Scenes Of Desolation and Misery. Even Willing to Accept Gomez Spain's Alleged Eagerness to Secure Peace in Cuba." (1898, February 25). *New-York Tribune*, 3.

"De Lome on the President: Spanish Minister Alleged to Have Insulted Mr. McKinley in a Letter to Senor Canalejas. Called a 'Low Politician' Cuban Junta Issues a Copy of the Communication Which Is Said to Have Been Stolen by a Patriot." (1898, February 9), *New York Times*, 1.

"Details of the Battle: The Manila Victory." (1898, May 9). *New York Times*, 1.

"Dewey and The Filipinos: A Talk With Lieut. Commander Rees of the Admiral's Flagship. Says Trouble Will Be Brief. The Rebellion Is Chiefly in Luzon, He Says—Admiral Dewey's Recent Dispatches." (1899, March 6). *New York Times*, 1.

Dewey Arms the Rebels: Spanish Efforts to Win Them over by Promises Are Repelled by Chief Aguinaldo." (1898, May 30). *New York Times*, 2.

"Dewey Expected in July: The Route by Which He Will Sail Agitating the Entire Country." (1898, May 12). *New York Times*, 1.

"Dewey Gives Way Before Admirers: Day Full of Stirring Incidents for the Hero of Manila. Gets Farragut's Old Flag. Tears on the Admiral's Face as Commander Baird Presents It. The Governor Calls Col. Roosevelt. Greets Dewey and Addresses the Tars—Gen. Miles, Gen. Merritt, and Vermont Friends Also Pay Their Respects." (1899, September 29). *New York Times*, 1.

"Dewey May Report To-Day: The McCulloch Said to Have Gone Back to Manila After Hearing of the Battle. Now Expected at Hongkong. Rumors from Various Sources Receive No Credence at Washington—Possible Explanations of the Long Delay." (1898, May 7). *New York Times*, 1.

"Dewey's Big Victory: Dispatches from Him State That He Has Destroyed the Spanish Fleet. Batteries at Cavite Demolished." (1898, May 8). *New York Times*, 1.

"Dewey's Captains Rewarded: Commanders of the United States Warships Advanced on the Naval Register." (1898, June 3). *New York Times*, 3.

"Dewey's Crew of Heroes: Men Foremost in Battle Coming on the Olympia. Admiral's Adieu to Manila Last Orders to His Fleet Before He Weight Anchor And Capt. Barker's Order." (1899, July 19). *New York Times*, 4.

"Dewey's Troops Held Back: Reported that All Hands Will Congregate at Honolulu and Go to Manila Together." (1898, June 14). *New York Times*, 4.

"The Difference in Men." (1898, June 20). *New-York Tribune*, 6.

"Early Days of the Fighting: Gen. Anderson Describes the First Events of the Campaign." (1899, April 30). *New York Times*, 2.

"A Faithful Pilot at the Helm: President M'Kinley Will Uphold the National Honor, But Will Not Be Driven into War Nor Does Spain Want War Her Government Ready to Disavow All Complicity in the Maine Disaster. Reassuring Spain Racific Announcement from the Sagasta Cabinet." (1898, February 27). *New-York Tribune*, 1.

"Fierce Battle With The Filipinos: Six Killed and Forty-three Wounded on American Side. Rebels Were Finally Routed. Col. Stotsenburg and Lieut. Sisson of Nebraska Regiment Dead. Fourth Cavalry Loses Two Men—Enemy Fought Behind Breastworks Near Quingua—Thirteen of Their Force Killed." (1899, April 24). *New York Times*, 1.

"Fierce Fighting Around Manila: Dewey Arms the Rebels, but Will Not Let Them Enter the City."(1898, June 7). *New York Times*, 1.

"Fight Goes on: Rebels Running: Town of Malinta Taken After a Fierce Battle. Malabon Now in Ashes. The Filipinos Apply the Torch Before Leaving the Town. Col. Egbert Killed. Believed Enemy Will Make Its Last Stand at the Capitol, Malolos—American List of Casualties Increasing." (1899, March 27). *New York Times*, 1.

"Fighting Their Way to Malolos: Americans Defeat Aguinaldo, Leading His Army. The Enemy Forced Back. Left 100 Dead on the Field, Losing Many Prisoners. MacArthur Advances, Result of Seventy-two Hours of Battle Complete Rout and Flight of the Filipinos." (1899, March 28). *New York Times*, 1.

"Filipinos Becoming Friendly: A Volunteer Soldier's Estimate of the People of Manila—They Are Learning to Like the Americans." (1898, November 20). *New York Times*, 14.

"Filipinos Fleeing Before Americans: Aguinaldo's Forces Driven Back from Manila. Their Loss in Battle 5,500. Rebel Leaders Declare Americans Forced the Engagement." (1899, February 7). *New York Times*, 1.

"Filipinos' Losses Heavy: Their Dead Bodies in the Trenches Tell of Fierce Battle. Driven from Coast Towns. Gen. Lawton Finds Bacoor Deserted and Torn to Pieces by the Gunboats' Shells." (1899, June 15). *New York Times*, 4.

"Filipinos' Stern Lesson: Reverses at Manila and Iloilo May End Hostilities. The Administration Satisfied if the Rebels Come Peaceably into Camp They Need Fear No Further Chastisement." (1899, February 15). *New York Times*, 1.

"Fleet Now Due at Manila. A Hongkong Report Says that Our Warships Are Already at the Philippines. A Naval Battle Imminent." (1898, April 20). *New York Times*, 1.

"A Futile Protest." (1898, May 25). *Los Angeles Times*, 8.

"Gen. F. V. Greene's Report: The Part Taken by His Brigade in the Battle Which Resulted in the Capture Of Manila. Troops Are Warmly Praised. Opposition of the Spaniards With a Loss Comparatively Insignificant—Special Commendation for Several Officers." (1898, October 03). *New York Times*, 3.

"Gen. Harrison on the Victory: He Says the Battle at Manila Recalls Farragut and Mobile Bay." (1898, May 3). *New York Times*, 2.

"Gen. Shafter Criticised: Officers Engaged at El Caney Express Surprise at Inaccuracies in His Report. Bravery of the Spaniards, Their Magnificent Fighting Against Heavy Odds—Scant Justice Done Those Who Participated in a Brilliant Charge." (1898, September 16). *New York Times*, 4.

"General Lawton to His Men: He Praises the Second Division for Gallant Work in The Santiago Campaign. Criticism of the Campaign." (1898, August 16). *New-York Tribune*, 2.

"Glad Tidings Cheered: Naval Victory Brings Joy to Patriotic Hearts. Scenes When News Is Received. Immense Throng Gathers at the Post Building and Makes City Ring with Cheers as Dispatches Are Received Long-Suppressed Anxiety and Excitement Find Vent in a Patriotic Outburst—Rejoicing at the White House. All Thoughts on the Philippines. Great Victory Assured. News Spread Everywhere." (1898, May 2). *The Washington Post*, 2.

"Hear The Eagle Scream: Rejoicing At Washington Over Dewey's Victory. News From the Philippines Affords the Greatest Satisfaction to the Administration—Prediction in Made That Spain Will Quit." (1898, May 2). *Los Angeles Times*, 1.

"The Hero of El Caney: Brilliant Military Record of Maj.-Gen. Henry W. Lawton." (1898, August 28). *Los Angeles Times*, 9.

"Hopes to Avoid War: Administration Will Not Rush into a Conflict. Waiting Naval Court's Report. Policy of the President as Outlined to Friends at the White House—Spanish Government Not Believed to Have Been Involved in Any Plot to Blow Up the Warship—Any Demand for Indemnity, It Is Said, Is Likely to Be Met Promptly. Expects Spain to Pay. Would Congress Agree to It? No Important Developments. Public Is Fully Informed. Secretary Long's Statements. Information from Sigsbee. Sigsbee's Recommendations Approved." (1898, February 25). *The Washington Post*, 1.

"How Guanica Was Captured: Arrival of Miles's Army—Gloucester's Good Work in Clearing the War for Landing. The Gloucester Leads the War. Launch Lands Thirty Sailors Opening Fire on Spaniards. Enemy Could Not See The Ships. No Serious Fighting Expected." (1898, August 6). *New-York Tribune*, 1.

"In the Hospital at Manila: Comfortable Home Provided for Sick American Soldiers in the Philippine Islands." (1900, January 26). *New York Times*, 3.

"In Manila a Month Ago: Condition of the City at That Time as Seen by a Visitor. Admiral Dewey's Popularity: How the People of the Islands Have Been Robbed by Their Spanish Masters—Their Ignorance." (1898, July 4). *The Baltimore Sun*, 4.

"Kansas Men's Charge: Enemy Fights Every Foot of Ground and Suffers Heavy Losses—Our Casualties Slight." (1899, February 11). *New York Times*, 1.

"The Line of Battle: Filipinos Concentrated at Malabon and Caloocan and Opened Fire on Our Outposts." (1899, February 1). *New York Times*, 1.

"Looking Toward Manila: Naval Officers Expect to Receive the First Big War News from the Philippines." (1898, April 29). *New York Times*, 2.

"Maine Blown Up at Havana: The Battleship Destroyed and Many Lives Lost by an Explosion. Spanish Cruiser Aids in Rescuing Survivors. Captain Sigsbee, in Reporting the Disaster to the Navy Department, Advises Americans to Withhold Judgment till the Facts Are Ascertained—Cause of the Catastrophe Not Yet Know.—Lighthouse Tenders Sent from Key West—Sympathy Expressed by General Blanco." (1898, February 16). *New-York Tribune*, 1.

"Maine Court at Key West: It May Return to Havana on Wednesday. Nothing Divulged About the Results of the Inquiry So Far—Conferences with Admiral Sicard—Sensational Stories Ridiculed Have Reached No Conclusion, Have Little to Say, Conferring with Admiral Sicard Stories Easily Proved False. Belief in Havana That No Knowledge Has Yet Been Gained of the Hull Or Magazines of the Main. False Stories of Discoveries. Was General Lee's Life Threatened? Activity at a Spanish Dockyard." (1898, February 28). *New-York Tribune*, 1.

"Maine Court Heard from: First Official News Reaches the Navy Department. Captain Sampson's Letter Puts a Quietus on Rumors That a Definite Conclusion Has Already Been Reached—The Court Will Return to Havana Strengthening the Accident Theory. Belligerent Feeling Subsiding. The Coming Elections in Spain, Belief That the Liberal Party Will Remain in Power. Cardinal Gibbons's Good Counsel Calmly Await the Court of Inquiry's Verdict, He Says Suppression of Filibustering a Report from Secretary Gage Sent to the House. Work at Fort Hamilton. No Day Leaves of Absence for the Men." (1898, March 1). *New-York Tribune*, 1.

"The Maine Inquiry: Feeling of the American Naval Officers on the Subject. Gravity of the Outcome Thoroughly Realized in Havana—Wild Stories to Be Sifted—Complete Failure of Autonomy—Gomez Moving Toward Havana. Divers at Work About the Wreck. Their Efforts as Yet Directed toward Salvage Only." (1898, February 20). *New York Tribune*, 1.

"Maine Inquiry Begun: The Naval Court at Havana in Session on the Lighthouse Tender Mangrove, Near the Wreck. Captain Sigsbee the First Witness. The Inquiry Begins Was Able to Answer All Questions. An Accident, Says Sagasta, the Spanish Premier Announces That. More Bodies from the Maine. Two of the Victims Recovered by Divers. Adding to Pacific Coast New Guns to Be Mounted." (1898, February 22). *New-York Tribune*, 1.

"Maine Now At Havana: Exchange of Courtesies with Spanish Officials. Sigsbee Confers With Gen. Lee. Arrival of Warship Occasioned Surprise and Aroused Curiosity, but City Remains Tranquil—Maine Likely to Remain in Port Some Time—Commander Sigsbee to Call on Acting Captain General Parrado—Much Gratified by His Reception." (1898, January 26). *The Washington Post*, 1.

"The Maine Sent to Cuba: Battleship Leaves Key West for Havana, Supported by the Whole of Admiral Sicard's Fleet. Secretary Long Explains It, Says It Is a Friendly Call Merely—Spain Notified of the Course to be Taken—A Concession to the Demand for Action." (1898, January 25). *New York Times*, 1.

"Mangled Men: Peace Hath Horrors No Less Than War. Fifty-nine Seamen Suffering Tortures in Silence. Two Hundred and Fifty-eight Silent in Death. Awful Scene At Havana. Proud Battleship Maine Lies a Helpless Wreck. Naval Officers Hope to Save Her for Further Service. Theory of Spanish Treachery not Received With Favor. Explosion of Her Magazine. The Cause Still a Mystery—Capt. Sigsbee Thrown from Bed—Guncotton Flooded—President and Cabinet Advise." (1898, February 17). *Los Angeles Times*, 1.

"Manila Awaiting Attack: Commodore Dewey Trying to Establish Communications with the Rebels, Says a Dispatch. Fleet Not Yet Heard From." (1898, May 1). *New York Times*, 1.

"The Manila Expedition: Delay in Sending the Second Detachment Explained by the War Department." (1898, June 4). *New York Times*, 2.

"Manila Hero Welcomed Home: Chief Gunner on the Olympia Sees His Son for the First Time."
(1899, January 6). *New York Times*, 3.
"Manila Situation Serious." (1898, May 35). *New York Times*, 1.
"Mighty Task For God: Wounded and Sin Stranded World to Be Reclaimed. Creation Required
Word Heathenism, Mohammedanism, Alcoholism and the Evils of War to Be Overcome,
Talmage Says—Would Not Give Lives of a Hundred Brave Americans for Cuba, the
Sandwich Islands, and All of Spain—Eminent Divine Gives Statistics. What Might God Do?
Working to Make Light. A Mighty Task. Only Spoke the Word. Corrupt Lives of Merchants.
Curse of Mohammedanism. Astronomy the First Science. Alcoholism's Throne of Skulls."
(1898, February 28). *The Washington Post*, 9.
"More Divers Sent To Cuba: Capt. Sigsbee Says No Examination Has Been Made of Area of
Explosion. Disaster's Cause Still Unknown. Certain Havana News Discredited. Mote Divers
Sent to Havana. Official Telegrams Exchanged. No Investigation of Explosion. The Proposed
Congressional Inquiry. The Maine Appropriation Passed. For a Monument to Sailors of the
Maine. Attitude of House Leaders on Cuba." (1898, February 22). *The Washington Post*, 1.
"The Morning Battle: Details of the Struggle Before Malolos at the Dawn of Good Friday."
(1899, March 31). *New York Times*, 1.
"Navy Battle Imminent: Dewey's Squadron Sails from Hongkong to Capture the Philippine
Fleet." (1898, April 28). *New York Times*, 2.
"Navy's Work in the East: The Surrender of Zamboanga to Commander Very. Natives Face
Starvation. Rice Was Brought Them by the Manila and Joy Followed Woe—No Trouble
Anticipated." (1900, January 7). *New York Times*, 15.
"Never A Mine: Havana Harbor Said to Be Very Safe. Official Maps Do Not Indicate Signs of
Danger. No New Developments as to the Maine Disaster. Ship Sinking in the Mud. Plenty of
Money for Uncle Sam in Case of War. Russell Sage and Mark Hanna to the Rescue. Millions
for the Defense of the Government. Very Rocky Times in Spain." (1898, February 27). *Los
Angeles Times*, A1.
"News from the Inside: Some Recent Happenings in the City of Havana. An Escaped American
Tells Admiral Sampson What Is Going on at the Cuban Capital—Havanese Said to Be Eager
for War." (1898, May 6). *Los Angeles Times*, 2.
"News Since Midnight: A Good Stiff Fight. That's What Shafter's Soldiers Are Looking for.
Aguadores Will Probably Be the First to Fall—Garcia Expects Santiago to Hold Out Ten
Days. Cervera's Choice of Destruction." (1898, June 23). *Los Angeles Times*, 2.
"Next Battle at Bacolor: American Troops Plan to Clear Filipinos Out of the Town. Stubborn
Fight Expected. Force of Six Thousand Well-Armed Rebels Intrenched and Waiting with
Plenty of Ammunition." (1899, May 8). *New York Times*, 1.
"No Anxiety About Cuba: How the Outbreak Is Regarded In Washington Dispatches from
Consul-General Lee Do Not Betoken Trouble—A Warship Not to Be Sent—Senor De Lome
Assured That Tranquility Prevails in Havana. Lee Expects No Further Outbreak." (1898,
January 15). *The New York Tribune*, 2.
"No Cuban Crisis Near: Relations with Spain Practically Unchanged. The President's Policy
Remains as Announced in His Message to Congress—No New Instructions Sent to Minister
Woodford. The Negotiations in Madrid, President M'Kinley's Attitude No Change of Policy.
Confident The Cubans Will Win Colonel Funston Expresses The Belief That the War Will
End Within Six Months. Dr. C. N. Thomas's Observations—He Thinks the War Likely to
Last For a Long Time. Spanish Newspaper Comment the Time For American Intervention
Said to Be Past." (1898, February 1). *New-York Tribune*, 1.
"No Surrender of Manila." (1898, June 14). *The New York Times*, 4.
"No War Wanted: President M'Kinley Will Adopt a New Policy. Will Not Intervene in Cuba
without Heavy Provocation—House Will Do Nothing Now. Adjournment of Congress. Not
Likely Take Place at an Early Date." (1898, January 31). *Los Angeles Times*, 9.

"No Word of Dewey: His Fleet and the Enemy at Manila Alike Cut Off from the World." (1898, May 4). *New York Times*, 1.

"Not Evil, But Good." (1898, May 6). *New York Times*, 6.

"Occupation of the Philippines: Absolute Surrender Probable. The Forts Shelled by Our Mighty Asiatic Squadron and Spanish Soldiers Said to Have Fled Into Interior—Cable Cut Near Manila—Madrid Placed Under Martial Law on Account of Bitter Feeling Produced by the Defeat. Commodore Dewey's Victory Over Spanish Fleet and Land Forces Complete and Crushing." (1898, May 3). *The Washington Post*, 1.

"'Officers With Dewey' Records Some of the Men Who Fought Against the Spaniards at Manila. Many Were in the Last War Captains Who Added to Former Brilliant Records. Cadets on Their First Cruise in the Fight." (1898, May 6). *New York Times*, 1.

"Olney's Gift: Manner of Making it is Criticised. State Department Discredited by the Ex-Secretary. Blanco's March to Eastern Cuba a Total Failure. The Captain-General Returning to Havana—Gen. Pando's Plans Suspended—Spain and America Preparing for Hostilities." (1898, February 6). *Los Angeles Times*, A1.

"Opinion on Havana: Officers Anxious for Definite Information. Various Ideas As to the Cause of the Explosion—Spanish Official Courtesy—Captain Sigsbee Thinks That the Investigation Will Be Finished in Three Days. The Submarine Mine Theory, Palace Officials Anxious. Unfriendly Feeling Shown Spain, Expects Better Relations. The Maine's Disaster Expected to Increase the Good Feeling Between That Country and the United States." (1898, February 21). *New-York Tribune*, 1.

"Otis Describes the Battle: Administration Officials Note the Brilliancy of the Movement to Crush the Filipinos' Army." (1899, March 26). *New York Times*, 1.

"Otis Ready to Advance: Americans to Make a General Attack at Manila. The Lull Before the Battle." (1899, March 12). *New York Times*, 1.

"Our Victory at Manila: How Dewey Ran Past the Forts and Sank the Spaniards, by One Who Was Present. Nine wrecks Dot the Bay. Spanish Guns on Shore Silenced and Our Flag Hoisted over the Arsenal at Cavite—the Defeat Unparalleled." (1898, June 13). *New York Times*, 3.

"Outbreak in Congress: Excitement Over the Maine. Dramatic Appeal for a Congressional, in the House the Senate Speeches. No Time Senator. Confidence Too Much an Appeal. Mr. Lodge Eulogy. The Whole Salvage, Cost to Honor Protection Lieutenant. More Expressions, They Continue. President Cables Senor." (1898, February 19). *New-York Tribune*, 3.

"The Outcome of the War: The Rev. Dr. Newton Believes We May Be Forced to Retain The Philippines. Nation's Duty to the World. The Clergyman Thinks It Expedient That America and England Should Unite to Stop Wrongs and Enforce Peace." (1898, May 16). *New York Times*, 1.

"The Philippine Campaign: American Forces in Possession of the Peninsula. Many Hardships Encountered. Long Marches in Pursuit of Natives, Who Flee Without Offering Battle—Insurgent Attacks." (1899, June 7). *New York Times*, 2.

"Policy Doubtful One: Senator Wellington on Sending a Ship to Havana. Says He Is Not in Favor of War, But if the Maine Proves to Have Been Destroyed by Treachery, He Thinks the Sooner We Get into the Fight the Better—Believes, However, in the Accident Theory—Cubans, in His opinion, Incapable of Self-government." (1898, February 28). *The Washington Post*, 3.

"Praise for the President: Dr. Parkhurst Commends His Course and rhe Moderation of the Mass of the People. The Colored Man's Attitude, What Thomas Dixon Would Do, What Dr. Watson Said. Fairness in International Questions. Peace Only With National Honor. Inspecting the Auxiliary Fleet. Lieutenant Commander Kelley, However, Says That It Is Merely His Regular Routine." (1898, February 28). *New-York Tribune*, 2.

"Praise for Volunteer Troops: Report of Brig. Gen. Charles King on the Work of His Brigade." (1899, June 17). *New York Times*, 7.

"The President's Attitude: No Expectation of a Conflict with Spain on Account of the Maine Disaster Entertained. Cuba Yet a Menace to Peace. Just How American Intervention Will Be Brought about Not Clear Apparently to Mr. McKinley's Closest Friends." (1898, March 2). *New York Times*, 1.

"Quiet Filipinos in Manila: Lieut. Braunersreuther Describes Them as 'Easy to Handle'." (1899, April 1). *New York Times*, 2.

"Rally to the Flag: Davis Calls for Support for The Administration. A Vigorous Adders by the Assistant Secretary of the Interior. Republicans Out in Force. Hazard's Jammed with a Great Public Meeting. Appeal to the Glorious Memories of War—The Man at the Helm and His Patriotic Achievements." (1898, October 30). *Los Angeles Times*, B10.

"Rejoicing in Washington: News of the Victory at Manila Causes Great Excitement at the Capital. Spanish Reports Believed. It Is Thought, However, that the Full Extent of Commodore Dewey's Success Is Not Yet Revealed—No Official News." (1898, May 2). *New York Times*, 1.

"Report from Gen. MacArthur: Describes Events in and Near Manila after the First Insurgent Attack." (1899, May 25). *New York Times*, 3.

"Results of the War: Spain Forced to Extremities in Less Than Two Months. Important Developments in American Nation Policy—Achievements of the Army and Navy. The Burden on the Navy, Its Meaning Not Realized. Future Conduct Of War." (1898, June 20). *New-York Tribune*, 1.

"Revelling *(sic)* in Rumors' Sensation-Mongers Declaring War on Spain but the General Public Manages to Keep It's *(sic)* Head and Wait Patiently for Authentic Reports About the Disaster to the Maine—Wild Stories and Denials of Them. A Time to Keep Cool. General Tracy Urges That Public Judgement Be Suspended Until After the Investigation. Senator Aldrich Says 'Go Slow.' The Main's Sailors Assaulted. A Letter grom One of the Crew Tells of a Fight with Residents pf Havana. Sympathy for the Victims." (1898, February 4). *New-York Tribune*, 4.

"Rewards for the Victors: Will Fight for Manila." (1898, May 10). *New York Times*, 1.

"Right to Cut Cables in War: Admiral Dewey Created a New Precedent Under the Law of Nations in Manila Bay." (1898, May 24). *New York Times*, 2.

"Riotous Spanish Officers: They Start in to Wreck Newspaper Offices in Havana. Filibustering Vessel Caught Fishing Smack from Jamaica Taken by a Spanish War Vessel. Is The Maine Going to Havana?" (1898, January 13). *New York Tribune*, 2.

"Rout of the Filipinos: American Loss at San Fernando Placed at Thirty-Four. Troops Are Now at Angeles." (1899, August 10). *New York Times*, 3.

"Sagasta's Work Fails: Momentous Movements in Cuban Internal Policies. Significance of the Proposition of the Radical Autonomists to the Insurgents—What Might Be Gained by an Armistice Might Be Saved by an Armistice." (1898, February 25). *New-York Tribune*, 3.

"Senate's Cuban Policy: Opposed to Taking Action or Making Declarations While the Maine Inquiry Is in Progress. A Time for Patient Waiting. Proposition of Mrs. Allen for Granting Belligerency to Cubans Rejected—He Offers a Resolution for an Investigation." (1898, February 24). *New York Times*, 3.

"Sermons on the Maine: Many Pastors of Various Denominations Refer to the Disaster in Havana Harbor. Dr. Parks on Senator Mason. He Criticises the Illinois Man and Sensational Journalism in His Talk to Sons of the Revolution." (1898, February 21). *New York Times*, 2.

"Spain Had No Hand in It: Secretary Long's Opinion of the Maine Disaster. He Says the Element of Official Spanish Participation in The Explosion Is Practically Eliminated—No Warship Going to Havana at Present Accepted as the Administration View to Take the Maine's Place." (1898, March 2). *New York Tribune*, 1.

"Spain Held Guiltless: Secretary Long's Own View of the Maine Disaster. Still a Question of Liability. Semi-official Statement Showing that a Demand for Indemnity, Directly or Indirectly, Must of Necessity Be the Basis of Any Action by This Government Following the Report of the Naval Court on the Destruction of the Battle-ship." (1898, March 2). *The Washington Post*, 1.

"Spain's Brutal Sport: Nation Seeks Consolation in the Killing of Bulls. Scenes In The Madrid Bull Ring. Spaniards, Men and Women of All Classes, Gather to Applaud the Picador, While the Kingdom Crumbles—Spectacular Torture of Dumb Brutes Their Delight—Accurate Description of the Degrading Horror Which Dons Consider Sport. In the Madrid Ring. Parade of the Fighters. Scenes of Brutal Slaughter. Not Admired by Americans." (1898, June 19). *The Washington Post*, 26.

"Spain's Cruel Rule: Condition of The Philippines as Bad as That of Cuba. Frightful Atrocities Practised on the Insurgents and Those Suspect of Sympathizing with Them—Unable to Subdue the Rebellion. The Inquisition Revived. Polavieja Worse Than Blanco. Early News From Hong Kong. Captain Concha's Last Message to His Children. The Cable Shut Off, Rebel Help On Shore." (1898, May 3). *New-York Tribune*, 2.

"Spain's Despair in the Philippines: Captain General Augustin Appeals to Madrid For Help." (1898, June 18). *New York Times*, 1.

"Spaniards Renew the Fight: Shots Fired from Bushes. Marines Abandon the Hill Camp Anxiously Awaiting Invaders. Washington Comment on the Fight. Spanish Story of Santiago. Fight Contradicts American Reports. Difficulties of a Band Attack Spanish Strength in Eastern Cuba Ensign Palmer's Bravery. After a Brief Attack the Enemy Disappear." (1898, June 14). *New-York Tribune*, 1.

"Spirit of American Press: Representative Newspapers Deprecate Jingoism. Public to Be Calm." (1898, February 25). *The Washington Post*, 4.

"Stay at Home Patriots: The Rev. Charles H. Eaton Preaches Upon Their Duties, at the Church of the Divine Paternity." (1898, May 2). *New-York Tribune*, 12.

"Suffering in Cuba: Mr. Russell, of the Department of Justice, Tells His Observations of Two Weeks in the Island." (1898, January 12). *The New York Tribune*, 7.

"The Taking of Manila: Gen. Anderson Files His Official Report of the Philippine Engagement. The Astor Battery's Work. Words of Praise from the Commander of the Second Division for the Work of the New York Artillerists." (1898, October 2). *New York Times*, 22.

"Terms With Aguinaldo: He Stipulated for the Philippines as Cuba Shall Receive." (1898, June 12). *The New York Times*, 2.

"To Fight at Malabon: Aguinaldo Will Stake His Cause on a Battle. Rebels' Condition Desperate. Fear American Shells and Bayonet Charges and Are Short of Supplies." (1899, March 25). *New York Times*, 1.

"To Keep Conquered Flags: There Is a Law That They Must Be Delivered to the President. Some Are Missing." (1898, June 21). *New York Times*, 3.

"Too Soon for Treaties: Suggestions of the Cuban Government Premature. Autonomy in the Island Labors Under a Heavy Handicap—the Maine's Timely Visit to Havana Demands Imprisonment for Weyler. The Public Prosecutor Wants Him Sentenced for Two Months." (1898, January 1). *New York Tribune*, 1.

"Troops Are Now at Calulet: American Lines Advance—Filipino Loss in San Fernando Battle Was 100 Dead and 300 Wounded." (1899, August 11). *New York Times*, 1.

"Troops Sail For Manila: Relief Expedition Under Gen. Anderson Leaves San Francisco Amid Great Enthusiasm." (1898, May 26). *New York Times*, 2.

"Twas a Mine That Caused the Maine Disaster. Such is Said to Be the General Belief at Havana. American Officers Convinced That Spain Did It. Divers Inspecting The Hull. Accident Theory Adhered to at Washington. But the War Department is Very Active. Great Activity in Military and Naval Circles. Victims of the Explosion. Relief Measures for the Sufferers Inaugurated—Cruiser Viscaya's Visit to New York—Spain Trying to Be Friendly." (1898, February 20). *Los Angeles Times*, A1.

"The Uses of War." (1898, May 24). *New-York Tribune*, 8.

"Victorious Battle in the Philippines: Aguinaldo's Rebel Army Flanked and Cornered. Fierce Jungle Fighting. Towns and Railroads Captured by United States Troops. Advance on

Malolos. McArthur's Division Sweeps the Country North of the Pasig—Losses on Both Sides." (1899, March 26). *New York Times*, 1.

"Warships Draw Throngs: Thousands of People Go to See the Big Sea-Fighters. Ferryboats and Excursion Craft Crowded All Day—Many Visitors Go on Board—Incidents of The Day. "Information" Freely Given Estimates of the Crowd. Departure of the St. Paul Interest in the Oregon." (1898, August 24). *New York Times*, 1.

"A Week Of Victories. Washington Authorities Think Decisive Successes at Manila and Cuba Are Near. Dewey Is Relied on to Take the Philippines. No Spanish Guns on Shore Believed to Equal the Batteries on the American Warships. Complaint that There Are Too Many Officers and Too Few Privates in the Army Now Assembling." (1898, May 1). *New York Times*, 1.

"With Dewey At Manila: The Graphic Story Told by the Surgeon on the Flagship. The Brave Fight They Made. The Spaniards, Too, Fought Pluckily And Desperately, But Their Gunners Shot Like Children." (1898, June 19). *The San Francisco Chronicle*, 15.

"With Dewey's Jack Tars: Stories of Men Who Served the Guns at Manila. Humble Champion of Schley. Forecastle's Reverence for the Great Admiral, Who Is Kind to the Youngest Apprentice." (1899, September 28). *New York Times*, 3.

"Women and Children Killed in Moro Battle: Mingled with Warriors and Fell in Hail of Shot. Four Days of Fighting. Nine Hundred Persons Killed or Wounded—President Wires Congratulations to the Troops." (1906, March 11). *New York Times*, 1.

"Worthless Cuban Rebels: Described by Returning Army Officers as Fit for Nothing but Loafing and Pillage. Means Trouble For America. Insurgents' Continuance of the Fighting Considered a Bad Sign—Plans to Feed the Needy Poor." (1898, August 24). *New York Times*, 2.

"Wyoming's Plucky Battle: An American Victory in Japanese Waters 37 Years Ago. Ships Sunk, Forts Silenced. The Gallant Fight Which Blazed the Way for Admiral Dewey's Achievement in Manila Bay." (1900, July 16). *New York Times*, 10.

APPENDIX B: PRINT NEWS MEDIA ARTICLES ANALYZED IN CHAPTER THREE, WORLD WAR I: AMERICAN SERVICE

Note to the Reader

The articles cited here represent a substantial sample of all news articles examined in the aforementioned chapter (in addition to those cited in the main text of the chapter itself). These articles dealt with a variety of topics related to the American presence in and action during the broader conflict that came to be known as World War I. When possible, the full citation of all articles examined for this section of the larger work, including the attributed author, is provided. Where an attributed author is not provided, readers may assume the article in question was contributed by a staff writer or supervising editor. Articles published in the *Los Angeles Times* during this period were very typically published unattributed. Articles presented by Special Cable to the *New York Times* were contributed by Edwin L. James or G. H. Perris, embedded journalists with the American military in France during this period, unless otherwise specified. Article headlines in the cited list below are occasionally abbreviated for the purposes of editorial brevity and contemporary citation practices as compared with those of a century ago.

Print News Articles

"11th Engineers Are Cited: Rendered Fine Service at St. Mihiel and in Meuse-Argonne." (1918, December 24). *New York Times (1857-1922)*, 7.

"89th Division's Record Distinguished Itself in St. Mihiel and Meuse-Argonne Drives." (1918, December 21). *New York Times (1857-1922)*, 11.

"120,000 Americans Killed or Wounded at Meuse-Argonne: War Department Statistics Show Tenth of U. S. Force Was Disabled; Total Dead of War 2 Per Cent." (1919, June 27). *New-York Tribune*, 9.

"Admit Our Argonne Gaines. Germans Report that Americans Advanced a Kilometer at Exermont." (1918, October 6). *New York Times*, 6.

"Advance of 77th Division in Argonne-Meuse Battle." (1919, May 4). *New York Times*, 80.

"Allied Attack Failed, Germans Are Told: But It Was Delivered 'In Front of Our News Positions' Behind Cambrai." (1918, October 11). *New York Times*, 1.

"Allies Attack at Many Points While Warships Extend their Operations Along the Belgian Coast Along Ostend." (1914, December 22). *New York Times*, 2.

"America Pays Honor to Valor at Verdun: Herrick Bestows the Only Medal This Country Has Given to Any Community. Poincare Defense France, Denies Imperialism and Says Germany Has Been Treated With Moderation." (1922, June 5). *New York Times*, 1.

"Americans Drive on in Furious Fighting: Germans Throw in Everything Along the Meuse, but Are Unable to Stay Advance. Crown Prince in Flight, Moves His Quarters from Mazieres in Hot Haste—5,700 Prisoners in Four Days." (1918, October 13). *New York Times*, 1.

"Americans Hammering Germans' Flanks: Enemy Arc is Sagging; 'Very Satisfactory' Progress Made; AUN Armies Return Blow for Blow in Effort to Cover Withdrawal; Franco-American Pressure Is Being Maintained Constantly. Allies Hammer Flanks of Hun." (1918, July 28). *Los Angeles Times*.

"American's Pressure Cracks Hun Defenses: Most Vital Sections In France Slowly Yield to Desperate Onslaught." (1918, October 27). *Los Angeles Times*.

"Americans Pursue Fleeing Army of Crown Prince as Allies Push Line Forward: Americans After Huns." (1918, July 29). *Los Angeles Times*.

"Americans Reach Freya Defenses: Forge Ahead on Northern Edge of Bantheville Forest and in Region of Bourrot. Begin Night Air Patrols Lieut. Bernhemier of News Flies Low in a Heavy Rain Over Enemy's Lines." (1918, October 21). *New York Times*.

"Americans Took 60,000 Prisoners: Revised Statistics Show More Than 59,000 Major Casualties Among U.S. Troops. Captured 12,000 Guns. 357,000 Men Sent as Replacements to Reinforce Divisions on the Battle Line." (1919, July 6). *New York Times*, 1.

"Argonne-Meuse, Greatest Battle in Our History," (1919, April 27). *New York Times*, 49.

"Armistice Day Hero Named by Gen. Pershing: Sergeant Samuel Woodfill Captured Three Machine Guns, Killing 19 Germans, Taking 3 Prisoners Used Pick as a Weapon Indiana Soldier Promoted and Decorated for Valor in Meuse-Argonne Drive." (1921, November..01). *New-York Tribune*, 1.

"Army Telegraphers Back: Warm Welcome Given to Returning 403D And 404TH Battalions." (1919, June 29). *New York Times*.

"Attacks Are Futile on Western Front: French Forces Checked Near Souchez and Germans on the Meuse Heights." (1915, July 19). *New York Times*, 3.

"Battle Across Vesle Rages: Allies Force Crossing After Bitter Struggle; Furious Counter-Attacks by Enemy Fail to Drive Foch's Troops Back a Foot." (1918, August 08). *Los Angeles Times*, 1.

"Berlin Tells of Ground Lost: Admits Retiring Near Lille—Insists Americans Are Checked." (1918, October 17). *New York Times (1857-1922)*.

"Cambrai Evacuation Admitted by Berlin: German War Office Explains Retreat of Forces Before the Americans." (1918, October 11). *Los Angeles Times*.

"City's Soldiers Cited For Valor: 154 of 77th Division Named for Heroism Along the Vesle and in Argonne Forest. Many in 306th Mentioned Regiment Took Part in Notable Battles Referred to in Gen. Pershing's Report." (1919, January 6). *New York Times*, 9.

"Demand True Spirit in War Memorials: Speakers Discuss Plans to Commemorate America Valor at Arts Federation Meeting." (1919, May 16). *New York Times*.

"Development of the Monstrous Struggle From Its Diplomatic Beginnings, to Which Is Added a Diary of the Ante-Bellum Period: 1914: A Record of World Events in the Year of the Greatest War." (1915). *New York Times*.

"Drive Germans From Air: American Aviators Sweep Sky Clear of Huns in Meuse-Argonne Region." (1918, October 06). *Los Angeles Times*.

"Foch Sends Tribute to People and Army of United States: Allied Commander Says Our War Effort Astonished Foe And Spoiled German Plans. Recalls Stirring Events Outstanding Feats of Arms of Our Forces Recapitulated in Order They Occurred. Won in All Major Attacks." (1921, July 04). *New York Times*.

"Foe Fighting to Avoid Rout, Says Staff Chief: Germans Massing Reserves to Hold Open Jaws of Foch's Trap; One Railway Only Aids Retreat." (1918, July 25). *Los Angeles Times*.

"Gains by Allies in Terrific Fighting; Two-Mile Advance." (1918, July 25). *Los Angeles Times*.

"General Pershing's Complete Story of Our Army in France: From the Organization of the Expeditionary Force Until the Capture of Sedan, When 'We Had Cut the Enemy's Main

Line of Communications and Nothing But Surrender or an Armistice Could Save His Army From Complete Disaster'." (1918, December 5). *New York Times*, 1.

"German Artillery Pound Allied Front: Heavy Cannonading Is Begun from Belgium to the Aisne and on the Meuse." (1915, July 4). *New York Times*, 7.

"Germans Close Swiss Frontier: Sudden Action, Coupled With Greater Vosges Activity, May Mean A New Drive. Not Even Mails Can Cross Foreigners in Germany, It Is Said, Won't Be Allowed to Leave For Twenty Days." (1916, April 27). *New York Times*.

"Germans in Headlong Flight as Allies Smash On: Americans Open Way; Thrust at Center Hurls Hun Back; German Retreat Again in Full Swing After Defeat at Cierges; Fierce Attack of Pershing's Men Breaks Enemy's Front Line. Our Men Open Way For Allies." (1918, August 2). *Los Angeles Times*.

"Germans in Raids Take Americans: Attack East of St. Die and Southeast." (1918, June 25). *New York Times*, 1.

"Germans Regain Ground on Meuses: In a Wide Attack Near Les Eparges They Recover Some Lost Trenches. Hard Fighting in Vosges. Violent Cannonading Continues in the Argonne— Sappers Are Busy on the Aisne." (1915, July 8). *New York Times*, 3.

"Germans Repulsed by Curtain of Fire. Attempted Argonne Offensive Breaks Down in Face of the French Guns. French Fail in Champagne. Germans Beat off Their Assaults over a 1,000-Meter Front North of Le Mesnil." (1916, January 13). *New York Times*, 3.

Grasty, C. H. (1918, November 06). "Huns Mass Before Yanks." *Los Angeles Times*.

Hartzell, Captain Arthur E. (1919, August 10). "Devil Dogs: Second Division Won Its Fame in France by Hard Fighting And Limitless Endurance." *New York Times*.

"Heroic Family Near Reunion: Christopher's Sons and Wife to Come From France: All Three Youths Decorated for Gallantry in War; Household Scattered during the past Ten Years. Heroic Family near Reunion, Returning to Civil Life, Bringing High Honors of War." (1919, September 1). *Los Angeles Times*.

"'History of the Fourth'. Division, Now in Germany, Took Vital Part in Aisne and Argonne Offensives and Lost 12,948 Men Division in Reserve. Advance Is Checked. Fighting on the Meuse. Capture of Bois de Fays Ordered Into Germany." (1919, June 15). *New York Times*, 64.

"Huge Guns Blast Way: Cannon Take Toll of Hun Mass; Quarter of German Army Now Fighting In Pocket Along Marne; Foch's Drive Still Gaining, Gen. March Tells the Public. Allies Blast Way With Guns." (1918, July 28). *Los Angeles Times*.

"Huge Naval Gun Pounds Enemy: Yankee Sailors, Firing Land's Greatest Projectiles, Help Pershing's Troops yo Win Three Victories Along The Meuse River." (1918, October 26). *Los Angeles Times*.

"Huns Battle to Save Soissons: American Cavalry In Action North Chateau Thierry." (1918, July 25). *Los Angeles Times*.

"Huns in Haste Leave Huge War Munitions: Acres of Shells, Miles of Cartridges, Found by Allied Forces." (1918, July 31). *Los Angeles Times*, 1.

"Huns Lose 180,000 Men in Ten Days: Foch's Men Still Gain; Germans Struggle to Hold Line. Foch Continues to Make Gains." (1918, July 24). *Los Angeles Times*.

James, Edwin L. (1918, July 12). Special Cable to the *New York Times*. "Pins War Crosses On 37 Marines: Heroes of Belleau Wood, Bouresches, and Vaux Honored in Ceremony Held on Marne. More Than 100 Are Cited 'Stood Like a Stone Wall Against Enemy Advance on Paris,' Says Official Order." *New York Times*, 1.

——— (1918, September 30). Special Cable to the *New York Times*. "Pershing's Army Pushes On: Captures Two Towns, One of Them on the Kriemhilde Line. Sweeps All Barriers Aside in Three Days. Our Men Cut Through Defenses That Had Stood For Four Years." *New York Times*, 1.

——— (1918, October 6). "Furious Fighting Along Our Front. Germans Concentrate Artillery in Effort to Check American Advance. Airmen in Many Battles. One Battalion of Americans, Surrounded, Cuts Its Way Out—Hill 240 Is Ours." *New York Times*, 1.

—————— (1918, October 9). Special Cable to the *New York Times*. "Americans Win Battle for Hill: 1,000 Geran Dead Left on the Field After Fierce Struggle in the Argonne. Fight in Blinding Storm Gains Toward Lancon and West of Fleville Weaken Foe's Hold in Forest." *New York Times*, 1.

—————— (1918, October 10). Special Cable to the *New York Times*. "Our Men Smash Through: Crush Enemy's Main Line in Hard Fighting West of the Meuse. German Losses Terrific. Advance Brings Our First Army in Sight of Open Country Beyond Defenses." *New York Times*.

—————— (1918, October 23). Special Cable to the *New York Times*. "Our Army Engaging 34 Enemy Divisions: Germans Draw From All Parts of Front to Hold the Line North of Verdun. Contests Gains Bitterly. Americans Succeeding in Task Not to be Measure by the Territory They Capture." *New York Times*, 3.

—————— (1918, October 27). Special Cable to the *New York Times*. "Pershing Hitting Foe Hard: 20,000 Prisoners in the Foe's Casualty Total North of Verdun." *The New York Times (1857-1922)*, 1.

—————— (1918, November 2). Special Cable to the *New York Times*. "Heavy Blow By Pershing: Our Men Push Forward 4 Miles in New Drive East of Argonne. A Dozen Towns Are Freed. American Artillery Preparation Was the Greatest Yet Attempted By Our Forces." *New York Times*, 1.

—————— (1918, November 3). "Pershing Wins Long Fight: Frey Line Smashed in a Battled That Cost For 100,000 Men. Trucks Rushed in Pursuit—Americans Lose Contact With Enemy After Dash By Auto North to Briquenay." *New York Times*, 3.

—————— (1918, November 5). Special Cable to the *New York Times*. "Our Big Guns Cut German Railway: Make Breach at Montmedy and Conflans While Pershing's Drive Progresses. Bitter Fighting at Meuse. Three Days' Gains Total Fifteen Miles and Net an Immense Lot of Material. Attack East of Meuse. Heavy Fighting Near Halles." *New York Times*, 1.

—————— (1919, February 13). Special Cable to the *New York Times*. "Argonne Region a Silent Desert: Snow-Clad Battlefield from Forest to Meuse is a Scene of Desolation." *The New York Times (1857-1922)*, 3.

"Liggett Comes to West Coast: Commander of First Army Returns to America; Defends Attitude of Haig in War Credits Speech; Democratically Choose to Pose With Doughboys." (1919, July 22). *Los Angeles Times*.

"Ligget Says Truce Put Troops in Danger. Cessation of Hostilities Would Have Left 2 Divisions, Astride Meuse, Exposed, He Explains." (1920, January 21). *The New York Times*, 3.

Local, C. (1918, July 28). "Hero of Two Wars: Maj. McCloud Killed in Battle Last Thursday, A Former Glen-Dale Resident." *Los Angeles Times*.

"Loss of St. Quentin Admitted by Berlin: Success Claimed in Raids Against the Americans West of the Meuse. Driving Close to Throughout, Allies Push Ahead for Gains All Along Northern Line." (1918, October 3). *The New York Times*, 2.

Murphy, M. F. (1918, August 17). "Huns Near Collapse? Tether-End Closer Than Suspected; Losses In Present Battle Estimated At 360,000 Men, 1,700 Guns; Inferior Depots Empty And Boys of 1920 Class Used in Garrisons." *Los Angeles Times*.

"New Foe Retreat Near: U.S. Men Again Push Forward. Huns Fall Into Trap, German Force Is Annihilated." (1918, August 1). *Los Angeles Times*.

"Our Drive Unchecked: Obtain Objectives Day by Day; Enveloping Forces Gradually Drawing Noose of Sack Tighter; Enemy Desperately Clings to Vantage Spots in Hills And Woods. Drives Still Goes Forward." (1918, July 27). *Los Angeles Times*.

"Only Huns Now South of Marne Dead or Prisoners." (1918, July 21). *Los Angeles Times*.

"Our Indian Soldiers on Marine Baffle Germans." (1918, July 23). *Los Angeles Times*.

"Our Men Overseas Exceed 2,000,000: March Says Influenza Epidemic Among Pershing's Men is Checked." (1918, November 3). Special to The New York Times. *The New York Times*, 14.

Perris, G. H. (1918, October 12). Special Cable to the *New York Times*. "Allies Closing in on Huntier's Army: Germans Making Desperate Efforts to Avert Retreat From St. Gobain

Posiiton. French Extending Barrier. Last Remaining Fragments of The Hindenburg Line Are Being Swept Away." *New York Times.*

Perriss, P. M. (1918, July 2). "War's Highest Roll of Honor: Seventy-Eight Winners of the Congressional Medal, of Whom Twenty-Four Were Killed and Four Have Disappeared." *New York Times.*

"Pershing and Baker Review Two Divisions: Decorations Conferred on Members of 99th—33d Parades on Eve of Homecoming." (1919, April 24). *New York Times,* 2.

"Pershing Reports Captures: 1,000 More Prisoners Taken by Our Men West of the Meuse." (1918, October 19). *New York Times,* 1.

"Pershing Tells of Activities: Describes Several Days' Work of Our Men Near Belleau Wood." (1918, June 27). *The New York Times,* 2.

"Picked Prussian Guards Fail to Stop Americans: Desperately Resisting, Enemy Is Ejected From More Than Half Salient." (1918, July 30). *Los Angeles Times.*

"Retreat to Suippe Admitted: Berlin Also Notes the New American Attack in the Argonne." (1918, October 8). *The New York Times,* 5.

Roosevelt, Lt. Col. George E. and Lt. Col. G. Edward Buxton, Jr. (1919, June 8). "The All-American Division: Thrilling History of 82d in 26 Days' *(sic)* of Fighting during Meuse-Argonne Offensive." *New York Times,* 59.

Simonds, Frank. H. (1919, September 28). "The Birthday of the Greatest Battle in Our History: The Meuse-Argonne Struggle One of the Most Terrific Contests in World's War Annals Allied Victory in 1918 Due Only to Freshness of American Troops." *New-York Tribune,* B3.

"Stonewall Division's Record: Work of the Men of the 81st in the Meuse-Argonne Offensive Was Praised by General Pershing." (1919, June 8). *The New York Times,* 60.

"Thrills in War News: Capital Electrified By Reports; Rumors of Decisive Victory Are Spread through Washington; Crown Prince Captured; Army Trapped Is Wild Assertion." (1918, July 26). *Los Angeles Times.*

"Thousands More Prisoners Taken in War's Most Gigantic Battle: German Losses More than Two Thousand Men. German Losses Are Terrific." (1918, July 26). *Los Angeles Times.*

"Town of Forges Captures: But Advance on Commanding Hill West of Meuse Is Repulsed. North Front under Fire Fresnes Is Also Severely Bombarded, but No Infantry Attack Is Made." (1916, March 7). *New York Times,* 1.

"Trap Closing on 500,000 Germans: Germans Outfought and Outwitted But May Attack Again." (1918, July 26). *Los Angeles Times.*

"Two-Man Tanks Wipe Out Huns: French-Built Machines Operated By American Troops; Alabama Soldier Tells Work Done by Iron Clads; Chauffeur Killed by Bullet Through Peephole." (1918, December 1). *Los Angeles Times.*

"Two Miles Gain Made: Counter-Blows by Guard in Vain; Sweep on through Barrage as Deadly as Germans in Months Have Laid; Fighting North of The Ourcq Heaviest Yet Experienced by Our Men. Our Men Make Two-Mile Gain." (1918, July 31). *Los Angeles Times.*

"Two Decorated for Valor: Newark Men Receive Awards for Heroism in Belleau Wood." (1919, November 9). *The New York Times,* 12.

"War Story of Pershing's Observer: Frederick Palmer's Estimate of the American Army's Share in the Victory Over Germany, from Belleau Wood and Chateau-Thierry to the Argonne." (1919, March 23). *New York Times,* 72.

Williams, H. A. (1921, September 25). "Recalls Glory, Horror of War: Reunion Here of Wild West Division Wakens Memory of Suffering, Hardships and Final Triumph of the Ninety-First on Battle-Front. Scenes of Their Victory Live Again For Veterans Here. Stirs Memories of Ear. Wild West Division's Reunion Here Recalls Days of Hardship Ending in Victory. At the Front With Ninety-First." *Los Angeles Times.*

"With Gas and Flame Germans Make Gain: They Win Ground on the Meuse Heights, but Paris Reports They Lost It Again." (1915, June 26). *The New York Times,* 2.

APPENDIX C: PRINT NEWS MEDIA ARTICLES ANALYZED IN CHAPTER FOUR, WORLD WAR II: THE GOOD WAR

Note to the Reader

As with other case study chapters in this work, the articles cited here represent a sample set of news articles examined in this work's Chapter 4, entitled "World War II: The Good War." The articles mentioned below were examined for the presence of discursive frames to do with the American military during World War II, along with those cited in the main text of the chapter itself. Whenever possible, the full citation is provided along with the author's first and last name. For a number of news pieces reviewed for this study, however, articles were provided only with titles and publication information but were appended with no byline crediting a specific author with the work. In those cases below, all available publication data is provided beginning with the article title first. The news items listed here and those used in the text of this case study chapter, represent publications sampled from across the country and taken from reputable and otherwise authoritative voices in the distribution of printed news in the United States. The overall assessment in this chapter as in other case study chapters in this work, then, is of a given discourse formed by a series of narrative frames, which then contributed to the structuring of public knowledge about the role of the U.S. military in World War II and about the centrality of the U.S. military in the structuring of conceptions of the American self during the time period reviewed and into future decades.

Print News Articles

"5 Million Casualties Listed By Japanese." (1945, September 7). *New York Times*, 3.

"25 Ships Sunk or Set Afire off Luzon; Carriers Strike Formosa and Okinawa: MacArthur's Fliers Cause Much Luzon Damage—New Landings Made on Mindoro—Leyte Casualties Go Up to 121,064 25 Ships Are Sunk Or Fired Off Luzon. Japanese Report on Luzon." (1945, January 4). *New York Times*, 1.

"46 Jap Ships Smashed Off San Fernando: Port Is Shelled; Yanks 12 Miles Inland on Luzon; Drive Unchecked." (1945, January 13). *The Washington Post*, 1.

"Americans 4 Miles Into Luzon on Solid Front; Win 4 Towns, Airfield; Japanese Moving Up; Nazis Quitting Western Tip of Belgian Bulge: MacArthur's Troops Reach Central Plain 100,000 Start Drive on Manila, 100 Miles Off; Meet Little Resistance Foe Rushes Tanks To Agno River Line." (1945, January 11). *New York Herald Tribune*, 1.

"Americans Cut Luzon in Half, Gain in Manila: 6th Division Battles Way to Dingalan Bay; 3 Forces in Capital Are Linked." (1945, February 13). *New York Herald Tribune*, 1.

"Americans Reach Clark Field, Japanese Fail to Make a Stand: Motorized Patrols Also Near Fort Stolsenburg; Corrigedor Is Bombed; Luzon Casualties 3,145, With 657 Killed; Foe's Dead, 6,449 Moving the Luzon Battle Line Closer to Manila Incomplete Source." (1945, January 25). *New York Herald Tribune*, 1A.

Baldwin, Hanson W. (1945, January 1). "MacArthur's Next Step: In Luzon Invasion Our Forces Face Hazards of Approach in Narrow Waters Possibility of Neutralization Handicaps to Thrust From East Roads of High Importance." *New York Times*, 12.

——— (1945, January 8). "Luzon a Major Military Venture: Presence of Garrison of at Least 150,000 Japanese Gives Prospect of the Greatest Pacific Test So Far A Pistol Pointed at Luzon Japanese Military Mind." *New York Times*, 3.

——— (1945, January 10). "U.S. Effort Mounting: Battles of Ardennes Bulge and Luzon Point to Peak of Our Military Power The Political-Military Link The Army Nurse Problem." *New York Times*, 6.

——— (1945, January 19). "The Puzzle of Luzon Resistance: Japanese Fear of American Armor and Air Superiority Seen as Factor in the Lack of Enemy Opposition Japanese Outwitted." *New York Times*, 3.

——— (1945, January 26). "Luzon Battle Has Yet to Reach Peak: Foe Expected to Neutralize U.S. Armor by Fight in Hills—Deadlier U-Boats Pose Growing Threat to Ship Lanes 3 Luzon Divisions Identified German Measures Still Awaited U-Boats Again Menace Lanes." *New York Times*, 10.

——— (1945, February 3). "Why We Win on Luzon: U.S. Rules Air and Sea So Our Gains Are Ahead of Schedule Japanese Mystery Deepens Enemy Weakness Explained." *New York Times*, 4.

——— (1945, August 13). "A Full Re-study of Our National Defense Needed: Technological Revision of Entire Set-Up Necessitated by Atomic, Other Weapons A Re-Evaluation Necessary Offensive Triumphs Again. New System Vitally Needed." *New York Herald Tribune*, 1.

——— (1945, October 25). "Atomic-Age Lessons: Good Intelligence Service, Air Power and Industrial Leadership Our Best Defenses Intelligence Service First Line Quibbling on Details Hit Scientists Oppose Secrecy." *New York Times*, 10.

"Battle of Luzon: Prelude to Battle of Japan Widespread Blows Invasion Scene Weapon of the Air The Road Back Jungle Battles The Road Ahead Damage to the Foe." (1945, January 1). *New York Times*, B1.

Berger, M. (1945, March 18). "Havoc Blazed From Attu to Luzon By Old Battleship Pennsylvania: Old Pennsylvania Nemesis To Japan. Her Guns Speak Off Luzon." *New York Times*, 1.

Bigart, Homer. "Half of Manila Won, Troops Pour Into City: 1st Cavalry First in From the East, 37th Infantry Follows From the North Santo Tomas Falls, U. S. Captives Free Room-to-Room Battle Is Waged; Foe Retreats to Pasig River for Stand." (1945, January 18). *New York Herald Tribune*, 1A.

"Chief of Staff Gives His Ides of What We Require to Prevent Another Catastrophe: Beyond the Call of Duty Information and Recreation Soldier Talent Used Educational Program Army Management Service Forces' Tasks Demobilization for the Common Defense. Martial Strength Sapped. No Third Chance Aspect of Total War Conclusion of the Report Proposes Universal Military Training for a Citizen Army." (1945, October 10). *New York Times*, S11.

Compton, Arthur H. (1945, October 28). "Atom Is Force to Destroy—Or Humanize Man: Atom Power Can Destroy or Humanize." *The Washington Post*, B1.

Crozier, Emmett. (1945, January 8). "Japan Reports Big Battle in Lingayen Bay: Says U. S. Task Force Is Standing Just Offshore to Pound Luzon Base Navy's Planes Join Army's in New Raids Pacific Fleet Bombards Paramushiro, Dueling With Shore Batteries Tank Guarding Nazis as Others Drove On to Bastogne." *New York Herald Tribune*, 1.

Daniel, Raymond. "Hard Year Pledged: American And German Treatment of Prisoners Contrasted. Demands That Axis Surrender Unconditionally Now Are Made by the Prime

Minister. Hostages Must Be Freed Turns to Western Front Britons Were Not at Hand Troops' Bravery Lauded." (1945, January 19). *New York Times*, 1.

Elliot, George F. (1945, January 11). "Battle for Luzon Seen as Test Of Real Quality of Japan's Army: Its Ability to Fight Large-Scale Action in Mechanized War Likely To Be Shown in Struggle to Prevent Loss of 'Door' to China Coast and Raw Materials." *New York Herald Tribune*, 17A.

——— (1945, January 16). "New Luzon Landing Seen Likely After Foe Commits Main Force: MacArthur Believed Awaiting Yamashita's Decision on Where to Make a Stand—Perhaps Try to Keep Roads Open—Before He Hurls in Flank Blow." *New York Herald Tribune*, 17.

——— (1945, January 17). "Burma Fighting Seen Indicating Japanese Army's Weaknesses: Yamashita May Be Dodging Mechanized Battle on Luzon Because He Knows Artillery, Armor and Tactical Air Force Are Outmatched." *New York Herald Tribune*, 21.

——— (1945, January 11). "Greatest Pacific Battle Building Up on Luzon: American Air Superiority May Prevent Japs From Exploiting Advantageous Central Position." *Los Angeles Times*, 7.

——— (1945, December 24). "Armed Forces' Demobilization Is Called Hasty and Disorderly: Qualitative Reduction Is Deplored; Retention of Draft Is Urged Until Volunteers Fill Gaps and a Policy Is Set on Universal Training." *New York Herald Tribune*, 13.

Fleisher, Wilfrid. (1945, February 11). "Loss of Luzon May Compel Foe To Abandon South Asia Empire: Cutting of Sea Route and Insecurity Of Railway Lines May Force Japanese to Select China as the Scene of Final Showdown Battle." *New York Herald Tribune* (NYC), A4.

"Foe's Manila Garrison Wiped Out; 2,146 Civilians Freed in Camp Raid: Batttle of Manila Ends in Old City." (1945, February 25). *New York Times*, 1.

"Invasion of Luzon Near, Says Enemy: Japanese Expect Blow Before Americans Overrun Mindoro, German Dispatch Reports Japanese Raid Mindoro Enemy Bands Roam Hills." (1945, January 1). *New York Times*, 12.

"It Had To Be Used." (1945, August 13). *New York Herald Tribune*, 16.

"Japanese Menace Broken At Midway: Way to Tokyo Hacked in Fierce Jungle War, Many Invasions, Great Sea-Air Battles. Gudalcanal First Step. New Guinea, Philippines, Iwo, Okinawa Milestones on Way to Japan's Fiery Conquest Death March of Bataan Japanese Meet Adversity Decisive Battle of Guadalcanal an Entire Enemy Fleet Sunk Twilight for Japan." (1945, August 15). *New York Times*, 10.

"Japs Reap Fruits of Misdoing." (1945, August 25). *Los Angeles Times*, A4.

Jones, George E. (1945, January 29). "Key Town Seized In Northern Luzon: Americans Win Rosario After 2-Week Battle, Drive Near Manila's Defense Line. Key Town Seized in Northern Luzon. Progress on Road to Manila Stiffest Fight on Luzon." *New York Times*, 1.

——— (1945, January 30). Parrott, Lindesay. "Savage Luzon Fight Won By Americans. They Wreck 49 Tanks, Rout Foe at San Manuel--Win San Fernando, Drive on Manila. Bitter Luzon Fight Won By Americans. San Fernando Hails 6th Army New Luzon Landings Reported." *New York Times*, 1.

Kelley, Frank. (1945, January 19). "Kinkaid Says Luzon Loss Will Blockade Japan: Sees Americans Strangling Sea Routes From Foe's Empire to the Homeland." *New York Herald Tribune*, 5.

——— (1945, January 27). "Artillery Duel Rages in Battle At Clark Field: Americans Hold Firm Grip on 3 of 17 Strips as Foe Makes Stand at Bamban Americans Meet Heavier Japanese Resistance on Luzon." *New York Herald Tribune*, 1A.

——— (1945, March 6). "6 Divisions Lost By Japanese in, Battle on Luzon: 4 Others Are Bottled Up in Mountains; U.S. Units Close on Clark Field Pocket The Sergeant Who Planted the Flag on Suribachi." *New York Herald*, 9.

Lawrence, W. H. (1945, November 9). "Monopoly of Atom Seen As Visionary: Four Leading Nuclear Physics Experts Tell Congress That No Defense Is Yet Feasible Experts Give Unsought Views Research Held Stifled Army Policies Criticized." *New York Times*, 3.

Lindley, Ernst. (1945, October 10). "U.S. Won't Be Mightiest Much Longer." *The Washington Post*, B5.

"MacArthur Congratulated: Stimson Terms Luzon Battle 'One of Most Brilliant in History'." (1945, February 16). *New York Herald Tribune*, 26.

"MacArthur Rides Into Battle to Visit San Manuel Front." (1945, January 29). *The Washington Post*, 2.

"Mexican Airmen Deliver First Blow at Japs on Luzon." (1945, June 10). *The Washington Post*, M4.

"Midanao Battle Rages at Airfield: On Luzon Trapped Japanese Are Pounded East of Manila—Wide Air Attacks Made Thirty Positions Knocked Out Yangtze Area Bombed." (1945, May 20). *New York Times*, 3.

Middleton, Drew. "Nazi Bulge Sagging: Americans Reach Within 4 Miles of Escape Road—British Pare Tip Gap Is Now 11 Miles. Germans Jab Nearer to Strasbourg in South—Storm Halts Fliers" (1945, January 10). *New York Times*, 1.

"New Army Invades Luzon in Bataan Area: Foe Caught Completely by Surprise Without Single Man Being Lost. New Army Hits Luzon." (1945, January 31). *Los Angeles Times*, 1.

Parrott, Lindesay. (1945, January 20). "Japanese Counter-Attacks Swiftly Smashed on Luzon: The General Returns With His Armies To Luzon. Japanese Attacks Smashed on Luzon. Squeeze Play on Japanese 12 Enemy Tanks Destroyed New Manila Bombing Reported." *New York Times*, 1.

"Peace on Earth." (1945, August 15). *Newsday*, 19.

Sebring, Leivis B. (1945, January 14). "Americans Cut Luzon in Luzon Landing Miraculous Feat: MacArthur Started Back With Little Equipment. Half, Gain in Manila: 6th Division Battles Way to Dingalan Bay; 3 Forces in Capital Are Linked." *New York Herald Tribune*, A4.

Sullivan, Mark. (1945, November 21). "Military Training Held Needed to Make United Nations Work: Mark Sullivan Says a Strong U. S., Equal to Russia in Might, Is Required to Prevent Fatal Flaw in Constructing World Peace Organization." *New York Herald Tribune*, 21A.

Tait, Jack. (1945, August 8). "Invasion Plan Holds Despite Atomic Bomb: Army Readies 6 Million Men, Refuges to Free Troops; Ultimatum to Foe on Way." *New York Herald Tribune*, 1.

——— (1945, September 25). "Army Explores Effect of Bomb on Its Victims: Doctors Find Few Symptoms of Radioactivity; Japan Lags in Atom Research." *New York Herald Tribune*, 13A.

"Tokyo Promises Long Guerrilla War on Luzon: Says Battle for Philippines Has 'Just Begun' and U.S. Will Pay Heavy Toll." (1945, February 7). *New York Herald Tribune*, 7.

"U. S. Flyer Fells 7 of Foe in 1 Battle Over Luzon." (1945, January 13). *New York Herald Tribune*, 2A.

"U. S. Gliders Land Behind Foe on Luzon: Air-Borne Force Attacks Near Captured Aparri to Speed Mop-Up of Isle Joins Guerrillas in Drive up River Cagayan Province Capital Held by Patriots in Bitter 3 -Day Battle." (1945, June 25). *New York Herald Tribune*, 1.

"Yank Troops Start Drive for Bataan: Americans Kill Japs 6 to 1 in Furious Battle Near Baguio U.S. Widens Beach Head: Drive on Bataan Begun." (1945, January 18). *Los Angeles Times*, 1.

APPENDIX D: PRINT NEWS MEDIA ARTICLES ANALYZED IN CHAPTER FIVE, AMERICA IN VIETNAM

Note to the Reader

As with previous case study chapters in this work, the news articles cited in this Appendix constitute a small sample set of roughly a thousand news articles examined in this work's Chapter 5 entitled "America in Vietnam." Given the longevity of the American political and military commitment in Southeast Asia during the 1960s and 1970s, it is understood that the sample provided here, like the articles examined in Chapter 5 in this work themselves, represents only a small fraction of print news coverage of the American war in Vietnam. As such, the citations provided below are intended to point the reader in the direction of the authoritative news articles analyzed for discursive constructions in Chapter 5 of this work, but they are not meant to represent an overall sample of printed news during the Vietnam era. Given the media attention and length of time of this particular American war, it is this author's contention that such a sampling would be unwieldy in the extreme should its collection be undertaken. Instead, what is provided below is a list of news items whose texts were investigated for discursive frames, narrative tropes, or frames of representation, which then, within themselves, helped to construct particular forms of public knowledge and distribute information about the role of the U.S. military in Vietnam. As with previous case study chapters and as with those to come, the overall assessment in this chapter is a focused effort at discerning the presence of a given discourse formed about the U.S. military by the authoritative print and news media and distributed to attendant readership across America. Conclusions about the form and structure of that discourse, or at least an intellectually significant part of it as the Vietnam War was waged in Southeast Asia, are to be found in Chapter 5 of this book.

Print News Articles

Aarons, Leroy. (1969, April 17). "Protesters in Army Are Increasing: Servicemen's Rebellion: Sharp Divisions, but One Goal Eight Demands Primarily Antiwar Drummed Out of Army Expansion Is Aim." *Washington Post*, F1.

Alsop, Joseph. (1968, May 12). "Press Can't Win in Vietnam War: Dismissed Westmoreland." *The Washington Post*, B1.

Apple, R. W. (1968, September 11). Special to the *New York Times*. "Humphrey Hails Unity On Vietnam. Says Stand by Candidates Raises Hope on Talks—Joint Statement Urged." *New York Times*, 1.

Arnett, Peter. (1969, April 15). "After 2 Years in Mekong Delta, U.S. Goal Is Elusive." *The New York Times*, 12.

Baldwin, Hanson. (1968, February 1). "News Analysis: Public Opinion in U.S. and South Vietnam Is Viewed as Main Target of New Offensive by Vietcong." *New York Times*, 12.

————— (1968, February 17). Special to the *New York Times*. "Washington Feels Vietcong Offensive Failed to Gain Maximum Objectives." *The New York Times*, 2.

Bigart, Homer. (1967, May 21). "Court Martial: Levy Pleads the 'Nuremberg Defense' Complexion Changes Defense Strategy Soldier's Rights." *New York Times*, E4.

Buckley, Tom. (1967, August 5). Special to the *New York Times*. "40,000 South Vietnamese Are Said to Evade Draft." *New York Times*, 3.

————— (1968, January 30). Special to the *New York Times*. "Vietcong Attack 7 Cities; Allies Call Off Tet Truce: Rockets Destroy 6 U.S. Planes at Danang—Prisoners Freed. For Opens Drive: Truce Canceled." *New York Times*, 1.

Chriss, Nicholas C. (1966, August 15). "U.S. Will Stay: President Adds That Nobody Can Predict Length of War Viet Reds Can't Win, Johnson Says." *Los Angeles Times*, 1.

Frankel, Max. (1966, October 27). Special to the *New York Times*. "President Visits G.I.'s (*sic*) in Vietnam in Surprise Trip: Spends 2 Hours at Base at Camranh Bay, Greeting Men And Praising Them Presents Decorations. He Jests AndShakes Hands—After Return to Manila, He Flies On to Thailand The President Salutes American Fighting Men in Person on Secret Trip to Vietnam." *New York Times*, 1.

————— (1967, December 23). Special to the *New York Times*. "President Visits Base in Vietnam After Thai Stop: Tells Soldiers at Camranh Bay Enemy Knows 'He Has Met His Master'. Talks With Wounded. Rome Prepares for Arrival of Johnson Although His Plans Are Not Divulged Foe 'Holding Desperately'." *New York Times*, 1.

"GI Morale Called High in Vietnam." (1968, May 8). *The Washington Post*, A8.

Harwood, Richard, and Laurence Stern. (1969, December 3). "Need for Inquiry Into Vietnam War Obscured by Oratory Over Mylai." *Newsday*, A15.

Hoffman, David. (1969, November 30). *Washington Post* Foreign Service. "Cemetery Is Mylai's Reminder: There Are No Flowers to Mark the Graves of Mylai No Provocation Fortified Pits U.S. Protection Immediate Response Hamlet's Name." *The Washington Post*, 1.

Hoffman, Nicholas V. (1967, May 25). "Tortures Usual in War, Levy Trial Witnesses Say: War Tortures Are Described Man Tied Up on Floor Tells of Ears Cut Off." *The Washington Post*, A1.

Homan, Richard. (1969, December 5). "Army Panel Hears Calley Testimony: Army Panel Hears Calley Testimony Dec. 5 Issue Problems With Meadlo Investigation Packard 'Sickened'." *The Washington Post*, A1.

————— (1969, December 5). "Medina Defends His Role: Says Stories Are Told by Problem GIs Median Says There Was No Massacre Suddenly 'Hot' Coldberg, Jurists Urge Probe of War Conduct Relax Witness Ruling Move Aggressively." *The Washington Post*, A1.

Johnson, Thomas A. (1968, April 29). Special to the *New York Times*. "The U.S. Negro in Vietnam: The Negro in Vietnam: Strides Toward Partnership Contrast With Lag at Home Military Career A Road to Dignity But Cost in Lives Is High—Many Civilians Attracted Abroad by Premium Pay." *The New York Times*, 1.

Kamm, Henry. (1969, November 17). Special to the *New York Times*. "Vietnamese Say G.I.'s Slew 567 in Town: Vietnamese Assert G.I.'s Killed 567 Unarmed Civilians in Village." *New York Times*, 1.

————— (1969, November 23). "Songmy 2: The Toll of Frustration and Fury." *New York Times*, E2.

Keatley, Robert, and Peter R. Kann. (1968, March 5). "Faltering Under Fire: Americans Say Attack During Tet Underscored Saigon Regime's Defects Heroic Acts Overshadowed By Bickering, Indecision, Exploitation of Citizens Glimmers of Reform Again Faltering Under Fire: Critics Say Tet Attack Showed Regime's Flaws." *The Wall Street Journal*, 1.

Kihss, Peter. (1969, November 30). "A 'Real Tight' Company And Its Test at Songmy: A 'Real Tight' Company of American Soldiers and Its Test at the Village of Songmy A Seargeant Says Men Were Angry, Notes Losses Before Attack at Site of Alleged Killing of Vietnamese Civilians." *New York Times*, 1.

———— (1969, December 1). "Lawyer Says Capt. Medina Gave No Massacre Order: Bailey Asserts Officer Was Told Village Was Full of Vietcong Lawyer Says Capt. Medina Gave No Massacre Order." *The New York Times*, 1.

Krebs, Albin. (1969, November 29). "Some Reap Financial Returns From Alleged Massacre at Songmy." *New York Times*, 15.

Langguth, A. J. (1968, May 5). "General Abrams Listens To a Different Drum: Abrams and the ARVN Since Tet, ARVN Criticism of U.S. Methods Has Mounted." *New York Times*, SM28.

"The 'Massacre' at My Lai." (1969, November 25). *Los Angeles Times*, A6.

Mayer, Robert. (1969, August 31). "When Good Boys Got to Vietnam." *Newsday*, 3B.

McArthur, George. (1968, March 20). "U.S. Troop Morale in Vietnam Held Still High: Reds' Tet Offensive Improved Spirit in Many Cases, Field Survey Shows." *Los Angeles Times*, A16.

———— (1968, May 27). "U.S. Troop Morale in Vietnam Held Still High: Reds' Tet Offensive Improved Spirit in Many Cases, Field Survey Shows." *Los Angeles Times*, 1.

Mohr, Charles. (1968, January 24). Special to the *New York Times*. "5,000 Men Massed At Khesanh By U.S.: Marines Rushed In as Foe Builds Up Force in Area Supply Planes Fired On. A Search for Safety in the Midst of an Enemy Attack." *The New York Times*, 1.

———— (1968, February 2). Special to the *New York Times*. "Street Clashes Go on in Vietnam, Foe Still Holds Parts of Cities: Enemy Toll Soars: 'Offensive is Running Out of Steam,' Says Westmoreland Street Clashes Continue in South Vietnam; Enemy Still Controls Parts of Cities. Letup Is Foreseen By Westmoreland But He Expects an Assault on Marines at Khesanh." *New York Times*, 1.

Moskos, Charles C. Jr. (1967, September 24). "A Sociologist Appraises the G.I.: From His Experiences Living with the Enlisted Men of Rifle Squads in Vietnam, a Professor Draws a Profile of the American Combat Soldier and His Attitudes toward the War in Which He Finds Himself. The G.I. (Cont.) In Combat, the 'Hero' Is 'One Who Endangers the Safety of Others'." *New York Times*, 251.

"My Lai Shock Waves Widening." (1969, December 1). *Newsday*, 3.

"My Lai Slides 'Sicken' Senators." (1969, November 28). *Newsday*, 3.

Nelson, Jack. (1967, May 25). "Vietnamese Atrocities 'Accepted,' Court Told: Witness for Levy Reports Saigon Troops With U.S. Forces Beat, Killed Prisoners." *Los Angeles Times*, 5.

Rao, Nguyen N. (1968, March 17). Special to the *Washington Post*. "Thieu's Rule Unshaken by Tet: Ky Suggests Adding 300,000 to Army." *The Washington Post*, A16.

Roberts, Gene. (1968, March 16). Special to the *New York Times*. "Allied Units Open The Biggest Drive Of Vietnam War: 50,000 Men Seek to Capture or Destroy Enemy Forces Believed Near Saigon Allied Units Open Biggest Operation." *The New York Times*, 1.

———— (1968, May 6). Special to the *New York Times*. "U.S. Officers Find Some Improvement In Saigon's Army: U.S. Officers Find Some Improvement in South Vietnam's Army Personnel Shifts Spurring Reform But Arms and Equipment Remain Scarce—Reliance on Americans Persists." *The New York Times*, 1.

Robinson, Douglas. (1968, June 30). Special to the *New York Times*. "Enemy Destroys A Fishing Village: 88 Civilians Dead: 103 Vietnamese Wounded During Attack on Military Unit Camped Nearby U.S. Terms It Atrocity. 15 Pacification Workers Listed Among Casualties—5 of Foe's Men Slain 88 Civilians Killed in Attack At South Vietnamese Village." *New York Times*, 1.

Sheehan, Neil. (1965, December 22). Special to the *New York Times*. "North Vietnamese Fear B-52's, A Deserter Reports in Saigon." *New York Times*, 7.

———— (1967, November 23). "Westmoreland Sure of Victory: Calls Dakto Battle Start of 'Great Defeat' for Foe." *The New York Times*, 1.

Smith, Hendrick. (1967, April 7). Special to the *New York Times*. "Vietnam To Get 3 U.S. Hospitals: Field Units to Treat Worst Civilian Casualties of War." *New York Times*, April 7, 1967, 2.

Smith, Robert. (1969, November 25). Special to the *New York Times*. "Army Will Review Study Of '68 on Alleged Killings." *New York Times*, 16.

Sterbas, James P. (1969, August 20). Special to the *New York Times*. "Lawyer Says Army Has 'Just No Case' Against the Berets: 'Just No Case' Against Berets, Lawyer Asserts." *The New York Times*, 1.

"Stop Weeping, Get On With War, U.S. Told." (1969, November 22). *Los Angeles Times*, 3.

Taylor, Frederick. (1967, June 20). "Mekong Delta Project Shows the Difficulty Of Pacification Effort: Vietcong Murder Government Workers, Raid Outposts; Key Canal Remains Closed A Mekong Delta Project Shows The Difficulty of Pacification Effort." *Wall Street Journal*, 1.

Taylor, Maxwell. (1967, October 15). "General Taylor Says—The Cause in Vietnam Is Being Won." *The New York Times*, 251.

"Tet Offensive Called Failure." (1968, April 24). *The Washington Post*, A16.

Thompson, Robert. (1967, January 22). "Vietcong Peg Victory Hope on Long-Term Viewpoint of 'Revolutionary War': Plan Is Switched Superb Underground Vietcong Victory Hopes Always Gaining Time Hopes For Collapse." *The Washington Post*, E1.

"Troop Morale in Vietnam Is High, House Unit Says: Troop Morale." (1968, May 8). *The Los Angeles Times*, 1.

Tuohy, William. (1968, February 14). "Tough, Resilient: Marines Thumb Noses at Death at Khe Sanh." *New York Times*, 1.

———— (1968, May 27). "Progress in Vietnam Seen by Congressman: Tunney of Riverside, Ending 9-Day Tour, Says Tot Attack Shocked People to Action." *The Los Angeles Times*, 14.

"Two Johnson Aides Hail Vietnam Drive." (1 April 1968). *New York Times*, 26.

"VC Document Gives Failures Of Tet Drive." (1968, March 30). *The Washington Post*, A14.

"Viet Situation Getting Better, Taylor Asserts." (1965, May 18). *Los Angeles Times*, 13.

"Vietnam U.S. Began Withdrawal From War." (1969, December 28). *Los Angeles Times*, H7.

Weinraub, Bernard. (1968, June 8). Special to the *New York Times*. "Pacification Role Shifts in Vietnam: Emphasis Is Now Being Put on Security in Hamlets." *New York Times*, 8.

———— (1968, July 6). Special to the *New York Times*. "Americans' Impact on Vietnam Is Profound: American Impact on Vietnam's Economy, Politics and Culture Is Profound." *The New York Times*, 1.

Wentworth, Eric. (1966, October 30). "U.S. Surgeons in Danang Work To Help War's Innocent Victims: U.S. Medics Aid War's Victims Not All Accidents Conditions Difficult Water Is Polluted Lack Control Navy Men Help." *Los Angeles Times*, A1.

APPENDIX E: PRINT NEWS MEDIA ARTICLES ANALYZED IN CHAPTER SIX, IRAQ PART I: SANITIZED WAR, UBIQUITOUS PATRIOTISM

Note to the Reader

The sample of articles here represents a subset of hundreds of articles reviewed for lexical choice and discursive positioning in the construction of the media analysis section of a chapter of this book entitled "Iraq Part I: Sanitized War, Ubiquitous Patriotism." Certainly, as compared with previous case study chapters examining wars of long durée like World War II and Vietnam, the print news media sample for this particular investigation was smaller and much more focused given the relatively quick buildup and prosecution of this specific American war. Still, like with all other case studies in this work, the sample size was still fairly large, numbering well into the hundreds, given the attention paid to the American military and its prosecution of the Gulf War in late 1990 and early 1991. Likewise, and as with previous case study chapters and those to come, news articles analyzed were sourced from Main or World sections of nationally distributed newspapers published in large American cities and published contemporary to the events that occurred during the First Gulf War. Editorials or other opinion articles were not considered for this specific study, given that they may not constitute a standard, institutional, or otherwise authoritative news perspective. What is given here, though, is a small sampling of all of those articles reviewed and assessed for discourse construction in the form of print media framing, story selection, emotive narration, and other forms of discernible print news discourse in news coverage of the First Gulf War. As discussed in some detail in the pages of this chapter itself, these discursive strategies are considered to be foundational in the creation of public knowledge and collective information regarding the U.S. military, its actions through the course of the war, and its place within the American state and society in the early part of the 1990s.

Print News Articles

Armstrong, Jenice. (1990, September 11). "Neighbors Remember Their Soldier in Mideast; Yellow Ribbons Bedeck Swann Street NW." *The Washington Post*, (D04).

Bailey, Eric. (1991, May 19). "200,000 Cheer Troops in O.C. Victory Parade Celebration: Gulf Veterans Get a Warm Welcome Home. Spectators View Military Might on Land and in Air." *Los Angeles Times*, 1.

Benfield, Karen. (1991, March 28). "Lasting Impressions: Gulf War, Too, Was Good for Tattoos: The Desert Storm Special Is Proof That Patriotism Is More Than Skin Deep." *The Wall Street Journal*, A1.

Boulard, Garry. (1991, February 5). "It's Flags and Yellow Ribbons for Mardi Gras." *Los Angeles Times*, 14.

Broad, William J. (1991, January 21). "War in the Gulf: High Tech: War Hero Status Possible for the Computer Chip." *Chicago Tribune*, A8.

Brown, Malcolm W. (1991, February 26). "Invention That Shaped the Gulf War: The Laser-Guided Bomb." *New York Times*, C1.

Brownstein, Ronald. (1991, February 27). "War Shows Its Unique Ability to Unite Public: Patriotism: Americans Rally around the Flag, a Contrast to Their Reaction to Domestic Crises." *Los Angeles Times*, OCA20.

Cannon, Lou. (1991, March 19). "From Pearl Harbor to the Persian Gulf." *The Washington Post*, A18.

Cawley, Janet. (1991, March 1). "Sorrow Settles in the Alleghenies Small Towns Mourn 13 Neighbors Killed in Scud Blas." *Chicago Tribune*, 5.

Charles, Eric. (1991, March 10). "Gulf Victory Celebration Draws 500 to District: Marchers Express Firm Support for Veterans." *The Washington Post*, A26.

Drew, Christopher. (1991, January 24). "Iraq Uses Scud Missiles to Terrify, Not for Mass Destruction, U.S. Says." *Chicago Tribune*, 9.

Enrico, Dottie. (1991, May 1). "Sponsors Are Gung Ho On Giving to Military." *Newsday*, 40.

Falk, William B. (1991, January 27). "A Patriotic Show of Support in Port Jefferson." *Newsday*, 49.

"A Father's Pride, A Yellow Ribbon." (1991, January 9). *New York Times*, A8.

Fritz, Sara, and Ralph Vartabedian. (1991, January 18). "High-Tech Warfare—A New Era: The Success of the Once-controversial Tomahawk Cruise Missile Is Emblematic, Experts Say, of Improvements in Electronic Weaponry. But Many Remain Skeptical." *Los Angeles Times*, SDA1.

Gellman, Barton, and Rick Atkinson. (1991, February 20). "Infrared Detection, Smart Bombs Said to Devastate Iraqi Armor." *The Washington Post*, A27.

Goodman, Ellen. (1991, May 3). "Ties that Bind Behind Ribbons, War Enthusiasm Reflects Yearning for Community." *Chicago Tribune*, 8.

Goodman, Walter. (1991, June 11). "TV Reporters Compete in Yellow Ribbon Game." *New York Times*, B5.

Gorman, Tom. (1991, March 10). "No Place Like Home: Months of Waiting End in Joyous Reunion for an Oceanside Couple." *Los Angeles Times*, SDB1.

Gugliotta, Guy. (1991, January 20). "High-Flying War May Next Come Down to Earth; Ground Must Still Be Won." *The Washington Post*, A27.

Harris, Scott, and Josh Meyer. (1991, May 20). "Gulf Troops Welcomed With Hollywood Flair Parade: Hundreds of Thousands Watch Them March in Festive Display. Veterans of All Conflicts Are Honored." *Los Angeles Times*, 1.

Hart, Maxwell, and Jeremy W. Jones. (1991, March 19). "T-Shirts to Die For: Desert Storm Is Hotter than the Simpsons." *New York Times*, A23.

Healy, Melissa. (1991, January 18). "Radar Choreographed the Allies' Aerial Ballet: Tactics: An Elaborate Network Coordinated 24 Types of Aircraft from Five Nations during Iraq Raids." *Los Angeles Times*, A7.

Hsu, Evelyn. (1991, June 7). "Condominium Managers Bar Anti-War Sign; Others in Alexandria Complex Are Allowed to Fly Flags and Yellow Ribbon." *The Washington Post*, B04.

Hubler, Shawn. (1990, September 30). "There Will Be Morale in the Persian Gulf, Thanks to South Bay Patriots." *Los Angeles Times*, 4.

Johnson, Ted. (1991, January 31). "Corona Shows Its True Colors Support: The Civic Center Is Awash in Yellow Ribbons as Employees Pay Tribute to Troops." *The Washington Post*, 11.

Leroux, Charles. (1991, January 20). "'Smart' Weapons at Head of Class." *Chicago Tribune*, 1.

Luttwak, Edward N. (1991, January 30). "Splendid Sorties, Tangential Targets War: Big Air Statistics Suggest Much Is Being Accomplished. But Little of that Reduces the Need for a Ground Offensive." *Los Angeles Times*, 7.

McFadden, Robert C. (1991, January 19). Special to the *New York Times*. "War in the Gulf: Air Commander; General Who Planned Air Assault, With Lessons of Vietnam: Charles Albert Horner." *New York Times*, 1.

McGrory, Mary. (1991, March 10). "On a Hill Of Yellow Ribbons." *The Washington Post*, D01.

Quintanilla, Michael. (1991, March 8). "Patriotism: The Latest Hot Seller: Commerce: Patriotism Has a Sweet Ring for Business. After the Gulf Victory, Manufacturers Are Creating Items that Wave the Flag and Celebrate the U.S. Troops." *Los Angeles Times*, (OCE6).

Quintanilla, Michael, and Kathleen Kelleher. (1991, February 8). "Good As Gold: 'Tie a Yellow Ribbon' Remains a Symbol of Support for Troops Stationed in the Persian Gulf." *Los Angeles Times*, E1.

Ramos, George. (1991, February 11). "Field of Yellow Ribbons Waves as Street Sends 5th Son to Gulf Series. Five U.S. Servicemen in the Middle East Hail from a Single East Los Angeles Street. One in a Periodic Series of Reports from the Neighborhood." *Los Angeles Times*, 9.

Ransom, Franki V. (1991, January 31). "Rallies Planned Throughout the Valley to Support Troops." *Los Angeles Times*, 2.

Richards, Evelyn. (1991, January 27). "Lowdown on High-Tech Weapons in Gulf War: Systems Could Be Better if Pentagon Kept Pace With Advances in Electronics, Experts Say." *Washington Post*, A9.

Roberts, Roxanne. (1991, April 4). "The Yellow-Ribbon Special; From Andrews, CBS's 'All-Star Salute to Our Troops." *The Washington Post*, D01.

Sands, Shannon. (1991, January 17). "Pupils Show Support of U.S. Troops." *Los Angeles Times*, OCB3.

Schmitt, Eric. (1991, February 24). War in the Gulf: Pilots; Racing through the Darkness in Pursuit of Scuds." *New York Times*, A17.

Seaberry, Jane. (1991, February 27). "Flying Symbols of Patriotism; Home Decorations Show Support for Troops in Gulf." *The Washington Post*, D01.

Siegel, Jessica. (1991, March 26). "Thanksgiving for Gulf Veterans Late but Great." *Chicago Tribune*, 7.

Specter, Michael, and Laurie Goodstein. (1991, June 11). "Millions Honor Gulf Vets At Parade in New York: 'Desert Storm Homecoming in New York'." *The Washington Post*, June 11, 1991, A1.

Stall, Bill, and Cathleen Decker. (1991, March 4). "Feinstein Heaps Praise on Bush Politics: A Chill Falls over State Democratic Convention as She Says There Aren't Enough Yellow Ribbons and Flags at Meeting. She Is Running for Sen. Seymour's Seat." *The Los Angeles Times*, 3.

Stanley, Alessandra. (1991, February 3). "War In The Gulf: Home Front; War's Ribbons Are Yellow With Meaning of Many Hues." *New York Times*, A1.

Sullaway, John. (1991, January 27). "Colors Flying in Support of Troops." *Los Angeles Times*, 3.

Sullaway, John. (1991, February 7)."Rallies, Flags and Yellow Ribbons." *Los Angeles Times*, SGJ1.

"Tomorrow, It'll Be Ticker-Tape City: A Big Apple Salute to the Heroes of the War in the Gulf." (1991, June 19). *Newsday*, 19.

Toner, Robin. (1991, July 28). "The Nation; Tying a Yellow Ribbon 'Round the Election." *New York Times*, A1.

Treadwell, David, Doug Conner, Caleb A. Gessesse, Lianne Hart, and Susan Pinkus. (1991, February 7). "Some Black Veterans Find Yellow Ribbon Bittersweet." *Los Angeles Times*, A1.

Treaster, Joseph B. (1991, January 22). Special to the *New York Times*. "War in the Gulf: Bombers; Giant B-52 Grows Old Virulently." *New York Times*, A9.

Wicker, Tom. (1991, February 27). "Yellow Fever," A27.

Zamichow, Nora. (1990, October 11). "Military Wives Battle Harassment on Home Front: Deployment: Operation Desert Shield Families Are Finding that Signs of Support for Troops—Yellow Ribbons, American Flags—Are Sending the Wrong Message to Some." *Los Angeles Times*, (SDB1).

APPENDIX F: PRINT NEWS MEDIA ARTICLES ANALYZED IN CHAPTER SEVEN, IRAQ PART II: INVASION, OCCUPATION, AND IMPERIAL OVERREACH

Note to the Reader

Included in this final Appendix within this study is a sampling of authoritative print news media articles reviewed and examined in connection with the discourse analysis performed in Chapter 7 of this book entitled "Iraq Part II: Invasion, Occupation, and Imperial Overreach." As with appendices connected to the preceding case study chapters within this work, what follows is a small subset of the many hundreds of articles reviewed for frames of representation in the presentation of an authoritative discourse on the American war of choice in Iraq spanning from the spring of 2003 through until the substantial drawdown of military personnel in 2011. As with the examinations performed for long durée wars in the recent American past, the sample presented below in no way represents a complete collection of news materials that were produced and disseminated during that period of time. Instead, what is offered below constitutes some of the text documents that were reviewed and critiqued in the chapter within this work connected to this appendix as a point of reference for those readers interested in the guiding methodology that sustained this media study. In most cases, the articles mentioned here were deconstructed within the aforementioned chapter as examples of authoritative news media texts presenting both overt and subtle meaning through print language in the conveyance of presumption, narrative framing, and/or ideological positioning in discussions of individual and collective actors connected with America's second Iraq war. And, as with previous article samples, some of the media texts presented here were applied in the associated case study chapter for multiple occurrences of a given discursive frame, while others were examined for one prevalent intellectual position emphasized within their text.

Print News Articles

Abram, Ruth J. (2004, May 30). "Save Abu Ghraib; Iraq Needs the Prison to Recall Its Past." *The Washington Post*, B02.

Allen, Mike, and Michael D. Shear. (2004, June 1). "Bush, Kerry Pay Tribute to Veterans at Events in Virginia: Saluting U.S. Veterans." *The Washington Post*, A1.

"Beyond Those Sick Images." (2004, May 4). *Los Angeles Times*, B12.

Brinkley, Joel. (2004, May 19). "9/11 Set Army Contractor On Path to Abu Ghraib: The Struggle for Iraq: A Civilian Interrogator, and the Karbala Tangle." *The New York Times*, A13.

Brookes, Peter. (2004, May 9). "The Rule of Pain; Torture, An Unreliable Way to Extract Information." *Chicago Tribune*, 1.

Bumiller, Elisabeth. (2004, May 15). "Bush, at a Commencement, Hails 'Honor' of U.S. Troops in Iraq." *New York Times*, A18.

——— (2004, May 25). "Bush Lays Out Goals for Iraq: Self-Rule and Stability: A Vow to Raze Hated Jail if Iraqis Wish." *New York Times*, A1.

Casillas, Ofelia. (2003, April 11). "Love of Service, Country ; Soldiers Killed in Iraq Devoted to Military, Their Families." *Chicago Tribune*, 1.11.

Chan, Sewell. (2004, May 6). "Rage Is on Display During Prison Tour: General Touts Reforms, New Facilities." *The Washington Post*, A19.

Cooper, Christopher, and Greg Jaffe. (2004, June 1). "Under Fire: At Abu Ghraib, Soldiers Faced Pressure to Produce Intelligence; Analysts, Interrogators Say Many Were Ill-Prepared; Quotas, Unsafe Conditions; In a Tent, as the Shells Flew." *Wall Street Journal*, A1.

Daniszewski, John. (2003, April 13). "Discovering Doubt and Death On Drive Toward Baghdad." *New York Times*, A1.

——— (2003, April 20). "After the War: A Battered Baghdad Showing New Life; Workers Are Returning to Their Jobs and Shops Are Reopening. Iraqi Police Hand the Former Finance Minister over to the Americans." *Los Angeles Times*, A3.

Daniszewski, John, and David Zucchino. (2003, July 19). "The World; U.S. Toll in Iraq Higher Than in '91 Gulf War; The Combat Fatalities Reach 149 after a Bomb Attack and Shooting Kill Two Soldiers. Agitation against the Occupation Continues to Grow." *Los Angeles Times*, A11.

Dao, James, Paul V. Zielbauer, and Fox Butterfield. (2004, May 6). "Abuse Charges Bring Anguish In Unit's Home." *New York Times*, A1.

Drogin, Bob. (2004, May 16). "Abuse Brings Deaths of Captives Into Focus; At Least 18 U.S. Detainees in Iraq and Afghanistan Died from Apparent Ill Treatment or Shootings." *Los Angeles Times*, A1.

Filkins, Dexter. (2004, May 6). "A Prison Tour With Apologetic Generals." *New York Times*, May 6, 2004, A16.

"GI's 'Sharp Moral Compass'." (2004, August 26). *The Christian Science Monitor*, 08.

Goldberg, Nicholas. (2003, November 9). "Iraq: Place the Fate of Iraq Above U.S. Politics; The Truth Is a Mixed Bag: Most People Are Better off, but Crime and Chaos Have Risen." *Los Angeles Times*, M1.

Graham, Bradley. (2004, May 20). "No Pattern of Prisoner Abuse, General Says: All Who Are Found Guilty Will Be Held Accountable, Abizaid Tells Senators." *The Washington Post*, A23.

Grier, Peter, and Faye Bowers. (2004, May 20). "Military Denies Pattern." *The Christian Science Monitor*, 01.

Higham, Scott, Josh White, and Christian Davenport. (2004, May 9). "The Struggle For Iraq: Prisoner; Iraqi Tells of U.S. Abuse, From Ridicule to Rape Threat." *The Washington Post*, 9.

Hoagland, Jim. (2004, May 9). "End of Empire." *The Washington Post*, B7.

Horan, Deborah. (2004, June 11). "Works in Plaster, Paint and Outrage; Exhibit Shows that Many Iraqis View U.S. through Prism of Abu Ghraib, Says the Tribune's Deborah Horan." *The Chicago Tribune*, 14.

"Iraq: One Plea In, One Rogue Ally Out: A Nation Seeks Its Moral Compass." (2004, May 23). *New York Times*, WK2.

Jehl, Douglas, and David Johnston. (2004, August 29). "C.I.A. Expands Its Inquiry Into Interrogation Tactics." *New York Times*, N10.

Krane, Jim. (2004, May 10). "Army Denies Medals for MP Prison Brigade." *Chicago Tribune*, 8.

McDonald, G. J. (2004, May 26). "Why Are They Smiling? The Stresses of War Can Distort Morality and Draw Out the Worst in Human Nature, Psychologists Say, but Sadistic Behavior Is Not Inevitable." *The Christian Science Monitor*, 15.

McDonnell, Patrick J. (2004, May 9). "The World; New Chief of Prisons Defends His Role in Iraq; Maj. Gen. Miller Headed a Team that Suggested Last Summer that U.S. Guards at Abu Ghraib Take a More Active Role in Interrogations." *Los Angeles Times*, A1.

McDonnell, Patrick J. (2004, September 12). "The Conflict In Iraq; Military Intelligence Soldier Sentenced in Abu Ghraib Case; The Defendant Pleads Guilty to Two Counts Related to the Abuse of Iraqi Prisoners." *Los Angeles Times*, A9.

Miller, Greg. (2004, June 4). The Conflict In Iraq; Abu Ghraib Intelligence Soldier Describes Iraq Abuse in Detail." *Los Angeles Times*, A1.

Morello, Carol. (2004, July 11). "Soldiers Return to Rejoicing; 22-Month D.C. Guard Deployment Ends After Stint at Guantanamo Bay." *The Washington Post*, C01.

"New Day in Ancient Land." (2003, April 10). *Los Angeles Times*, B14.

Osnos, Evan. (2004, May 6). "Military Gives Media Tour of Infamous Jail; U.S. Tries to Block Fallout of Scandal." *Chicago Tribune*, 17.

Parker, Kathleen. (2004, May 12). "Weapons of Mass Photography; Hysteria Skews Our Perspective on Iraq." *Chicago Tribune*, 23.

Peterson, Scott. (2003, May 2). "Iraqi Teen Shares Her Diary of War." *The Christian Science Monitor*, 8.

Phillips, Michael N. (2004, May 10). "The Abu Ghraib Fallout: Marines in Iraq See Prison Photos Creating Enemies." *The Wall Street Journal*, A10.

Press, Associated. (2003, July 23). "Home At Last: Jessica Lynch, Months after Being Injured in Iraq, Returns to West Virginia." *Chicago Tribune*, 3.

Ricks, Thomas E. (2004, August 26). "In Iraq's Guerrilla War, Army Intelligence Faces a Tough Job." *The Washington Post*, A18.

Ricks, Thomas E., and Anthony Shadid. (2003, June 2). "A Tale of Two Baghdads; As U.S. Soldiers Perceive Warm Welcome, Residents Express Anger." *The Washington Post*, A01.

Rubin, Alissa J. (2003, June 29). "The World; U.S. Finds War in Iraq Is Far From Finished; Guerrilla- Style Attacks Are Growing. A Military Official Vows to Stay the Course in Quelling Resistance and Rebuilding the Nation." *Los Angeles Times*, A1.

——— (2003, August 10). "The World; Iraq Seen as Terror Target; Anti-Western Extremists Have Been Infiltrating and May Be Looking to Attack Symbols of America and Its Allies, Officials Say." *Los Angeles Times*, A1.

"Rumsfeld Visits Iraq, Tours Abu Ghraib." (2004, May 14). *The Washington Post*, 6.

Schiraldi, Vincent, and Mark Soler. (2004, September 19). "Locked Up Too Tight; It's Harder to Prevent Abuse in Prisons Like These." *The Washington Post*, B05.

Schraeder, Esther. (2004, May 5). "Accountability at Issue in Abuse of Prisoners; With Public Outrage Growing, Lawmakers and Others Are Asking where Responsibility Will Settle and whether Higher-ups Will Be Punished." *Los Angeles Times*, A4.

Schreiber, Cynthia. (2003, October 29). "Soldier's Brother Gets Donations To Help Supply Some Iraq Schools." *Wall Street Journal*, B4.

Schwartz, John. (2004, May 13). "Experiments in 1971 Foreshadow Abuses; Situations Drove Subjects to Do Horrible Things." *Chicago Tribune*, 8.

Serrano, Richard A., and Greg Miller. (2004, May 8). "Iraq Prison Scandal; A Combustible Mix at Iraq Prison; At the Abu Ghraib Facility, the Combination of MPs' Poor Training and Heavy Demands on Interrogators Resulted in a Disregard for Rules." *Los Angeles Times*, A10.

——— (2004, May 23). "The Conflict in Iraq: Documents Provide New Details of Abuse; Army Investigators Heard Accounts from Inmates of Abu Ghraib and Intelligence Officers." *Los Angeles Times*, A1.

Shanker, Thom. (2004, May 15). "Busy Rumsfeld Keeps Working at Both Ends of Whirlwind." *New York Times*, A9.

Stevenson, Richard W., and Stephen R. Weisman. (2004, May 6). "Bush, on Arab TV, Denounces Abuse of Iraqi Captives." *New York Times*, A1.

White, Josh. (2004, August 4). "MPs Blamed for Abu Ghraib Abuse." *The Washington Post*, A14.

Williamson, Elizabeth. (2004, July 8). "Hostile Mission for Recruiters; Prison Scandal Discourages Enlistment in 372nd MP Unit." *The Washington Post*, A01.

Wright, Robin. (2004, May 23). "President Plans Drive To Rescue Iraq Policy; Speeches, U.N. Action Will Focus on Future." *The Washington Post*, A01.

Zernike, Kate. (2004, August 4). "Soldier Who Held the Leash at Iraq Prison Goes to Court; Defense Says She Was Obeying Orders." *Chicago Tribune*, 1.

INDEX